Frames
of Mind

A Text Filters Through from First Thoughts to Finished Version

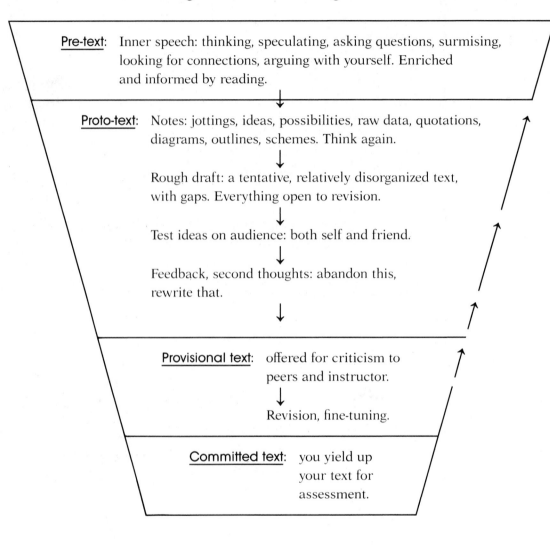

Pre-text: Inner speech: thinking, speculating, asking questions, surmising, looking for connections, arguing with yourself. Enriched and informed by reading.

↓

Proto-text: Notes: jottings, ideas, possibilities, raw data, quotations, diagrams, outlines, schemes. Think again.

↓

Rough draft: a tentative, relatively disorganized text, with gaps. Everything open to revision.

↓

Test ideas on audience: both self and friend.

↓

Feedback, second thoughts: abandon this, rewrite that.

↓

Provisional text: offered for criticism to peers and instructor.

↓

Revision, fine-tuning.

Committed text: you yield up your text for assessment.

Frames of Mind

A Course in Composition

Judith Summerfield
Geoffrey Summerfield

both of Queens College, The City University of New York

Random House **New York**

First Edition
987654321
Copyright © 1986 by Judith Summerfield and Geoffrey
Summerfield

Library of Congress Cataloging-in-Publication Data

Summerfield, Judith.
    Frames of mind.

    1. English language—Rhetoric.   I. Summerfield,
Geoffrey.   I. Title.
PE1408.S7798   1985   808'.042   85-25766
ISBN 0-394-33795-6

Book Design: Glen M. Edelstein
Cover Design: Katherine Von Urban
Cover Photo: *Mr. Hulings' Rack Picture,* 1888, by William
M. Harnett. Courtesy of The Regis Collection.

Manufactured in the United States of America

Permissions Acknowledgments

DOUGLAS ADAMS Reprinted from *The Hitchhiker's Guide to the Galaxy* by Douglas Adams. Copyright © 1979 by Douglas Adams. Used by permission of Harmony Books, a division of Crown Publishers, Inc. Used by permission of Pan Books Ltd.

JAMES AGEE From *Let Us Now Praise Famous Men* by James Agee and Walker Evans. Copyright © 1939 and 1940 by James Agee. Copyright © renewed 1969 by Mia Fritsch Agee. Reprinted by permission of Houghton Mifflin Company.

W. H. AUDEN "Eden" from *The Dyer's Hand and Other Essays* by W. H. Auden. Copyright © 1962 by W. H. Auden. Reprinted by permission of Random House, Inc.

SAMUEL BECKETT From *Watt* by Samuel Beckett. Reprinted with permission of Grove Press, Inc. All rights reserved. First published in 1953 by the Olympia Press.

ELIZABETH BISHOP "Twelve O'Clock News" from *Geography III* by Elizabeth Bishop. Copyright © 1973 by Elizabeth Bishop. Reprinted by permission of Farrar, Straus & Giroux, Inc. Originally appeared in *The New Yorker.*

BLACK'S MEDICAL DICTIONARY "Fever" from *Black's Medical Dictionary*, 31st ed., 1976, ed. William A. R. Thomson, M.D. Reprinted by permission of Barnes & Noble Books, Totowa, N.J.

COLIN BLAKEMORE From *Mechanics of the Mind* by Colin Blakemore. Reprinted with the permission of Cambridge University Press.

DIRK BOGARDE From *A Postillion Struck by Lightning* by Dirk Bogarde. Copyright © 1978 by Dirk Bogarde. Reprinted by permission of Holt, Rinehart and Winston, Publishers.

EDITH BONE From *Seven Years Solitary* by Edith Bone. Reprinted by permission of Bruno Cassirer Publishers Ltd.

DEREK BROMHALL From *Devil Birds* by Derek Bromhall. Reprinted by permission of AP Watt Ltd.

JEROME BRUNER From *Toward a Theory of Instruction* by Jerome Bruner. Reprinted by permission of the publishers from *Toward a Theory of Instruction* by Jerome Bruner, Cambridge, Mass.: The Belknap Press of Harvard University Press, Copyright © 1966 by the President and Fellows of Harvard College.

DONALD BURNHAM From Donald Burnham, "Strindberg's Inferno and Sullivan's 'Extravasation of Meaning,' " IX, 1973. Reprinted by permission of Donald L. Burnham.

H. H. and E. V. CLARK From *Psychology and Language* by Herbert H. Clark and Eve V. Clark. Reprinted by permission of Harcourt Brace Jovanovich, Inc.

THOMAS EAKINS By permission of Smithsonian Institution Press from *The Thomas Eakins Collection of the Hirshhorn Museum and Sculpture Garden*, by Phyllis D. Rosenzweig, pp. 336–37. © Smithsonian Institution, Washington, D.C. 1977.

ALBERT EINSTEIN From Helen Dukas and Banesh Hoffman, *Albert Einstein, the Human Side: New Glimpses from His Archives.* Copyright © 1979 by the Estate of Albert Einstein. Excerpt pp. 25–28, 108–109 reprinted by permission of the Hebrew University of Jerusalem and Princeton University Press. Reprinted by permission of Princeton University Press.

F. SCOTT FITZGERALD From *Correspondence of F. Scott Fitzgerald*, edited by Matthew J. Brucolli and Margaret M. Duggan. Copyright © 1980 by Frances Scott Fitzgerald Smith. Reprinted by permission of Random House, Inc.

SIMON FRITH From *Sound Effects: Youth, Leisure, and the Politics of Rock 'n' Roll*, by Simon Frith. Copyright © 1981 by Simon Frith. Reprinted by permission of Pantheon Books, a division of Random House, Inc., and by Constable Publishers.

ERVING GOFFMAN From *Frame Analysis: An Essay on the Organization of Experience* by Erving Goffman. Copyright © 1974 by Erving Goffman. Reprinted by permission of Harper & Row, Publishers, Inc.

THOM GUNN "Yoko" from *Jack's Straw Castle* by Thom Gunn. Copyright © 1971, 1973, 1974, 1975, and 1976 by Thom Gunn. Reprinted by permission of

Farrar, Straus & Giroux, Inc. and by permission of Faber and Faber Ltd.

NAZIM HIKMET "Ninth Anniversary" from *The Epic of Sheik Bedriddin* by Nazim Hikmet. Copyright © 1977 by Randy Blasing and Mutlu Konuk. Reprinted by permission of Persea Books, Inc.

VIRGINIA CARY HUDSON "Melvin," "Etiquette," and "Gardening" from *O Ye Jigs and Juleps!*, by Virginia Cary Hudson. Reprinted by permission of the author.

TED HUGHES From an essay entitled *Myth and Education* by Ted Hughes. Copyright © 1970 by Ted Hughes. Reprinted by permission of Olwyn Hughes. "Wodwo" and "The Thought Fox" from *New Selected Poems* by Ted Hughes. Copyright © 1962 by Ted Hughes. Reprinted by permission of Harper & Row, Publishers, Inc.

GEORGE KENNAN *Memoirs 1925–1950* by George F. Kennan. Copyright © 1967 by George Kennan. Reprinted by permission of Little, Brown and Company in association with the *Atlantic Monthly.*

DAVID KILLINGRAY From *A Plague of Europeans*, pp. 68, 72 (Penguin Education 1973) by David Killingray. Copyright © 1973 by David Killingray. Reprinted by permission of Penguin Books Ltd.

D. H. LAWRENCE From *Studies in Classic American Literature* by D. H. Lawrence. Copyright 1923 by Thomas Seltzer, Inc., renewed 1950 by Frieda Lawrence. Copyright © 1961 by The Estate of Frieda Lawrence. Reprinted by permission of Viking Penguin, Inc.

DENISE LEVERTOV "Writing in the Dark" from *Candles in Babylon* by Denise Levertov. Copyright © 1982 by Denise Levertov. Reprinted by permission of New Directions Publishing Corporation.

ROSS MACDONALD From *The Zebra-Striped Hearse* by Ross Macdonald. Copyright © 1962 by Ross Macdonald. Reprinted by permission of Alfred A. Knopf, Inc.

DAVID MALOUF From *An Imaginary Life* by David Malouf. Reprinted by permission of the publisher George Braziller, Inc., New York, and by permission of Chatto & Windus.

WILLIAM LEAST HEAT MOON From *Blue Highways: A Journey into America* by William Least Heat Moon. Copyright © 1982 by William Least Heat Moon. Reprinted by permission of Little, Brown and Company in association with the *Atlantic Monthly.*

EDWIN MORGAN From "Innsbruck July 1971," "London June 1971," "Naples February 1972," "Death of Marilyn Monroe," and "Translunar Space March 1972" from *Poems of Thirty Years* by Edwin Morgan. Copyright © 1982 by Edwin Morgan. Reprinted by permission of Carcanet Press Ltd, Manchester, England.

VLADIMIR NABOKOV From *Speak Memory* by Vladimir Nabokov. Copyright 1947, 1948, 1949, 1950, 1951 by Vladimir Nabokov; copyright © 1960, 1966 by Vladimir Nabokov. Reprinted by permission of Vera Nabokov, Trustee.

MYLES NA GOPALEEN "The Best of Myles" from *Myles na Gopaleen* by Myles na Gopaleen. Copyright © 1983 by Myles na Gopaleen. Reprinted by permission of Brandt & Brandt Literary Agents, Inc.

JOHN NEIHARDT From "All Is But a Beginning" by John G. Neihardt. Copyright © 1972 by John Neihardt. Published by Harcourt Brace Jovanovich, Inc. 1972. Reprinted by permission of Hilda Neihardt Petri, trustee of the John G. Neihardt trust.

IRIS ORIGO Excerpts from *Images and Shadows*, copyright © 1970 by Iris Origo. Reprinted by permission of Harcourt Brace Jovanovich, Inc., and with kind permission of John Murray (Publishers) Ltd.

MIMI POND Excerpted from *The Valley Girls' Guide to Life* by Mimi Pond. Copyright © 1982 by Mimi Pond. Reprinted by permission of Dell Publishing Co., Inc.

GEORGE PALMER PUTNAM Excerpts from *Soaring Wings*, copyright 1939 by George Palmer Putnam; renewed 1967 by Margaret H. Lewis. Reprinted by permission of Harcourt Brace Jovanovich, Inc.

SALMAN RUSHDIE From *Midnight's Children* by Salman Rushdie. Copyright © 1981 by Salman Rushdie. Reprinted by permission of Alfred A. Knopf, Inc., and Jonathan Cape Ltd.

SEI SHŌNAGON From *The Pillow Book of Sei Shōnagon* translated and edited by Ivan Morris. © 1967 by Ivan Morris. Reprinted by permission of Oxford University Press.

WILLIAM STAFFORD "Bess" from *Stories That Could Be True: New and Collected Poems* by William Stafford. Copyright © 1966 by William Stafford. Reprinted by permission of Harper & Row, Publishers, Inc. "Things I Learned Last Week" from *A Glass Face in the Rain: New Poems* by William Stafford. Copyright © 1982 by William Stafford. Reprinted by permission of Harper & Row, Publishers, Inc.

MAY SWENSON "By Morning" from *New and Selected Things Taking Place* by May Swenson. Copyright 1954 by May Swenson. First appeared in *The New Yorker* as "Snow by Morning." Reprinted by permission of Little, Brown and Company in association with the Atlantic Monthly Press.

DALTON TRUMBO From *Additional Dialogue: Letters of Dalton Trumbo* edited by Helen Manfull. Copyright © 1970 by Dalton Trumbo. Reprinted by permission of the publisher, M. Evans and Co., Inc., New York, NY 10017.

BARBARA TUCHMAN "Biography as a Prism of History" from *Telling Lives: The Biographer's Art* by Barbara Tuchman. Copyright © 1979 by Barbara Tuchman. Reprinted by permission of Russell & Volkening, Inc., as agents for the author.

EVELYN WAUGH From *The Letters of Evelyn Waugh* edited by Mark Amory. Copyright © the Estate of Laura Waugh 1980. Copyright © in the introduction and compilation Mark Amory 1980. Reprinted by permission of Ticknor & Fields, a Houghton Mifflin Company.

EUDORA WELTY From *One Writer's Beginnings* by Eudora Welty. Copyright © 1983, 1984 by Eudora Welty. Reprinted by permission of Harvard University Press.

VIRGINIA WOOLF Excerpts from *Moments of Being* by Virginia Woolf, copyright © 1976 by Quentin Bell and Angelica Garnett. Reprinted by permission of Harcourt Brace Jovanovich, Inc.

RICHARD WRIGHT From *Black Boy* by Richard Wright. Copyright 1937, 1942, 1944, 1945 by Richard Wright. Reprinted by permission of Harper & Row, Publishers, Inc.

MARGUERITE YOURCENAR Excerpts from *Memoirs of Hadrian* by Marguerite Yourcenar. Copyright © 1954, renewed copyright © 1982 by Marguerite Yourcenar. Reprinted by permission of Farrar, Straus & Giroux, Inc.

Nine articles as they appeared in *Daily Times:* May 4, 1983, B, p. 1; "6-year-old boy quite a driver," May 10, 1983; "Vandals hit Stonehenge," "Chimney gets him into a jam," "Pep talk," "Garden Invite," May 15, 1983; "Getting out of the rain almost ruined the wedding," May 23, 1983; "Don't just sit there—gripe about it!" April 16, 1984. Three articles as they appeared in *The New York Times:* "Ruttman Gets Pole Spot," "200 Cheer as Grocery Collapses into Ground," and "Basketball Player Dies," May 15, 1983. Reprinted by permission of The Associated Press.

Two articles from the *Daily Times:* " 'Mother Superior' becomes nun at 68," "Getting out of the rain almost ruined the wedding," May 23, 1983. Reprinted by permission of the *Daily Times* (Mamaroneck, NY).

"The Murder They Heard," by Stanley Milgram and Paul Hollander, *The Nation,* June 15, 1964. Reprinted by permission.

Six articles from *The New York Times:* "Queens Woman Is Stabbed to Death in Front of Home," March 14, 1964; An editorial comment, March 28, 1964; "That Naive Naked Man Waving His Hand," by Edward Rothstein, October 18, 1981; "A Tireless Search for One Lost Soul," by Anna Quindlen, September 15, 1982; "Toys as a Serious Business," by Anna Quindlen, February 9, 1983; "Meet the Flash, Who Fixes Trains in a Flash," by Anna Quindlen, April 20, 1983. Copyright © 1964/81/82/83 by The New York Times Company. Reprinted by permission.

Seven articles from *The New York Times:* "A Sunny World in a Window," May 11, 1983; "Ruttman Gets Pole Spot," May 15, 1983; "200 Cheer as Grocery Collapses into Ground," May 15, 1983; "Basketball Player Dies," May 15, 1983; "Mary Lou Cohalan's Caveat," April 19, 1984; "Cabby Doesn't Want to Feel Left Out," May 11, 1984; David K. Shipler, July 1, 1984. Copyright © 1983/84 by The New York Times Company. Reprinted by permission.

Two articles from *The New York Times:* "Taking a Stand Against Standing for the Pledge of Allegiance," by David Margolick, November 30, 1984; Extracts from *The York Times* of December 2, 1984. Copyright © 1984 by The New York Times Company. Reprinted by permission.

Two articles as they appeared in *The Logan Herald Journal:* "Class by himself," and "Goose is cooked," June 12, 1983. Reprinted with permission of United Press International, Inc.

One article as it appeared in *The New York Post:* "Woman awakes at funeral," May 21, 1984. Reprinted with permission of United Press International, Inc.

To the Student Using This Book

Frames of Mind: what exactly *is* a frame of mind? A convenient dictionary definition is "a mental or emotional disposition or state." That's a useful beginning, especially since it acknowledges that we all have both a *mental* and an *emotional* life. Many people would agree that these are often so closely intertwined that it's virtually impossible to separate them.

"A mental *or* emotional disposition": what is "or" doing there? *Either* mental *or* emotional? Surely, we reply, the energy of some emotional disposition and the activation of some part of the mind are *absolutely* inseparable? Curiosity—wanting to find out—and the work of satisfying or answering our curiosity—these are surely both emotional and mental. So is the experience of doing anything worthwhile.

Consider "frame" as a verb, and you will discover some of its oldest and strongest uses:

> "to contrive, to compose, to put into words" (earliest known written record: 1514)
> > "to form in the mind" (1597)
> > "to articulate" (1609)
> > "to enclose in or as in a frame" (1705)

You will see that, even with only four of its older uses, "frame," the verb, gathers together some rich, active meanings.

We hope that you will discover, when working through this book, that texts—your texts—can be well formed, strongly articulated, verbally satisfying, and clearly edged. And that making a text will give you satisfaction in expressing and realizing one or more of your own frames of mind. And that you will find further satisfaction when you discover that your text can affect others, can have an effect on them.

Through taking on—or entering—a variety of roles, you will have the opportunity to experience and verbalize a great variety of frames of mind, and end up representing them in a great variety of texts.

Enough! Go to it! In the words of Shakespeare, "Put your discourse into frame."*

Hamlet, Act III, scene 2, line 321.

To the Instructor

In a letter to a college student, Albert Einstein wrote, "If we speak of the purpose and goal of an action we mean simply the question: which kind of desire should we fulfill by the action or its consequences ... ?"

Our purpose in offering *Frames of Mind* is to help student writers fulfill some of their desires in writing—both personal desires and also those desires or needs that are framed, shaped, and defined by the institution.

What the book contains has come directly out of our work with students. That work and those students have rarely bored us. Why is this so? We believe that there are two answers. They concern the *what* and the *how*. What they have attended to in their writings has almost always been of interest both to them and to us. How they have gone about writing, how they have managed, how they have tried to meet the demands of the enterprise—this, also, has mostly interested us.

Jerome Bruner, in his essay on teaching a native language,* made an eloquent case for the sheer usefulness of exercise and also expressed the hope that teachers might find a way to help students discover that "the conscious deployment of language" is, in the event, "more lovable" than they had suspected.

We endorse both Bruner's plea and his hope. If we got this book right, then maybe, through all the various occasions it offers for writing a variety of texts, the students using it will indeed find that they can, to some degree, unaffectedly love the "conscious deployment" of their language.

The fulfillment of desire and falling in love are strange terms to use of a composition course. We only hope that your students will prove us right.

*See page 368.

Acknowledgments

Many people have contributed to our work on *Frames of Mind,* and we wish to thank them. From start to finish, our students, some of whose texts we quote, have reaffirmed our belief that teaching composition is worth the candle. Colleagues and friends, mostly in New York and Utah, but also in California, New England, and other places, have allowed us to bounce our ideas off them, and keep the ball in play.

Whenever our line got tangled, Steve Pensinger, our editor, consoled us with his own fishing stories (the truth of which we will not swear to); Jennifer Sutherland, Cynthia Ward, Jean T. Davis, and Evelyn Katrak benignly licked our text into shape. Our readers—James Catano, Tulane University; James Collins, State University of New York at Buffalo; Cy Knoblauch, State University of New York at Albany; Charles Schuster, University of Washington; and Carol Singley, Brown University—struggled through the tangled wood of an early draft and reported usefully on their experiences.

Theoretically, our greatest debt is to Jimmy Britton, but our minds also derived valued sustenance from W. H. Auden, Eric Auerbach, Roland Barthes, Hugh Brody, Jerome Bruner, Edmund Epstein, Henry Glassie, Erving Goffman, Michael Halliday, D. W. Harding, Barbara Hardy, Seamus Heaney, Shirley Brice Heath, Dorothy Heathcote, Ted Hughes, Dell Hymes, Henry and William James, Frank Kermode, William Labov, Denise Levertov, Perry Meisel, Michael Oakeshoot, Walter Ong, Richard Poirier, Michael Polanyi, Mary Louise Pratt, Barbara Herrnstein Smith, Virginia Tufte, Lev Vygotsky, and D. W. Winnicott.

Contents

Chapter 4: Dear Sir or Madam, You Don't Know Me, But . . . Writing for/to Strangers   63

Part 2
Roles and Texts   85

Chapter 5: "What/Who Do You Want to Be When You Grow Up?"   87

Chapter 6: Proteus Could Change His Shape at Will: Varieties of Role and Varieties of Text   111

Chapter 7: Seeing from Within: Participant Texts   133

Chapter 17: Frames of Mind: Writing as a Member of an Academic Community   350

part **1** | Self
and
Others

1 | Dear Me, . . .
Writing for Ourselves

Why Do We Write for Ourselves? Practical and Reflective Texts

WHY? BECAUSE IT FREES OUR MINDS

Take a simple case: yesterday we jotted down on a pad that sits near the toaster in the kitchen: "Dog biscuits." What were we doing? What had happened that made us write those words? Our guess is that you (a total stranger) will have very confident answers to those questions. You probably believe, and rightly so, that you have a 99.999 percent chance of being right.

We didn't want to spend the rest of the day continually reminding ourselves to buy a fresh supply of dog biscuits, because we had *more important things to do with our minds.* The alternative to writing it down and so having an instant externalized memory was (a) to have to keep thinking about those necessary dog biscuits and spoiling everything else that our minds should have been engaged in and enjoying or (b) to feed the dog on rather unhealthy scraps.

As soon as we learn to write, we can begin to free our minds of relatively trivial chores, and so free them to live a better, more satisfying life.

So, our first purpose in writing for ourselves is to remember, to be more efficient, to organize, to gain some degree of control over tomorrow, to give ourselves a better chance of avoiding a nervous breakdown through circuit overload inside the brain. We shall call this purpose *practical.*

The function of *practical writing for ourselves,* then, is simply to be more efficient in controlling our environment.

WHY? BECAUSE IT REPRESENTS THE LIFE OF OUR MINDS

The purpose of the other main kind of writing that we do for ourselves is more mysterious and therefore more difficult to write about. If you yourself haven't already done it, you may have some difficulty in understanding it, even if we explain it very clearly. Put it another way:

3

when we explained the purpose of practical writing for ourselves, you probably grasped the point very quickly. But now you may need to slow down.

Unlike other forms of life—chimpanzees or pigeons—human beings not only need to control their environment, they also need to make sense of their worlds. Your worlds include all your personal relationships, your past, your future, your very complex emotions, your sense of being a person with needs, desires, hopes and fears, your intentions, and your regrets. Even as you read these words, this book and the course of which it is a part are now two of your "worlds." And even as you occupy this world, other worlds will keep breaking in: your private worlds, your state of health or of unhealth, your feelings about other people, both friends and strangers. Above all, fragments of the past will irresistibly keep breaking in, uninvited. Your concerns and preoccupations, your enthusiasms, passions, and anxieties do not wait to be invited into your consciousness: they enter without even knocking at the door. The question that we put to you is this: what do you do with this hurly-burly, this richness, these crowds, these voices that comprise the life of your mind? Do you find that the interior drama of your mind is merely a chaos or a place of boredom or of overload? Do you find that good things evaporate? That some nagging questions are never answered, never clear?

If you do find that to be the case, then you are perfectly normal. But *if you never write things down for yourself alone*, then you are missing out on an important source of satisfaction. Let us try to explain why we believe this to be so.

It is very difficult for anyone to "read" their own thoughts. Even as we are thinking about what we think, the phone rings, the dog starts to attack the cat, the cat starts to terrorize the canary, there's a knock at the door. And even when things are quiet, the thought that we want to hold on to and explore (e.g., "Why was X so impatient with me this morning?") may well be pushed to one side by other thoughts that insist on invading our minds. Our control over the floods of consciousness is pretty feeble. The dam leaks in thousands of places.

But once our fleeting thoughts are *written down*, they are given a very useful kind of permanence. We can hold on to them, retain them. Not only retain them, but look at them, read them again. And as we read them, we can reconsider them, shuffle them, modify them, extend them, even quarrel with them. Those thoughts that came so quickly that as we jotted them down our handwriting scrawled, desperately trying to keep up, our typewriter almost collapsed—those lightning-quick thoughts are amazingly slowed down, taken into custody, never to escape. That perplexing question that yesterday seemed insoluble, even impenetrable—there it sits in our notebook, and now it feels as if it has been tamed, reduced to something manageable, comprehensible. We can change its shape, put it another way, extend it, tease out its implications—all those parts that lie buried inside it, waiting to be teased out. The energies of the mind—of your mind and of our minds—those energies are unpredictable and never altogether under our conscious, deliberate, willed control. They break out like flash floods, and they disappear and evaporate just as suddenly. All the more reason, then, for holding on to the produce, the fruits, of the bout of energy as it happens, whenever and wherever it may happen. *Get it down!* No matter that you scribble illegibly, in a strange private shorthand. The words are for your own eyes alone. No one is looking over your shoulder with a red pencil and a grim scowl.

The alternative to such momentary acts of holding on is quite simply the terrible wastefulness, the loss, that comes with forgetting. And as you read over what you have written, you will find that the scribbly chaotic little text that sits so roughly on your page will serve you well. It will animate your memory; it will lead to new discoveries; it will generate amazing extensions and elaborations. Above all, as you read what you have snatched from the throat of time, you will recognize the reassuring fact that the life of your mind is in itself very interesting, very rich, very valuable!

One last word: this kind of text does not have the same kind of usefulness as the practical texts; its value is of a different kind. We shall call these texts *reflective*.

MAKING NOTES

In this chapter we shall ask you to look at a variety of *texts-for-the-self*. Some will be easily recognized as practical. Others will be reflective, serving a variety of needs, intentions, purposes, and functions. (Reflective texts are as various as people's minds.)

You will also be invited/required/instructed/asked to write. Above and beyond what your instructor/professor requires of you, we suggest that you buy a small notebook that will fit almost invisibly in your pocket or your purse, in order to build up a store of texts for yourself, reflective texts. For example, you may overhear a hilarious conversation on the bus. With a small notebook handy, you can jot it down there and then. The oddness of what people say is often not so much in the general meaning (e.g., she told him off) but in the actual words spoken. It's the actual words spoken that we can too easily forget, so losing the flavor, the taste, the relish.

We cannot convince you that keeping a reflective notebook is very satisfying; this is something that *you* must experience for yourself.

But here is one of our students, Katia Michailidis, musing on the usefulness of making notes:

"I Let a Song Go Out of My Head"
Duke Ellington

I let a thought go out of my head never to return, but thanks to my notebook, I have started to trap them before they fly away.

I trap them, use them for a while, then they can go. It's not that I

hurt them. I don't. I just hold on a little, then they are free to go wherever thoughts go.

I think they just float around in the air, and the reason you or I get
one, is because we walk into them the right way—so they can enter our
heads, or the winds and breezes are such that they bang into us. That's
what I think, but I can't say for sure.

I think when we're sleeping and all is calm and quiet they land on
us, like the dust that settles on my dresser; then we dream.

If that is true I should no longer sleep with my window open because
then they get blown away. But then again, with the window open, I get
a new bunch every night, so I guess I'm doing the right thing.

Whenever you meet the sign *Notes* in this book, it means that we
recommend you at such a point to write down your thoughts—for one of
two reasons:

1. To be able to make a contribution to class discussion

2. To collect raw material for a text you may/will write

Regulating Our Lives by Writing Texts

Texts-for-the-self are not intended for sharing—not at first, when they
are written. They are written solely for the writer's benefit. But later, when
people come to write about their lives for a wider audience, a readership,
they often include some of those little private texts in order to show
exactly how they were thinking and managing their lives.

A LIST OF "THINGS TO BE DONE"

When people publish those texts that they had written for themselves,
they are allowing us to "read over their shoulder." Here is a simple example. We shall offer you no clues at all to help you make sense of it. See how
much you can guess about the writer and about what he (it was a he) was
trying to accomplish. You will have no difficulty in deciding that it's a
practical text, since it's clearly about things that have to be *done:*

(1) To set up, on each farm, an eight-year rotation.*
(2) To start ditching, draining, and the building of dykes and dams on
the steep clay hills, and of banks in the river-bed in the valley, so as to be
able to cultivate land at present either flooded or water-logged.

---

*"The sowing, in the first year, of barley and oats interspersed with lupins and
alfalfa; in the second and third years, of only lupins and alfalfa; in the fourth, of
wheat. In the fifth the soil was to lie fallow, while in the sixth we would sow
white and red clover, in the seventh clover only . . . in the eighth, wheat again."

(3) To increase further the arable land by arresting erosion on the hillsides, and by extirpating rocks and boulders in the fallow land.

(4) To rebuild and modernize the existing farms, as well as rebuilding the granaries, cellars, store-rooms and machine-sheds of the *fattoria*, and to renew the whole machinery for making oil.

(5) To increase the acreage of olive-groves and vineyards.

(6) To build new roads.

(7) To build new farms.

(8) To increase the number, and improve the quality of the cattle, sheep, and pigs and, for this purpose, to increase the acreage of alfalfa and clover.

(9) To suspend all cutting down of trees for at least eight years, and then to establish a regular rotation of twelve years' growth.

(10) To increase facilities for education and medical care.

WHAT NOW? READING OVER THE WRITER'S SHOULDER

1. What kind of picture can you build up of the writer's environment?
2. What was wrong with that environment at the time of writing?
3. What did he propose/hope to do to change it?
4. Why?
5. Which country was he living in?
6. How do you know? (If you're not sure and your answer is therefore tentative, feel free to say so. Many of your most intelligent thoughts are *tentative*, as opposed to certain or sure.)
7. If 1 to 10 is not only the order of his list but also the order in which he will do the work, first 1, then 2, and so on, do you think he has got them in the right order?
8. If he were including this in a letter to a friend on the other side of the world who knew nothing about the writer's new life, what explanations would you expect the writer to provide so as to help the reader to make sense of it?
9. Does item 10 on his list make a big difference in the way you imagine the writer? In terms of what kind of person he was?
10. What sorts of things did he have to do before writing his list?
11. If you know about flow charts or critical path analysis, here is an extra question for you: Translate his list into a flow chart or a diagram of a critical path. What do you gain in clarity?

When you have finished jotting down your answers, compare them with those of others. How well did you do? Did you overlook something that is now very obvious?

What are the advantages of collaboration, of working with someone else? What was the usefulness of jotting your ideas down in writing?

How did you go about answering question 5? Most of our students who find the correct answer do so by putting various "clues" together. For instance, olive groves and vineyards, oil and hills. Those four, taken together, suggest Italy. This is confirmed by the one word in italics: *fattoria* (Italian for "factory," the part of the farm where machinery is kept).

Context   Now that you have exercised your mind, we will explain the *context* for that list of farming tasks. In 1924, Iris Origo, a young Anglo-American woman, married an Italian, and they went to live in Italy, making their home together in the main house of a large estate that included many farms. These were very run-down, having been neglected for years. The tenant farms were inefficient and produced very little; so Iris's husband set to and made a plan for the improvement of the whole estate. Item 10 on his list is a recognition of the fact that the bodies and minds of the farmers' daughters and sons had been neglected also; this neglect Origo proposed to remedy. But there were other things that were more urgent.

IRIS ORIGO'S LIST

Later in her life, on a particular occasion, Iris Origo compiled the following list:

> Don't ask all the questions.
> Don't know all the answers.
> Don't hurry.
> Don't worry.
> Don't probe.
> Don't pry.
> Don't linger.
> Don't interfere.
> Don't compare—or at least don't complain.
> Don't try too hard.

This was a practical list for herself. Can you identify the occasion on which she would have been likely to find such a list helpful? (Years later she confessed: "These precepts, of which the last is the most important, were not, I need hardly say, all kept.")

If you can't think your way through to an answer that satisfies you, try collaborating with someone. If your combined resources still draw a blank, ask your mothers, or—better still—your grandmothers. See page 375 for the answer.

Notes   →   Do rules help? Or is the composing of rules itself useful as a way
Journal   of concentrating the mind, even if you don't keep to them? Make notes in your notebook, reflecting on that question.

You get to know that elusive entity, your self, by studying other people and engaging in comparisons. True? Our knowledge of ourselves is not absolute but comparative. True?

"I am *relatively* tranquil," we say. Or "I'm *comparatively* restless." Allowing for differences in age and circumstance, how do you compare with your grandmother/grandfather? With your mother/father? brothers? sisters?

If today were New Year's Eve, what resolutions would you be inclined to make?

What do your best friends think are your worst faults? Your best virtues? Do you agree?

If you once decided that you had some unattractive or deplorable characteristics, how did you set about changing them?

Make notebook entries, reflecting on the above questions.

Making Ourselves

Many people try to use their will power to take control of their lives. The most common example of this is New Year's Resolutions; these usually take the form of a list of Do's and Don't's, designed to promote good behavior and prevent foolish behavior. You may find it interesting to discuss how sensible, realistic, and effective it is to try to regulate one's conduct for a month or a year ahead. Obviously, many people believe that they can shape, if not their personalities, at least their lives.

JAY GATSBY'S RULES

Here is how the hero of F. Scott Fitzgerald's novel *The Great Gatsby* set about making resolutions when he was still a boy. Notice that Jay Gatsby's words were written for himself alone; here, as they read it, others are snooping:

> "Look here, this is a book he had when he was a boy. It just shows you."
> He opened it at the back cover and turned it around for me to see. On the last fly-leaf was printed the word SCHEDULE, and the date September 12, 1906. And underneath:

Rise from bed	6.00	A.M.
Dumbbell exercise and wall-scaling	6.15–6.30	"
Study electricity, etc.	7.15–8.15	"
Work	8.30–4.30	P.M.
Baseball and sports	4.30–5.00	"
Practice elocution, poise and how to attain it	5.00–6.00	"
Study needed inventions	7.00–9.00	"

GENERAL RESOLVES

No wasting time at Shafters or [a name, indecipherable]
No more smokeing or chewing.
Bath every other day
Read one improving book or magazine per week
Save $5.00 [crossed out] $3.00 per week
Be better to parents

How much of your earlier adolescent self do you recognize in that schedule and list of resolutions? What do you understand about Jay Gatsby's needs and concerns—maybe even his anxieties—from his schedule? Do you smile when you read the last but one of his "resolves"? If so, why?

WHAT NOW?

Push Gatsby's list forward in time by 80 years; what would an adolescent schedule probably include in 1986? In 2006?

Write a schedule and list of resolves that would represent the kind of person you were at 14 or 15.

What "rules" have you evolved for keeping your father off your back? For keeping your mother happy? For not annoying or shocking your grandparents?

If you have a boyfriend/girlfriend, what "rules" have you formed in order to be acceptable to his/her parents?

BEN FRANKLIN'S RULES

When he was in his twenties, Benjamin Franklin compiled a list of rules designed to help him walk the road to "moral perfection," and added to it a "progress chart," to measure his actual conduct against his ideal. By comparing the two—the ideal and the actual—he was "surprised to find myself so much fuller of faults than I [had] imagined." Are you surprised? Don't we *all* find ourselves falling short of our ideal?

Here, then, are Franklin's rules; we have added a few glosses in the margin to explain words that have either changed their meaning or dropped out of the language since he was writing:

°**elevation:** inebriation/ drunkenness (One wonders why "elevation," when drunks *fall down.*)

1 TEMPERANCE Eat not to fulness; drink not to elevation.°

2 SILENCE Speak not but what may benefit others or yourself; avoid trifling conversation.

3 ORDER Let all your things have their places; let each part of your business have its time.

4 RESOLUTION Resolve to perform what you ought; perform without fail what you resolve.

5 FRUGALITY   Make no expense but to do good to others or yourself—i.e., waste nothing.

6 INDUSTRY   Lose no time, be always employed in something useful; cut off all unnecessary action.

7 SINCERITY   Use no hurtful deceit; think innocently and justly, and, if you speak, speak accordingly.

8 JUSTICE   Wrong none by doing injuries, or omitting the benefits that are your duty.

9 MODERATION   Avoid extremes, forbear resenting injuries as much as you think they deserve.

10 CLEANLINESS   Tolerate no uncleanliness in body, clothes, or habitation.

11 TRANQUILLITY   Be not disturbed at trifles, or at accidents common or unavoidable.

°**venery:** sexual activity (from Venus)

12 CHASTITY   Rarely use venery° but for health and offspring, never to dulness, weakness, or the injury of your own or another's peace or reputation.

13 HUMILITY   Imitate Jesus and Socrates.

Here now is part of his progress chart:

I made a little book, in which I allotted a page for each of the virtues. I ruled each page with red ink, so as to have seven columns, one for each day of the week, marking each column with a letter for the day. I crossed these columns with thirteen red lines, marking the beginning of each line with the first letter of one of the virtues, on which line, and in its proper column, I might mark, by a little black spot, every fault I found upon examination to have been committed respecting that virtue upon that day.

I determined to give a week's strict attention to each of the virtues successively. Thus, in the first week, my great guard was to avoid every the least offence against *Temperance,* leaving the other virtues to their ordinary chance, only marking every evening the faults of the day. Thus, if in the first week I could keep my first line, marked T, clear of spots, I supposed the habit of that virtue so much strengthened, and its opposite weakened, that I might venture extending my attention to include the next, and for the following week keep both lines clear of spots. Proceeding thus to the last, I could go through a course complete in thirteen weeks, and four courses in a year. And like him who, having a garden to weed, does not attempt to eradicate all the bad herbs at once, which would exceed his reach and his strength, but works on one of the beds at a time, and, having accomplished the first, proceeds to a second, so I should have, I hoped, the encouraging pleasure of seeing on my pages the progress I made in virtue, by clearing successively my lines of their spots, till in the end, by a number of courses, I should be happy in viewing a clean book, after a thirteen weeks' daily examination.

TEMPERANCE.						
EAT NOT TO FULNESS; DRINK NOT TO ELEVATION.						
S.	M.	T.	W.	T.	F.	S.
T.						
S.	•	•		•		•	
O.	••	•	•		•	•	•
R.			•			•	
F.		•			•		
I.			•				
S.							
J.							
M.							
C.							
T.							
C.							
H.							

The precept of *Order* requiring that *every part of my business should have its allotted time,* one page in my little book contained the following scheme of employment for the twenty-four hours of a natural day.

°**prosecute:** carry out (i.e., follow through)

THE MORNING.
Question. What good shall I do this day?

$\left\{\begin{array}{l}5\\6\\ \\ \\ \\7\end{array}\right.$ Rise, wash and address *Powerful Goodness!* Contrive day's business, and take the resolution of the day; prosecute° the present study, and breakfast.

$\left\{\begin{array}{l}8\\9\\10\\11\end{array}\right.$ Work.

NOON.

$\left\{\begin{array}{l}12\\1\end{array}\right.$ Read, or overlook my accounts, and dine.

$\left\{\begin{array}{l}2\\3\\4\\5\end{array}\right.$ Work.

°**diversion:** amusement or recreation

Question. What good have I done to-day?

$\left\{\begin{array}{l}6\\7\\8\\9\\10\end{array}\right.$ Put things in their places. Supper. Music or diversion,° or conversation. Examination of the day.

NIGHT.

$\left\{\begin{array}{l}11\\12\\1\\2\\3\\4\end{array}\right.$ Sleep.

> I entered upon the execution of this plan for self-examination, and
> continued it with occasional intermissions for some time. I was sur-
> prised to find myself so much fuller of faults than I had imagined; but
> I had the satisfaction of seeing them diminish.
>
> —*The Autobiography of Benjamin Franklin*

How did you find that extract from Franklin? Did it strike you as ridiculous? Charming? Silly? Self-conscious? Did Franklin strike you as too
wrapped up in himself?

The way you react to Franklin, on the wide spectrum of approval–
disapproval, will tell others something about you. Even as you read about
how he gets through his day, you will irresistibly be thinking also about
your day. When we read a text, any text, all that we can bring to it is
what we already know; in this case, what we know of how we feel about
time and the use of time, and of how we control or regulate our own
conduct, and of how our hopes and ideals, our needs and intentions carry
us through our days.

Your overall impression may well be something to do with how the
world has changed since Franklin's time. This sense of a time shift is a
part of our responses to any text written in the past.

LAWRENCE'S RULES VERSUS FRANKLIN'S

When D. H. Lawrence, the twentieth-century novelist, read Franklin's
rules, he reacted very strongly, as you will now see.

> Here's my creed, against Benjamin's. This is what I believe:
>
> *"That I am I."*
> *"That my soul is a dark forest."*
> *"That my known self will never be more than a little clearing in the
> forest."*
> *"That gods, strange gods, come forth from the forest into the clearing of
> my known self, and then go back."*
> *"That I must have the courage to let them come and go."*
> *"That I will never let mankind put anything over me, but that I will try
> always to recognize and submit to the gods in me and the gods in other
> men and women."*
>
> There is my creed. He who runs may read. He who prefers to crawl, or
> to go by gasoline, can call it rot.
>
> Then for a "list." It is rather fun to play at Benjamin.
>
> 1 TEMPERANCE   Eat and carouse with Bacchus, or munch dry bread with
>   Jesus, but don't sit down without one of the gods.
>
> 2 SILENCE   Be still when you have nothing to say; when genuine passion
>   moves you, say what you've got to say, and say it hot.
>
> 3 ORDER   Know that you are responsible to the gods inside you and

to the men in whom the gods are manifest. Recognize your supe-
riors and your inferiors, according to the gods. This is the root of
all order.

4 RESOLUTION   Resolve to abide by your own deepest promptings, and
to sacrifice the smaller thing to the greater. Kill when you must,
and be killed the same: the *must* coming from the gods inside you,
or from the men in whom you recognize the Holy Ghost.

5 FRUGALITY   Demand nothing; accept what you see fit. Don't waste
your pride or squander your emotion.

6 INDUSTRY   Lose no time with ideals; serve the Holy Ghost; never
serve mankind.

7 SINCERITY   To be sincere is to remember that I am I, and that the
other man is not me.

8 JUSTICE   The only justice is to follow the sincere intuition of the
soul, angry or gentle. Anger is just, and pity is just, but judgment
is never just.

9 MODERATION   Beware of absolutes. There are many gods.

10 CLEANLINESS   Don't be too clean. It impoverishes the blood.

11 TRANQUILLITY   The soul has many motions, many gods come and go.
Try and find your deepest issue, in every confusion, and abide by
that. Obey the man in whom you recognize the Holy Ghost; command when your honour comes to command.

12 CHASTITY   Never "use" venery at all. Follow your passional impulse,
if it be answered in the other being; but never have any motive in
mind, neither off-spring nor health nor even pleasure, nor even service. Only know that "venery" is of the great gods. An offering-up of
yourself to the very great gods, the dark ones, and nothing else.

13 HUMILITY   See all men and women according to the Holy Ghost that
is within them. Never yield before the barren.

If we pinned you in a corner and said, "You can follow Franklin or
Lawrence—that is your only option," who would you choose? Does your
reading of those two—and your reactions to them—help you to know more
clearly what you *believe*? If so, how?

Franklin wrote his rules for his own eyes; Lawrence wrote his for
publication in his book on American literature. Lawrence's readers would
expect something resembling a history textbook. Do you think he surprised them? Do you think that this was probably part of his purpose?
(It may help you to know that Lawrence spent most of his adult life shocking and provoking people; either intentionally or because he didn't care.)
Do you find Lawrence's tone of voice rather aggressive? Conceited? Is he,
do you think, writing a text-for-himself or deliberately setting up a certain kind of relationship with his readers—rather like shouting at them
or giving them a sharp kick? Do you like his tone of voice?

WHAT NEXT?

1. Compile a list for the kind of day when you feel like avoiding real work; make it as plausible as possible, so as to convince anyone who sees it that you are not wasting your time.
2. a. How many ways do you try to avoid doing what you feel disinclined to do? Do you have different strategies for avoiding different tasks?
   b. Compile a list of all the things you do when you want to avoid writing.
3. Arrange a meeting in a bar or restaurant between Franklin and Lawrence, and have them engage in dialogue. What do they *recognize* in each other? Does Lawrence, for example, recognize that Franklin is more than a narrow-minded Puritan? If so, how does Franklin enable him to recognize this? Does Franklin recognize in Lawrence the same degree of moral passion as exists in himself? Do they end by agreeing or disagreeing? How many moods do they move through in the course of their conversation? Who eats the most? Does one of them get drunk?
4. If you had to take sides either with Franklin or with Lawrence, who would you ally yourself with? Who would you prefer as a roommate? Traveling companion? Husband? Father? Son?
5. Franklin forces Lawrence to gather, consider, and formulate his own convictions. Which of your friends or acquaintances has a similar effect on you?

Keeping a Pillow Book √

So far, you have been looking at practical texts—writing designed to regulate or guide some action, or doing, or conduct. Now we invite you to turn to a *reflective text-for-the-self*. It comes from one of the oldest surviving books written by a woman, Sei Shōnagon. She was a terrible snob, or so we gather, but she was very observant, very acute. And what she wrote way back in the tenth century is now both a long way away from us—representing bits of a life lived in a very different kind of society—and yet, simultaneously, very familiar. We have taken a few extracts from the book for which she is still remembered, even though she wrote for herself alone. The title of her book is *Makura no Sōshi*, which is Japanese for *Pillow Book.*

What was a pillow book? Can you possibly guess? What purposes do you think it served? What satisfactions do you think it could have provided?

A pillow book was simply a small notebook that could be kept under the pillow, so that if thoughts, memories, ideas came to you at night, you could jot them down without losing time. The Japanese still keep similar note-books today; they are called *Zuihitsu*—random notes.

SEI SHŌNAGON'S "THINGS"

Here is one of her pillow notes:

Things Without Merit

Rice starch that has become mixed with water. . . . I know that this is a very vulgar item and everyone will dislike my mentioning it. But that should not stop me. In fact I must feel free to include anything, even tongs used for the parting-fires. After all, these objects do exist in our world and people all know about them. I admit they do not belong to a list that others will see. But I never thought that these notes would be read by anyone else, and so I included everything that came into my head, however strange or unpleasant.

Let us share with you our reactions to that. First of all, we have no idea why she regards a mixture of starch and water as vulgar; maybe it has something to do with her social class, something such as "I wouldn't soil my precious hands with that stuff—that's the servants' business." We are simply not sure. What interests us about this passage is something else: it's the way she recognizes the freedom, the irresponsibility of anyone who writes a text-for-the-self. When you write a text-for-the-self, you are accountable to no one else. You are "free to include anything." You can include "everything that comes into your head, however strange or unpleasant." When we read her words, we are like eavesdroppers who have slipped through a time warp, we are like a fly on the wall of Sei Shōnagon's bedroom.

Her next pillow-book note is about things that embarrass her. Before you read it, jot down some *Notes* of the things that embarrass you; then you can compare notes with her and with us.

Embarrassing Things

While entertaining a visitor, one hears some servants chatting without any restraint in one of the back rooms. It is embarrassing to know that one's visitor can overhear. But how to stop them?

A man whom one loves gets drunk and keeps repeating himself.

To have spoken about someone not knowing that he could overhear.

Parents, convinced that their ugly child is adorable, pet him and repeat the things he has said, imitating his voice.

An ignoramus who in the presence of some learned person puts on a knowing air and converses about men of old.

A man recites his own poems (not especially good ones) and tells one about the praise they have received—most embarrassing.

Lying awake at night, one says something to one's companion, who simply goes on sleeping.

In the presence of a skilled musician, someone plays a zither just for his own pleasure and without tuning it.

Some of these things will never embarrass us. We have never had servants and we never will. But other items in her list ring a bell. We also find it embarrassing when friends drink too much and behave foolishly. And we have also been disconcerted when we discovered that someone we had been talking about had heard every word we said!

WHAT NEXT?

Which of Sei Shōnagon's items do you share? If you were to grade your experiences of embarrassment on a scale of (a) slightly, (b) very, or (c) almost unbearably, which kinds of situation would you include in each category?

What are the most obvious differences between Sei Shōnagon's world and yours?

Here is another interesting group:

Squalid Things

The back of a piece of embroidery.
The inside of a cat's ear.
A swarm of mice, who still have no fur, when they come wriggling out of their nest.
The seams of a fur robe that has not yet been lined.
Darkness in a place that does not give the impression of being very clean.

If you didn't know the meaning of the word *squalid*, how would you deduce it from these examples?

We ourselves find that the back of a piece of furniture is sometimes squalid: the visible parts are so finely finished and polished, and then we discover that the invisible parts are rough and tacky. But the inside of a cat's ear? That strikes us as very neat, very ingeniously formed, delicate yet strong, and strangely shiny. Maybe the lady was nauseated by wax?

Even as we are reading her list, we find our own alternatives are rising into our minds unbidden, uninvited; we can't shut the door of the mind on them.

When Sei Shōnagon speaks of hateful things, she seems to have in mind socially deplorable behavior:

Hateful Things

One is in a hurry to leave, but one's visitor keeps chattering away. If it is someone of no importance, one can get rid of him by saying, "You must tell me all about it next time"; but, should it be the sort of visitor whose presence commands one's best behaviour, the situation is hateful indeed.

A man who has nothing in particular to recommend him discusses all sorts of subjects at random as though he knew everything.

How do you react to these?

Things That Give an Unclean Feeling

A rat's nest.
Someone who is late in washing his hands in the morning.
White snivel, and children who sniffle as they walk. . . .
Little sparrows.
A person who does not bathe for a long time even though the weather is hot.
All faded clothes give me an unclean feeling, especially those that have glossy colours.

Things That Have Lost Their Power

A large boat which is high and dry in a creek at ebb-tide.
A woman who has taken off her false locks to comb the short hair that remains.
A large tree that has been blown down in a gale and lies on its side with its roots in the air.
The retreating figure of a *sumō* wrestler who has been defeated in a match.
A man of no importance reprimanding an attendant.
An old man who removes his hat, uncovering his scanty top-knot.
A woman, who is angry with her husband about some trifling matter, leaves home and goes somewhere to hide. She is certain that he will rush about looking for her; but he does nothing of the kind and shows the most infuriating indifference. Since she cannot stay away for ever, she swallows her pride and returns.

Things That Give a Clean Feeling

An earthen cup. A new metal bowl.
A rush mat.
The play of the light on water as one pours it into a vessel.
A new wooden chest.

Things That Make One's Heart Beat Faster

Sparrows feeding their young. To pass a place where babies are play-ing. To sleep in a room where some fine incense has been burnt. To notice that one's elegant Chinese mirror has become a little cloudy. To see a gentleman stop his carriage before one's gate and instruct his attendants to announce his arrival. To wash one's hair, make one's toilet, and put on scented robes; even if not a soul sees one, these prepara-tions still produce an inner pleasure.

It is night and one is expecting a visitor. Suddenly one is startled by the sound of rain-drops, which the wind blows against the shutters.

Notice that the items in this last pillow note fall into two main categories: things that were come upon unexpectedly, such as the sparrows, and things that were set up, such as washing one's hair. Our hearts beat faster when we are aroused, startled, or excited—pleasurably or otherwise—when the pulse quickens, even before the mind has time to reflect on the experience. There is the beginning of a short story in the last one!

And finally:

Things That Arouse a Fond Memory of the Past

Dried hollyhock. . . . To find a piece of deep violet or grape-coloured material that has been pressed between the pages of a notebook.

It is a rainy day and one is feeling bored. To pass the time, one starts looking through some old papers. And then one comes across the letters of a man one used to love.

Last year's paper fan. A night with a clear moon.*

WHAT NOW? YOUR "THINGS"

What is it that most powerfully triggers off your memory? What do you experience when something from your past leaps into your mind? Do you see an image, hear a voice, or what? And what are your fondest memories?

You may have noticed that Sei Shōnagon, like many of us, uses the word "things" to refer to objects, animals, insects, people, the way people behave, and situations.

Consider the following categories, and provide your own examples:

Things that disconcert me

Things that upset me

---

*Notice the consequences of the fact that Sei Shōnagon is writing for herself and not for others. If she had been deliberately writing for a remote audience—remote in time and/or place—she would have had to explain how/why some of these items arouse a fond memory in *her* time and place.

Things that make me hysterical

Things that confuse me

Irresistible things

Puzzling things

Mysterious things

Things best avoided

Things that make me glad I'm no longer an adolescent

Things that make me feel optimistic/pessimistic

Things that make me shudder

Things that set my teeth on edge

Things that get me out of bed

Things that make me feel like staying in bed

Advice: don't generalize; particularize.

SOME OF OUR STUDENTS' "THINGS"

Things That Have Lost Their Power

Electric lights when you don't pay the bill
Old turtles
Broken can openers
Elastic on old underwear
Clothespins without the spring
As and Fs, because I no longer strive for the former and never get the latter
Miss America 1984 in 1985

Things That Give a Clean Feeling

Fresh sheets blowing in the wind
Curling up in a clean bed
Linen closets with moth balls
Ammonia and furniture polish
Freshly brushed teeth
New car upholstery

Things That Make My Heart Beat Faster

A first-time kiss
A last-time kiss

The phone ringing in the middle of the night
Seeing a squirrel run in front of a car and make it to the other side
Getting a good grade on a not-good paper
Roller coaster rides
Comebacks in the 4th quarter of a football game
Fire escapes
Large dogs, barking like all hell from behind a fence on a dark night
as you pass by
Riding waves
Cliff diving
A mountaintop view
Special reports interrupting a TV program

Things That Are Phony

Prepackaged Easter baskets filled with all that green grass
A smile that doesn't quite reach the eye of the giver
Being called "Dear" or "Honey" at the doctor's office (oh, brother!)
Corny, canned supermarket music
McDonald's "doing it all for me"

Embarrassing Things

Mismatched socks in the event of a bus accident
Wedding nights
A trip to the gynecologist when you're sixteen
Being in love and trying to hide it
Your bathing suit lost in a sudden wave
Calling your present boyfriend your ex-boyfriend's name three times
in the same day

Annoying Things

A toothpaste tube squeezed from the middle
Fingernails scratching a blackboard
Being at the end of a long line
The sound of the alarm clock every morning
Having someone smarter than you disagree with you
People who talk during a movie
A continuously ringing phone that no one will answer
Making unerasable mistakes
The line "Where's the beef?"
Someone telling you where

Things That Make Me Angry √

People who have no respect for others' property
Kids who tie up the phone lines day and night

Time—it's always too slow or too fast
All the injustice in the world
People who are never on time
Envy, especially my own, and greed
People who discard their animals when they move away
People staring in church at a crying baby (weren't they young once?)
Helplessness

Things That Are Hateful

People who think they're better because they have money
People who hurt animals
Being the class bully and getting away with it
People who never say please or thank you, ever
Being humiliated and having to swallow your pride
Waking up in a blue mood
People who categorize, standardize, and have their lives sorted out on shelves
Prejudice, racism, and extreme nationalism
McDonald's commercials

—From the "Pillow Books" of Marina Berkovitch, Sharon Fishbein,
Linda Higgins, Michael Morgan, and Elderina Pepe

The Move Outward to Others

If you have started to keep a reflective notebook, you will probably have discovered an interesting fact about it—and therefore about yourself. It's this: Even though you write entries in your reflective notes primarily for yourself, even exclusively so—at least that's what you "intended"—you will soon discover an extraordinary fact about yourself and about those expressions of your mind. It's this: you are a *social* being.

In other words, you have probably felt a distinct inclination to share some of your thoughts with others. It may even feel like a need. Our advice is this: don't deny that impulse, that inclination. As you write in your notebook, and then browse through what you have written, you will discover that the life of your mind is much more interesting, much more alive, than you had ever suspected.

The inclination to share some of the fruits of your writing with others is an absolutely normal and healthy one. So do it. Choose parts that you can most easily share, or parts that you have good reason to believe will interest others, even though you are not quite sure why this is so.

If you offer such little texts to others, you will find that the act of offering is in itself satisfying and that a further strong satisfaction you reap is the pleasure of being accepted or recognized. All human beings need some degree of acceptance and recognition—not stars or prizes—

simple recognition. At that point your texts will begin to turn irresistibly toward others; they will become social. One of the fundamental social pleasures we all need is to discover that we are like others and that we are unlike others.

WHAT NEXT?

As soon as you have written about 20 or 30 entries in your notebook, however short they may be, you will be in a position to select those that you would like to extend, to take further, to elaborate on, to explore further. To discover what it is that you want/need to write about—that is a very important moment in your development as a writer. Better sooner than later.

2 | Dear You, . . . Writing for/to Others

Talking to Yourself Is All Very Well, But . . .

Imagine for a moment a world in which you were never again allowed to talk to anyone else or communicate with them in any way. What do you think would happen to your mind, to your language? That question is one way of helping you to recognize that your *relationships with others* are the most important part of your life as a human being. Your absolute need, like ours, is to have others to talk to and to listen to. We do not use the telephone or write letters merely to pass the time. We all need to share our view of our world with others—to interact.

THE LISTENERS/READERS INSIDE AND OUTSIDE YOUR HEAD

In this chapter you will read texts through which individuals are sharing. In every case the sharing is achieved through writing—sometimes to someone in particular, as in a letter, and sometimes to a larger unknown readership, through the printed word (as in the case of this whole book).

In Chapter 1, most of the texts were written for/to the writer herself/himself. Now we shall see writers reaching out to others, "speaking" to them, often in order to have some kind of effect on them, to affect them.

Even before the writer puts pen to paper, or finger to typewriter, there is someone else inside his/her head. Who exactly is it, you ask. Or do you already know? (Do you?)

Think of your closest friends for a moment. Our guess is that, if you are like us, you spend a fair amount of your time "talking" to them even when they are not with you. This act of addressing someone who is physically absent is a perfectly normal human act, a result of the gift of language. There is nothing to be gained by trying to determine exactly where they are, inside your head. It really doesn't matter. The important thing is that they really do feel as though they are there. You, like us, can enjoy the sense of their presence, their proximity. And they oblige us by listening and by usually understanding what we say. When our friends are inside our heads they are usually very cooperative, very obliging.

When you write a letter to your friends, the situation is both the same and different. You sit at your table, and the words to them flow pretty easily. That is what friends are for! (And not to pick critically at every word we offer—unless we specifically invite them to read our text as critic or editor.) But—and it's an important but—they are also living their own independent lives out there in the world, separate from you.

When we write, then, we write to two friends, two in one: the totally congenial friend inside our heads, and the actual absent friend who is out there somewhere in the world. The first, internalized, friend helps us to "speak"; but the actual friend out there has *needs that we must recognize.*

To understand the nature of these needs, let us look briefly at the differences between talking to friends and writing to them. When you are engaged in a conversation with a friend—you are sitting at the same table—whenever you sell her short by failing to explain or by talking vaguely or imprecisely, she has the power to ask you to do it properly. Most talk is dialogical—an interaction between two or more. Whenever you refer to something within your immediate environment, you don't need to do much more than "point." "Look at that crazy guy over there," you say. And she turns to look in the direction that you have already indicated by the mere direction of your eyes. It is only when you refer to an experience elsewhere of which she was not a part that you will need to "put her in the picture." And if you neglect to do so, she can give you the appropriate cue. Then you will obligingly specify, describe, characterize, and contextualize*; as she begins to nod emphatically, you know that you have supplied the necessary clues. She can then say, "I see!" meaning not that she sees, literally, but that your verbal representation is adequate for her needs.

Now consider the situation in which you are writing to a distant friend. As we have pointed out, friends are already in one sense internalized within your consciousness, but they are also elsewhere. It is to the actual friend elsewhere that you will have to take care to give as much as he needs in order to reconstruct your intended meaning from your words on the page. You can't be there to say, "Oh, I meant. . . ."

We usually make a pretty good job of letters to friends; it is when we are writing for complete strangers that we can fall flat on our faces. Why is this so? In general, because we can't be absolutely sure of (a) what they know, and (b) what they don't know. Every text that you read will have made assumptions about what you, the absolutely unknown reader, knows—that is, can reasonably be expected to know—and what you don't know and *therefore need to be told.*

---

*Contextualize: to present the surrounding "field" of your particular topic so that your reader will have enough grasp of when and where to be able to "place" and make sense of what follows. In conversation we signal: "Yesterday [time], at Mary's house [place]."

"Talking" to Others

THE NATURE OF OUR SOCIAL SATISFACTIONS

In Chapter 1 we suggested that normal human beings like you and us talk to themselves, literally, inside their heads, and also "talk" to themselves in writing, by making notes of various kinds. We suggested that we do this kind of writing-for-the-self for two main reasons: one we called practical, the other we called reflective.

At the end of Chapter 1 we suggested that such writing, like talking, turns or veers irresistibly out toward others.

The reasons for this turning to others are not very hard to find. Any person who spent his whole life talking only to himself would strike most people as in some sense abnormal, odd, and probably mad. And this is not at all surprising, because our most "normal" use of language is precisely to sustain and extend our social lives as human beings. A useful definition of a human being—as opposed to an ape or a pigeon—is "one who makes conversation."

Another way of putting this is to claim that for human beings no experience can be said to be complete until they have *verbalized* it. It is through our gift of language that we are able to think about anything that has happened to us, and also to share that thinking with someone else. And the inclination, impulse, and need to share our thoughts, to represent them to another person, are again a definitive part of what is meant by being human.

We have thousands of reasons for representing our thoughts to others. We are sure that if you reflect for a few minutes on your own life over the past week you will be able to recall many occasions when you have talked to others for some reason or other. It is so much a matter of habit, of what we normally do, that we rarely stop to think about it.

We stay sane by sharing our thoughts with others. We recount to friends an experience we have had and explain to them how we behaved, how we reacted, how we feel about it. And in our telling, either explicit (stated) or implicit (unstated, left for them to pick up on) is the question "What do you think?" or "How would you have reacted?" or "Do you think I am/was right?" That is why we have friends—for interaction, reconsideration, reassurance, checking it out, or consolation.

REPRESENTING AND PRESENTING

So we write little texts, both reflective and practical. We can call these *representations*—ways of representing in words our thoughts and feelings, and also ways we have invented or discovered for getting things done. And we can present these to others.

When we present our reflective texts to others, what are we doing? What are we intending? What are we hoping for? The answer is: some kind of recognition. In effect, we are saying: "This is how this bit of the world strikes me. This is how I interpret this or that bit of experience. Do you recognize it?"

And what reaction are we hoping to receive in return? Total recognition: "That's just what I think"? "That's exactly how it struck me too"? "Yes, that's how I felt too"? Or "Yes, but . . ."?

The value of presenting our representation, our text, to others may well lie in the fact that they recognize it *to some degree*—enough to allow us to go on believing that they and we share values, beliefs, and convictions. But others also do something perhaps even more useful. They do recognize; but they also say such things as "Haven't you overlooked so-and-so?" "Aren't you forgetting something?" "I'm not sure that I understand this bit. Can you make it clearer?" and so on.

When we wrote, we may have been so caught up in it that, yes, we see now that we slipped up a bit here, and we repeated ourselves there, and we failed to make that bit clear *for the other person*. The main difference between experienced writers and inexperienced writers is possibly this: that experienced writers develop a habit of having those kinds of conversations inside their own heads. In other words, they have gradually internalized an independent reader who reacts in useful ways, as a reader, even while the text is going onto the paper. Certainly, we know that *our* failures as writers tend to occur when the reader inside our heads has gone to sleep.

(Our assumption at this moment is that you already, in some sense, know what we are "saying"; and that our task is to remind you of it, because to be conscious of this knowledge will probably help you to write more effectively.)

Let us now have a look at some writers addressing their absent readers.

Sharing What We Have Learned

HENRY DAVID THOREAU COUNTS HIS PENNIES

Here is Thoreau writing about how he built a house very inexpensively:

> Before winter I built a chimney, and shingled the sides of my house, which were already impervious to rain, with imperfect and sappy shingles made of the first slice of the log, whose edges I was obliged to straighten with a plane.
>
> I have thus a tight shingled and plastered house, ten feet wide by fifteen long, and eight-feet posts, with a garret and a closet, a large window on each side, two trap doors, one door at the end, and a brick fire-place opposite. The exact cost of my house, paying the usual price for such materials as I used, but not counting the work, all of which was done by

myself, was as follows; and I give the details because very few are able to tell exactly what their houses cost, and fewer still, if any, the separate cost of the various materials which compose them:—

Boards	$8 03½	{ Mostly shanty boards.
Refuse shingles for roof and sides	4 00	
Laths	1 25	
Two second-hand windows with glass	2 43	
One thousand old brick	4 00	
Two casks of lime	2 40	That was high.
Hair	0 31	{ More than I needed.
Mantle-tree iron	0 15	
Nails	3 90	
Hinges and screws	0 14	
Latch	0 10	
Chalk	0 01	
Transportation	1 40	{ I carried a good part on my back.
In all	$28 12½	

These are all the materials excepting the timber, stones, and sand, which I claimed by squatter's right. I have also a small wood-shed adjoining, made chiefly of the stuff which was left after building the house.

—Henry David Thoreau, *Walden*

Did you notice how Thoreau writes "I give the details because . . ."? Why should any writer explain, or feel the need to explain, why he has "given" a particular part of his text? Do you think he suspects that otherwise we might suspect him of boasting? ("See how clever I was!") Or is he afraid we might turn away? ("Oh, all these tedious, unnecessary details!")

The writer's assured and earned position, after he has supplied such a wealth of particular detail, down to half a cent, is that the reader can never afterward claim that he or she has been misled or deceived; there is no trace of vagueness here, no airy generalizing. The writer is scrupulously specific. Even at the risk of giving us too much, he has taken care to give us enough.

MARY LOU COHALAN'S CAVEAT

What, then, of this?

- "Make sure your schedule is flexible so you have enough time to spend on the building site. It's best if your job and home are not more than a half-hour away, and you should always be accessible for phone calls.

- "Don't take on the job of a general contractor without some prior knowledge of construction.
- "Don't get carried away, making lots of changes in the architect's basic plans without figuring the additional costs first.
- "The biggest mistake I made was hiring people simply because of bottom-line prices. And find out as much as possible about all the workmen hired, either through references or personal experience.
- "Be sure you have insurance to cover workmen's accidents and stolen materials."

—New York Times, April 19, 1984

Mary Lou Cohalan, who wrote those words for a newspaper, had built a house on a limited budget: not $28, but $85,000. There's inflation! As a result of some unfortunate experiences, she decided to share, not the details of her experience, but rather what she had learned, with others, so that her readers might benefit from her mistakes. Her decision to write her text may have been inspired in part by anger and irritation at having been "ripped off"; but it was also presumably informed by a wish to help others, if only by saving them from the same pitfalls that she had encountered.

Even as you were reading her words, you may well have been thinking not of house building but of some mistake that you had made, either through not knowing enough or through misjudgment. If you were, we urge you not to think of that train of thought as a symptom of an inability to concentrate. It's not. Rather, it is a perfectly normal way of reading what someone else offers you. Even as you are receiving their representation of their experience, it can give rise in your reader's mind to the awareness of something similar or analogous, from your own life. (You will have noticed how, when someone tells of an experience, his or her last words are often hotly pursued by the words of someone else. For example, "Just like what happened to me in Utah last year. . . .")

WHAT NOW?

Write a short text to share with your class: "I hope you can learn from my experience. . . ."

Sharing Our Sensations

In writing for others, we usually have a purpose. The purpose of Cohalan's text seems pretty clear. Thoreau's is perhaps more complicated, a case, perhaps, of mixed motives. Albert Einstein once suggested that "If we speak of the purpose and goal of an action we mean simply the question: which kind of desire should we fulfill by the action or its consequences . . . ?"

Here, the action can be taken to mean writing (and being published, and therefore read); the consequences, the effect of a text on the writer and the readers.

JAMES AGEE'S SENSATIONS: AN EXERCISE IN PARTICULARIZATION

Let us now look at a text that is hardly more than a list and see what desires and consequences have to do with it. In this text, a short quotation from his *Let Us Now Praise Famous Men*, James Agee offers an account of some of the sensations that give him a strong sense of well-being. We have set them out as a list, so that each item is more distinct.

the fracture of sunlight on the facade and traffic of a street

the sleaving up of chimneysmoke

the rich lifting of the voice of a train along the darkness

the memory of a phrase of an inspired trumpet

the odor of scorched cloth, of a car's exhaust, of a girl, of pork, of beeswax on hot iron, of young leaves, of peanuts

the look of a toy fire engine

the stiffening of snow in a wool glove

the odor of kitchen soap, of baby soap

the flexion of a hand; the twist of a knee; the modulations in a thigh as someone gets out of a chair

the bending of a speeding car round a graded curve

the taste of turnip greens; of a rotted seed drawn from between the teeth

of rye whiskey in the green celluloid glass of a hotel bathroom

the breath that comes out of a motion-picture theater

the memory of the piccolo notes which ride and transfix Beethoven's pastoral storm

the odor of a freshly printed newspaper

the stench of ferns trapped in the hot sunlight of a bay window

the taste of a mountain summer night

Here, now, are a few thoughts that we would like to share with you about our reading of that passage of Agee's. You will see that we take up Einstein's point about the fulfillment of desires and also his distinction between an action (in this case the act of writing) and its consequences (the effects of the text both for the writer and for readers).

The Satisfactions of Writing

What we know about Agee—from reading pretty well everything he ever wrote—is that he had a very active, even restless, mind and also loved the life of his senses. For example, he had a very acute sense of smell and also loved to drive cars fast and recklessly just for the pleasure of speed, of hectic motion. We also know that he was a compulsive talker and writer: he could talk all night, until his friends were snoring on the sofa. In this passage, Agee is probably fulfilling his desire for the satisfaction of representing some of his most intense pleasures, pleasures of the senses. When we write keenly of a remembered pleasure, it is almost as if we re-experience it. Doubtless this was true for Agee too.

He also had a very strong desire to share his pleasures. "O.K.," he seems to say, "I can't take you there, but I can tell you about it." Then there is the pleasure for him of the act of writing, of sheer representation, of finding the right word, of making it vivid and strong, sharp and "close up."

The Satisfactions of Reading

That is the pleasure of the writer. What, then, of *our* action and its consequences? Our act is that of reading, of reaping the harvest that is both on the page and also in what the text arouses in our minds, drawing on our memories of pleasures of a similar kind. He reminds us of sensations we had forgotten until this moment: "Ah, yes! Baby soap! What a delicate fragrance! What beautiful dim memories it stirs!" And even as we read, we hear a train in the distance, raising its desolate, restless, lonely sound in the night: "the rich lifting of the voice. . . ." We wouldn't have thought of expressing it like that, and so his phrase adds to our pleasure. It provides another way of saying and therefore of "seeing" it.

And one of the consequences is that we are reminded of many half-forgotten pleasures—modest, simple pleasures, no less valuable for their modesty. And we have the joy of discovering someone who uses strong, vivid words, so that we are pleasured once more—this time by the language.

Effective Particularizations

What if Agee had brushed by all this sensation, merely glancing? What if he had written: "There are various sensations that give me pleasure"? Such a statement would have been of very limited interest. Why so? Because it is very generalized; it fails to specify; it fails to particularize. And it's merely a claim. We have to take it on trust. It offers no "proof"; it is merely a rather vague statement. There is nothing in that general statement to savor, to enjoy, to "feel," to be aroused by. It leaves us pretty well where it found us—and maybe disappointed too.

Agee offers not just whiskey, but rye whiskey; not just rye whiskey, but in the green celluloid (celluloid was a kind of cheap plastic) glass of a hotel. Not just a hotel, but a hotel bathroom. He drank his whiskey out of a cheap glass, the kind you use for cleaning your teeth! Out of something so cheap, he drank with relish. Intense pleasure and a suggestion of squalor: the mixture is very rich! And it is sharply particularized.

Tell about your favorite sensations. Jot them down in your notebook. Then choose half a dozen—the most idiosyncratic, vivid, or memorable—to share in class. Make sure your text effectively particularizes.

Sharing Someone's "Normal Day"

The following text is a short extract from a letter written by one of the best letter writers of the twentieth century—Dalton Trumbo, the novelist and Hollywood scriptwriter; it was written to Elsie McKeogh, his agent (she was responsible for selling his writings and for getting a fair price for them). She was also a friend.

How much did she need to know in order to understand his letter?

> Things otherwise go well. We have a dining room but no furniture, so I've fixed it up as a work room and it's excellent. Melissa is a fine kid, and I believe we enjoy her more than the others when they were babies because we're more experienced and not so afraid of her as we were of them. Chris fell today from some great height at school and has an egg on his forehead. Nikola fell from a bicycle and has the skin of half her knee gone. Cleo spent too much time under the sunlamp and fried herself. Our dog was run over and recovered after an operation for ruptured stomach. I am quite broke. Everything normal.
>
> —Dalton Trumbo, *Additional Dialogue*

It's obvious that you know far less about Trumbo than did Elsie McKeogh. What, then, do you guess or assume or infer about the people mentioned in his letter?

And what do you guess/assume/infer about his sense of humor? What is the effect for you of Trumbo's last sentence?

WHAT NOW?

Make a note of about a dozen domestic calamities that have occurred in your house over the past few years. Write an account of them as if they had *all* occurred *in one day*, then end with Trumbo's last sentence. How do you like the effect?

WHAT NEXT? FACT OR FICTION?

1. Was Trumbo telling the literal truth, telling lies, embroidering, or creating a little domestic fiction to amuse his friend?

   The question is unanswerable. What is of interest here is not your answer in itself but the way in which you work to get it.

2. Which of the following is most likely?
   a. Trumbo is a liar, and all his children know it.
   b. His children say, "Our father loves exaggerating and teasing."
   c. Trumbo enjoys other people's pain.
   d. The Trumbo children are all exceptionally careless.
   e. Trumbo is more interested in his dog than he is in his children.
   f. Trumbo cannot pay the rent.

In the rest of this chapter we invite you to look at two kinds of texts, reflective and practical, intended for others.

Taking Stock of Last Week

One of the main things we do when we reflect is to go over our recent past experiences. We are confident you will agree with that statement and will also be able to provide many examples. (Why are we so confident?)

Here is the American writer William Stafford reflecting for himself and for his readers on what he learned last week:

Things I Learned Last Week

Ants, when they meet each other,
usually pass on the right.

Sometimes you can open a sticky
door with your elbow.

A man in Boston has dedicated himself
to telling about injustice.
For three thousand dollars he will
come to your town and tell you about it.

Schopenhauer was a pessimist but
he played the flute.

Yeats, Pound, and Eliot saw art as
growing from other art. They studied that.

If I ever die, I'd like it to be
in the evening. That way, I'll have
all the dark to go with me, and no one
will see how I begin to hobble along.

In The Pentagon one person's job is to
take pins out of towns, hills, and fields,
and then save the pins for later.

Human beings are both like and unlike one another. In what ways are you like the learner in that text? In what ways unlike?

Some people know things that others do not know. Which references in Stafford's text do you *not* recognize? (Let us guess: probably "Schopenhauer" and possibly one or two of "Yeats, Pound, and Eliot.") Our further guess is that you recognize every other reference in the poem; you don't need to check anything in an encyclopedia. Right?

The trickier question goes beyond the recognition of references. It is this: Do you recognize his various states of mind? You will do so only if you yourself have experienced similar states of mind. In other words, *you will recognize him only if you recognize yourself also in his text.*

In the first two lines, we can say he has *noticed something.* It may be important, it may be trivial. We notice lots of things. Some stay with us and provoke reflection; others simply evaporate. They were noticeable, even noteworthy, for a moment; then our minds dropped them.

As for that mysterious character, Schopenhauer, he was a not very good nineteenth-century German philosopher. Do not worry about identifying him. Think rather of anyone who is a pessimist *but* plays the flute. What, then, do you make of that connecting "but"? Why "but"? What difference would it make if you substituted "and" for "but"?

Isn't there something *implicitly optimistic* about playing any musical instrument? How come that a pessimist *plays*? Is there some kind of contradiction in anyone who claims to be a pessimist and yet plays the flute?

Don't push this too far. Don't worry it to death. One of the reasons we talk to others is to enjoy the pleasure of teasing them, of mystifying them, of provoking and activating their gray matter. It's pleasurable to hear our friends cry out, "Hey, wait a minute! What's that got to do with this? What's playing a flute got to do with pessimism?"

WHAT NOW? WHAT DID YOU LEARN LAST WEEK?

Write a text, using either the same kind of patterns as Stafford or your own, which represents what you "learned last week." And remember, you don't have to tell the truth.

Writing in the Dark I

We don't know how Sei Shōnagon actually wrote her *Pillow Book.* Certainly pencils had not been invented. Maybe she used a brush and ink. And she probably had a low light burning in her bedroom—a small lamp or a candle. Here now is a text about writing, not by a dim light, but without benefit of any light: writing in the dark.

It's not difficult.
Anyway, it's necessary.

Wait till morning, and you'll forget.
And who knows if morning will come.

Fumble for the light, and you'll be
stark awake, but the vision
will be fading, slipping
out of reach.

You must have paper at hand,
a felt-tip pen—ballpoints don't always flow,
pencil points tend to break. There's nothing
shameful in that much prudence: those are your tools.

Never mind about crossing your t's, dotting your i's—
but take care not to cover
one word with the next. Practice will reveal
how one hand instinctively comes to the aid of the other
to keep each line
clear of the next.

Keep writing in the dark:
a record of the night, or
words that pulled you from depths of unknowing,
words that flew through your mind, strange birds
crying their urgency with human voices,

or opened
as flowers of a tree that blooms
only once in a lifetime:

words that may have the power
to make the sun rise again.

—Denise Levertov, "Writing in the Dark"

That again is a reflective text, is it not? Or is it also practical? Does
it contain a set of instructions that will be useful to us? Clearly it does.
But it is not entirely, exclusively, a practical text, is it?

Take out all the bits of directly practical instructions, and what do you
have left?

1. A reassurance: "It's not difficult."

2. An assertion: "it's necessary."

3. A warning: "you'll forget."

4. Another warning: "Fumble for the light, and . . ."

5. Another reassurance: "There's nothing shameful...."

6. An encouragement: "Keep writing...."

7. A list of new possibilities—of what we can do, even though we had never perhaps thought of such possibilities before.

What, then, is this text up to? Apart from giving very down-to-earth, practical advice, it seems to want to affect us, to have an effect on us, to change our minds and possibly, therefore, what we do with our lives. If our minds are changed, then other things change too.

In reflective texts we can not only express our hopes and ideals, as when we write for ourselves; but when we present our text to others, we can express what we hope for others too; and those hopes may become theirs also.

WHAT NOW?

Recall the last time you helped a friend to do something, or the last time a friend helped you to do something, by offering advice or instructions. Did reassurance, warnings, and encouragements accompany the practical parts? How important were they in keeping up morale?

Writing in the Dark II

In June 1928, Amelia Earhart became the first woman to fly the Atlantic. In January 1935, she made the first solo flight from Hawaii to California. In 1937, she had almost completed a flight around the world when her plane disappeared without trace.

On her Atlantic flight—the one that made her famous—she flew with two men, Bill Stultz (pilot) and Slim Gordon (mechanic). For two weeks they were held up by fog and had to wait in Trepassey, Newfoundland, until they finally received news of better weather. Her publicity manager, George Putnam, cabled her from the United States while she was waiting:

SUGGEST YOU TURN IN AND HAVE YOUR LAUNDERING DONE

She replied:

THANKS FATHERLY TELEGRAM   NO WASHING NECESSARY
SOCKS UNDERWEAR WORN OUT   SHIRT LOST TO SLIM AT RUMMY
CHEERIO AE

Stultz, the pilot, had a serious drinking problem, and when the time came to set off, he was drunk. Amelia and Slim dragged and lifted him into the plane, Amelia threw out a bottle she found concealed in the cockpit, and after three attempts, they got the plane into the air.

Amelia Earhart in 1932

Earhart's plane *Friendship* in 1928, after her transatlantic flight

Throughout the flight, which lasted more than 20 hours, Amelia kept a log. For many hours the night sky was pitch-black, and she couldn't put a light on because it would have reflected off the dials and dazzled Stultz. So she wrote in the dark.

Here is what her logbook looked like:

You probably found that rather difficult to read, so here are some extracts from the logbook, printed normally:

140 m.p.h. now. Wonderful time. Temp. 52. The heater from cockpit warms the cabin too.

Bill says radio is cuckoo. He is calling now.

There is so much to write. I wonder whether ol' diary will hold out.

I see clouds coming. They lie on the horizon like a long shore line.

I have just uncurled from lying on Major Woolley's suit for half an hour. I came off this morn with such a headache that I could hardly see. I thought if I put it to sleep it might get lost in the billows of fog we are flying over.

There is nothing to see but churned mist, very white in the afternoon sun. I can't see an end to it. 3600 ft. temp. 52, 45 degrees outside. I have et a orange, one of the originals. At T. our infrequent oranges came from Spain, under-nourished little bloods.

4:15. Bill has just opened the motor to climb over this fog. We are 3800 and climbing.

Creatures of fog rear their heads above the surroundings. And what a wallop we get as we go through them.

Bill has just picked up XHY British Ship Rexmore, which gives us bearing. 48 no. 39 west 20:45 GMT. The fog is growing patchy and great holes of ocean can be seen. XHY will inform NY of our position.

As I look out of the window I see a true rainbow—I mean the famous circle. It is of course moving at our speed and is on our right, sun being to port a trifle. I have heard of color circles in Hawaii.

The sun is sinking behind a limitless sea of fog and we have a bright rainbow, a fainter ring and, if I am not seeing things, a third suggestion on the edge. The middle is predominately yellow with a round grey shadow in the center. Is it caused from us or our props?

The pink vastness reminds me of the Mojave Desert. Also:

> J'ai miré dans ma prunel
> Petite minute éblouie
> La grande lumière éternele.

(Bill gets position. We are out 1096 miles at 10:30 London time,)—and having done so he is content to die. I wish I had that poem here.

One of the greatest sights is the sun splashing to oblivion behind the fog, but showing pink glows through apertures in the fog. I wish the sun would linger longer. We shall soon be grey-sheathed.

We are sinking in the fog.

4000 ft.

The light of the exhausts is beginning to show as pink as the last glow of the sky. Endless foggies. The view is too vast and lovely for words. I think I am happy—sad admission of scant intellectual equipment.

I am getting housemaid's knee kneeling here at the table gulping beauty.

It is* about 10. I write without light. Readable?

The sea was only a respite. Fog has followed us since. We are above it now. A night of stars. North the horizon is clear cut. To the south it is a smudge.

The exhausts send out glowing meteors.

How marvellous is a machine and the mind that made it. I am thoroughly occidental in this worship.

Bill sits up alone. Every muscle and nerve alert. Many hours to go. Marvellous also. I've driven all day and all night and know what staying alert means.

We have to climb to get over fog and roughness.

Bill gives her all she has. 5000 ft. Golly how we climb. A mountain of fog. The north star on our wing tip.

Fog and cloud persisted. The radio had failed. They could not get a bearing. They didn't know where they were.

We are going down. Probably Bill is going through. Fog is lower here too. Haven't hit it yet, but soon will so far as I can see from back window. . . . Everything shut out.

Instrument flying. Slow descent, first. Going down fast. It takes a lot to make my ears hurt. 5000 now. Awfully wet. Water dripping in window. Port motor coughing. Sounds as if all motors were cutting. Bill opens her wide to try to clear. Sounds rotten on the right.

3000 ft. Ears not so painful. Fog awful.

Motors better, but not so good.

It is getting lighter and lighter as day dawns. We are not seeing it dawn, however. I wish I knew radio. I could help a lot.

We are over † stratum now. At 3000. Bill comes back to radio to find it on the blink.

We are running between the clouds still, but they are coming together. Many clouds all about . . . shouldn't bother. Port motor coughing a bit. Sounds like water. We are going to go into, under or over a storm. I don't like to, with one motor acting the way it is.

How grey it is before; and behind, the mass of soggy cloud we came through, is pink with dawn. Dawn "the rosy fingered," as the Odyssey has it.

Himmel! The sea! We are 3000. Patchy clouds. We have been jazzing from 1000 to 5000 where we now are, to get out of clouds. At present there are sights of blue and sunshine, but everlasting clouds always in the offing. The radio is dead.

---

* A misprint for 'Tis? Compare with her handwriting.

†

That is the way it is written in the logbook. So far no one can make out that word before "stratum." Can you?

The sea for a while. Clouds ahead. We ought to be coming somewhat in the range of our destination if we are on the course. Port motor off again. 3000 ft. 7 o'clock London.

Can't use radio at all. Coming down now in a rather clear spot. 2500 ft. Everything sliding forward.

8:50. 2 Boats!!!!

Trans steamer.

Try to get bearing. Radio won't. One hr's gas. Mess. All craft cutting our course. Why?*

"Why?" That was the last entry in her log. Within a few minutes they had landed at Burry Port in Wales. When Amelia climbed down out of the plane, all she carried were two scarves, her toothbrush, and her comb.

When she returned to America and a tickertape parade, a reception at the White House, and inescapable fame, she holed up in George Putnam's house in Rye, New York, and wrote her account of the flight, *20 Hours 40 Minutes.*

In her book, she explained:

> Have you tried to write in the dark? I remember sitting up in bed at school composing themes after lights. During those night hours on the Friendship the log was written with the help of my good left thumb. I would not turn on the electric light in the after cabin lest it blind Bill at the controls. And so I pencilled my way across the page of the diary thankful for that early training with those better-late-than-never themes. The thumb of my left hand was used to mark the starting point of one line. The problem of this kind of blind stenography is knowing where to start the next line. It didn't always work. Too often lines piled up one on the other and legibility suffered.

Take another look at those extracts from Amelia's logbook. Is the text practical or reflective? What do you think her log had to do? What were its essential functions? Why did she have to write it? What did she write that was not absolutely (functionally or practically) necessary?

If you work out your answers to those questions, you will know that her log was both practical and reflective. In other words, it was not only a reasonably reliable record of data; it was also (equally important for later flights?) an account of *how a human being was experiencing* the flight, a representation of her state of mind. So her log constitutes both a practical, useful record and also an account of *how it felt*—an account that would "preserve" the experience, as she went through it moment by moment, for herself. It was also something she could present to others, so that they could *share* her feelings, the life of her mind, the pleasures of her senses.

---

*She had expected by now to see small craft in the ocean, with observers on the lookout, but failed to see any.

What, then, makes her log an especially exciting text? We believe that its most compelling feature is this: that it was *concurrent*, or *simultaneous*. It is a representation of an experience not written later, looking back from a cozy armchair, but scribbled *even as she was participating in the experience.*

In a word, her logbook is a *participant text*. Whereas the book she wrote a few weeks later was a *spectator text*.

TWO KINDS OF TEXT: PARTICIPANT AND SPECTATOR

A participant text is simply a text that is written even as you are doing something else. Some activities obviously don't *allow* you the opportunity to scribble in a notebook at the same time as you are doing whatever it is you are doing! Let's take an extreme case. Imagine you are learning to be a tightrope walker. No way are you going to agree to keep a written record of your sensations, your lurchings and swayings, while you are up there on the rope.* Your instructor, of course, may be doing just that— making a moment by moment record of your mistakes. But he/she is a spectator.

Many forms of scientific lab work clearly demand that you keep such a record. And people who have volunteered as guinea pigs in biological experiments have kept such records.

WHAT NEXT? WRITING A PARTICIPANT TEXT

In Chapter 7 we will look at participant texts in greater detail. Meanwhile, try this: Next time you find yourself in one of the following situations, take out your notebook, and jot down your observations: in a laundromat; in a cafeteria; babysitting; riding the subway; on a bus, an airplane, or a train; at a lecture; in a hairdressing salon; in a doctor's or dentist's waiting room; training your dog or cat; fighting a bout of flu; dieting; trying to stop smoking. (Some of those texts will involve writing over a period of half an hour, others over a period of maybe a few weeks.)

---

*NASA solved this problem by using radiotelephones, so that even as the pioneer astronauts were having hitherto unknown experiences, they could talk their way through them. The talk was recorded and then transcribed to form a participant text, even though the astronaut had not literally written it down.

3 | Dear John, . . .
Writing for/to People We Know

Here is a brief recapitulation, to begin with:

1. Talking to ourselves is a private activity.
2. Writing for ourselves is also a private activity.
3. Talking to someone else is a social activity.
4. Writing to someone else is also a social activity.
5. We often do 1 and 2 in order to prepare ourselves to do 3 and 4.

Proximity/Distance

Let us take a closer look at item 3 in the above list, talking to someone else. How many people have you talked to in the last 24 hours? How would you place them on a diagram of proximity—that is, a simple chart of relationships from intimate/close to the other extreme of distant/stranger?

CLOSE	LESS CLOSE	EVEN LESS CLOSE	DISTANT
family	neighbors	instructors*	someone who got a wrong number
boyfriend/ girlfriend	classmates	college secretary	
			a stranger on the bus

We don't need to tell you that your ways of talking at the extreme left-hand end of that chart are very different from those at the extreme right-hand end. You may, incidentally, quarrel with some of the placements

---

*As the semester progresses these may move somewhat to the left.

on our diagram. Obviously this crude little chart is a simplification of all the subtle differences, the imperceptible gradations, of your proximity to/distance from other people.

But let us simply stress this point: if it is true that you intuitively and without thinking choose the appropriate voice for any social interaction, this must be because you have learned to do it—not by taking a course in social skills but by learning and correcting yourself while actually doing it and observing feedback. In this chapter and in Chapter 4, we shall invite you to look at how writers also operate on something like the same grid of proximity/distance and find—or fail to find—the appropriate "voice" or language for each of their occasions.

WRITING TO A CLOSE FRIEND

In this chapter we shall start with proximity.

The easiest, most relaxed writing that you do is when you write a letter to a close friend. Why do we believe that to be generally so? ("Generally," because after a misunderstanding, for example, you might have to "choose your words" very carefully.) Consider the following observations, and see if you agree with them.

When you write to close friends:

1. You feel as if you are simply talking to them.

2. You are hardly aware of writing, because . . .

3. Your thoughts come so easily and quickly.

4. You have plenty to say.

5. You are confident that your words to them will be acceptable and welcome.

6. No door will be slammed in your face. You will not be told to wipe your feet.

7. Your language feels comfortable, like a good old pair of shoes that never pinch your toes—so comfortable, you don't even realize you are wearing them.

8. In your mind's eye, you can see your friend enjoying your letter.

9. In your mind's ear, you can hear him/her muttering little sounds of approval and interest.

10. You never pause to ask: "Why am I writing this letter?"

When we write to close friends or to members of our family, we fulfill some of our own desires and simultaneously fulfill some of theirs. Those are good things to do, and writing is only one of many ways of doing them.

For our present purposes, we want you to focus on why it is that in intimate letters you suffer no pangs of nervousness about your *ability to write*. What, then, are the conditions in which you yourself enjoy a sense of confidence as a writer? Let us try to guess. If we omit something that seems to you important, then drop us a line.

You enjoy confidence as a writer when:

1. You are free from the awful feeling that someone not altogether sympathetic is breathing down your neck.

2. Your purpose for writing, your intention, is so clear that you don't need to think about it.

3. You concentrate on WHAT is to be represented and don't feel distracted by the question HOW.

4. You concentrate so keenly on what is to be said that you are in no way self-conscious.

5. Your act of concentrating is more like a feeling of being possessed than like a deliberate effort of will.

THE INTENDED READER AFFECTS THE WRITER

Two Letters from the Hospital

Here are two letters written from the hospital:

September 26, 1984

Dear Grandma,

Just a note to tell you I'm feeling just great. The doctors say my appendix is no longer an appendage! I'll be on solid foods soon—in the meantime, it's jello for breakfast, lunch, and dinner.

Should be home soon. Mom will let you know exactly when. Thanks for the flowers; they're really lovely. And tell Sam I asked about him.

Love,
Jo

September 26, 1984

Hi!

Remember saying, "Stay cool!" Well, Jane, I'm not, I'm really not. This place scares the hell out of me. All these guys rushing in and out, the noise, the lights, day and night. I can't get any sleep. It really got to me last night—would you believe I cried into my pillow? Oh, you're probably saying, that's Jo, all right, but, really—sometimes it's the smallest thing that makes you feel weak and I do. And, okay, so it was only an appendectomy—a routine operation, but, well, I don't know, I feel strung out.

And the stitches are no picnic. And the food—I'm dying for a steak and a ton of French fries. You should see the food they throw at you— cream of wheat, mashed potatoes, jello. Well, maybe I'll fit into *your* Calvin Klein's when I get out.

They didn't have a semi-private room, and so here I am stuck in this ward—with seven other people. All I can see out the window is these boring trees and a flagpole. But you should see the woman next to me. Would you believe she's a woman wrestler!!! Like, she's covered in plaster. And she never stops joking. Says she's gonna show me her tattoos when the casts come off. I honestly don't know whether to believe her. But you should see the freaked-out guys who come to visit her, and what they write on her casts. I can't even write those words down. Tell you when I get home. And I don't care—I'm getting out of here soon.

In the meantime, say Hi to you know who . . .

Keep your fingers crossed,
Jo

P.S. Stay cool.

Notes How does the intended reader affect the writer? In order to consider that question, first make a note of any differences you can detect between the two letters from the hospital. Then compare your observations with ours.

1. The most obvious difference is that Jo has far more to say to Jane than she has to say to her grandmother.

2. Jane-as-audience seems to release far more of Jo's energy.

3. In her letter to Jane, Jo feels able to admit to emotions that are not even mentioned in her letter to Grandma. She explores her fear, her feeling of weakness, her gluttonous desire for a gross quantity of dubious food. And she is clearly excited by the woman wrestler, even though she does not say so explicitly.

4. In the second paragraph of her letter to Grandma, she seems to be casting around for things to say.

5. It is reasonable to infer that letter 1 is a duty letter, one that Jo felt obliged to write, whereas letter 2 is a letter she wrote from desire.

Notes 1. If Jo had put her letters in the wrong envelopes and sent Jane's letter to Grandma, how do you imagine Grandma would have reacted?

2. If Jo had chosen to tell Grandma about the female wrestler, how would her account probably have differed from the one she gives to Jane?

3. If someone observed that these two letters showed "two sides of Jo," what would you take that remark to mean?

4. Why do you think that her letter to Jane is so much more interesting than her letter to Grandma?

5. Consider now a more difficult question: Do you feel that you are a more interesting person when you are with some people than with

others? Can you account for this notion? (It is in fact shared by many people but tends not to receive much attention.) When you are with X you feel that you have a lot to say, but when you are with Y you search desperately for something to say—anything to break your silence. Do you think this is because X is more genuinely interested in you than Y is?

6. If we say that in her first letter Jo is in the role of dutiful grand-daughter and that in writing to Jane Jo is in the role of close friend, do you think that Jo deliberately took on those roles, or is it something that most of us do as we move from one relationship to another and do *as a matter of habit,* without really thinking about it?

Letters of Advice

A FATHER'S SURPRISING LETTER TO HIS SON

In 1956, Dalton Trumbo's son, Christopher, reached the age when most young people are ready to leave home. To mark the occasion, Trumbo wrote the following letter to his son as a kind of welcome to the world of adults.

My dear son:

When a young man leaves the house of his parents for the first time it is altogether proper that his father impart to him certain basic truths by which the son can guide his actions, solve his difficulties, enrich his mind and increase the scope of his activities. I append, therefore, a few homilies for your consideration:

Stealing: Never steal more than you actually need, for the possession of surplus money leads to extravagance, foppish attire, frivolous thought and other vices which ought, especially among the young, to be discouraged.

Borrowing: Give not security, for such is the lowest form of borrowing. In this context, it can be accomplished only in the circle of your dearest friends, the circle itself diminishing by one with each transaction, since if your friend refuses to lend he is no longer your friend, while if he yields to your importunities you can no longer afford to be his. It follows that not only are there fewer opportunities to borrow than to steal, but that borrowing is also immensely more difficult, requiring as it does the most artful admixture of wit, intuition and intelligence. Contrary to the rule for stealing, prudence commands the borrower to think not only of present but of future needs, from which we derive the formulation: either borrow not, or over-borrow.

Lying: The art of lying is the art of the practical. It ought never be indulged for the pure pleasure of the thing, since over-usage dulls the instrument, corrodes the character and despoils the spirit. The important thing about a lie is not that it be interesting, fanciful, graceful or even pleasant, but that it be believed. Curb, therefore, your imagination. Let the lie be delivered full-face, eye to eye, and without scratching of the scalp. Let it be blunt and forthright and so simple that you can repeat it in detail and under oath ten years hence. But let it, for all its simplicity, contain one fantastical element of creative ingenuity—one and no more—designed to capture the attention of the listener and to convince him that, since no one would dare to invent the improbability you have inserted, its mere existence places the stamp of truth upon everything you have said. If you cannot tell a believable lie, cling then to truth which is always our surest succor in time of need, and manfully accept the consequences.

Girls: Girls are what boys want, young men get, and old men think about. I have long intended to counsel with you on this matter as a father should, and will delay it no longer.

The most agonizing problem for a young man of your age upon encountering a girl who suits his taste is this: If I ask her for a date will she accept me?—or will she reject me? One shivers with joy at the prospect of acceptance: one trembles with shame and mortification at the mere thought of rejection. The following mode of conduct, being an infallible guide for determining in advance whether your request for a date will be granted, can save much heartburn and embarrassment:

Let us assume you are at a dancing party, and a girl strikes your fancy, and you ask her to dance, and she accepts, and you dance. Be not too uplifted by this, for your case is really very little advanced. Although she dances with you, she also dances with others, while the date you wish to make with her involves, I trust, your own company alone.

Therefore, at some moment during the dance when the music is soft and languorous, draw your lips close to her left ear and whipser—distinctly but not so loudly that others can overhear—a sequence of lewd and obscene words. Do not weave them into a sentence, and if inadvertently you do, in no circumstances allow the sentence to conclude with a question mark. Far better the short, simple, sturdy words in artful arrangement, and nothing more.

If she draws back slightly and regards you with a look of wild surmise, say nothing. Compose your mouth into a gentle leer and lower your left eyelid slowly until the eyeball is entirely covered. Then, just as slowly, open the eye. Arch the neck slightly, and, showing plenty of white in both eyes, gaze at her with admiration.

If she turns from you and runs across the floor to her mother's arms, chattering away and pointing at you, put her down for a prude, and turn your eyes otherwise, content in your knowledge that if you had asked her for a date she would most likely have refused. If, however, she smiles and resumes the dance, you have the strongest assurance that a call on the morrow will neither be misunderstood nor ungraciously received.

In this fashion, working your way slowly through the group, you will by the end of the evening have discovered those who favor your cause and those who do not, without once having made an advance or lain yourself open to rejection. The number who turn away from you may be considerable, but in them you have lost nothing. If, however, among all that company of girls, just one continues to dance with you—oh my boy, my boy!

Your mother and I send our blessings. Cherish us in your heart and honor us by your conduct.

I am, sir,

Your father,
Dalton Trumbo
—from *Additional Dialogue*

Does that letter strike you as intimate or as formal? Or both at once? Does it surprise or disconcert you? Do you feel as if you are eavesdropping? prying? Could you imagine yourself using that kind of language in writing to someone in your family—a younger sister or brother?

Anyone familiar with the movies for which Trumbo wrote scripts—for example, *The Fixer, Thirty Seconds over Tokyo, Johnny Got His Gun, Spartacus*—will know that he had a very wide repertoire of "voices" at his disposal: he could find a way of speaking to suit anybody. He also had a well-developed sense of the dramatic: he could write words for a character that, when spoken, would create a strong sense of tension or a powerful, unmistakable effect. We gather from reading his letters that he was a modest, good-humored man, with a well-developed sense of the ridiculous and a hatred of self-important or pretentious people. How then can we explain the formal tone of this letter? Surely such formality is not appropriate to an intimate letter? "I append, therefore, a few homilies for your consideration"—indeed! But Trumbo was too clever a man to have gotten it so badly wrong! So what exactly is his game?

The fact that his language sounds not only formal but also old-fashioned—perhaps this is a clue? In the old days, what did the father of a well-to-do family do when his son was about to enter the adult world? He called the young man to his room, stood erect in front of the fireplace, tucked his thumbs into his vest, and delivered a high-sounding sermon on how a man should behave. This seems to be exactly how Trumbo is performing—by his manner. But *what* is he saying? Is his advice conservative, old-fashioned, pious, solemn? Hardly! So perhaps the peculiar pleasure of reading this text comes from the contradiction between Trumbo's manner and his matter.

WHAT NOW?

Try one of the following:

1. Write a straight or ironic letter of advice to a younger friend who is about to go to college. Help him/her to learn from your own experience.
2. Write a sympathetic letter to a younger brother or sister who has just been jilted for the first time and who appears to need emotional sympathy and consolation.

3. Write a conciliatory letter to a friend who is persistently avoiding you as a result of a foolish misunderstanding.
4. Write a tactful letter to your parents explaining one of the following: (a) why you wish to change your major, (b) why you need more money, (c) why you have taken a part-time job, (d) why you are leaving college to go to Finland to work as a lumberjack, a waitress, or whatever "unsatisfactory" occupation you fancy.
5. Write the letter that Christopher Trumbo might have written to his father a year later giving an account of why his advice was either so successful or so disastrous. Or write the letter that Christopher's girlfriend might have written to Trumbo explaining why his advice to his son had proved to be so calamitous or so effective.

A FATHER'S HARSH LETTER TO HIS DAUGHTER

In 1938, the novelist F. Scott Fitzgerald wrote the following letter to his daughter, Scottie. She had broken some rules at her boarding school, and had been asked to leave. Her father was afraid that this would prevent her from getting into Vassar College, which was where *he* specially wanted her to go. At this time Fitzgerald's wife, Zelda, was in a mental hospital; Fitzgerald himself died in 1940.

[Metro-Goldwyn-Mayer Corporation]
[Culver City, California]
July 7, 1938

Dearest Scottie:

I don't think I will be writing letters many more years and I wish you would read this letter twice—bitter as it may seem. You will reject it now, but at a later period some of it may come back to you as truth. When I'm talking to you, you think of me as an older person, an "authority," and when I speak of my own youth what I say becomes unreal to you—for the young can't believe in the youth of their fathers. But perhaps this little bit will be understandable if I put it in writing.

When I was your age I lived with a great dream. The dream grew and I learned how to speak of it and make people listen. Then the dream divided one day when I decided to marry your mother after all, even though I knew she was spoiled and meant no good to me. I was sorry immediately I had married her but, being patient in those days, made the best of it and got to love her in another way. You came along and for a long time we made quite a lot of happiness out of our lives. But I was a man divided—she wanted me to work too much for *her* and not enough for my dream. She realized too late that work was dignity, and the only dignity, and tried to atone for it by working herself, but it was too late and she broke and is broken forever.

It was too late also for me to recoup the damage—I had spent most of my resources, spiritual and material, on her, but I struggled on for five years till my health collapsed, and all I cared about was drink and forgetting.

The mistake I made was in marrying her. We belonged to different worlds—she might have been happy with a kind simple man in a southern garden. She didn't have the strength for the big stage—sometimes she pretended, and pretended beautifully, but she didn't have it. She was soft when she should have been hard, and hard when she should have been yielding. She never knew how to use her energy—she's passed that failing on to you.

For a long time I hated *her* mother for giving her nothing in the line of good habit—nothing but "getting by" and conceit. I never wanted to see again in this world women who were brought up as idlers. And one of my chief desires in life was to keep you from being that kind of person, one who brings ruin to themselves and others. When you began to show disturbing signs at about fourteen, I comforted myself with the idea that you were too precocious socially and a strict school would fix things. But sometimes I think that idlers seem to be a special class for whom nothing can be planned, plead as one will with them—their only contribution to the human family is to warm a seat at the common table.

My reforming days are over, and if you are that way I don't want to change you. But I don't want to be upset by idlers—inside my family or out. I want my energies and my earnings for people who talk my language.

I have begun to fear that you don't. You don't realize that what I am doing here is the last tired effort of a man who once did something finer and better. There is not enough energy, or call it money, to carry anyone who is dead weight and I am angry and resentful in my soul when I feel that I am doing this. People like _____ _____ and your mother must be carried because their illness makes them useless. But it is a different story that *you* have spent two years doing no useful work at all, improving neither your body nor your mind, but only writing reams and reams of dreary letters to dreary people, with no possible object except obtaining invitations which you could not accept. Those letters go on, even in your sleep, so that I know your whole trip now is one long waiting for the post. It is like an old gossip who cannot still her tongue.

You have reached the age when one is of interest to an adult only insofar as one seems to have a future. The mind of a little child is fascinating, for it looks on old things with new eyes—but at about twelve this changes. The adolescent offers nothing, can do nothing, say nothing that the adult cannot do better. Living with you in Baltimore (and you have told Harold that I alternated between strictness and neglect, by which I suppose you mean the times I was so inconsiderate as to have T.B., or to retire into myself to write, for I had little social life apart from you) represented a rather too domestic duty forced on me by your mother's illness. But I endured your Top Hats and Telephones until the day you snubbed me at dancing school, less willingly after that. . . .

To sum up: What you have done to please me or make me proud is practically negligible since the time you made yourself a good diver at camp (and now you are softer than you have ever been). In your career as a "wild society girl," vintage of 1925, I'm not interested. I don't want any of it—it would bore me, like dining with the Ritz Brothers. When I do not feel you are "going somewhere," your company tends to depress me for the silly waste and triviality involved. On the other hand, when occasionally I see signs of life and intention in you, there is no company in the world I prefer. For there is no doubt that you have something in your belly, some real gusto for life—a real dream of your own—and my idea was to wed it to something solid before it was too late—as it was too late for your mother to learn anything when she got around to it. Once when you spoke French as a child it was enchanting with your odd bits of knowledge—now your conversation is as commonplace as if you'd spent the last two years in the Corn Hollow High School—what you saw in *Life* and read in *Sexy Romances*.

I shall come East in September to meet your boat—but this letter is a declaration that I am no longer interested in your promissory notes but only in what I see. I love you always but I am only interested by people who think and work as I do and it isn't likely that *I* shall change at my age. Whether you will—or want to—remains to be seen.

Daddy

P.S. If you keep the diary, please don't let it be the dry stuff I could buy in a ten-franc guide book. I'm not interested in dates and places, even the Battle of New Orleans, unless you have some unusual reaction to them. Don't try to be witty in the writing, unless it's natural—just true and real.

P.P.S. Will you please read this letter a second time? I wrote it over twice.

—*The Letters of F. Scott Fitzgerald*

Notes   How did you react to that letter? Did it annoy you? Distress you? Disconcert you? Did you identify more with Scottie or her father? Does Fitzgerald's frankness about his marriage and its failure surprise you? Do you think it was fair of Fitzgerald to impose such knowledge on his daughter?

What does Fitzgerald appear to want for himself? For his daughter? Do you find him self-centered? Or could it be that his presentation of the failures and sorrows of his own life could help his daughter? How would you react to receiving such a letter from your father or mother? When do you think daughters and sons should know the worst about their parents—if ever?

Consider his proposition: "The adolescent offers nothing, can do nothing, say nothing that the adult cannot do better." Do you agree at all with that point of view? (Or is it perhaps a statement of fact?) What do you think his purpose was in writing it?

Do you agree with our notion that this would be a very difficult letter to answer? How many different conflicting reactions might one have to it, coming from one's father? If it were your duty to answer it, how would you do it? Should you respond warmly to your father's need for sympathy? (Does he deserve it?) What could you say about his marital confessions?

When we write, we can use language to get close to the other person or to put distance between ourselves and them. Where in the text do you see Fitzgerald using language to hold Scottie at arm's length?

"A Quarrel in the Streets"

Let us share with you some of our reactions to Fitzgerald's letter. Even after having known it for twenty years or so, we still feel rather like intruders when we read it again. Does anger or indignation clear one's head or confuse it? It seems that for Fitzgerald it made him see things very starkly, in terms of almost absolute right and wrong. But he must have known his daughter very well, and presumably knew how much she could take. Since this is a text from real life—unlike, say, a letter in a novel—we are at a disadvantage. Whereas the novelist would have provided all the knowledge of his characters that we would need in order to evaluate the letter (e.g., is it unkind, too harsh, overbearing?), in the case of a letter from someone's life we are not in a position to make those kinds of informed judgments or to draw the appropriate inferences. But the letter leaves us feeling not depressed or indignant, not defensive for Scottie or sorry for her father, but *exhilarated*. It's possible that the reason for this lies in John Keats's observation in a letter to his brother, George: "Though a quarrel in the streets is a thing to be hated, the energies displayed in it are fine."

How does the letter leave you?

Fitzgerald as Spectator and Participant

In his letter to Scottie, we see Fitzgerald engaging in an action designed to affect his daughter: the written equivalent of giving her a good talking to. Before he could participate in this action, he must have spent months as a spectator of her conduct, slowly forming judgments of her, evaluating the way she was living—he would have said wasting—her life. On a longer time scale, as he points out, he had participated in a marriage that had slowly gone badly wrong; now he sits at his typewriter as a spectator of his own past and is able to evaluate both his wife and his marriage.

When we are actively involved in an action or a situation, we are so busy participating that we cannot stand back and evaluate it. But as we withdraw from participation, we find that we have the psychological elbow room or breathing space to see it as a whole, from outside, as a spectator. It is then that we find ourselves saying: "Wow, that was a ridiculous waste of time" or "That was a great party!" or whatever.

Notice that Fitzgerald's representation of his marriage is his and only his. For a more complete account, we would have to know other versions: how his wife saw it, not to mention anyone else involved, such as Scottie. Note also that when we are participants in an experience from moment to moment, we cannot know what is going to happen next.* It is only afterward, when it is all over, that we can see that experience from beginning to end, make sense of it, decide what it meant, and evaluate it.

---

*A good example of this is to be found in Amelia Earhart's logbook (p. 39).

Letters of Reassurance

A YOUNG AMERICAN IN PARIS WRITES A LETTER TO HIS MOTHER

In 1866 Tom Eakins arrived in Paris, a 22-year-old student. He wrote many letters to his mother, back in Philadelphia. He believed that his drawing was better than his writing, so he often drew little pictures in his letters to make things clearer.

Paris, Nov. 8, 1866

My dear Mother,

Having a great desire to write to you and having the time, I will tell you about my room for want of something more interesting. It is as comfortable a one as can be found in Paris as far as I know. The house is across the way from the old palace of Luxembourg, and by going out into the entry, I can look down into the garden. Besides, it is close to my school, not more than half a mile, and on the same side of the river. Besides that, there is an arsenal or some such place right back of the house, and the soldiers of this place and of the Luxembourg wake me up at the right time in the morning with their trumpets and drums. Besides that there are no bugs and not even fleas which bother the Americans very much in Paris, as I am told. So taking everything together, I am as well off as I can be out of my home. My room is not as large as my bed chamber at home, but it is large enough and has a big window in it, which gives plenty of light. The walls are papered, and the ceiling is nicely whitewashed. The floor is of stone or rather a sort of brick painted red, but a big piece of carpet in the centre of the room covers half of it.

The grand houses still have waxed wooden floors. They are very slippery, and I came near falling when I first went to the Luxembourg palace to see the pictures. Before trying to find my way in, I stopped and asked a soldier for directions. He said they depended on what I wanted to see, so I told him the pictures. Well then you must go in that door over in the corner, but have you seen the throne, it is far more worth seeing. I told him no, and then he showed me where I must enter. I represented to him that I had rather see the pictures first, but he was eloquent for the throne. I finally told him I was going to be a painter. He didn't say another word. I fell at least a hundred degrees in his estimation. I am yet ignorant about that throne and whose it was.

My room is well furnished, and the principal piece is of course the bed. It is kept clean and tidy. The French bedsteads all seem to have curtains. They add to the beauty, and help keep out the light which would be of advantage to those who don't need to get up early. I'd like to know when you would be up if you had long curtains to your bed. There is a big flat pillow half the size of the bed which goes down at the foot and covers the legs after one is in bed. It is not a bad idea, for when the feet are right warm there's no necessity for a heavy bunch of bed-clothes. But comfortable as it is, I've spent more miserable hours in it lying awake, thinking of home during my trouble. But I will not think less of my home now that

it is ended, but it will be with another feeling. The next thing I've drawn for you is a chair with a velvet seat to it. I have two of these besides the little one with a cane seat. These will do for my friends when any of them will come to see me. Crépon has promised to come sometime, and so have one or two of my new friends.

The next thing is my bureau, and this I make that Aunt Eliza's mind will be a little eased about a place to put my clothes. The next thing is the wash stand, but I believe there is nothing worth mentioning about it. The next thing is the stove which is just in the corner of the room. It is necessary to build a fire every two or three days, to dry the room and purify it, even if you are not going to sit in it. To make a fire you take a little ball of resinous shavings. These balls are about as long as one's finger and twice as thick. You light it and put a bunch or half bunch of little sticks on top and then a couple of big pieces over them and then pull down the gate in front. After the fire is well started you can put up the gate or whatever it is called and throw some coke in on top of the wood. The next thing I've drawn is a mahogany box with a door and a drawer to it. I think you would have had a good deal of trouble guessing its use if I hadn't left the door a little open. The lowness of the French bedstead has given rise to this piece of furniture, which I first saw at the Hotel of Lille & Albion. It was sometime before I thought of looking there for what I wanted. On this page I make my armchair. This I sit in when I have a fire.

Nov. 9th

When I got home from school today, I sat down to draw my table for you, but it got so dark in a few minutes that I couldn't see, the days are so short here, but I guess you can make out that it is a table with a cover and some books on it. There is yet another table to write on, and this one has two little drawers in it, and completes the furniture of the room. There is no closet but there are some big wooden pegs on the wall to hang the clothes upon, and a curtain can be drawn over them which will keep them from getting smoked.

When I came home yesterday, the old doorkeeper opened her little window and told me she had received a letter for me. I grabbed it and made for my room, and lit my candle as soon as I could. It was a miserable little business card. I had gone to Monroe's, American Banker, to see a paper & had registered my name & address, and this man of business I suppose copies down all the names of all the Americans who come to Paris. Advertising is a good thing but it's carried too far when it takes the private letter form. I'll be careful never to go to that store. . . .

When you write me don't forget about little Caddy and her progress, and tell me about Mrs. Lewis & Uncle Emmon's family. I am very anxious to receive my first letter from home. I expected one today, but I am afraid I've another week to wait. It's likely when the mail comes I'll get a whole bunch of them. How is Billy Crowell? I hope he didn't go home that rainy night; for he had been very sick. Have Max and Johanna taken supper at our house since I left. I have often used her present. I found no great difficulty in sewing buttons on. It was necessary to take a peep at the other buttons & remember the old civil engineering rule I learned

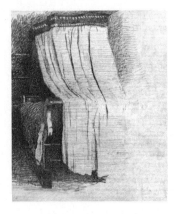

at school that to gain stability you must widen the base and distribute evenly the strain.

I have had a little darning to do too and I don't think I've done it badly. The hole wasn't very big though. I see it will require more talent to mend a stocking with big ones in it. When they get beyond darning and want patch work I'll go and buy a new pair for I remember that Aunt Eliza with all her experience was not always successful in this line although always brilliant. When you get this letter I suppose it will be thanksgiving day. Of course they don't have any in France. We had a holiday here last week & they shut the school. It is called the day of all the saints. Next day was the day of the dead, and all Paris goes to the cemeteries to put wreaths on the graves of their friends. Mrs. Moore says the Chinese carry food to their graves in California. . . .

—Phyllis D. Rosenzweig, ed., *The Thomas Eakins Collection of the Hirshhorn Museum and Sculpture Garden*

Here is an edited version of a classroom discussion of Tom's letter:

G.S.:   Anyone in this class write letters as long as that?

[Much head-shaking, expressions of incredulity]

ROSEMARY: I don't. But my phone calls last for hours!

LISA: I reckon most of us use the phone. . . .

G.S.:   Rather than write letters, you mean?

LISA: Sure.

G.S.:   O.K. Let's see if we can find out something about ourselves by asking Eakins—his text—some questions. What purposes does his letter serve?

DON: He's telling her about his new life.

UNIDENTIFIED: Sending information.

G.S.:   Agreed. But what is all this information—about his room, the museum, the garden, the hole in his sock—why do you think he tells her so much?

LOIS: If she's anything like my mother, she probably wants to know everything!

ALMA: She wants to know, and she needs to know.

G.S.:   And what exactly is this *need to know*? Does her life depend on it?

BARBARA: She *needs* to know—it's a kind of reassurance. He's away from home for the first time. She needs to be sure—assured—he's

O.K. And maybe *he needs* to reassure her. To feel comfortable in himself.

LISA: He couldn't *call* her—the phone wasn't invented—so he had to put his *voice on paper* and say, "I'm O.K. I hope you're O.K." He *cares*. And she *cares*. It's a long letter. She'd have to care, to take the time to read it.

DEAN: It's a way of getting her off his back. He writes this letter, puts it in the mailbox, and says, "Ha! I can get on with my life now."

STEVE: She's not going to pester him if she gets letters like this. She'll stop worrying about him, and she'll stop worrying him!

G.S.: So, do you think he said to himself, "I'll sit down and write a long letter to Ma, and reassure her, and then she'll stay off my back"?

DEAN: Not in so many words, in those words. But that would be what he wanted—that would be his purpose, even if he didn't say so to himself.

G.S.: Explicitly?

DEAN: Right. He wouldn't be explicit. It's more a matter of how he felt, what he felt, without putting it into words, explicitly.

G.S.: So, what role is he playing?

BARBARA: In Paris?

G.S.: By writing the letter.

BARBARA: In Paris, he's in the role of student, art student; and writing the letter, he's in the role of good, dutiful son, reassuring son.

DON: He's not yet grown away from his family, his mother, so he's not in the role of stranger even though Paris must seem strange to his mother. His role is "member of family who's a long way from home."

Notes   One of the features of Tom Eakins's letter that we didn't attend to in that discussion was that it is very different from the kind of letter that most of us would write on a similar occasion. All that talk about furniture! the detail he offers about individual pieces of furniture. Is it possible to explain this, without knowing more about Eakins or his mother? Is it that Mrs. Eakins would like to be able to *see* his room, and that this is the closest she can come? That she is exceptionally inquisitive, and he has to represent everything in order to satisfy her curiosity?

Could you tell the whole truth about your room to your parents? If you needed to reassure your mother, what features of your room, what parts of your life would you concentrate on? What parts would you pass over in silence?

WHAT NOW?

Write an account of last night in such a way as to reassure your mother.

Write an account of the same time span in order to convince a friend that your life is full of excitement. Use a plausible mixture of fact and fiction.

Putting Your Cards on the Table

A TRUE STORY

George Putnam, Amelia Earhart's public relations manager, proposed to her several times, and on each occasion she declined his offer. She was, she told a friend, "unsold on marriage." In September 1930, her father, an unsuccessful lawyer, died. "His big case was lost and we told him he won." A few weeks later, Amelia and George went to the Lockheed aircraft factory in Burbank, and once more he proposed marriage. She patted his arm, accepted, then took her new plane up to see how it handled. They were married in February 1931. But before the ceremony, she handed him a letter and asked him to read it. This is what he read:

> Dear GP,
>   There are some things which should be writ before we are married. Things we have talked over before,—most of them.
>   You must know again my reluctance to marry, my feeling that I shatter thereby chances in work which means so much to me. I feel the move just now as foolish as anything I could do. I know there may be compensations, but have no heart to look ahead.
>   In our life together I shall not hold you to any medieval code of faithfulness to me, nor shall I consider myself bound to you similarly. If we can be honest I think the differences which arise may best be avoided.
>   Please let us not interfere with each other's work or play, nor let the world see private joys or disagreements. In this connection I may have to keep some place where I can go to be myself now and then, for I cannot guarantee to endure at all times the confinements of even an attractive cage.

I must exact a cruel promise, and this is that you will let me go in a year if we find no happiness together.
I will try to do my best in every way.

A.E.

—*Letters from Amelia*

It is surely strange for us to be able to read that very private letter. Do you feel like a prying intruder, a voyeur? The private made public— that shift, that exposure, can be very disconcerting, rather like those awful dreams most people have in which they appear in public with no clothes on.

But how do you react to AE's letter? Do you find that your mind is immediately inclined to pass judgment? "How could she! So heartless! How could he marry her after that?"

How do you think he reacted, there and then? Later, when he'd had time to reflect on it? At the time, he simply smiled and nodded; then they were married. (She kept her own name.) Later he described the letter as "brutal in its frankness but beautiful in its honesty." Do you think that is a mature, well-judged, finely tuned response? Can you accept the paradox that something can be simultaneously "brutal" and "beautiful"?

AE never took silly risks, but she tested experimental planes and pushed herself to the limit. And she had prepared for her own death well in advance. In 1928 she wrote the following sealed "popping-off letter" to her mother. In 1937, after the search for AE's plane in the Pacific had been called off, her mother finally opened that farewell letter; this is what she read:

Dear Mother,
Even though I have lost, the adventure was worthwhile. Our family tends to be too secure. My life has really been very happy, and I don't mind contemplating its end in the midst of it.

Amelia Earhart wrote her "popping-off letter" while she was alive, well, and with no reason for believing in the imminence of her death. This may help to account for its cheerful and unsentimental tone. But how do people manage to write anything coherent when faced with the inescapable fact of approaching death? How can anyone conceivably write under such pressure?

MICHAEL SMITH'S MESSAGE

About one hundred years ago, Michael Smith was one of about 40 miners trapped deep in a coal mine after an explosion. He wrote a final message to his wife, Margaret, scratching his words on a tin water bottle.

See if you can decipher his writing. You will have to guess a few words, where the text disappears around the back. (See below for the full text.)

Here is Michael Smith's full text, transcribed by someone who was able to read it from the bottle itself. The transcriber made some changes; can you spot them? (Answer on page 375.)

> Dear Margaret,
>   There was 40 of us altogether at 7 a.m. Some was singing hymns, but my thoughts was on my little Michael that him and I would meet in heaven at the same time. Oh Dear wife, God save you and the children, and pray for me. . . . Dear wife Farewell. My last thoughts are about you and the children. Be sure and learn the children to pray for me. Oh what an awful position we are in.
>
>   Michael Smith, 54 Henry Street

WHAT NOW? PUTTING *YOUR* CARDS ON THE TABLE

"But I never realized that you . . ." people say when serious misunderstandings arise. One way to prevent them is to ensure that the other person knows exactly where you stand. In order to make your position perfectly clear, a letter is far more effective than talking. When you try to *say* it, face-to-face, interruptions can throw you off your stride. A letter allows you to take control of your words without distraction. And you can work away at it, modifying, revising, until you're sure it says exactly what you need to say. And your words, being written down, cannot be misrepresented.

Think of a situation in which it is very important that someone should be very clear about where you stand, and write an appropriate letter.

Notes
Saying Goodbye

When Michael Smith realized that he would probably not escape from the mine, his thoughts turned to his wife and children. For reasons that we cannot explain, he singled out "little Michael" for special mention: it's possible that the child was in fact dying or had just died—infant mortality was commonplace a hundred years ago.

If you found yourself in a desperate situation—and God forbid!—who would you write to? What feelings would you feel the need to express?

Suggesting a Cure

An English parson once received a letter from a woman friend, Georgiana, in which she confessed that she was seriously afflicted by deep depressions. Here is his reply:

> Dear Lady Georgiana,—Nobody has suffered more from low spirits than I have done—so I feel for you.
> 1st. Live as well as you dare.
> 2nd. Go into the shower-bath with a small quantity of water at a temperature low enough to give you a slight sensation of cold, 75° or 80°.
> 3rd. Amusing books.
> 4th. Short views of human life—not further than dinner or tea.
> 5th. Be as busy as you can.
> 6th. See as much as you can of those friends who respect and like you.
> 7th. And of those acquaintances who amuse you.
> 8th. Make no secret of low spirits to your friends, but talk of them freely—they are always worse for dignified concealment.
> 9th. Attend to the effects tea and coffee produce upon you.
> 10th. Compare your lot with that of other people.
> 11th. Don't expect too much from human life—a sorry business at the best.
> 12th. Avoid poetry, dramatic representations (except comedy), music, serious novels, melancholy, sentimental people, and everything likely to excite feeling or emotion, not ending in active benevolence.
> 13th. *Do good*, and endeavour to please everybody of every degree.

14th. Be as much as you can in the open air without fatigue.
15th. Make the room where you commonly sit gay and pleasant.
16th. Struggle by little and little against idleness.
17th. Don't be too severe upon yourself, or underrate yourself, but do yourself justice.
18th. Keep good blazing fires.
19th. Be firm and constant in the exercise of rational religion.
20th. Believe me, dear Lady Georgiana, Very truly yours,—

Sydney Smith
—*The Smith of Smiths*

WHAT NEXT? HOW TO CURE A COMMON AILMENT

Which of the following ailments have you suffered from?

An excessive addiction to ice cream

Procrastination

Blushing

Indolence

Untidiness

Excessive borrowing

The inability to find anything

Chronic unpunctuality

Unconvincing excuses for not doing work

Illegible handwriting

Write a letter to a friend who now suffers from the same ailment, and prescribe your cures.

4 Dear Sir or Madam, You Don't Know Me, But . . . Writing for/to Strangers

Three Responsibilities

When we write to strangers, there are three cardinal responsibilities to bear in mind. The first is the need to "put the reader in the picture." We cannot assume that the stranger-reader knows what we know, shares our viewpoint, has an identical frame of reference. Things must be spelled out, not taken for granted, if we want that stranger to understand what we are saying. (And why write to/for others at all if only to be misunderstood?)

The second need has to do with social skills, with understanding our private and public worlds and how they differ. As soon as we attempt to relate to a stranger, either in talking or in writing, we must first be aware of having moved from our own cozy, relaxed, private world, into the public world. And this shift has important consequences for the way in which we use language in order to present ourselves.

We can *prepare* for such encounters in the enclosed space of our own room, in our own inner speech, in our own notebook, wearing our old pajamas. But when we actually present ourselves to the other person, if we are still wearing our old, mussed-up pajamas, they are—you guessed it—going to be shocked, disconcerted, even provoked to anger.

When it's a matter of clothes, appearance, or manners, we learn very early the social skills that prevent our making such blunders. It is a subtler and more demanding task to transfer such social common sense into the sphere of written communication and work out its consequences for our expectations of our writing.

The third need is to be aware of *degrees* of social distance. Look again at the chart on page 43. You will see at a glance that "strangers" are at the extreme right-hand side of the proximity/distance continuum. Consequently the way in which we write to/for a stranger should differ radically from the way in which we write to a close friend.

As you read this chapter, ask yourself how well the writer of each text has followed through on these three basic responsibilities. We begin with letters to a very famous stranger.

Writing to Einstein

It is a generally recognized fact that the price of fame is a flood of letters from total strangers, who write for all sorts of reasons, very few of them better than greed or idle curiosity. When Albert Einstein was the most famous scientist in the world, he was no exception. Letters from strangers poured into his mailbox from around the world. But often, instead of throwing them away, he answered them with remarkable patience, courtesy, and even sympathy. Here are accounts of three strangers' letters to Einstein and how he replied to them.

THE MEANING OF LIFE

In Princeton, early in December 1950, Einstein received a long handwritten letter from a nineteen-year-old student at Rutgers University who said "My problem is this, sir, 'What is the purpose of man on earth?' " Dismissing such possible answers as to make money, to achieve fame, and to help others, the student said "Frankly, sir, I don't even know why I'm going to college and studying engineering." He felt that man is here "for no purpose at all" and went on to quote from Blaise Pascal's *Pensées* the following words, which he said aptly summed up his own feelings: "I know not who put me into the world, nor what the world is, nor what I myself am. I am in terrible ignorance of everything. I know not what my body is, nor my senses, nor my soul, not even that part of me which thinks what I say, which reflects on all and on itself, and knows itself no more than the rest. I see those frightful spaces of the universe which surround me, and I find myself tied to one corner of this vast expanse, without knowing why I am put in this place rather than another, nor why this short time which is given me to live is assigned to me at this point rather than at another of the whole eternity which was before me or which shall come after me. I see nothing but infinities on all sides, which surround me as an atom, and as a shadow which endures only for an instant and returns no more. All I know is that I must die, but what I know least is this very death which I cannot escape."

The student remarked that Pascal saw the answers to be in religion but that he himself did not. After elaborating on the cosmic insignificance of man, he nevertheless asked Einstein to tell him where the right course lay, and why, saying "Pull no punches. If you think I've gone off the track let me have it straight."

In responding to this poignant cry for help, Einstein offered no easy solace, and this very fact must have heartened the student and lightened the lonely burden of his doubts. Here is Einstein's response. It was written in English and sent from Princeton on 3 December 1950, within days of receiving the letter:

> I was impressed by the earnestness of your struggle to find a purpose for the life of the individual and of mankind as a whole. In my opinion there can be no reasonable answer if the question is put

this way. If we speak of the purpose and goal of an action we mean simply the question, which kind of desire should we fulfill by the action or its consequences or which undesired consequences should be prevented? We can, of course, also speak in a clear way of the goal of an action from the standpoint of a community to which the individual belongs. In such cases the goal of the action has also to do at least indirectly with fulfillment of desires of the individuals which constitute a society.

If you ask for the purpose or goal of society as a whole or of an individual taken as a whole the question loses its meaning. This is, of course, even more so if you ask the purpose or meaning of nature in general. For in those cases it seems quite arbitrary if not unreasonable to assume somebody whose desires are connected with the happenings.

Nevertheless we all feel that it is indeed very reasonable and important to ask ourselves how we should try to conduct our lives. The answer is, in my opinion: satisfaction of the desires and needs of all, as far as this can be achieved, and achievement of harmony and beauty in the human relationships. This presupposes a good deal of conscious thought and of self-education. It is undeniable that the enlightened Greeks and the old Oriental sages had achieved a higher level in this all-important field than what is alive in our schools and universities.

WHO TO MARRY?

On 28 October 1951 a graduate student in psychology sent a beautifully worded letter to Einstein in Princeton asking for advice. The student was an only child and, like his parents, Jewish though not orthodox. A year and a half before, he had fallen deeply in love with a girl of the Baptist faith. Knowing the pitfalls in a mixed marriage, and the unintended wounds that could be inflicted by the thoughtless remarks of others, the couple had mixed socially with friends and acquaintances and found that their love was able to withstand the stresses. The girl, unprompted, had expressed a willingness to convert to Judaism so that their children would have a more homogeneous family life. While the young man's parents liked the girl, they were frightened of intermarriage and gave voice to their objections. The young man was torn between his love for the girl and his desire not to alienate his parents and cause them lasting pain. He asked whether he was not right in believing that a wife takes precedence over parents when one ventures upon a new mode of life.

Einstein drafted a reply in German on the back of the letter. The reply may very well have been sent in English, but only the German draft is in the Einstein Archives. Here is a translation of it:

I have to tell you frankly that I do not approve of parents exerting influence on decisions of their children that will determine the shapes of the children's lives. Such problems one must solve for oneself.

However, if you want to make a decision with which your parents are not in accord, you must ask yourself this question: Am I, deep down, independent enough to be able to act against the wishes of my parents without losing my inner equilibrium? If you do not feel certain about this, the step you plan is also not to be recommended in the interests of the girl. On this alone should your decision depend.

I THOUGHT YOU WERE DEAD

From a boarding school in Cape Town, South Africa, on 10 July 1946, a British student wrote a long and naively charming letter to Einstein in Princeton asking for his autograph. Here is an excerpt: "I probably would have written ages ago, only I was not aware you were still alive. I am not interested in history, and I thought that you had lived in the eighteenth century or somewhere near that time. I must have been mixing you up with Sir Isaac Newton or someone." The student, mentioning a friend, went on to tell that they were much interested in astronomy and would creep past the prefect's room at night so as to observe the stars and planets despite being caught and punished a few times. The student confessed an inability to understand curved space. And ended by saying with sturdy patriotism, "I am sorry that you have become an American citizen. I would much prefer you in England."

On 25 August 1946 Einstein replied in English as follows:

Dear Master . . . ,

Thank you for your letter of July 10th. I have to apologize to you that I am still among the living. There will be a remedy for this, however.

Be not worried about "curved space." You will understand at a later time that for it this status is the easiest it could possibly have. Used in the right sense the word "curved" has not exactly the same meaning as in everyday language.

I hope that you and your friend's future astronomical investigations will not be discovered any more by the eyes and ears of your school-government. This is the attitude taken by most good citizens towards their government and I think rightly so.

Yours sincerely,

The student was thrilled to receive this autographed letter, even though Einstein had mistakenly thought, from her unusual first name, that she was a boy. In her reply, dated 19 September 1946, she wrote: "I forgot to tell you . . . that I was a girl. I mean I am a girl. I have always regretted this a great deal, but by now I have become more or less resigned to the fact." And later in the letter she said: "I say, I did not mean to sound disappointed about my discovery that you were still alive."

Einstein replied:

I do not mind that you are a girl, but the main thing is that you yourself do not mind. There is no reason for it.

—Helen Dukas and Banesh Hoffman, eds., *Albert Einstein, The Human Side*

What problems did this young girl have in regulating her relationship with her reader, Einstein? First, she failed to put him in the picture—pointing out that her name could be mistaken for a boy's but that she was in fact a girl. She failed to recognize or identify what he would *not* know. What then saves her from giving offense or causing annoyance? We suspect that Einstein was charmed by her innocent naïveté. He was also a generous man. Even she seems to realize, in her reply, that it was she who had caused misunderstandings.

WHAT NOW? WRITING TO EINSTEIN OR TO . . .

Let's agree that it is impudent to write to famous people. But let us immediately add that there is something very tempting about the idea, the fantasy.

Choose the one famous person to whom you feel most desirous of writing. Invent a very convincing reason for intruding into his/her privacy—a reason that will convince your classmates, that will strike most of them as sufficiently plausible—something much better than "I've always wanted your autograph" or "I've often wondered whether you wear pajamas."

Write your letter.

Submit it to the jury of your class to see if you really did find a good reason as well as a satisfactory tone in your writing, neither obsequious nor presumptuous.

One Way of Answering a Stranger's Request: "Tell Me about Yourself"

The request, coming from a stranger, is very direct, unsubtle, and can even sound rude. But we don't have to answer it directly. We can answer it *in*directly. Just as the contents of our pockets, our purses, or our rooms will tell about ourselves, represent parts of us, similarly our ideals and wishes speak of us, are ways of presenting something of who we are.

One of our most ambitious and most hopeless ideals is our vision of an ideal world, a utopia or Eden, a world fashioned according to our needs and desires.

AUDEN'S EDEN

Here is how the writer W. H. Auden represented his ideal world. You may find it in some ways a very strange place, but don't be surprised by that, for W. H. Auden was in some ways a very strange person. And just remember the old proverb: one man's meat is another man's poison.

Eden

Landscape
Limestone uplands like the Pennines plus a small region of igneous rocks with at least one extinct volcano. A precipitous and indented sea-coast.

Climate
British.

Ethnic origin of inhabitants
Highly varied as in the United States, but with a slight nordic predominance.

Language
Of mixed origins like English, but highly inflected.

Weights & Measures
Irregular and complicated. No decimal system.

Religion
Roman Catholic in an easygoing Mediterranean sort of way. Lots of local saints.

Size of Capital
Plato's ideal figure, 5040 about right.

Form of Government
Absolute monarchy, elected for life by lot.

Sources of Natural Power
Wind, water, peat, coal. No oil.

Economic activities
Lead mining, coal mining, chemical factories, paper mills, sheep farming, truck farming, greenhouse horticulture.

Means of transport
Horses and horse-drawn vehicles, canal barges, balloons. No automobiles or airplanes.

Architecture
State: Baroque. Ecclesiastical: Romanesque or Byzantine. Domestic: Eighteenth Century British or American Colonial.

Domestic Furniture and Equipment
Victorian except for kitchens and bathrooms which are as full of modern gadgets as possible.

Formal Dress
The fashions of Paris in the 1830's and '40's.

Sources of Public Information
Gossip. Technical and learned periodicals but no newspapers.

Public Statues
Confined to famous defunct chefs.

Public Entertainments
   Religious Processions, Brass Bands, Opera, Classical Ballet. No movies, radio or television.

—The Dyer's Hand

WHAT NOW? YOUR UTOPIA

Auden used 17 categories to classify the essential ingredients of his utopia. You can probably think of categories that he left out but that you would want to include. Use his categories, and others of your own choosing, to construct a representation of your ideal world.

Note: In fact, Auden lived much of his life in New York City, a place very unlike his Eden. Perhaps it was living in New York that inspired him to create an alternative fantasy world so very different.

Notes   How would your mother's ideal world differ from yours? Your father's? How would your utopia as conceived now differ from the one you might have envisaged at the age of 15?

WHAT NEXT? IMAGINE THIS

You have won first prize in a competition: two weeks' vacation in Auden's Eden. You know nothing about it before you arrive.

1. Write a letter to your folks back home, after you have been there for a week.
2. Write some notebook entries about the surprises you encounter.
3. Enter the Eden of one of your classmates, and make notes of what delights/amazes/surprises/shocks you.

Any Complaints?

Creating the fantasy of an ideal world and complaining about the world as it is—these are two sides of the same coin.

COSIMO'S BOOK OF COMPLAINTS

In Italo Calvino's amusing short novel *The Baron in the Trees,* 12-year-old Cosimo quarrels with his tyrannical father. Rather than accept a beating, the boy rushes out of the house and climbs up into his favorite tree. "I'll never go down, ever again," he tells Viola, the girl next door. He is very much in love with Viola and wants to impress her. So he stays up there and learns to scramble from tree to tree. He ends up by spending the rest of his life in the trees. One day he realizes that many of the people that come to talk to him feel a sense of grievance; many are vexed by petty injustices. He decides it's time for them to write them all down in a book of complaints. Predictably, it was possible to identify each group from the evidence of what they chose to complain about.

> To explain what "books of complaints" were, Cosimo said: "Let's try and make one." He took a school notebook and hung it on the tree by a string; everyone came there and wrote down whatever they found wrong. All sorts of things came out; the fishermen wrote about the price of fish, and the vineyard men about those tithes, and the shepherds about the borders of pastures, and the woodmen about the Commune's woods, and then there were all those who had relatives in prison, and those who had got lashes for some misdeed, and those who had it in for the nobles because of something to do with women; it was endless. Cosimo thought that even if it was a "book of complaints" it need not be quite so glum.... He got the idea of asking everyone to write down what they would like most. And again everyone went to put down their ideas, sometimes rather well. One wrote of the local cakes, one of the local soup; one wanted a blonde, one a couple of brunettes; one would have liked to sleep the whole day through, one to go mushrooming all the year round; some wanted a carriage with four horses, some found a goat enough; some would have liked to see their dead mother again, some to meet the gods on Olympus. In fact, all the good in the world was written down in the exercise-book, or drawn—since so many did not know how to write—or even painted in colors. Cosimo wrote too—a name—Viola. The name he had been writing everywhere for years.

Bearing in mind that compared with most people in the world you are in fact very well off, reflect now on the nature of *your* complaints. What are they directed toward? What provokes your most serious complaints? What can you do to put things right? Is it enough to complain? It is only when we compare notes with others that we sometimes discover that many others feel the same way. Is that, perhaps, how revolutions begin?

There are two kinds of complaints: reasonable and unreasonable. In the case of reasonable ones, others will agree that you have good grounds for them; considering all the circumstances, yes, it seems that you are reasonably entitled to complain. Or, to put it another way, the situation can be rectified without too much trouble, and in general the change will make others happier, too. Every new movement of ideas—the women's movement is an example—may appear to be overinclined to complain. But the reason for this appearance is not far to seek: there is a great deal that can be improved or put right.

WHAT NOW? YOUR COMPLAINTS

1. What irritates or annoys you most? The cosmos? The cold war? Your friend's smoking? The weather? Your car? Your college or university? Your courses? All of them? Lack of time? Your own untidiness? Your roommate? Make a completely undiscriminating list of all your various causes of complaint, and then separate them into two categories: trivial and serious. Then divide the serious items into two further subcategories: those that you can perhaps do something about and those that you can in no way influence.

2. What, then, do you intend to do about those you believe can be put right? At the very least you can draw the matter to the attention of someone who may be in a position to make changes. In other words, you can use your own words to try to make a difference.

   Don't just sit there, complain! Take that first list of complaints—ones you can perhaps do something about—and write a letter of complaint. But remember this: abusive, insulting, offensive, or hysterical letters will go straight into someone's wastepaper basket.

Your tone of voice is *your* responsibility. It is a matter of choice. Obsequiousness—making your words "crawl"—is usually as revolting as vulgar abuse. It is your responsibility to steer a middle course between those two extremes, if your letter is to have any hope of making someone change his/her mind.

This is not to say that the writing of terribly abusive letters can't be very satisfying—for the writer. Try it. But make sure that your abuse then goes straight into your wastepaper basket!

Many politicians are very attentive to public opinion. Now is the time for you to begin to take your place in the world. And don't forget to celebrate Griper's Day:

Don't just sit there—gripe about it!

Just because you missed National Griper's Day, that's no excuse to keep complaints to yourself.

Griper's Day founder Jack Gilbert of Columbus, Ohio, will listen to a troublesome tale any day in his effort to give the disgruntled, disappointed and depressed a sympathetic audience.

The 55-year-old Columbus man—who marked the first National Griper's Day on Sunday—said he invented the holiday of sorts to bring back old-time personal communication.

"If I am right that it's becoming more and more difficult to have people listen to you, the whole idea of having people call is good," Gilbert said. "The second purpose is just to get people to feeling like people again and not afraid of high technology and computers and all that stuff."

Gilbert doesn't stop at promoting National Griper's Day. The free-lance writer also publishes his phone number and address so people can use him as an outlet for their frustrations.

He hopes to compile the complaints he gets into a humorous griper's newsletter that could be sent to government officials so they know what really irks constituents.

Gilbert said complaints range from consumer costs to chemicals in food. The oddest gripe, he said, came from a Texas man who believes there is too much satellite debris in outer space. "The first permanent space station should be a garbage truck," he wrote to Gilbert.*

—*Daily Times* (Mamaroneck, New York), April 16, 1984

TRUMBO'S TRUCULENCE: A MODEL OF PARTICULARIZATION

The most effective complaints are the most specific; the most specific complaints are the most effective. A successful complaint is the opposite of vague. It does all it can to *particularize:* it names names, it specifies the time of day, the place, the circumstance, the relevant elements in the context—all those details that will prevent the offender from wriggling out of or side-stepping the issue.

The successful complaint doesn't throw insults around—however strong the temptation. It chooses rather to state the facts as precisely as possible and then draws out the implications of those facts; or it simply leaves the facts to speak for themselves.

Dalton Trumbo's letter to the manager (mismanager?) of the La Canada branch of the Bank of America is a classic, a perfect demonstration of how to complain.

Los Angeles, California
November 23, 1957

My dear sir:

Attached to this letter please find notice of a $20 overdraft against the account of Cleo and/or Dalton Trumbo, together with your customary $1.50 charge for such service. Permit me to suggest that you would have been a wiser man and a better banker had you paid the check instead of returning it and charged me under the category of "Paid against insufficient funds." . . .

In passing, I may add this isn't the first time I have received similar intimations of your disesteem. I am a writer, and a bad mathematician, and a poor bookkeeper, and I may upon occasion be briefly and minutely overdrawn. But most of the expense to which I have been put by your idiotic charges, and most of the embarrassment I have suffered by returned checks, have been the result of your own inefficiency, rather than mine.

Example: I have deposited checks drawn against the Sunset and Clark Branch of the Bank of America in my account in the La Canada Branch,

---

*This complaint is not as silly as it may appear. Space is already strewn with debris, which interferes with radio-astronomy and its exploration of the universe.

and drawn against the deposit, and had my checks returned because my deposit had not been cleared between your branches. No telephone call was made to the Sunset and Clark Branch—which is, after all, the same bank—to see whether my deposit was backed by sufficient funds in that bank. (It always was, for the signature to the Sunset and Clark Branch checks was the Paul Kohner Agency, which is one of the wealthiest talent agencies in Hollywood.) Nor was any call made to me. The checks I'd drawn were simply returned. You have grown so enormously as a system of banks that you are no longer one bank. You don't trust your own accounts and apparently you have no way of verifying them. You don't just shoot first and think later: you shoot and never think at all.

Example: Upon a certain Friday afternoon I was so stupid as to deposit by mail a check drawn on the Sunset and Clark Branch in the sum of $2,700 in your La Canada Branch for my account. On the following Tuesday a businessman telephoned me that he was holding my returned check for $80 odd. I told him to run it through again, since I had made a substantial deposit. He differed with me. He had just talked with your branch, and had been informed my account did not have sufficient funds to redeem my check.

I telephoned your bookkeeper. True enough, my account held less than $80.00 and there was no record of any $2,700 deposit. I told her of my Friday mail deposit which certainly should have arrived in La Canada in Monday's (the previous day's) mail. She bestirred herself. She reported back that the check had, indeed, arrived the preceding (Monday) morning before the opening of the bank. I then asked why the check hadn't been posted to my account, and why, some thirty hours later, you were giving out information over the telephone that was not only hundreds of dollars wrong, but thousands. She then tried to explain to me a new and dazzling system of posting checks by which you penalize depositors by delays of up to two days in placing his own funds at his disposal.

I then asked the young lady to telephone the aggrieved businessman to whom she had given her misinformation. I requested this small favor so that the gentleman in question would cease thinking me a liar, so he would understand that it was the bank that had erred and not I. She promised effusively to do so. At five o'clock that afternoon I telephoned the businessman. She had not called him. She clearly had no intention of doing so. You will briskly advertise a man's small accounting errors to all his associates, and charge him for it to boot, but you will not make the slightest effort to rectify your own by the same route.

Example: During the spring a thousand-dollar deposit in my account was erroneously entered twice by your teller in my bank book. My wife quite naturally entered both deposits in our check book. About six weeks later we were rewarded with a blizzard of returned checks, to each of which an appropriate charge was attached. Again I got on the telephone, and again I ran down the error, and again it lay at your door. One ten-cent telephone call, one decent little business courtesy, would have stopped the whole sequence at the outset. But you don't do business that way. The only recognition of error I got out of you was a series of charges against my account which placed me in the happy—from your point of view— position of standing the bill for a typical banker's blunder.

I am not a rich man, and I am not a bookkeeper, but neither am I a pauper or a hot-check artist. I have a $26,000 equity in a house which you yourself approved for a $10,000 loan. I carry $60,000 of insurance on my own life, and $34,000 more on the lives of my family, plus two family health policies. I own four insured automobiles, a great deal of furniture and household and office equipment, a large library, certain valuable copyrights, blocked sums of money in various foreign countries, and other real estate. My income is all earned personal income, and most of it, although not all of it, has been deposited in your branch. My present deposit book accounts only for the past twenty-three months. I find that I have deposited in that period some $76,630.46, for a rough average of $3,330 per month. It's not a large account nor a large income, but I am informed by your extensive advertisements that you are eager to accommodate such small accounts as mine. What the ads don't say is that you are inefficient, unaccommodating, as inclined toward error as you are toward delay, and eager at all times to destroy the good names of your depositors.

I have selected my new bank very carefully. I have gone over these figures and examples with them in order to make certain I shall not be subjected at their hands to the same stupidity I have encountered at yours. They assure me that they handle such matters with intelligence, good faith, efficiency and reasonable celerity. I ask for nothing more.

I shall allow a week for present checks to clear, and then close my account. I have an escrow pending with you. Cancel it and return whatever funds remain in it to my account. I recently ordered two new checkbooks printed up. Cancel the order. If I am too late for cancellation I shall, as usual, pay the bill and leave them with you as my last gift to the Bank of America.

Very truly,
Dalton Trumbo
—Additional Dialogue

Consider for a moment the various satisfactions that Trumbo must have derived from writing that letter:

The pleasure of action—as opposed to merely putting up with it passively

The anticipation of some desirable consequence: at least to cause some embarrassment, to shake people out of their complacency, and presumably to receive an apology

The satisfaction of having done it: a sense of having wrapped it up and brought it to a close

The writer's satisfaction in shaping the text so that it would bite, sting, or jab his reader

The satisfaction of never descending into mere insult or abuse—mudslinging—but of conveying a tone of powerful and impressive disapproval

A Speculative
Reconstruction of
the Evolution of
Trumbo's Letter

How did Trumbo arrive at the point at which he could sit down and write his letter to the bank manager?

1. He engages in transactions with the bank and things seem normal.

2. He continues to participate in bank transactions, and is disconcerted by little discrepancies.

3. He takes time out and reflects on these discrepancies. He is now a spectator of his own past transactions and of the bank's handling of them.

4. He continues to participate in the transactions—paying money in and withdrawing it, paying checks, etc. But now his frame of mind is different from what it had been. He is more alert. He notices more errors.

5. He sits back and evaluates the bank's performance.

6. As a result of his evaluation—totally negative—he begins to participate in the composition of a letter. He does sums, checks his stubs, and begins to form appropriate phrases inside his head.

7. He commits himself to active participation: he sits at his typewriter and writes a first draft.

8. He becomes a spectator of his first text and evaluates it, posing questions: Is this sentence really clear? Is that sufficiently emphatic?

9. As a result of evaluating his own first text, he revises it, types it up, pops it in an envelope, and rushes out to mail it before he can fall prey to an attack of tolerant forgiveness.

WHAT NOW?

We all experience a sense of annoyance, frustration, or irritation, in the same way as Trumbo did. Choose an aspect of your life that you wish to complain about, and first write an intemperate letter simply to let off steam and release the pressure. Then read your text carefully, and moderate its tone so that the result of your revision is that, even though the tone is less intemperate, less abusive, it gets its point across very strongly and clearly, yet politely.

Three Scenarios for Your Participation and/or Spectatorship

We now offer you three "situations." One is fictional, one is actual, and one we are simply not sure about. You may enjoy trying to decide which is which. Each of the scenarios or situations will, we trust, involve you in various ways. You will find yourself reacting to each of them, and from your reactions you will be able to compose a **reactive text**, just as Dalton Trumbo did when he finally lost patience with his bank. The most difficult of these texts will probably be letters to strangers, where you will have to take care to write with moderation and fairness, but at the same time with a sense of clear conviction.

VIRGINIA'S SITUATION

The first episode occurred early in this century, and the account of it comes from a book written by one of the participants, Virginia Cary Hudson, who was about ten years old when she wrote her text. To help you form an impression of Virginia, we first offer you her account of gardening and of etiquette.

> Gardening is growing things. First you find somebody to dig up the ground, and when he tells you what he charges, you say "Too much" and get another somebody. After he digs and rakes, you start planting.
>
> You start in the front with parsley, and lettuce, and onions, and radishes. Get a long string and two sticks and keep your lines straight. Then comes the beets, and the carrots, and the peas, and the bunch beans. The potatoes are over in a field by themselves. Then comes the asparagus, and the celery, and last of all the pole beans, and the butter beans, and the sweet corn. Then you bound your garden on the north and the east with cantelopes and on the south and the west with watermelons. Then you plant sunflowers and hollyhocks in the back corners. Then you pray for the rain to come and if too much comes, you pray for it to stop. It keeps you busy all summer praying and hoeing.
>
> Etiquette is what you are doing and saying when people are looking and listening. What you are thinking is your business. Thinking is not etiquette.

Here now is Virginia's "situation":

> One day we got tired of playing hopscotch and skin the cat, so Edna Briggs said, "Let's play Baptizing." I said to Mrs. Williams, "Can we, I mean may we play Baptizing in your rain barrel?" And she said to me, she said, "Yes, indeed," and she just went on tatting. So I put on my father's hunting breeches and got Judge Williams' hat off the moose horn rack, and I dressed up like the Baptist preacher. That was when Edna ran to get all the kids. And I said to them I said, "The Lord is in his Holy Temple, keep silent and shut up." And then I said, "All you sinners come forward and hence." And nobody came but Melvin Dawson. He is just two years old. Poor little Melvin. He is so unlucky. I got him by the back of his diaper and dipped him in the rain barrel

once for the Father, and once for the Son, and when it came time for the Holy Ghost, poor little Melvin's safety pin broke and he dropped in the bottom of the rain barrel, and everybody ran, and nobody would help me, and I had to turn the rain barrel over to get him out, and then I galloped him on his stomach on my pony to get the water out of him, and then I sat him inside his house, and then I went out to Mrs. Harris' house and got under her bed, and when she looked under there and saw me, all soaking wet, Mrs. Harris said, she said, "Rain and hail in Beulah land, what has happened now?" And when I told her what had happened she just patted her foot and sat, and sat, and then she said, "You know what?" and I said, "What" and Mrs. Harris said, "The Bishop sure needs just such a barrel in the church yard to give some members I know just what little Melvin got." And then Mrs. Harris said, "Let's talk about fishing." And we did.

Thank God for fishing. Thank God for Mrs. Harris and God bless poor little Melvin. Amen.

—O Ye Jigs and Juleps!

WHAT NOW? WRITING TO RESOLVE TENSION

There were no telephones in Virginia's town, and the mothers of the kids in that escapade were either too angry or too embarrassed to visit and talk the matter over. So the letters and notes flew fast and furious. But however furious, we must remember that people then were bound by very strict notions of courtesy and decorum.

Mrs. Dawson writes a letter to Mrs. Hudson.

Mrs. Hudson writes a reply.

Mrs. Hudson and Mrs. Dawson are still not speaking; Mrs. Harris decides to pour oil on troubled waters. She is not sure she can say the "right thing"—her sense of humor tends to run away with her; so she writes to both Mrs. Hudson and to Mrs. Dawson.

The Bishop gets in on the action, too, and writes a pastoral letter to everyone in town to try to bring back the peace of the good old days before Melvin's trauma.

Assume the role of any one of these characters and write his/her letter.

WHAT NEXT? MODERN TIMES

Bring the episode into the 1980s. Mrs. Hudson sends Virginia to a child psychiatrist, who then writes a letter to convey his/her diagnosis and recommendations to Mrs. Hudson.

Virginia writes a letter to her best friend, giving an account of her session with the psychiatrist.

Write one of these letters.

LORD GLASGOW'S SITUATION

During World War II in Britain, people who owned stately homes and lots of land often received a letter from the government informing them that an army unit would be lodged on their estate for a while. There was simply nowhere else to pitch the tents, and the rolling acres of the estate would be ideal for training.

Evelyn Waugh, the novelist, was an officer in a unit that was lodged on the estate of an elderly landowner, Lord Glasgow. One day, Waugh wrote the following letter to his wife:

°**Cmdo:** Commando

°**sixpence:** a coin as small as a dime

°**DSO:** a medal
°**subaltern:** junior officer

No. 3 Cmdo° were very anxious to be chums with Lord Glasgow so they offered to blow up an old tree stump for him and he was very grateful and he said don't spoil the plantation of young trees near it because that is the apple of my eye and they said no of course not we can blow a tree down so that it falls on a sixpence° and Lord Glasgow said goodness you are clever and he asked them all to luncheon for the great explosion. So. Col. Durnford-Slater DSO° said to his subaltern,° have you put enough explosive in the tree. Yes, sir, 75 lbs. Is that enough? Yes, sir I worked it out by mathematics it is exactly right. Well better put a bit more. Very good sir.

And when Col. D. Slater DSO had had his port he sent for the subaltern and said subaltern better put a bit more explosive in that tree. I don't want to disappoint Lord Glasgow. Very good sir.

Then they all went out to see the explosion and Col. D.S. DSO said you will see that tree fall flat at just that angle where it will hurt no young trees and Lord Glasgow said goodness you are clever.

So soon they lit the fuse and waited for the explosion and presently the tree, instead of falling sideways, rose 50 feet into the air taking with it ½ acre of soil and the whole of the young plantation.

And the subaltern said Sir I made a mistake, it should have been 7½ lbs not 75.

Lord Glasgow was so upset he walked in dead silence back to his castle and when they came to the turn of the drive in sight of his castle what should they find but that every pane of glass in the building was broken.

Lord Glasgow gave a little cry & ran to hide his emotion in the lavatory and there when he pulled the plug the entire ceiling, loosened by the explosion, fell on his head.

This is quite true.

Notice that because Waugh is writing a private letter, a letter to his wife, he has cut corners and not taken the trouble to punctuate his text as he would have done if intending to publish it.

If Waugh had been writing this story for publication, what other changes would he have made, do you think? (E.g., would he have revised it, so as to get rid of all those *and*'s? "him and ... grateful and ... eye and ... sixpence and ... clever and ...")

Notes   You have been a spectator, observing that incident through Waugh's representation of it. Since Waugh was also only a spectator—not involved or implicated in the action—we can assume that his account is probably a fair one, with no particular bias for or against any of the participants. But how would the participants later give their versions of what happened? Would you expect Glasgow's version to be exactly the same as that of Durnford-Slater?

What kinds of desires or needs would each of the participants have when they later came to give their versions of the episode? Would their versions depend in part on who their audiences were?

WHAT NEXT? VERSIONS

1. The subaltern writes to his girlfriend.
2. The subaltern submits an official report to the local army commanding officer, who is conducting an inquiry to determine responsibility.
3. Glasgow writes to his lawyer.
4. Glasgow writes to his daughter.
5. Durnford-Slater writes to his brother.
6. Durnford-Slater writes to Lord Glasgow.
7. Glasgow writes to the newspaper, complaining about the behavior of the army.
8. A patriotic individual, on reading Glasgow's letter in *The Times*, writes a reply arguing that everyone must make sacrifices during wartime.
9. Another reader of the paper replies to the patriot, attempting to reconcile Glasgow's and the patriot's points of view.
10. The senior administrative officer of the mental hospital where Glasgow is recuperating writes to Glasgow's daughter, giving an account of his slow recovery.

Take on the role of one of those writers. Before you write, think about the needs and desires of the character you are impersonating. What effect do you wish to have on your reader?

JEAN L'ANSELME'S SITUATION

Dear Sir,

By the time I arrived at the house where you sent me to make repairs, the storm had torn a good fifty bricks from the roof. So I set up on the roof of the building a beam and a pulley and I hoisted up a couple of baskets of bricks. When I had finished repairing the building there were a lot of bricks left over since I had brought up more than I needed and also because there were some bad, reject bricks that I still had left to bring down. I hoisted the basket back up again and hitched up the line at the bottom. Then I climbed back up again and filled up the basket with extra bricks. Then I went down to the bottom and untied the line. Unfortunately, the basket of bricks was much heavier than I was and before I knew what was happening, the basket started to plunge down, lifting me suddenly off the ground. I decided to keep my grip and hang on, realizing that to let go would end in disaster—but halfway up I ran into the basket coming down and received a severe blow on the shoulder. I then continued to the top, banging my head against the beam and getting my fingers jammed in the pulley. When the basket hit the ground it burst its bottom, allowing all the bricks to spill out. Since I was now heavier than the basket I started back down again at high speed. Halfway down, I met the basket coming up, and received several severe injuries on my shins. When I hit the ground, I landed on the bricks, getting several more painful cuts and bruises from the sharp edges.

At this moment I must have lost my presence of mind, because I let go of the line. The basket came down again, giving me another heavy blow on the head, and putting me in the hospital. I respectfully request sick leave.

—Jean L'Anselme, *The Ring Around the World*

WHAT NOW?

Write one of the following letters:

1. The bricklayer's employer replies to that letter.
2. The bricklayer's wife visits him in the hospital, and then writes a letter to her sister.
3. The employer writes a circular, which is sent out to all the bricklayers in his employment.
4. A pedestrian who happened to be passing and who was shaken by what she/he saw later writes to the local newspaper about it.

Impersonations   A few months ago we invited our students to "become" building inspectors, responsible for ensuring that all building regulations are observed, and to report on that episode in a reactive text—an official letter. Here are two of their letters. First, John Lynch's:

Inspector #G6287
Report #29
March 3, 1984

The recent epidemic of poorly trained bricklayers has not found its end in District 23. The following report of incompetence in this district may seem like fantasy, but I assure you it is not. Out of the 34 bricklayers whom I inspected this week, only 7 met the Department's standard qualifications check. It would be understandable for you to assume my judgment harsh based on the ratio of those failed to those passed. I insist that this is not the case. As you surely know from my long career in the Department, I always test by the book.

Where these inept bricklayers are receiving their training I do not know. In one case the problem was so severe that I checked with personnel to make sure the bricklayer's license was not a forgery. Without going into too elaborate an account of the incident: the workman had either not received or had completely forgotten the most elementary brick hoisting techniques. This ignorance almost cost the man his own life in the course of lowering bricks from the roof of a two-story unit he had been repairing. An accident resulting from a simple hoisting operation can only represent total incompetence in more complicated procedures. Surely you must agree that my credentials check was not overzealous.

I feel, out a sense of fraternity, that I must leave names out; however, on checking this man I found he was indeed licensed. The only possible way he could have procured one is through bribery. I'm sure you are aware of the seriousness of this inference. However, my duty as a professional leaves me no choice but to insist that you pursue this matter with the licensing department.

Now, Robert Hammer's:

I am writing this report at your request on the bricklayer, Mr. Jean L'Anselme.

On Feb. 28, 1984, we observed him for the first and only time. He was working on 103 E. Cortland Ave. in Oceanside, Long Island. A storm had recently occurred, damaging many of the bricks on the roof. We had chosen Mr. L'Anselme at random from the ACME Brick & Brack Co. Our office had received a few complaints about the quality of their work.

After one day's worth of observation, I feel due to gross incompetence on Mr. L'Anselme's part he should have his license revoked and further investigation into his company is necessary. We base this on the following observations.

1) He brought up well in excess of fifty more bricks than he needed. This excess of bricks can create dangerous working conditions which can not only injure himself but any passerby on Waukena Avenue.

2) The beam was from our vantage point fifty yards away at too great an angle and could have fallen at any time.

3) The pulley did not look strong enough to hold up the weight it was supposed to carry. It could have broken at any time.

4) His bricks were unsorted from our visual inspection and included many bad bricks, some of which may have been used in the repair of the roof.

5) The basket used to carry the bricks up and down was of poor quality. This was proven by the accident in which the basket fell to the ground and burst its bottom.

6) We inspected the rope and it was strength A rope which is weaker than Industry F rope. It may have ripped at any time.

7) He untied the line while it was holding up bricks which resulted in himself being subsequently injured and hospitalized.

On the basis of these observations we believe Mr. L'Anselme's license should be revoked for a period of at least two years, for his safety and that of the general public.

Yours truly,
R. Hammer
Building Inspector

Neither John nor Robert is actually an inspector of buildings. We can say, then, that their texts are **impersonations**. Which of them strikes you as the more convincing? Are there any details in each letter that strike you as specially convincing? Any which reveal that the writer is impersonating? Do the tone and style of each strike you as properly official?

Notes   Many students who take part-time jobs feel during the first few days or weeks that they are involved in an act of impersonation—that on the job they are "pretending." But gradually they settle in, and later, even though they are still doing exactly the same kind of work, they no longer feel that they are pretending. How do you account for this change? Have you had a similar experience? (You will find more on role-playing on page 87.)

Writing for Your Instructor

Until you get to know your instructors, think of them as Einsteins-with-power—strangers who are authorized to judge, assess, nudge, and criticize your texts.

As you work through this book and through the semester, you will begin to form a reasonably clear sense of your instructor's expectations. For example, some professors insist that students type all their papers; others are willing to strain their eyes almost blind deciphering a handwritten scrawl that seems committed to total illegibility. How do *you* measure up in terms of basic manners, courtesy, or considerateness? Is your writing clear and comprehensible, or does it mutter unintelligibly out of the side of your mouth?

Let us now work through the process. You have been assigned a topic. What next?

Think in terms of (a) what you need to do and (b) what you need to know. Most departments have guidelines on how to do research, how to use a library, and so on. If such guidelines are not available to you, consult a good handbook. That will take care of what you need to know. But what about what you need to do?

Make sure you have grasped the meaning and intention of the topic, then talk your way through it, both through inner speech and in your notebook. Develop a habit of speculating, surmising, chasing associations, posing questions to yourself. If the topic demands an examination and an assessment of competing points of view, then argue both sides while you take a shower. But don't let any ideas go down the drain. Get them down in your notebook. At this stage, concentrate entirely on the matter in hand; elbow your instructor out of your head.

On the basis of your notes, some of which you will probably throw out (as your grasp of the topic and its boundaries evolves, some items in your notes will be self-evidently useless or irrelevant), you can then begin to shape a text. Write this first text as if for yourself—or for a friend. When it is complete, walk away from it. Sleep on it, if possible. Then come back to it as a first-time reader. Become a spectator of your own text, as if it had been written by someone else. At this point you must focus on writing *as a social act*. Has this text put the reader in the picture, or will he/she be left with countless unanswered questions? Does it point the way, or will he/she get lost moving from this to that paragraph? Is that reference too vague? Is the tone overfamiliar? too pretentious? *(Read it with your ear.)*

Finally, shift gear, and read it as you imagine your instructor (not *any* stranger) would read it. Try to envision his/her reactions, the ways in which your text may affect him/her. Put yourself in your instructor's shoes.

Reciprocally, when he/she returns your text, with comments, you may well discover that your instructor has done precisely that—put himself/herself in your shoes. He/she has recognized a particular segment of your text where you knew all along you were experiencing difficulties, has discerned the symptoms of those difficulties and demonstrated ways of resolving them.

COMMENTARY

We always encourage our students to write little supplementary notes for us, which they attach to their texts. In these notes they pose questions that let us into the ways in which they were thinking while they were writing—questions that reflect as openly as possible on the life of their minds when engaged in writing. They also offer specific invitations to us, for example, "I'd like some advice on how to handle the semicolon," or "Please recommend something to read further about this." These notes are very useful, because they help us to avoid the rather frustrating guessing game that takes place whenever one tries to understand *how* someone else thinks. (See page 107 for such a note.)

In writing this section, we are not trying to supplant your own instructor. The best help you will receive as a student-writer will come not from us or from any other book but from that individual who knows your current writing best, both its strengths and its limitations.

And please remember that as you develop as a writer, much of the above advice will fall into the limbo of the no-longer-necessary!

part 2 | Roles
and
Texts

5 | "What/Who Do You Want to Be When You Grow Up?"

Texts Written in Role: Perspectives

LOOKING BACK

Looking back on their lives, elderly people can often see the kinds of people they had become at various stages in their lives. (See, for example, a writer's impression of the emperor Hadrian looking back on his life later in this chapter.) Such knowledge is available only after the event, when we can take a long, retrospective, spectator's view of our past selves, and perceive changes—both improvements and deteriorations—in our character. When we are going through those changes, as participants in our daily lives, they are so gradual as to be imperceptible.

LOOKING FORWARD

As we look forward in time, we are continually preparing to meet the demands we know, or surmise, tomorrow will make. These acts of preparation are very various, some of them overt and obvious, others so subtle that we are hardly aware of them. Checking our hair or our necktie before an important interview; going to college; cramming for a test; learning to conduct ourselves appropriately in a new job; anticipating the boss's requirements; reminding ourselves not to swear when visiting grandma—in fact, evolving an adequate and appropriate language for all situations, especially those that are socially or professionally demanding.

How, then, does a young woman or man become, say, a lawyer? We believe that people prepare themselves for a variety of social and professional demands by role-playing. *Not* acting. *Not* pretending. But role-playing. What, then, is role-play?

Types of Role-play

First we need to distinguish between two main kinds of role-play: the kind that takes place inside our heads (fantasy) and the kind that takes place out in the world.

FANTASY

Most of us stop fantasizing only when we stop breathing. And we fantasize in two ways: (a) as if we were someone else, and (b) as an idealized self.

Fantasy as if Another

When we become intensely involved or caught up in a movie or a novel, it is *as if we become* someone else. We identify with particular characters. We impersonate them. We feel their anxiety, their joy, their sorrow, and so on. Their states of mind and of feeling possess us. When we put the book down, or leave the theater, and re-enter the world of our daily lives, we often feel a sense of anticlimax. Some people, when they finish a long novel in which they have "lived"—experienced powerful **forms of life***—are often restless for hours and even days afterward, finding it very difficult to re-enter actual dailiness. Norman Mailer put it well when he observed: "The psychological heft of role has more existential presence than daily life."

Fantasy as Idealized Self

Inside our heads we are continually rehearsing scenes for tomorrow. We have to meet a friend with whom we have had a painful quarrel; or the boss wants to see us about some serious mistake we made in the accounts. Preparing, rehearsing, we play the encounter within our minds. It is as if we are already there. And we play our role most eloquently, talking persuasively, with sharp wit and clear head, never at a loss. We hear ourselves delivering the ultimate punch line. It is exhilarating. Whatever the situation requires, we can produce, like a rabbit from a hat. Our assurance and style are perfect and invulnerable.

Fantasy as idealized self is an arena for some of our most energetic and productive verbal activity—mostly in the form of inner speech, but if alone, we may begin to vocalize our words, especially when we are anxious or agitated.

Note that both of the above kinds of fantasy take place inside our minds. But we also "make believe" out in the real world.

ROLE-PLAYING OUT IN THE WORLD

Becoming Another Self

Here is a simple example of becoming another self out in the world: You take a part-time job as a bank teller. For a few days you feel strange, wearing a slightly uncomfortable polite smile and your best clothes. At times you feel fraudulent, fake, or ridiculous. You are *not* playacting. The money you handle is real money; your customers are actual customers. But you may feel as if you are acting, especially since, like an actor, you have been given lines to speak: "Have a nice day [smile]." Gradually, the sense of faking, of pretending, wears off, and you then know that you have not only assumed the role but have internalized it. It now fits

---

*Forms of life: Being amused, feeling anger, being intrigued, finding something ridiculous—these are examples of forms of life—the whirlings of organism, the signs that someone is really alive and responsive.

comfortably. "How strange that I felt so strange before!" Your role is now second nature. Even so, as you go home from work each day, you shift from one role—bank teller—to the central role of being your private self. Your voice may even change in the process.

Becoming an
Other

Now here is an example of becoming an other. Your mother's nerves are bad, she is difficult to live with, and you can never say the right thing. One day, exasperated, she simply says, "Put yourself in my shoes." You think about it and decide to try it. The world begins to look quite different. You are now role-playing as an other.

Women writers produce convincing representations of men, and vice versa. They are role-playing as an other. You are a law-abiding citizen, yet you write a short story that offers a convincing view of the world from the point of view of a criminal psychopath. Your friends are shocked. They don't realize that you have been role-playing.

ALTERNATING AS PARTICIPANT (THE "POETICAL CHARACTER") AND SPECTATOR

You have to write a history paper about pioneers. The subject is dead for you, without interest. Then you daydream yourself into role-playing a pioneer, translating dry information into the eventfulness of a pioneer's days—its activities, frenzies, fears, relaxations, states of mind, hopes, plans. You find more material than you can make room for. Then you pull back, become a historian and view the pioneer's days as a spectator, evaluating and summing up. You have produced an interesting and satisfying paper by taking on two roles: pioneer-participant and historian-spectator. In the process your daily self disappeared; or, to quote John Keats, you solved your problem by becoming, by discovering within yourself what Keats called "the poetical character."

"It is not itself," Keats wrote. "It has no self—it is every thing and nothing —It has no character—it enjoys light and shade; it lives in gusto, be it foul or fair, high or low, rich or poor, mean or elevated—It has as much delight in conceiving an Iago as an Imogen."* It is in that *state of mind* that you could/can "become" anyone. "What shocks the virtuous philosopher, delights the chameleon poet. It does no harm from its relish of the dark side of things any more than from its taste for the bright one; because they both end in speculation. A poet . . . has no identity—he is continually informing and filling some other body." (For a text by a student who independently discovered the truth of Keats's words, see p. 106.)

We believe that if you have practice in writing texts of another self, you will learn to produce more effective practical texts, and that if you practice writing texts as another, you will produce more effective reflective texts.

---

*Letter to Richard Woodhouse, October 27, 1818.

In the rest of this chapter you will become more familiar with these two ways of writing in role and gain experience in doing so. But first let us summarize briefly what practical and reflective texts are.

Practical and Reflective Texts

Practical texts are the kinds of texts that, as you saw in Chapter 1, help you organize your activities, and which you will have to produce as part of your professional work in the world. They will be judged by how well they help to get a job done. If successful, they will perform some task efficiently, economically (without beating about the bush and wasting others' time and effort), and in a language that is appropriate to its professional context. When a lawyer addresses the jury, he tends not to say, "Hey, there was this guy, and he. . . ." On the contrary, he or she uses the language of lawyers, a professional jargon that seems to many of us to create a kind of smoke screen to keep ordinary folks in the dark. But it has in fact evolved into a distinctive language because of the nature of law, with its necessary concern for precision of meaning, identification, verifiability, and specification. Similarly, when a historian prepares a paper for the State Department, to fill them in on the history of some obscure country whose history he knows very well, he or she will use the kind of language that we learn to expect when we read history. And within history, each subcategory has formed its own dialect, so that a social historian's language uses terms different from those of an economic historian. The younger you are, the easier it is for you to master these various dialects. Think of the language of computers, for example. Many people over 40 believe that they will never master the novel and strange language of computer science.

Reflective texts, in contrast—fiction, autobiography, journals, poems—are primarily used to represent a particular personal experience or state of mind for nonpractical purposes. By sharing such texts we can remind ourselves what it means to be a human being.

When we write reflective texts we may wish to realize (make "real" to ourselves) and represent both our own experiences, states of mind, and forms of life, and those of others. To do this we need to "become" others. There is no other way to do it. But the great satisfaction of doing this, of entering or taking on a role, is that as we do it we escape from ourselves. If you do it, you will for a while no longer be "a student in English Composition."

Notes   Read over this chapter so far, and make some informal notes in your notebook about your own experiences of fantasy and role-play, and of your entry into new roles at various stages of your life. Can you distinguish various distinct "voices" or styles of talk? What sort of person is your idealized self? romantic? philanthropic? extravagant? foolhardy?

Sundry Voices

FINDING VOICES

We have been delighted and surprised by the ability of our students to take on a variety of roles, to find the appropriate voice for each and so create an "authentic forgery"—a text written from inside a role that is plausible, convincing, like the real thing.

And needless to say, we have asked them how they manage to do it. (We know how we do it, but we want to know how they do it so that we can compare notes.) Before we share their answers with you, take time out to reflect and make notes on where your "voices" come from. If they come from within you, then how did they get in there? Reading the following text may offer you some clues.

Frank, Get Up!

At that instant, in the final frontier, "Quickly, Scotty! Warp-factor 3! The Klingon ship is firing its phasers at the Enterprise. I need warp-speed!"

"Sorry, Captain, I don't know if I can hold it much longer. We've already lost three di-lithium crystals, and the rest are going fast."

Meanwhile high above the U.K., buzzzzzzzzzz zzzz!

"So, Mr. Bond, now that I have control of your helicopter, I'll bet you're eager to tell me where the secret tracking devices for the Polaris and Trident fleet are."

"On the contrary, comrade, you're quite a good pilot. Besides, Uncle Sam is a personal friend."

"Goodbye, 007!"

Back in Gotham City, "Golly gee, Batman, of all the underhanded dastardly things to do—that Joker!"

"Quick, Robin, try to reach your bat utility belt!"

"Holy Heat Wave! We'll be bat-snacks!"

"If only I could reach my bat-freon in my utility belt . . ."

Over in Oz: "No, no! Leave me alone!!"

"I'll get you, my little pretty! And your little dog, too!"

"Please, please! Don't hurt me!"

"Why, my little party's just beginning!"

Whoosh! Back in Texas: "Attention, all units! Be on the lookout for a black Trans-Am, headed east on I 46."

"I'll get you, you sumbitch bandit! Nobody makes a fool out of Buford . . ."

"Frank!"

"No! No! I'll be in Georgia in ten minutes."

"Frank, get up. It's time to live your own life!"

"Aw, Mom."

—Frank Cuttita

HEARING VOICES

Our students agree that they do *not* invent or make up their other voices; on the contrary, they simply "hear" them with the inner ear, the ear of the mind or of memory.

In eighteen years or so, they have heard and retained hundreds—some say thousands—of voices and have internalized them. An example they offer is the distinctive voice of a grandmother or a grandfather. At the drop of a hat, they can "tune in" and hear those voices again.

Almost as important as the voices of family and neighbors are the voices mediated by TV and the movies. Take the "voice of the psychiatrist": very few of our students know any psychiatrists, and even fewer have visited one. Yet, when asked, they can produce a convincing impersonation of one. Where does it come from? From soap operas and similar sources. Needless to say, the students do not need to rest content with the kind of stereotype encountered in soaps; the stereotype merely provides the "scaffolding" that supports their own construction of a plausible psychiatric voice.

In brief, we are all "funded" with a repertoire of "voices" that we can tune in to when the occasion demands. Everyone's funding contains the memories of voices raised in anger, voices expressing affection or concern, voices associated with good humor, voices that register short temper, and so on; each distinctive tone of voice expresses a form of life, a frame of mind, or an attitude. By listening to such voices, we are enabled to find appropriate language for a greaty variety of texts.

REAPING THE VOICES IN OTHER WRITERS' TEXTS

When we speak of a "voice" (or "voices") in a text, we put the word in quotation marks for the simple reason that in a literal sense there is no vocal sound coming from the page. In a literal sense, every printed page is silent. But once you begin to develop the pleasurable habit of reading with your ear, of hearing the words, their rhythms, weight or lightness, punch or stroke, haste or leisure, pace and feel, and above all their "tone of voice"—cheerful, measured, calm, polite, amusing, sorrowful, or whatever—once you begin to do this, you will be making an important contribution to your own development—not only as a reader but as a writer too. For how can you make a text if you cannot recognize and appreciate the salient characteristics of others' texts? The most effective way to internalize an extensive repertoire of writerly voices (and so to be able to use them in your own way) is simply to read, preferably with your inner ear.

It is clear that confident and dependable writers float on a sea of extensive and intensive reading. They read and reread not only their own texts but also others' texts: novels, nonfiction, mysteries, newspapers, magazines, and so on. No one is born a good writer. The effective writer becomes so by reading widely and unresistingly, discovering that reading offers some fulfilment of desire.

You cannot ask your instructor to wave a magic transmogrifying wand and turn you into a competent writer. What you can do is this: read extensively for pleasure, looking through the text at the "world" that the text presents to you. And reread some parts of your extensive readings. And change gear into a different kind of reading: choose a segment, a page, an episode, that you specially relish, and this time read the text. That is, look not through but *at the text*. What is it, not in what is presented but in how the words do their work, that specially satisfies you? alerts you? intrigues you? amuses you? affects you to a notable degree?

Most experienced writers are compulsive readers and suffer from print hunger if cut off from reading matter for any reason. If you want to develop as a writer, the best favor you can do yourself is to join the secret club of compulsive readers.

Marguerite Yourcenar as the Emperor Hadrian; Hadrian as an Ambitious Young Roman

THE PART SHE PLAYED

Marguerite Yourcenar, the French-American writer, spent about thirty years, on and off, thinking and making notes about the Roman emperor Hadrian, who—to put it mildly—intrigued her. (From the notes she made during the first ten years of her work, she saved only one sentence.) In her remarkable book *The Memoirs of Hadrian*, a twentieth-century woman "became" a man who had lived over 1,800 years earlier and created a convincing illusion of participating in his ways of thinking and feeling, his states of mind, and his forms of life. Working from mountains of historical documents, she discovered that her attempt to re-create Hadrian was no different from anyone's attempt to re-create their earlier self:

> We lose track of everything, and of everyone, even ourselves. The facts of my father's life are less known to me than those of the life of Hadrian. My own existence, if I had to write it, would be reconstructed from externals, laboriously, as if it were the life of someone else: I should have to turn to letters, and to the recollections of others, in order to clarify such uncertain memories.

As for the frustrating gaps in her knowledge of Hadrian, she organized her text so that the things she didn't know would coincide with the things that he might well have forgotten!

THE PARTS HE PLAYED

As a young man, a student, Hadrian was impatient of grammar, thinking it "absurd." In later life, he realized that grammar is simply one of

Marguerite Yourcenar

Hadrian

the means whereby we regulate our energies, achieving a balance of impulse (drive) and control, the power to dispose all the parts in a coherent pattern. But more important, in terms of preparing him for the demands of both political and military life, were the exercises in role-play that formed a major part of his early training in rhetoric, the art of persuasive speech. These exercises were not mere bits of imitation, of copying respected models. They went deeper than that, as he himself insists:

> As for the rhetorical exercises in which we were successively Xerxes and Themistocles, Octavius and Mark Antony, they intoxicated me; I felt like Proteus. They taught me to enter into the thought of each man in turn, and to understand that each makes his own decisions, and lives and dies according to his own laws.*

For us, the most important words in that passage are: *we were* (*were* — not "pretended to be" or "imitated" or "copied"); *intoxicated* — the exercises were not merely cold, analytical, dutiful task work, but so exciting as to make him feel intoxicated, raised above normal consciousness; *felt like* — the role-play was an outward expression of internalized, inwardly experienced forms of life; *enter into the thought of* — a kind of deep probing that was ensured by, infused by, the energy of feeling. How can one grasp

---

*"Xerxes . . . Antony": statesmen and generals of the classical era, some noted not only for skill in action but also for a persuasive eloquence. Proteus: a sea-god who could answer all questions. He had a magical capacity for changing his shape into anything or anybody, to avoid capture. Only if you trapped him in his original form would he have to answer your questions.

how a man is thinking unless one can feel how he is feeling? A person's words affect us when they enable us to sympathize with his or her feelings. Such are the benefits of role-play, which might be taken more seriously if it were called role-work.

As Hadrian matured, he moved through various phases of ambition, hope, desire:

> Different persons ruled in me in turn, though no one of them for long; each fallen tyrant was quick to regain power. Thus have I played host successively to the meticulous officer, fanatic in discipline, but gaily sharing with his men the privations of war; to the melancholy dreamer intent on the gods; the lover ready to risk all for a moment's rapture; the haughty young lieutenant retiring to his tent to study his maps by lamplight, making clear to his friends his disdain for the way the world goes; and finally the future statesman. But let us not forget, either, the base opportunist who in fear of displeasing succumbed to drunkenness at the emperor's table; the young fellow pronouncing upon all questions with ridiculous assurance; the frivolous wit, ready to lose a friend for the sake of a bright remark; the soldier exercising with mechanical precision his vile gladiatorial trade. And we should include also that vacant figure, nameless and unplaced in history, though as much myself as all the others, the simple toy of circumstance, no more and no less than a body, lying on a camp bed, distracted by an aroma, aroused by a breath of wind, vaguely attentive to some eternal hum of a bee. But little by little a newcomer was taking hold, a stage director and manager. I was beginning to know the names of my actors, and could arrange plausible entrances for them, or exits; I cut short superfluous lines, and came gradually to avoid the most obvious effects. Last, I learned not to indulge too much in monologue. And gradually, in turn, my actions were forming me.

Later, Hadrian was employed as a speech writer for the then emperor, Trajan:

> I succeeded all the better for having had practice in that kind of accommodation: in the difficult period of my apprenticeship I had often written harangues for senators who were short of ideas or turns of phrase; they ended by thinking themselves the authors of these pieces. In working thus for Trajan, I took exactly the same delight as that afforded by the rhetorical exercises of my youth; alone in my room, trying out my effects before a mirror, I felt myself an emperor. In truth I was learning to be one; audacities of which I should not have dreamed myself capable became easy when someone else would have to shoulder them. The emperor's thinking was simple but inarticulate, and therefore obscure; it became quite familiar to me, and I flattered myself that I knew it somewhat better than I did. I enjoyed aping the military style of the commander-in-chief, and hearing him thereafter in the Senate pronounce phrases which seemed typical, but for which I was responsible.

And in the hazardous — even treacherous — world of Roman politics, he learned to play his roles to good effect:

> I was deferent toward some, compliant to others, dissipated when necessary, clever but not too clever. I had need of my versatility; I was many-sided by intention and made it a game to be incalculable. I walked a tightrope, and could have used lessons not only from an actor, but from an acrobat.

Notes   As you became aware in adolescence of the variety of your life, and of what various people in various relationships, situations, or contexts, expected of you, what did you learn of versatility? How many roles did you learn to play?

WHAT NOW?

1. Project yourself forward forty or fifty years; then write an end-of-life reminiscence of some of your early roles.
2. Choose someone who has had authority over you at some stage in your life. Create a text, such as a letter of recommendation or a letter to your parents, in which the authority figure expresses either approval or disapproval of you. *Listen* to the "voice inside your head," and write. Then check to be sure that your text has captured an authoritative/authoritarian tone of voice.
3. As Hadrian learned to meet the various demands of Roman politics, he learned to play an increasing number and variety of roles. Choose three or four adults that you know, and consider what roles they seem to have mastered.
4. If you have already decided what career you intend to follow, try to outline the various roles that you think you will be required to play in your work.
5. Now flip back in your mind to earlier roles. How far back can you go? How did you "sound" at six, say, when you entered first grade? At nine? At thirteen? If you have younger siblings close by, then you may regularly hear the characteristic features of a younger voice. Try next to represent the voice of a child in a particular role and situation (playing with a friend, talking to an adult, going to the doctor, etc.).

Our Students in Role

Now meet one of our students, Meg Medina, as she creates a voice and a character.

MEG MEDINA'S "MAXINE CURIEL"

Maxine Curiel

Mommy says that I shouldn't talk to strangers, so it's a good thing that I know you. She says that she knows a few bad people who eat little girls so that's why I can't talk to people that I don't know 'cause you never know who's bad. But I know you won't eat me up 'cause your mouth isn't nearly big enough to fit me inside of. So we can talk, I guess.

But you can't call me Maxine when you talk 'cause I hate that name, Maxine, and only Miss Posy calls me Maxine. Daddy says she looks like she swallowed a lemon, Miss Posy, since she never does do anything but pucker up and make us write the 'lphabet a zillion, trillion times. But I like swallowing lemons with the skin and everything 'cause then I don't get thirsty. But I don't think I'm like Miss Posy who just puckers all the time 'cause I got lots of friends and they never said anything about me puckering up. So, anyhow, Max is what my best friend calls me whose name is Cynthia Stephonopolis, but I call her Snuff. Me and Snuff are best friends forever, 'cept she's in Greek for the summer. She's staying with her Grandma who lives there, but when she comes home, we'll still be best friends. Snuff is six years old, too, like me. Her birfday is just three weeks before mine is, which makes her bossy sometimes when she says that she gets the bigger half of the candy 'cause she's older. Mommy says that three weeks makes no difference and besides, I get more E's on my report card than she does, anyhow. Last year, I got 15 E's, 4 G's and no P's or F's. Snuff only got 12 E's, and 7 G's. So that's why she flat left me and got best friends with that big ugly Jenny Quigley kid until Quigley told ole' Snuff that she was a whole half of a year older, and Snuff got sick of havin' to do what she said. So we weren't best friends for a week, until I lent her Ballerina Barbie and then she was fine. So that's why Barbie is in Greek with Snuff 'cause she's still got her. I told her she could take her if she didn't bring her back with dark hair and skin like she's got on the count of Barbie is Irish like me and it wouldn't be right for her to be dark if she was Irish, see? She said O.K. and that's why she's over there at Snuff's Grandma's.

My Grandma's name is Erin Dempsey and she's pretty old, about 100 or so. She kinda smells funny all the time like Daddy's old sport coat that he lets me play with, the one that was my costume last year for Halloween. She's jumpy like Miss Posy and stands behind me when I go to the frigerata' to get milk and Bosco 'cause she says little girls always spill milk though I haven't spilt any since I was really little and Mommy says so. And she holds my hand when we go shopping at Mr. Barnes' store for food for Me and Mommy and Daddy 'cause she says little girls should always hold onto someone's hand when they're shopping. Mommy says that I should shut up my complaining about her hands which are too crinkly and have those spots 'cause they're not dirty or nothing, spots aren't catchy, and besides Grandma can't see no more and I've got perfec' vision and can see things coming like Mommy showed me how.

But I say that if those spots aren't catchy, how come all the old people gave 'em to each other? And I don't know about not seeing neither 'cause Grandma see O.K. when we play hopscotch in back of the house which I don't like to do 'cause she makes me pick up the stick for her on the count of her back will break, she says, if she bends over. That isn't hop-scotch, then, I say, but Daddy says to play 'cause Grandma needs a best friend and mine's away anyhow. So Grandma is being my best friend, but she's not like Snuff. Snuff knows how to play hopscotch right and I betcha Snuff's Grandma can play right, too, not like mine whose got spots.

I'm not allowed out near the street 'cause of the cars that go by here real fast and can hurt kids like me, even, Daddy says. So I gotta go. So bye-bye and come back when Snuff's here and I'll show you Barbie.

— *Meg Medina*

WHAT NOW? READING "MAXINE CURIEL"

1. What do you know about the voice, role, character, and situation from the very first line of the text? Who is "talking"? How old do you imagine the speaker to be? How do you know that this text is a fiction?
2. When do you first learn the sex of the speaker? Does Maxine "sound like" a little girl? What features, interests, perceptions, speech patterns, does Meg Medina (the writer) attribute to Maxine (her creation)? How might this character sound if she were a boy?
3. Think for a moment about the social situation in which this monologue takes place: little girl "captures" a person and talks non-stop for *x* minutes. Who might the person be? How do you know? Why do you suppose that Max speaks so fast, so breathlessly: "I told her she could take her if she didn't bring her back with dark hair and skin like she's got on the count of Barbie is Irish like me and it wouldn't be right for her to be dark if she was Irish, see?" Is it impatience, or excitement, or hysteria, or is it the way in which she traps her audience, not giving them a chance to break away?
4. How does Meg represent the logic of a 6-year-old? Is Max convincing as a thinker? Do her connections make sense for a 6-year-old? For example, her thinking about old people and freckles? How does she make these connections? Do you find her wise or silly?
5. *How* does Max make connections: what words other than *and* and *but* link her thoughts?
6. Do you find the text to be an effective "forgery"? Does Meg convince you that this *is* the voice of a child? How so? How not?

MIMI POND'S "LIKE, SHOPPING"

Impersonation can be either serious or comical. Roles can be played either in earnest or for fun. A medical student, on first working with patients in a hospital, will probably concentrate very hard to maintain the illusion of being a doctor, even though, inside, she/he may well feel uncomfortable, wrong-footed, and even fraudulent. But someone who has just witnessed an amusing scene and wishes to share it with friends will probably impersonate for comical reasons, to amuse others. In the following passage, is the real writer, Mimi Pond, being funny or serious— or both?

Like, Shopping

Shopping is the funniest thing to do, 'cause, o.k., clothes? They're important. Like for your image and stuff. I mean you don't want people to think you're some kind of spaz. Like, I'm sure. You have to look good. Everything has to match. Like *everything*. Like your earrings and your shoes and all your accessories and stuff. And you don't want to wear stuff that people don't wear. People'd look at you and just go, "Ew, she's a zod, like get away." And you have to brush your hair a lot in case any guys walk by.

Even if you don't have much billies, you can go hang out with your friends anyway and check out the dudes. Here's something you can buy if you don't have hardly any money: lipgloss, 'cause you *always* need lipgloss. I mean anyway you have to buy *something* or everyone will think you're wigged out.

You always have to go with at least three other friends, like your best friend and then maybe April and Shawn and Michelle. EVERYONE has to help you decide what to buy. You can't get it unless they say it's super darling on you. 'Cause how would you know by yourself? Like, I'm sure. Sometimes if you don't like one of the girls who's with you, you can get her to buy something totally grody. Then you always look better than she does.

All the shops like Judy's and Fashion Conspiracy and Charlotte Russe have real bitchen clothes but the girls who work there are total rags. Real beasties, like not from the Valley or anything. What Yvette and Danielle and me like to do is try on all this stuff we'd *never* buy and make the salesgirl keep bringing us belts and stuff. Then you tell them how ugly everything is and like how come they don't have anything good? Then you ignore them. Another good thing to do is pretend you're from somewhere else like New York or Europe or something and put on a fake accent.

I mean really the only reason we do it is not to be mean or anything, but just to excite our day. Make it fun, you know? Otherwise we might be known as boring people.

The other thing about the mall is all these dudes hang out there too. So you can sit on the planters and stuff and wink at them, or go, real loud, like you're talking to your friend, "GOD, WHAT A CUTE DUDE, HUH?" Or you just laugh real loud. Then sometimes they come over and talk to you, and maybe you exchange phone numbers or something.

If you do that, you always tell the dude opposite names. Like you said you were Heather and she said she was you. That way you call the dude and say it's your friend except it's you. Like you say it's April 'cause that's really you except he thinks it's your friend. Then you go, "Do you like

Heather? 'Cause she thinks you're a vicious babe." That way you find out if they like you. Then later if you go to the beach with him or something —it doesn't matter 'cause usually he just thinks he was confused. . . .

—*Mimi Pond*

WHAT NEXT? READING "LIKE, SHOPPING"

The following questions may help you to reread Mimi Pond's text more closely:

1. Who has Mimi Pond "become"? What evidence can you produce to sustain your answer?
2. How far did you read, first time, before you were pretty confident that you had recognized the "speaker" from her language? Line 1, 5, 15, or 20?
3. Do you find Pond's impersonation consistently convincing?
4. Is her text an attempt to represent utterance (i.e., talking)?
5. What do you think is the implied context? Is the speaker addressing a friend? A stranger? A parent? Is the situation of the "talking" formal or informal?
6. How would you characterize the tone of voice of the text? Boasting? Confessing? Confiding? Is the speaker guarded or unguarded?
7. Does the speaker sound silly? Frivolous? Giddy? Empty-headed? Would she be likely to describe herself in those terms? If not, why not?

TEXTS THAT REPRESENT UTTERANCE

Read this: "He came casually through the door. When he saw the body, he stammered, 'What, what . . . ah! Oh, no! Some, somebody tell me, tell me what's goin' on here! Oh, God! No!' He covered his eyes, and staggered out of the kitchen."

The words inside the single quotation marks represent **utterance**, that is, what someone actually said. If you substitute description for utterance—for example, "He expressed shock and confusion"—what do you lose? The reader can no longer "hear" the voice. The text tells you something; but that telling lacks the direct dramatic power of utterance, the words spoken. Part of the pleasurable variety of a good text lies in its offerings of utterance, so that one can "hear" directly, with one's inner ear. When texts incorporate utterance, they gain in vividness and variety.

Notice, however, that the *whole* of Mimi Pond's and Meg Medina's texts is utterance—the illusion of someone talking, talking, talking. . . .

As we shall show you shortly, it is possible for text to represent not only talk but also inner speech—the flow of language inside the head. In detective stories, the text often represents utterance, creating the illusion of this hard-bitten private eye talking to us, the readers, quoting what other people say to him, quoting what he says to them, and also offering his private inner speech, which tells *us* what he is really thinking. The other person in conversation with him can hear only what he says out loud, not what he is really thinking—that secret he shares only with us, his readers. (It makes things even more interesting when we remind ourselves that it is not the detective who is "talking" to us, but the writer at her typewriter inventing the words for him!) Much of the cool dry humor depends on the fact that we readers are allowed to be spectators of the detective's thoughts, whereas the characters he is talking to inside the story don't have the faintest idea what he is really thinking. So we feel privileged— and smart!

Switching Gender

LETTERS TO DIRK

As you will see in greater detail in Chapter 14, when the celebrated movie actor Dirk Bogarde was a boy, his father insisted that he leave home and go away to school. Dirk was extremely unhappy, and one day he sent a cry for help to his parents, asking them to let him return home. We asked our students to take on the role of either father or mother and reply. Here are some of the results.

First, Nick as the mother:

> My dear son,
>   The mailman delivered your letter today. I could tell its contents simply from the quivering handwriting on the envelope. I knew then what I know now; you should never have left home.
>   You must realize that I think of you each evening. I still remember cradling you in my arms, all wrapped up in a small, woolen blanket, resting your weary head on my bosom. Such thoughts a mother never forgets. A son will never be forgotten by a mother.
>   I want you to come home. I will aid you in every conceivable way. You have no life there, at least a chance here. Your father will give in, I know. He will allow you to become an actor. Dirk, you belong here with me. I am as discontented as you, and my greatest joy will be when I receive you at my front door. Come home, Dirk. I miss you.
>
> Lovingly yours,
Mother

Second, Michael as the father:

> Dirk:
>   Got your letter. I do not understand. Unhappy? When I have sent you to get an education in a job which most certainly is the best for you? When I have taken care of you, seen to your lodging with your mother's

sister? I am appalled at your rebelliousness and stupidity, you ungrateful wretch! *How dare you!*

Certainly, you may come home. I am your father, and this is your home. But I will not try to help you anymore, as you refuse my assistance. You'll have to learn your own trade. And *mark my words:* When you reach the age of a printer's apprentice, I will support you no longer. Out you shall go.

Yesterday, I mailed your food and lodging money to your uncle. Get the return fare from him, if you are so foolish as to wish to return.

Father

Finally, John as the mother:

My dearest Dirk,

I can only hope you receive my letter first, because I'm sure the one your father is writing will make you feel worse. I'm so sorry, Dirk. I've pleaded with your father to let you come home, but there is nothing I can do.

When I read your post card, I was in tears. Your father looked at it, tossed it aside, and asked me when dinner would be ready. When I asked him about you, he asked if I was joking. Under no circumstances are you to return, he said, until you've set your life in order.

An orderly life, to him, would be one which follows his orders. He still wants you to take up an "honorable profession." I still haven't told him of your hope to become an actor; I probably never will. He won't find out until you become a successful matinee idol. I know you can do it, son, even without his support.

I wish there was something I could do, but there is nothing. When you are a bit older, he will no longer be able to keep you at your uncle's house. Then I'll take you around to the studios, and who knows?

I have faith in you, Son. I know, you'll get through this and make me proud of you. I can't wait to see you again. I wish it could be sooner.

Love,
Mom

Our students say that in these letters the father holds his son at arm's length, whereas the mother draws close to him. What specific evidence can you point to, to support this impression?

What does the father omit in order to signal "I'm keeping you at a distance"? What does the mother include to show that she is reaching out? Do you think that those impersonations are merely stereotypes?

WHAT NEXT?

Take on the role of a firm but generous and sensitive father. Write a letter telling Dirk that he must stay where he is but doing it in such a way as not to hurt his feelings.

Take on the role of a mother who wants her son back primarily to satisfy her own needs. Without stating this directly in her letter, try to make it implicit.

THE SPEECH OF POLLY BAKER

You have just seen how Nick and John both impersonated a woman. In the next text, Benjamin Franklin does the same.

In order to challenge laws that he thought unfair, Franklin decided to argue against them *not as himself* but as a woman. As a man, a politician, and a pamphleteer, Franklin was a *spectator* of women being victimized by harsh laws; as Polly Baker, he became a *participant* (a) in the imagined experience of being a woman victimized by those laws and (b) in the act of speaking, as a victim, against those laws.

> The Speech of Miss Polly Baker before a Court of Judicature, at Connecticut near Boston in New-England; where she was prosecuted the fifth time, for having a Bastard Child: Which influenced the Court to dispense with her Punishment, and which induced one of her Judges to marry her the next Day—by whom she had fifteen Children.
>
> "May it please the honorable bench to indulge me in a few words: I am a poor, unhappy woman, who have no money to fee lawyers to plead for me, being hard put to it to get a living. I shall not trouble your honors with long speeches; for I have not the presumption to expect that you may, by any means, be prevailed on to deviate in your Sentence from the law, in my favor. All I humbly hope is, that your honors would charitably move the governor's goodness on my behalf, that my fine may be remitted. This is the fifth time, gentlemen, that I have been dragg'd before your court on the same account; twice I have paid heavy fines, and twice have been brought to publick punishment, for want of money to pay those fines. This may have been agreeable to the laws, and I don't dispute it; but since laws are sometimes unreasonable in themselves, and therefore repealed; and others bear too hard on the subject in particular circumstances, and therefore there is left a power somewhere to dispense with the execution of them; I take the liberty to say, that I think this law, by which I am punished, both unreasonable in itself, and particularly severe with regard to me, who have always lived an inoffensive life in the neighborhood where I was born, and defy my enemies (if I have any) to say I ever wrong'd any man, woman, or child. Abstracted from the law, I cannot conceive (may it please your honors) what the nature of my offense is. I have brought five fine children into the world, at the risque of my life; I have maintain'd them well by my own industry, without burthening the township, and would have done it better, if it had not been for the heavy charges and fines I have paid. Can it be a crime (in the nature of things, I mean) to add to the king's subjects, in a new country, that really wants people? I own it, I should think it rather a praiseworthy than a punishable action. I have debauched no other woman's husband, nor enticed any

other youth; these things I never was charg'd with; nor has any one the least cause of complaint against me, unless, perhaps, the ministers of justice, because I have had children without being married, by which they have missed a wedding fee. But can this be a fault of mine? I appeal to your honors. You are pleased to allow I don't want sense; but I must be stupefied to the last degree, not to prefer the honorable state of wedlock to the condition I have lived in. I always was, and still am willing to enter into it; and doubt not my behaving well in it, having all the industry, frugality, fertility, and skill in economy appertaining to a good wife's character. I defy any one to say I ever refused an offer of that sort: on the contrary, I readily consented to the only proposal of marriage that ever was made me, which was when I was a virgin, but too easily confiding in the person's sincerity that made it, I unhappily lost my honor by trusting to his; for he got me with child, and then forsook me.

"That very person, you all know, he is now become a magistrate of this country; and I had hopes he would have appeared this day on the bench, and have endeavored to moderate the Court in my favor; then I should have scorn'd to have mentioned it; but I must now complain of it, as unjust and unequal, that my betrayer and undoer, the first cause of all my faults and miscarriages (if they must be deemed such), should be advanced to honor and power in this government that punishes my misfortune with stripes and infamy. I should be told, 'tis like, that were there no act of Assembly in the case, the precepts of religion are violated by my transgressions. If mine is a religious offense, leave it to religious punishments. You have already excluded me from the comforts of your church communion. Is not that sufficient? You believe I have offended heaven, and must suffer eternal fire: Will not that be sufficient? What need is there then of your additional fines and whipping? I own I do not think as you do, for, if I thought what you call a sin was really such, I could not presumptuously commit it. But, how can it be believed that heaven is angry at my having children, when to the little done by me towards it, God has been pleased to add his divine skill and admirable workmanship in the formation of their bodies, and crowned the whole by furnishing them with rational and immortal souls?

"Forgive me, gentlemen, if I talk a little extravagantly on these matters; I am no divine, but if you, gentlemen, must be making laws, do not turn natural and useful actions into crimes by your prohibitions. But take into your wise consideration the great and growing number of bachelors in the country, many of whom, from the mean fear of the expenses of a family, have never sincerely and honorably courted a woman in their lives; and by their manner of living leave unproduced (which is little better than murder) hundreds of their posterity to the thousandth generation. Is not this a greater offense against the publick good than mine? Compel them, then, by law, either to marriage, or to pay double the fine of fornication every year. What must poor young women do, whom customs and nature forbid to solicit the men, and who cannot force themselves upon husbands, when the laws take no care to provide them any, and yet severely punish them if they do their duty without them; the duty of the first and great command of nature and nature's God, *encrease and multiply;* a duty, from the steady performance of which nothing has been able to deter me, but for its sake I have hazarded the loss of the publick esteem, and have frequently endured publick disgrace and punishment; and therefore ought, in my humble opinion, instead of a whipping, to have a statue erected to my memory."

Notes

1. Franklin (in the 1740s) was doing something very similar to what Mimi Pond was doing (in the 1980s). Do you agree?

2. If Polly Baker had used the eighteenth-century *equivalent* of the language of Mimi Pond's text, she would have lost her case. Do you agree?

3. "In speaking and writing, we draw on a repertoire of verbal patterns or formulas we have learned and used before, substituting, as the occasion requires, the variants that are appropriate to the particular needs of the moment" [Barbara Herrnstein Smith]. What would we *need* to know about eighteenth-century American speech to apply this generalization to Polly Baker's speech?

4. New slang is interesting/amusing/effective *because it is new.* As soon as it becomes a common, recurrent element in people's talk—a "verbal pattern or formula"—it loses its power and turns boring. Inevitably, it is displaced by still newer slang and mostly disappears. How many changes of slang have you lived through in the last ten years?

5. Polly Baker's strength is *in* her language (the language that Franklin has given to her), her tone of voice (how would you characterize it?), and the resourcefulness of her mind. How many of the following turns or strategies can you identify in her speech?

Concession

Explanation

Interpretation

Contradiction

Appeal to empathy

Justification

Use of evidence

Compromise

Appeal to natural justice

Distinction between law and justice

6. Franklin's text is a fiction. But assume for a moment that there was an actual woman, Polly Baker, who delivered this actual speech. If that were so, do you think this speech would have been delivered

straight out of her head, or must it first have been written down—a text—and then read to the court?

(What we are appealing to, here, is *your* capacity to recognize how people sound when they produce *unscripted* talk, as opposed to how they might sound when reading aloud from a script.) For a focus, you might consider the sentence "I take the liberty . . . child".)

VENGEANCE NIGHTMARE

In the following text, Michael Lee, in his "poetical character" role, takes on the identity of an angry, vindictive woman absolutely exasperated by her boyfriend's behavior. In the text, Michael gives vent to a kind of passionate fantasy of revenge. After you have read his text, take a look at his commentary, in which he offers a brief account of various reactions to his text.

Oh come on! I really don't deserve this. The abuse I'm taking. I'd rather be married than take this. I can't stand the summer; I hate the beach—all this sunlight burning away at the eyes and skin, and all this sand, getting all over. And that loud music! It's so loud, I think I'm gonna burst. Decadence, that's what it is, complete decadence. How am I supposed to get anything done under these conditions?

Now what? What the . . . is going on? Where's he going? What's he doing?

"Hey you! Idiot! Where are you going?" Oh no, not into the water—it's so cold! The waves are so rough. Ouch, I'm freezing. "Stop! Stop! You know I can't swim."

Oh, you're really going to pay for this. For the last five weeks, it's been the same craziness. Beach! Beach! Beach! Beach! Oh, finally, we're getting out of this liquid filth. Look at it—it's slimy and it stinks. . . . Now you just lie there. Finally, some rest. I sure need it. All those others destroying themselves just like you. You know, you really deserve it for treating me this way. All the incessant partying. Why don't you try to save yourself while you can? Even if you don't care about yourself, at least have a little respect for me.

Ah, you fell asleep, did you? Yes, yes, you really did, didn't you! Well, I think it's my turn to "play" a bit. Yes, I think it's time to repay you. Oh sweet revenge!

Let's see now. What shall I do? How about a headache? Would you like that? No, after those last few parties you've been to, you've probably become immune to headaches.

How about taking all sensation from your legs? When you wake up and try to stand—boom! Flat on your face!

No, no, no, that's no good. A dream . . . How about a dream? No, even better: a nightmare! Oh, isn't this great! Hmmmm? What shall this nightmare be about? Let's see—we'll need some sex. Maybe a little violence; no, change that: a lot of violence. Maybe even a little death. Okay, here we go.

If I remember clearly, you have a fear of speed and heights. All right, get set, 'cause here we go! You're driving on a mountainous road in the country. Yes, you're right—what a great day for driving! Hey, who's that? A girl—a really good-looking girl. Huh, what a fox! Just what you like.

Ho, ho, her car has broken down. Look—she sees you. Come on, come on, stop, you gullible fool, you. Give me a break: you could've used a better line than "Need a lift, babe?" You really are one sleazy person.

What did she say? She needs a lift to the nearest garage? Her car broke down? Come on! Take her! That's a good boy. Keep your eyes on the road.

What's that she's pulling out? A gun? It's a gun, and she's pointing it at you. What did she say? "O.K., big boy, let's see what you're made of!" Now, now, don't panic. She won't really hurt you. She'll probably kill you! Ha, Ha! You really deserve it. But I'll spare you—anyway, I'm not through with you yet.

Go on, give her all your money, and your watch, too. Uh, don't forget your gold chain. Did she really say that? "I oughta shoot you now"? Don't interrupt her. Let her finish: she says she wants to have some fun. What's that she wants? Wants you to go faster?

I know you're scared, but I don't think she's kidding. You'd better listen to her. Go faster yet. Boy, she's really going to kill you if you don't. 55, 60, 65, 70, 75, 85 miles an hour. You'd better be careful: there are cliffs at the side of the road. Don't fly over one! "Go faster," she said. You heard her. Come on, do it!

95 m.p.h. Look out for that turn! You're not going to make it. Watch it! Ha, ha, she jumped out of the car just in time. But you've just jumped off the road with your car. That's right, idiot—you're falling off the cliff—you have about five seconds to live.

Isn't this fun! Now, don't start screaming and crying, you cry-baby. You only live once. About one second, I figure, until you hit the bottom of the cliff. Here it comes!

Aww, back at the beach, are we? You are an idiot. Look at all your sweat. That nightmare must have cost you at least five pounds. . . . You idiot, you woke up screaming! People are laughing at you.

All right, all right, lie down, and try to relax. I wouldn't go to sleep, though. Never know what could happen.

Hey, who's that sitting next to you? Oh my God, you're right. It's her—the girl from your nightmare. Now, don't do that! Wait! Stop! Too late! You fainted.

But I can't believe it, either. I made her up for you. She can't be *here*. Hold on, Buddy, I think I'm gonna faint, too!

Michael's Commentary

When I first wrote this, I really loved it. I enjoyed writing it. I loved the idea. I felt you would like it, also. However, when I showed it to my mother and father, they hated it. They said it was disgusting and vulgar, and that I shouldn't hand it in.

I began to listen to them and had second thoughts, but then my sister read it. She liked it; she could identify with it better, I guess.

My mother asked if I was learning *anything* in English, and again I began to have second thoughts.

I had developed "writer's block" and couldn't finish it. After I'd spoken to you about it, I began to regain my confidence. I love this text. It's now finished, and I'm satisfied with it. I hope you are, too.

Our Commentary   It was an odd coincidence that we had just been rereading Keats's letter, in which he had written to his brother about his conception of "the poetical character," when Michael gave us the unfinished first draft of his text.

It seemed to us that although he had never read Keats's letter, Michael had himself discovered something of the strange power of the imagination, to enter/become others and to "live in gusto, be it foul or fair, high or low. . . ." Like a chameleon, he had changed his appearance, even his sex, and "heard" a compelling voice within himself.

Whether the woman who "speaks" in his text is pleasant or unpleasant is neither here nor there: what counts is the vividness, the power, the intensity of Michael's realization.

His ending is ingenious and ironic: the biter bitten!

Some Famous People Take Their Pick

Here are some extracts from the *New York Times*, December 2, 1984:

The Book Review asked a number of prominent people which character from a novel, or from a work of nonfiction, they would most like to be and why. Most respondents were sensitive to the difference between the character they would like to be and the character they are most fond of. Others ignored such subtle distinctions and just fantasized.

Margaret Atwood
Author

To be rather than *to have written*? Fiction? Not many women characters in fiction have a very good time. Elizabeth Bennet, in "Pride and Prejudice," manages to, but her scope is somewhat limited. How about Professor Challenger, in Arthur Conan Doyle's "The Lost World"? He gets travel, pterodactyls (which I've always lusted after) and temper tantrums (which I've never been able to have but feel I ought to). Also, he's a pig with women, and it would be interesting to know what that feels like from the inside. Nonfiction? Lady Hester Stanhope. Or Anna Jameson, who took her smelling salts and parasol into the 19th-century north woods and wrote about it.

Leon Botstein
President of Bard College

Since this symposium leaves little room for humility, my initial choice is Pericles, as portrayed by Thucydides in the "History of the Peloponnesian War." Pericles's integrity, intelligence and "respect for the liberty" of his people gave his leadership greatness. Ambitious, decisive and unsentimental, Pericles was also judicious and capable of restraint. His eloquence and rhetorical clarity triumphed over slogans and flattery. Although he had the misfortune of dying in a plague, he did not live to see his work undone.

Since Pericles may be a bit much and since I don't envy his early death, I would settle for Pierre Bezuhov in Leo Tolstoy's "War and Peace." Absent-minded but inquisitive, Bezuhov suffered imprisonment, deprivation, a bad marriage and loneliness. He explored serious ideas in his search for the meaning of life. Despite an unassuming appearance and a fondness for good food and comforts, he, unlike his fellow characters, made it to the very end. He married Natasha and found faith along with domestic bliss. He avoided becoming a bore. One would like to be as intelligent, resilient, observant and ultimately fortunate.

Laurie Anderson
Performance artist

I would like to have been Sei Shōnagon, who lived 1,000 years ago in Japan. She wrote "The Pillow Book," which was a series of impressions and lists ("Things That Cannot Be Compared," "Things That Quicken the Heart," "Things That Have Lost Their Power"). The only things we know about her life are the roles she gave herself: gadfly, social critic, stranger, voyeur.

Carlos Fuentes
Author

I am Don Quixote. Therefore I am Pickwick and Prince Myshkin. I can even become Madame Bovary. I am at the center of unity. I am on the farthest shore of difference. I leave my shelter. I travel. I am exhausted. I become Pierre Menard [from Jorge Luis Borges's story, "Pierre Menard, Author of the Quixote"], and he sends me back to my village. I am myself plus all my intentions. I am myself plus all my readers. I imitate the past. The present imitates me. I am what I read. I read what I am. I am Don Quixote.

Woody Allen
Actor

Gigi. I want more than anything to be Gigi. To meander, feather-light, down the boulevards of *belle époque* Paris in a little blue sailor dress, my sweet face framed by a flat, disk-shaped hat with two ribbons dangling mischievously past my bangs. And I would be squealing, *"Maman! Regardez! Maman!"* And my room would be paneled and perfect and cluttered with overstuffed pillows and a Victorian chaise and my bed, meltingly soft, with embroidered silk sheets, and everything would be warmly lit by sconces and table lamps whose globes were painted with buds and floral themes. And I would sit and brush my hair and put it up over my eyes, trying out new styles and giggling. And dinner would consist of a cup of thick chocolate beaten up with the yolk of an egg, some toast and grapes and for breakfast, soft-boiled eggs with cherries in them. (I would awaken refreshed each day in a nightgown and stretch like a kitten, rubbing the sleep from my saucer eyes with my tiny fists.)

And then, joy of joys—Gaston (who had delighted in me as a young girl but never dreamed that eventually I would blossom to stunning womanhood) would come to visit and, unable to believe his eyes, would suddenly realize that I am no longer the innocent, frail wisp of a child he has known but I have, obeying destiny, ripened into a creature of breathtaking loveliness. Now I toss my head, allowing my hair to bounce from shoulder to shoulder, offering Gaston the scent of perfume from my neck. Unable to resist, he cups my delicate face in his hands and asks me to go with him to Maxim's. From here it gets a little vague and the image of my black-rimmed glasses and shopping bag from Zabar's intrudes but by then I'm usually radiant and sobbing.

WHAT NOW? TAKE YOUR PICK

Now choose *your* character, and give the reasons for your choice. Remember to make the distinction between the character you are most fond of and the character you would most like to be.

6 | Proteus Could Change His Shape at Will: Varieties of Role and Varieties of Text

Academic Voices

In this section we present various texts written by writers in a role that is similar to the one your professors must take on when they prepare a lecture or a scholarly paper. They are then writing not as private individuals but in a public role.

WILLIAM JAMES AND HIS DOG

In this first text, a philosopher is asking philosophical questions and generating speculations about some of the differences between human beings and animals. The main difference resembles the one that test pilot Chuck Yeager once pointed to. When comparing the experimental chimps and the astronauts in the early days of the space program, he remarked that it was only the humans who knew that they were sitting on top of a rocket that could blow up under them.

Take our dogs and ourselves, connected as we are by a tie more intimate than most ties in this world; and yet, outside of that tie of friendly fondness, how insensible, each of us, to all that makes life significant for the other!—we to the rapture of bones under hedges, or smells of trees and lamp-posts, they to the delights of literature and art. As you sit reading the most moving romance you ever fell upon, what sort of a judge is your fox-terrier of your behaviour? With all his good will toward you, the nature of your conduct is absolutely excluded from his comprehension. To sit there like a senseless statue when you might be taking him to walk and throwing sticks for him to catch! What queer disease is this that comes over you every day, of holding things and staring at them like that for hours together, paralyzed of motion and vacant of all conscious life?

—William James, "On a Certain Blindness in Human Beings"

ERVING GOFFMAN ON OTTERS

Here, now, is a sociologist, Erving Goffman, examining the way in which otters play at fighting—role-play as fighters. You will probably find this text more difficult than the first. Our advice is this: Let your mind skip the phrases that are obscure, and read on right to the end so as to grasp the general drift of the passage. Once you have that, you can return for a second reading and focus on those little patches of difficulty. You may discover that they are mostly difficulties of reference—the writer is referring you to names or concepts that you have not yet met. It is counterproductive to be discouraged by difficulties of reference. All readers meet them, and mature readers can readily admit that they don't (yet) know everything. Such references often occur in parts of the text that are not essential to understanding the main argument. So do not panic, and do not be discouraged.

> During visits to the Fleishacker Zoo beginning in 1952, Gregory Bateson observed that otters not only fight with each other but also play at fighting. Interest in animal play has a clear source in Karl Groos' still useful book, *The Play of Animals,* but Bateson pointedly raised the questions that gave the issue its wider current relevance.
>
> Bateson noted that on some signal or other, the otters would begin playfully to stalk, chase, and attack each other, and on some other signal would stop the play. An obvious point about this play behavior is that the actions of the animals are not ones that are, as it were, meaningful in themselves; the framework of these actions does not make meaningless events meaningful, there being a contrast here to primary understandings, which do. Rather, this play activity is closely patterned after something that already has a meaning in its own terms—in this case fighting, a well-known type of guided doing. Real fighting here serves as a model, a detailed pattern to follow, a foundation for form. Just as obviously, the pattern for fighting is not followed fully, but rather is systematically altered in certain respects. Biting-like behavior occurs, but no one is seriously bitten. In brief, there is a transcription or transposition—a *transformation* in the geometrical, not the Chomskyan, sense—of a strip of fighting behavior into a strip of play. Another point about play is that all those involved in it seem to have a clear appreciation that it is play that is going on. Barring a few troublesome cases, it can be taken that both professional observers and the lay public have no trouble in seeing that a strip of animal behavior is play and, furthermore, that it is play in a sense similar to what one thinks of as play among humans. Indeed, play is possible *between* humans and many species, a fact not to be dwelt upon when we sustain our usual congratulatory versions of the difference between us and them.
>
> —*Erving Goffman*

WHAT NOW? ATTEMPT EITHER (1) OR (2)

1. Your task is to "become" both writers. Write a dialogue between them, arguing about the issues raised in their two texts, and including any other evidence and propositions you wish to produce. To make it easier

you may wish to think of William James, the first writer, as an elderly man who believes in common sense, and of Erving Goffman, the second writer, as a younger man who enjoys upsetting applecarts.

2. "Anthropomorphism" is the term given to the attribution of human characteristics to non-humans, e.g., animals. Put yourself in—or take on—two opposing roles, one promoting "anthropomorphism" and one refuting it. Write a dialogue in which the two points of view are both fairly aired, including any supporting evidence for both points of view. Whatever *your own* point of view may be, try to give each position an adequate showing, so that anyone reading your text would be unable to deduce where you yourself stand on the issue.

COLIN BLAKEMORE ON FORGETTING

Here now is another text by an academic. It is about the way in which the memory works or doesn't work. Read it first for interest's sake; some of it is about yourself.

Imagine that you are asked to remember the number "584." What could be easier? Whether you wanted to or not, the number would be yours to recall for the next few minutes. With the slightest effort of will you could remember it at the end of this chapter; and, if it were important enough, you would recollect it next month, next year or next century.

There is an American—let us call him Henry M.—who has been robbed of this precious power to remember; not partially and gradually, just by growing old, as most of us will be; but suddenly and almost totally, by the knife of a well-intentioned surgeon. From Henry we can learn about the nightmare of eternal forgetfulness—a condition that Franz Kafka would have been delighted to describe. Brenda Milner, at the Montreal Neurological Institute, has followed the case of Henry for more than 20 years. She once asked *him* to try to remember that very number, "584." He sat quietly, entirely undistracted, for 15 minutes, and, to her surprise, he *could* recall the number. But when asked how he did it, this is what he said:

"It's easy. You just remember 8. You see, 5, 8 and 4 add up to 17. You remember 8; subtract it from 17 and it leaves 9. Divide 9 in half and you get 5 and 4, and there you are: 584. Easy!"

Henry lives in a world of his own, restricted not just in space but in time. Ever since an operation on his brain in 1953, his world has been just a few minutes long. Without such elaborate and fantastic tricks of rehearsal, almost everything slips from his mind, like water through a sieve. Every moment has a terrible freshness. He never knows the day of the week, what year it is or even his own age. Even though Brenda Milner has spent countless hours with Henry, she is an utter stranger to him, and on each new occasion that they meet it is as if she were entering his transient world for the first time.

Henry works in a state rehabilitation centre, mounting cigarette lighters on cardboard frames, a task that he has learned to do skillfully. But still he can give no account whatever of his place of work, how he gets there, or the type of job that he does. So Henry has not lost the ability to learn new skills of *movement*; he is, quite simply, unable to remember the new contents of his *conscious* experience. His general intelligence is not at all reduced and he is painfully aware of his own shortcomings. He apologizes constantly for the absence of his mind. "Right now, I'm wondering," he once said, "have I done or said anything amiss? You see, at this moment everything looks clear to me, but what happened just before? That's what worries me. It's like waking from a dream; I just don't remember." . . . "Every day is alone in itself, whatever enjoyment I've had, and whatever sorrow I've had."

Henry still has his very old memories and habits, but cannot form new ones and even had amnesia for things that happened in the years immediately before the operation. Three years before, his favourite uncle died, but Henry suffers the same grief anew each time he is told of his uncle's death.

In 1892 the German physiologist Friedrich Goltz described a similar loss of memory in dogs after the cerebral cortex had been damaged. "They do not learn from past experience," Goltz wrote. "They do not *have* experiences, for only he who has memories can have experiences. The decerebrated dog is essentially nothing but a child of the moment." Henry is a "child of the moment," too; he is trapped, interminably, in the naïveté of infancy.

We discover from this special case that our memories have two forms: one of them is quickly created but fades within a few minutes, to be followed by a more persistent store, which can last for a lifetime. The most popular view is that short-term memories are converted or consolidated into the long-term ones, but it is just as possible that the two processes are totally independent. One thing seems certain; the embodiments of the two sorts of memory must be quite different. Henry has lost the power to form new long-term memories; or perhaps he *can* make them, but has no way to retrieve them again.

It is difficult to exaggerate the importance of *forgetting* in *mental* memory, too. The selection process that lets us store in long-term memory only a tiny fraction of the running contents of short-term memory is essential if the brain is to use particular instances to derive general principles, by a process of inference. The Russian psychologist Alexander Luria has described a man whose memory seemed to have no limit—a mnemonist whose mind was so extraordinary that Luria wrote of him in terms reserved for the mentally ill. He could commit to memory in a couple of minutes a table of fifty numbers, which he could recall in every minute detail many years later. His greatest difficulty was in learning how to forget the endless trivia that cluttered his mind.

—Colin Blakemore, *Mechanics of the Mind*

Role and
Audience

Please have another look at that text, and see if you can determine what kind of audience Blakemore was writing for: children? experts? intelligent nonexperts? people with defective memories? Support your choice by reference to particular bits of the text. Walk into anyone's house and you will probably find a television set. Would you be likely to find a copy of Blakemore's article? How would you characterize or typify the kind of home in which you would *not* be surprised to find it? Do you think Blakemore's target audience was less or more specialized than Goffman's? How do you know that Blakemore's text is very probably not an extract from a letter to a friend who happens to be interested in memory?

Both Goffman and Blakemore refer to other people—writers, scientists, and so on—in their texts. Why do you think they do this? Out of politeness? To support their own position? To show that they have read the "important" writers in their field of work? All three?

Who, of all three writers, particularizes most specifically? Why do you think this is so? What is the effect of the particularizing on you, the reader? How do the particular details work to support generalizations? Most readers find Blakemore clearer than Goffman. Why do you think this is so? Can you point to passages of obscurity in Blakemore's text? Who would you rather have a lecture from—James, Goffman, or Blakemore?

Blakemore's text is a version of a talk that he prepared for reading over the radio. Does it "sound" natural to you? Is it easier to read aloud than Goffman's? Which do you remember best?

DEREK BROMHALL ON DEVIL BIRDS

Finally, in this section, we offer a more extended passage from someone writing in the role of a disseminator of biological discoveries. As a biologist, Derek Bromhall uses a variety of techniques for acquiring new information about his chosen subject, the swift, a bird often confused with the swallow. As he amasses his new findings, they either fit into existing patterns of what is already known, or they contradict earlier "facts," which are displaced.

Out of masses of notes, jottings, records, statistics, and questions—the stock in trade of anyone devoted to the task of making and recording observations—he finally shaped a text that would make sense not only to other specialists but also to an interested general reader.

When a colony of swifts first nested in the tower of Oxford University's Museum of Science in 1976, they gave scientists an ideal opportunity for observing them at very close quarters, with the aid of some very sophisticated cameras; the use of the cameras produced an interesting discovery. On a larger scale, it was fortunate that by this time radar observation and tracking of aircraft was sufficiently refined to pick up the great flocks of swifts that every evening mysteriously left the lower air near the ground and began their startling ascent into the sky—their "Vespers flight"—going to bed in the sky!

In this passage, Derek Bromhall discusses both the newly observed vibrating of the head, recorded for the first time by high-speed cameras, and the extent of the evening flight and what was discovered about it.

Swifts

What had started as a heatwave in May 1976, before the eggs were even laid, extended into a long period of consistent sunshine and high temperatures. By 7 June, thermometers in the nest-boxes were recording temperatures exceeding 30° C (86° F) and as the sun continued to gain strength during the month temperatures in the Tower rose above 38° C (100° F) by mid afternoon. The sitting birds kept as cool as possible by panting with open beaks, losing heat by evaporation from the lining of the throat. At such times one can see that although the swift has a very small beak it has an enormous gape, in common with other birds that catch insects on the wing, in particular the nightjars, and notably the Australian frogmouth. The full extent of the gape can only be seen when the swift yawns, which it does not infrequently during incubation.

As well as panting and yawning the swifts occasionally vibrated head and beak very rapidly, for no more than two or three seconds at a time. Such behaviour, which occurs during the course of preening sessions in the nest, has not previously been reported. The vibration was so rapid, and was over so quickly, that it was difficult to be sure it had actually happened; in fact we were uncertain ourselves until we closely examined the film recording the event. What at first appeared to be a blurred and out-of-focus sequence of the swift's head proved, on analysis of the film, frame by frame, that the bird was in fact vibrating its beak and head at such a speed that the image on the film appeared as a blur. We later found that a photograph taken at 1/1000 second exposure was still too slow to freeze the movement of the head.

An explanation of such curious behaviour can only be tentative. It could be to dislodge parasites on the head, and perhaps in the nostrils, where mites congregate, but if so it has no effect that one can observe. More likely, in my view, is that it is a means by which the swift preens that part of its body which it cannot reach at all with its beak, and only very awkwardly and inefficiently with its claws. By vibrating the head at high speed, individual feathers separate, small particles of dirt and debris are shaken off and the feathers fit neatly into place again when the vibration ceases. A swift has special problems in preening, different from other birds. Being continuously on the wing it cannot rest to groom itself; its legs are so short that only with great difficulty can it scratch its head when in the nest, a difficulty presumably compounded when it is actually flying. One might suppose also that swifts have a particular need to groom the feathers of the head. They catch several thousand insects each

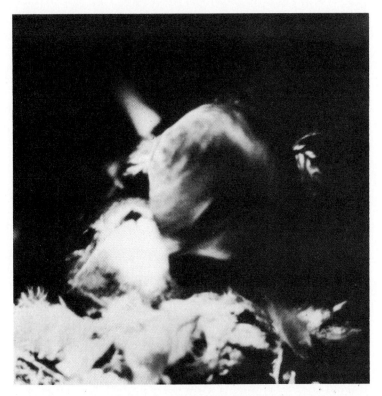

In preening, a swift sometimes vibrates its head so fast that it is blurred even when photographed with electronic flash at 1/1000 sec.

day, many of which are soft-bodied and easily damaged on impact with a swift travelling at high speed; it is to be expected that insect juices and small fragments, as well as the swift's own saliva, will adhere to the feathers around the beak and head. Indeed this can be seen when swifts which are feeding chicks bring back food in their throat pouches. It is possible that while on the wing the swift cleanses and grooms the feathers of its head by vibrating them at high speed, in a manner similar to the way we use ultra-sonic vibration to clean clothing. What we observed as a rare event in the nest-box may normally occur while the bird is in flight.

In good weather only one bird at a time occupies the nest-box during the day, but each evening the partner last out returns to its mate sitting on the eggs and they spend the night together, sleeping side by side. They give every appearance of sleeping profoundly, and the fact that they benefit from a good night's sleep increases the mystery of how swifts rest when they are not nesting, and spend night after night on the wing.

Each evening at the Tower as the sun sets and the breeding pairs settle down for the night, groups of birds circle the Tower, screaming from time to time and rising higher as the sky grows darker, to disappear completely as night closes in.

We know now that these swifts are the immature non-breeders, joined occasionally by mature birds spending the night away from the nest. Speculation that swifts fly all night and sleep on the wing persisted for many years before being accepted as fact. It is illustrative of the perversity of human nature that the improbable legend of swallows hibernating in lakes was believed for centuries, whereas reports from responsible witnesses of swifts spending all night on the wing, backed by considerable circumstantial evidence, were treated with scepticism and even disdain, perhaps because it is hard to believe that a small bird can fly continuously night and day and actually sleep on the wing.

As long ago as the First World War a French airman reported an encounter with a flock of swifts at night. He had climbed to 4400 metres (14,500 feet) before cutting his engine and gliding silently down over the German lines. At about 3000 metres (10,000 feet) he saw below him, showing up clearly against the white clouds in the light of a full moon, a scattered group of birds which appeared to be drifting above the clouds and showed no reaction to the presence of the plane. As he flew through the flock one of the birds was accidentally trapped in the fuselage, and it turned out to be a swift. Convincing evidence, one might suppose, and there were other reports too, of swifts being heard and seen on the wing at night, yet in 1952 a correspondent of *The Times*, in an article dated 22 July and entitled 'Spying on Swifts,' was asking sceptically 'Does the bird sometimes sleep on the wing, or at least spend the night flying, as some naturalists believe? That great authority, the *Handbook of British Birds*, says it is improbable. . . .'

By coincidence, in that same month David Lack saw for the first time a party of swifts, which had been feeding over the marshes along the Sussex coast, fly out to sea at dusk. He assumed then that they were returning to the Continent but in later years more detailed observations suggested that swifts which were either feeding along the coast or were in passage, responding to a major weather movement, regularly flew out to sea each evening, whatever the weather, to spend the night on the wing. It was not until *Swifts in a Tower* had gone to press that David Lack was able to confirm, in a postscript, that swifts in passage sleep on the wing, from having observed mass ascents of birds feeding over reservoirs, the swifts rising to a height of 100 or 200 feet before drifting away together.

A. S. Cutcliffe, in a contribution published in *British Birds* in 1955, describes how he saw and heard swifts flying well after dark on two occasions, on one of which he saw them flying through the searchlight beams of a warship lying at anchor.

In recent years the circumstantial evidence and eye-witness reports of swifts sleeping on the wing have been confirmed by studies in which sophisticated radar equipment has tracked large numbers of swifts as well as individual birds. Radar has proved very useful in bird studies, enabling migrant species and foraging birds, such as starlings, to be tracked over large areas. One of these studies, conducted by the Marconi Company, recorded on film a radar screen monitoring the sky over the London area and southern England, including the Channel. As the sun set and darkness fell all detail on the screen was blotted out as thousands upon thousands of swifts rose into the night sky, in what has come to be known as their Vespers flight.

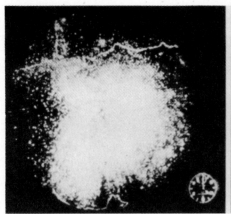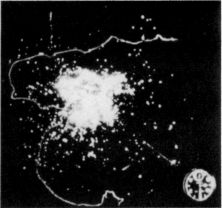

The Vespers flight of the swift over southeast England, as seen by radar.
A photograph of the radar screen at 9:00 p.m. in mid-summer (June 22); the echoes of planes (large points of light) flying between the Wash, to the north, and the English Channel, show up clearly against the outline of the coast. At 10:30 p.m., as darkness falls, all detail on the screen is obliterated as thousands of swifts rise into the night sky to sleep on the wing (from film *Devil Birds; courtesy:* The Marconi Co. Ltd)

In Switzerland swifts have been tracked by radar automatically, day and night. We now know that they spend the night high in the air in bad weather as well as fine, and when flying at night a swift alternates a phase of wing beats with one of rest. The beating phase is of 1 to 6 seconds duration, with wing-beat frequencies of 6 to 8 per second, while the resting phase lasts from 0.5 to 5 seconds. Non-migrating individuals fly at an air speed of about 23 k.p.h. (14 m.p.h.), while swifts migrating at night travel faster, at around 40 k.p.h. (25 m.p.h.). These studies have also confirmed eye-witness reports that the general pattern of migration of swifts is dominated by the passage of weather systems.

As far as is now known, the European swift is the only bird which ascends at night to sleep on the wing. For explanation we need look again at the unique way of life of a bird whose domain is the open sky. On the wing a swift is usually safe, but one that is brought down is in peril of its life. So unless some accident befalls it the swift leaves its refuge in the sky only when it is essential to do so, as when nesting, and for the minimum period of time. Swifts do occasionally cling momentarily to the outside of a building in which there are nests, as if in play, usually towards the end of the breeding season but these are probably young birds that have recently left the nest.

Swifts are not only seasonally migratory, travelling thousands of miles each spring and autumn between Europe and Africa, but they also fly great distances during the summer in response to weather movements. Those that are rearing young usually restrict their foraging to within a hundred miles or so of their nest, but the non-breeders are free to range where they will and may fly up to a thousand kilometres in a single day to avoid a region of bad weather. Mass movements of swifts occur throughout the summer, the birds avoiding depressions and congregating in their thousands where there is abundant food. When these movements occur the swifts fly against the wind, thus avoiding the centre of the depression. Ranging the length and breadth of Europe they would not find safe roosting places every evening, in localities with which they were not familiar. So it is safer for them to remain in the air overnight, and by rising high above any tall buildings, trees or other obstacles, or when they are near a coastline by flying over the sea, they stay out of danger.

Reading "Swifts"

Because we participate in the life of our own minds and bodies, we know what it means to be a human being. But in terms of knowing other organisms, we can never be more than spectators. As spectators, we can observe, record our observations, look for significant patterns or correlations, draw inferences, play hunches, engage in intelligent guesses, form hypotheses, and replicate our experiments in order to verify our findings—or disprove them.

Bromhall's text contains many of the characteristic features of good scientific writing. His explanation of the amazing Vespers flight is especially elegant. How does he organize it?

First he writes of the birds' disappearance in the evening and recognizes the fact that this disappearance had for many years given rise to a surmise, a speculative idea—namely, that the birds sleep in the higher air. He then steps sideways to compare this speculative notion with the superstition—the "improbable legend"—that the birds hibernate under water! (What is the crucial difference between a "reasonable" speculation and a "foolish" superstition?) He then traces the history of the observations, from World War I to the present day, separating out (a) circumstantial evidence, (b) eyewitness reports, and (c) radar confirmation of eyewitness reports. Note that (a) and (b) correlated neatly, but (b) had to be regarded as possibly, even probably, fallible. When (c) became available, it clinched the matter. In two decades the biologists moved the Vespers flight from improbability to confirmed or verified fact.

Bromhall's text, then, gives us not only the findings but also the nature of the quest, and it reinforces the essential empirical distinction between "it may perhaps be" and "it certainly is."

The Invisible Spectator

One of the first disciplines that the spectator-as-scientist has to accept is the discipline of **impersonality**. Good scientists never allow their own feelings to enter into their work, since their first duty is to refrain from tampering with their findings. It is one thing to *want* a certain kind of result; it is quite another to bend your work so that it appears to yield the desired result. So throughout the 95 pages of Bromhall's account of the swifts, he remains entirely *invisible*. This is not to deny that we assume him to be interested in the swifts. (Why otherwise would he be devoting all that time to them?) If, then, he wishes to express his own personal delight in the swifts, where can he legitimately do it? Bromhall found a neat answer by including such matter in his "acknowledgments":

Having now written a book and made a film about swifts I feel very much in their debt, a feeling which must be shared by others who have been privileged to study wild animals at close quarters. In special cases it may be possible to go some way towards repaying this debt directly, for instance where effective measures to save a species or its habitat may follow the appearance of a book or film; but in most instances repayment is indirect, with benefits accruing to wildlife in general.

In the case of the swift it might be supposed that its life is so remote from ours that our influence on it must be minimal. But almost unawares we have been providing swifts with nest sites in the roofs of our homes for centuries; equally unwittingly we may be denying future generations of swifts their traditional sites, as new buildings replace old and roof spaces are sealed off to conserve heat. The swift is in fact in greater potential danger now than at any time in the past.

To counteract this we should now be installing nest-boxes for swifts wherever this is feasible. There can be few birds as beneficial to man as the swift and certainly no greater scourge of insects. And for those who take the trouble and have the patience to establish their own colony, there will be the immeasurable reward of being able to observe, enjoy and discover for themselves what it is about the swift that makes it the most fascinating and challenging of all birds.

> Derek Bromhall
> Oxford
> March 1980

Nonacademic Voices

Learning to use an academic voice can be hard work; such learning takes time. Even more time may be needed to learn to feel natural when using it. Now, for relaxation, we invite you to regress.

THOM GUNN'S "YOKO"

First, read this poem by Thom Gunn.

Yoko

All today I lie in the bottom of the wardrobe
feeling low but sometimes getting up
to moodily lumber across rooms
and lap from the toilet bowl, it is so sultry
and then I hear the noise of firecrackers again
all New York is jaggedy with firecrackers today
and I go back to the wardrobe gloomy
trying to void my mind of them.
I am confused, I feel loose and unfitted.

At last deep in the stairwell I hear a tread,
it is him, my leader, my love.
I run to the door and listen to his approach.
Now I can smell him, what a good man he is,
I love it when he has the sweat of work on him,
as he enters I yodel with happiness,
I throw my body up against his, I try to lick his lips,
I care about him more than anything.

After we eat we go for a walk to the piers.
I leap into the standing warmth, I plunge into
the combination of old and new smells.
Here on a garbage can at the bottom, so interesting,
what sister or brother I wonder left this message I sniff.
I too piss there, and go on.
Here a hydrant there a pole
here's a smell I left yesterday, well that's disappointing
but I piss there anyway, and go on.
I investigate so much that in the end
it is for form's sake only, only a drop comes out.

I investigate tar and rotten sandwiches, everything, and go on.

And here a dried old turd, so interesting
so old, so dry, yet so subtle and mellow.
I can place it finely, I really appreciate it,
a gold distant smell like packed autumn leaves in winter
reminding me how what is rich and fierce when excreted
becomes weathered and mild
                              but always interesting
and reminding me of what I have to do.

My leader looks on and expresses his approval.

I sniff it well and later I sniff the air well
a wind is meeting us after the close July day
rain is getting near too but first the wind.

Joy, joy,
being outside with you, active, investigating it all,
with bowels emptied, feeling your approval
and then running on, the big fleet Yoko,
my body in its excellent black coat never lets me down,
returning to you (as I always will, you know that)
and now
            filling myself out with myself, no longer confused,
my panting pushing apart my black lips, but unmoving,
I stand with you braced against the wind.

Reading "Yoko"   At what point did you begin to recognize Yoko's voice as a dog's?
When did you feel certain that it was a dog?

Was the tone of voice that Gunn gave to Yoko misleading? Did you hear a rather serious human being until the other clues forced you into realizing that the speaker was a dog? Was there an interesting tension between your reading of "human" language and your realization that the language had been given to a dog?

Do you think Gunn is closer to James or to Goffman in his attitude to animals? Gunn is invisible inside his own poem; he gives all the space to Yoko. If Gunn had intruded and said directly: "I love Yoko" or "Yoko is a lovable old dog," would such direct telling have spoiled his text? What effect(s) do you think Gunn wished to have on you, his reader? Do Gunn's moments of particularizing help you to see Yoko more vividly? What else do they achieve?

Assume you are not a dog lover; quite the contrary. How might this text change your mind?

WHAT NOW?

1. Assume the role of a biologist observing Yoko's behavior, and make a record of all that he does in the text, as if you had observed it. (Assume that Gunn gave you permission to observe inside the house as well as outside). Recalling the texts of Goffman and of Bromhall, try to write in role as a scientific observer.
2. If you have (or have had) a pet, write *its* text about your life together.
3. Gunn's poem has been found in a high school poetry anthology by an extremely narrow-minded reactionary member of a PTA. Assume the role of this watchdog, and write a letter to your local newspaper demanding that the book be removed from the library and stating your reasons. Then assume the role of a good-humored tolerant member of the community, and write a defense of Gunn's poem.

"Writing" Even as You Read Someone Else's Text

When you read the sentence, "The cat sits on the mat," what happens inside your mind? How do you give meaning to the simple words forming that simple sentence?

Whose cat do you "see"? Which mat do you "see"?

If the text offers you no more to go on, then the cat you "see" must be a cat you know; and the mat must be a mat with which you are familiar. To put it another way, you recognize the meanings of the words because they provoke you to **re-cognizing**—knowing once more (by calling it up from your own past)—what you already know. If, however, you meet this sentence: "Floccinaucinihilipilification seems trivial to me," then there may well be absolutely no recognition, simply because you have not met this extravagant creature before.

When we say that you "write" as you read, we are referring to the fact that as you read the words on the page, you yourself are creating (a) a "text"—a text of images and memories both like and unlike the writer's text on the page—and also (b) words that may possibly come next. But if writers merely reminded you of what you already know, you would soon decide that there's not enough satisfaction for you in reading. We would agree. A good strong text gives readers both what they already know (reawakened knowledge that has been lying dormant) and what they don't already know. And as you read, what you already know about language allows you to predict an extraordinary amount of what will _____ _____. Your anticipations both of the text (the shape of its sentences, its word order) and of what it represents (the "virtual" world that it presents) are simultaneously satisfied and surprised, and your satisfactions in reading depend on that interplay between the expected and the unexpected. Our guess, then, is that Gunn's poem about Yoko had precisely this kind of pleasurable, double-edged effect on you.

"All today I lie in the bottom of the wardrobe"????!!!! (That's the kind of overblown punctuation that some of our students use until they learn that less is more.) Be honest. What surprised you about that sentence? After the perfectly cozy familiarity of "All day I lie . . . ," "in" comes as a shock as soon as we realize there's something odd about "bottom"—human beings don't lie *in* the bottom; *on* the bottom, maybe . . . But even as these half-thoughts move through our minds, we reach "the wardrobe." "In the bottom of the wardrobe"? What exactly is going on here? Our normal expectations about where and how *we* lie have been shaken up. "And lap from the toilet bowl" is even more startling; but at least we are learning in this text to expect to be disconcerted. A familiar world is being oddly defamiliarized. We experience a mixture of uncertainty and a feeling that we may be on to something—that we might be able to get to the bottom of this . . . so we read on.

"A dog goes for a walk." If that were all you were given by way of a text, whose dog would you read/write into the word? Where does your dog go walking? You envision your streets, your lampposts, your trees. But as Gunn's poem proceeds, the "dog" of *his* text, increasing in its distinctive particularities, displaces all stereotypes of "dog," all visions of the behavior of *your* dog; *his* increasingly realized dog enters your mind, takes it over, sniffs around, and curls up. You may not be sure whether you like him, but he is unmistakably *that* dog, presented by *that* text—specific, closely observed, registered, even relished, both in his typicality (otherwise you wouldn't recognize him as canine) and in his own distinguishing individuality.

WHAT NOW? ANTHROPOMORPHIC VOCALIZATIONS

Compose any one of the following monologues:

1. You are a dinosaur that has just crawled out of a cave in Central Park and are amazed that everyone thinks you should be extinct. Make a statement to the press.

2. You are a tiger that was captured when young and imprisoned in a zoo. Now you are very old and feel death approaching. Make a last plea for the opportunity to return to your homeland.
3. You are a chimpanzee in a laboratory being prepared for a painful experiment. Make a last appeal to the biologists as they fasten the electrodes on your skull.
4. You are a neglected alley cat. You never know the luxury of good food, but you love your freedom to roam the tiles. Speak to a cossetted, pampered pet cat that has never known freedom.
5. You are the last carrier pigeon in nineteenth-century America. Speak a warning to humans.

DOUGLAS ADAMS'S WHALE

One of the most popular books of recent years is Douglas Adams's *The Hitchhiker's Guide to the Galaxy,* an extravagant spoof on science-fiction fantasies. Impossible events take place on almost every page, none more so than the following cruel joke.

> Another thing that got forgotten was the fact that against all probability a sperm whale had suddenly been called into existence several miles above the surface of an alien planet.
>
> And since this is not a natural tenable position for a whale, this poor innocent creature had very little time to come to terms with its identity as a whale before it then had to come to terms with not being a whale any more.
>
> This is a complete record of its thought from the moment it began its life till the moment it ended it.
>
> Ah . . . ! What's happening? it thought.
>
> Er, excuse me, who am I?
>
> Hello?
>
> Why am I here? What's my purpose in life?
>
> What do I mean by who am I?
>
> Calm down, get a grip now . . . oh! this is an interesting sensation, what is it? It's a sort of . . . yawning, tingling sensation in my . . . my . . . well I suppose I'd better start finding names for things if I want to make any headway in what for the sake of what I shall call an argument I shall call the world, so let's call it my stomach.
>
> Good. Ooooh, it's getting quite strong. And hey, what about this whistling roaring sound going past what I'm suddenly going to call my head? Perhaps I can call that . . . wind! Is that a good name? It'll do . . . perhaps I can find a better name for it later when I've found out what it's for. It must be something very important because there certainly seems to be a hell of a lot of it. Hey! What's this thing? This . . . let's call it a tail—yeah, tail. Hey! I can really thrash it about pretty good can't I? Wow! Wow! That feels great! Doesn't seem to achieve very much but I'll probably find out what it's for later on. Now—have I built up any coherent picture of things yet?
>
> No.

Never mind, hey, this is really exciting, so much to find out about, so much to look forward to, I'm quite dizzy with anticipation . . .

Or is it the wind?

There really is a lot of that now isn't there?

And wow! Hey! What's this thing suddenly coming towards me very fast? Very very fast. So big and flat and round, it needs a big wide sounding name like . . . ow . . . ound . . . round . . . ground! That's it! That's a good name—ground!

I wonder if it will be friends with me?

And the rest, after a sudden wet thud, was silence.

WHAT NOW? AGAINST ALL PROBABILITY

Create an improbable event, in which things get out of control, and represent it through the thoughts, the inner speech, of someone caught up in the confusion, calamity, or crisis.

FILLING THE GAP: TED HUGHES'S "WODWO"

The gulf that yawns between the human race on the one side and the higher animals on the other has always intrigued human beings. Many societies and cultures have, indeed, invented mythical creatures to fill the space—a variety of creatures of an ambiguous kind, with some human characteristics and some animal qualities, melded to form an odd composite. The crucial question concerns the possession or otherwise of language. The general consensus today is that while the higher animals can make signs, they do not possess language. (If this distinction interests you, we recommend Walker Percy's exhilarating book *Lost in the Cosmos.*)

Scientific observation has established this fact beyond question: in the absence of human society, even human beings do not, cannot, develop language. The famous Wild Child of Aveyron, who had probably been abandoned soon after birth and had somehow survived in the forest, was captured when, according to his teeth, he was probably about 12 years old. Every effort to help him develop language failed.

In his poem "Wodwo," Ted Hughes revives a widespread medieval belief that the deep woods were inhabited by wild men or wodwos. Hughes gives his wodwo the benefit of the linguistic doubt and endows him with speech, at least the power to talk to himself. In his text, Hughes takes on the role of a wodwo.

Hughes himself has explained:

I imagine this creature just discovering that it is alive in the world. It does not know what it is and is full of questions. It is quite bewildered to know what is going on. It has a whole string of thoughts, but at the centre of all of them as you will see, is this creature and its bewilderment. The poem is called "Wodwo." A Wodwo is a sort of half-man half-animal spirit of the forests.

Wodwo

What am I? Nosing here, turning leaves over
following a faint stain on the air to the river's edge
I enter water. What am I to split
the glassy grain of water looking upward I see the bed
of the river above me upside down very clear
what am I doing here in mid-air? Why do I find
this frog so interesting as I inspect its most secret
interior and make it my own? Do these weeds
know me and name me to each other have they
seen me before, do I fit in their world? I seem
separate from the ground and not rooted but dropped
out of nothing casually I've no threads
fastening me to anything I can go anywhere
I seem to have been given the freedom
of this place what am I then? And picking
bits of bark off this rotten stump gives me
no pleasure and it's no use so why do I do it
me and doing that have coincided very queerly
But what shall I be called am I the first
have I an owner what shape am I what
shape am I am I huge if I go
to the end on this way past these trees and past these trees
till I get tired that's touching one wall of me
for the moment if I sit still how everything
stops to watch me I suppose I am the exact centre
but there's all this what is it roots
roots roots roots and here's the water
again very queer but I'll go on looking

—Ted Hughes

A Classroom Discussion

G.S.:   So, "Wodwo" is a *fiction*, yes?

NEIL: How can you be so sure it's a fiction?

[Many voices are heard, all at once; they are unintelligible, but it sounds as if several people are shouting, "Of course, it's fiction!" and several others are saying, "Right! How can you/How can we?"]

G.S.:   Hold it! Hold it just one second! Whose voice is "talking" in "Wodwo"? Stephanie?

STEPHANIE: Ted Hughes's voice. And it's *pretending* to be Wodwo's voice.

UNIDENTIFIED
STUDENT: Yeah, he's impersonating!

G.S.:   So Ted Hughes is not simply giving us a transcript of what someone else—some wild man—actually said?

STEPHANIE: No. He's making it all up. Like you said, it's fiction.

NEIL: But it doesn't *have* to be! Just imagine: there's this guy who's been
up in the mountains for years. His plane crashed. He got a concus-
sion, maybe he was in a coma for a few hours, even days. Then he
regains consciousness, but he's brain-damaged. He's gone right
back to being *very* simple....

DANNY: Like a small kid ... very young ... almost a baby. Regressing ...

NEIL: Right. Then he's got to start all over, to make sense of his environment, his world. Or he'll die, right?

LIZ: Of course he'd die! He's gotta eat and drink ... get moving ...
figure it all out, fruit, water, wild mushrooms—stuff like that ...
and quick!

G.S.:   O.K. So he's regressed to an earlier, more primitive, infantile level
of consciousness. Like senility. And finally he gets out of those
mountains, or somebody finds him. Then ...

NEIL: Then he gives an account of his experiences—how he explored,
and poked around, and sniffed, and tasted things, to see if they
were eatable—edible. And what he says, this account he gives, it
would be like "Wodwo."

DANNY: I doubt it!

CHRISTINE: No, it wouldn't! It would be like a narrative, and it would be in the
past, the past tense. He'd say things like, "When I came to, I had
this terrific headache. But I was so hungry, I didn't have time to
search in the wreckage."

HOWARD: What wreckage?

CHRISTINE: The plane, you dummy! What I'm saying is it would be the same
as when we give an account of what we did yesterday or two years
ago. But Wodwo's talking *now*. It's all in the present tense. And
that's impossible! Because when you're doing something by yourself, and talking to yourself about it *while* you're doing it, you're
not talking to anybody else, not really. Even if you imagine somebody's with you.

DANNY: Like when a guy I know is fixing his car, he talks to himself—out
loud!—all the time. "Now fix the carburetor," he says, and grabs the
wrench or the screwdriver. "Hey, this is stuck...." That sort of
thing....

LORI: You should hear what my boyfriend says when he's fixing *his* car!

G.S.:   O.K.! Let's see if we can pull all this together. See if you agree with this: The text "sounds like" Wodwo, especially when we read it aloud. Agreed? But as Christine says, it's the kind of utterance we produce when we're alone and talking to ourselves, talking through something complicated or new or delicate, when we're especially keen not to make a mistake. But Hughes isn't Wodwo, and he's never heard a wodwo talk; so he created the illusion. And we enjoy the illusion created by the words; it's *as if* we were tucked away inside Wodwo's mind, and could actually hear his thoughts.

DANNY: Impossible!

G.S.:   Exactly. So it *must* be a fiction.

> The function of reflective thought is to transform a situation in which there is experienced obscurity, of some sort, into a situation that is clear, coherent, settled, harmonious.
>
> —*John Dewey*****

Making Sense of a Text   In Hughes's fiction, Wodwo is engaging in a kind of reflective thought as he goes about his work; his reflective thought is an example of **synpraxis**—verbalizing your activity even as you do it. As we work toward an understanding of Hughes's text, we also engage in reflective thought: part of the task of *our* thought is to justify, make sense of, all the features of Hughes's text—both *what* it represents and also *how* it represents it—in order to reach a reading of the text that is "clear, coherent, settled, harmonious."

Here now are some students' comments on "Wodwo." Some are utterances, others are texts—you may care to decide which is which. Some are helpful, others are useless—again, you may care to decide which is which.

1. There seem to be a lot of misprints—the printer left out a lot of commas and periods.
2. It's sort of a kind of representation of somebody getting lost.
3. In the text, Wodwo is trying to make sense of its/her/his relationship with the environment, in order to satisfy its basic needs.
4. It's a set of binaries: known: unknown; familiar: strange; recognizing: being recognized; knowing: being known; ability: disability; moving: being still; lost: found; clear: confused; center: periphery; active: passive (doing: being done to); forward: back; in: out; water: dry land; coping: being overwhelmed; stagnating: progressing. At the end it says, "I'll go on looking," so there's hope for it; it should make progress, along a kind of zig-zag.
5. Wodwo? Eh, he's some kinda airhead!

**Intelligence and the Modern World*, ed. J. Ratner (New York, 1939), p. 851.

6. I don't think Wodwo's stupid—I know it's a fiction! But the surface uncertainty and confusion—all those mixed-up sentences—it all means he's really observant, and thinking hard, even though he doesn't know a lot. I think the punctuation—or lack of it—lets Hughes (or Wodwo) say two things at the same time. In line 3, for example, this is ambiguous: it could mean

> "What? Am *I* to split . . ." (Is it *my* task?)

or it could be

> "What am *I*, to split . . ." (Am I capable of splitting, am I worthy, do I have any right . . . ?)

7. What interests me is "who" is Wodwo, or "what" is a wodwo? I think he's got to be a mammal because, in lines 4–5, he seems to think of water as an element in which he doesn't really belong. And he confuses water (the river-water) and air—"here in mid-air." He's not a burrower; otherwise, he'd probably feel "rooted." He seems to have hands, to pick with, and we know he has a very good sense of smell, since his statement begins with his nose! I suspect that either he is young, even very young, or he has strayed into an unfamiliar environment, because the last ten lines or so all stress the tentativeness of his perceptions. To summarize, I think he is a young mammal with some humanoid characteristics; I see him as rather like a young, "intelligent," inquisitive chimpanzee.

8. The shape of a sentence is the shape of a relationship: for example, "I'll fix the car" expresses the *clear* relationship between the doer ("I"), the job ("fix") and what the job is to be done to ("the car"). If you have a clear sense of the relationships between yourself and things in your environment, this will be evident in what you say or write to express those relationships. If, on the other hand, you're not yet sure of your relationship with, say, unfamiliar objects, then one way in which that uncertainty is expressed can be in the uncertainty of your utterances, even if you don't admit explicitly that you're uncertain.

   Wodwo says, "me and doing . . . have coincided very queerly"—in other words, he's not yet clear about the relationship between himself and his actions. It's rather like when we say "I don't know why I did that." It may well be that he is guided or driven by instinct but doesn't know what instinct is and doesn't have a word for it.

9. The rush of the sentences from "But what shall I be called" right down to "for the moment" expresses the confused impulsive rush of his actions—he's almost in a kind of frenzy, and the running together of all those short sentences is an effective way of conveying, representing, the mad rush.

10. Punctuation—our system of "pointing"—comes from two separate traditions: one is *dramatic*—a set of signs telling the reader how to read *aloud*—and the other is *grammatical*, pointing to the separation of the parts (sentences, phrases, etc.). In "Wodwo," the punctuation is dramatic—it helps you to "hear" Wodwo's voice.

WHAT NEXT?

1. Assume that Wodwo is at a certain point in its evolutionary development. Consider what—at this point—it is capable of "saying" (therefore,
of thinking). Now push it a few notches *up* or *down* the evolutionary
ladder. Put it in the same environment, and compose its inner speech
in a style that is appropriate to and expressive of the stage of evolution (*more* or *less* advanced) that you have chosen.
2. Compose a dialogue between *two* wodwos. Show how two heads are
better than one when problems are to be solved.
3. Envisage a couple of superstitious peasants or two naïve children
traveling through the woods and sighting Wodwo for the first time.
Generate their conversation. (You will have to decide whether or not
they have already heard stories about such creatures.)
4. A team of anthropologists, equipped with television cameras, has discovered Wodwo. They film it as it is doing all the things in Hughes's
text. Later, in the studio, they edit the film and add a voice-over commentary by an expert. As Wodwo performs each action, the voice offers
a running commentary-explanation. The finished film is intended for
a nonspecialist audience; the commentary is intended to help the
viewers make sense of what, at each stage, they are observing. Use the
following format:

ACTION (IMAGE):   COMMENTARY (WORDS SPOKEN):

INNER SPEECH

What are we doing when we talk to ourselves? We take on the role of
speaker and the role of listener. The listening inner ear of the mind provides feedback to the speaking part of the mind.

This is very useful when we are learning to perform some complicated
task; the inner speaker talks us through it; the inner listener reacts in various ways, confirming, modifying, doubting, slowing it down, correcting,
reassuring, and so on.

Our inner speech expresses our choices and our decisions, our options
and uncertainties; and all the time, the listener inside us is responding
usefully.

About fifty years ago, it was realized that there is something consistently
characteristic of the sentences that we all produce in our inner speech:
they have no subject. For example, instead of saying, "I'm gonna do this,"
as we would in social (vocalized) talking, we say, "gonna do this." Instead
of saying, "The dog's scared," we say, "Scared," or " 's scared."

Why does inner speech omit the subject of its sentence? Speculate about this. Consider, for example, why it is that social speech names the subjects of its sentences. Remember that when we talk to someone, he/she needs to know what we are talking about! First we have to *identify* what it is we are talking about (name a subject); only then can we say something about it (provide a *predicate*).

Notes

You have seen how Wodwo talks to himself as he explores his environment and tries to solve its riddle and make sense of it. "Wodwo" was, of course, a fiction. But in many ways Ted Hughes gave it a kind of inner speech very close to your own: a stream of language that carries observations, speculations, surmises, guesses, wonderings, and questionings—a running commentary on the interactions between a mind and a world. In the next chapter, we shall invite you to explore inner speech more extensively, and more closely, but meanwhile we invite you to make notes on the various kinds of thinking that you perform when you are producing your unending stream of inner speech.

7 | Seeing from Within: Participant Texts

Writing from Within

Think for a moment of your past life. Choose a particular episode—a crisis, an extraordinary event, a red-letter day. How can you represent that event? You are now here, in the present, standing outside that past event, looking back at it—not at the event itself but rather at your memories of it. And of course you are not literally "looking back"; you may even have your eyes closed.

To represent that event in writing, you have two main options: (1) You can remain "outside" it and keep it in its place, in the past, while you observe it as separate from you, who are in the present. Or (2) You can reconstruct your experience of being "inside" the event, taking part in it from moment to moment. You can feel as if once more you are having that experience. The mental event becomes a powerful illusion of the actual event—so powerful that, for example, you even blush again as you relive a moment of embarrassment.

In this chapter, we shall offer you opportunities to discover what is involved in writing that second kind of representation. You had a brief encounter with such texts on page 42; now we shall explore them in greater detail. We call such texts **participant texts**, because even though you can no longer be an actual participant in your own past activities, such texts can effectively, convincingly, and satisfyingly present that sense of intimate, inner/inside knowledge that only those who are in the thick of an experience can have. Participant texts have a power to excite, to amaze, to arouse. Writing them can be intensely satisfying for the writer, and reading them can be intensely pleasurable for the reader. Such texts seem to give us direct access to consciousness itself: an intimate sense of the drama that is being played out inside the mind.

A RUSH OF RUSHDIE TO THE HEAD

Plunge straight in, now, and read the following text. Read it *out loud*.

No colours except green and black the walls are green the sky is black (there is no roof) the stars are green the Widow is green but her hair is black as black. The Widow sits on a high high chair the chair is green the seat is black the Widow's hair has a centre-parting it is green on the left and on the right black. High as the sky the chair is green the seat is black the Widow's arm is long as death its skin is green the fingernails are long and sharp and black. Between the walls the children green the walls are green the Widow's arm comes snaking down the snake is green the children scream the fingernails are black they scratch the Widow's arm is hunting see the children run and scream the Widow's hand curls round them green and black. Now one by one the children mmff are stifled quiet the Widow's hand is lifting one by one the children green their blood is black unloosed by cutting fingernails it splashes black on walls (of green) as one by one the curling hand lifts children high as sky the sky is black there are no stars the Widow laughs her tongue is green but see her teeth are black. And children torn in two in Widow hands which rolling rolling halves of children roll them into little balls the balls are green the night is black. And little balls fly into night between the walls the children shriek as one by one the Widow's hand. And in a corner the Monkey and I (the walls are green the shadows black) cowering crawling wide high walls green fading into black there is no roof and Widow's hand comes onebyone the children scream and mmff and little balls and hand and scream and mmff and splashing stains of black. Now only she and I and no more screams the Widow's hand comes hunting hunting the skin is green the nails are black towards the corner hunting hunting while we shrink closer into the corner our skin is green our fear is black and now the Hand comes reaching reaching and she my sister pushes me out out of the corner while she stays cowering staring the hand the nails are curling scream and mmff and splash of black and up into the high as sky and laughing Widow tearing I am rolling into little balls the balls are green and out into the night the night is black. . . .

Notes   Make notes on your *experience* of that text. Don't struggle to explain it; rather, give an account of how reading it felt. Feel free to write about your confusion, uncertainty, suspicion, or whatever was uppermost in your mind from moment to moment as you were in there, reading it.

Next read it again, and see if you can detect any patterns—patterns of repetition, of images, of emotions.

Now look at the structure of the sentences; what has happened to them? How do they compare with "normal" sentence patterns? What is the main effect of the abnormality?

Compare your notes on these questions with those of others. And do not be anxious to find a "right answer."

Slowing Down   We will now "come clean" and contextualize the passage. It comes
the Text   from a remarkable novel about India, *Midnight's Children*, by Salman Rushdie. Up to this moment in the novel, the text has been perfectly "normal," putting the reader in the picture, offering a clear narrative line, doing everything necessary to make sure that readers keep their bearings. Then

suddenly, without warning, this! "No colours except green. . . ." Why does the text suddenly go crazy? And what effect does this craziness have on us readers? We can only speak for ourselves and for friends who have shared their impressions with us. First, we will try to explain what we recognize.

Probably like you, we recognize confusion. A text behaves in this way only when either (a) the writer is losing his mind; or (b) the writer wishes to achieve an effect of the *narrator* losing his mind. Since we trust Rushdie, on the basis of the pages we have already read, we assume it is (b). In what way, then, is the narrator losing his mind? We recognize this kind of linguistic mess and this kind of confused jumble of delusions. How? We recall the experience of sitting by the bedside of someone who is suffering from delusions during, say, a bad attack of pneumonia accompanied by a very high temperature. We recognize a partial breakdown of the ability to distinguish between what is really present and what the sufferer is deluded into believing is present (cf. alcoholics).

As we plunge and stagger and grope our way through Rushdie's crazy text, we become increasingly convinced that it only appears to be out of control and that in fact the writer is very much in control. He is shaping his text to express, to represent as directly as possible, without explanation, the experience of extreme feverishness, from the point of view of a wretched participant. It is as if a tape recorder had been left running at the bedside and had picked up this meandering, perplexed, and perplexing onrush of words that express a condition of severe hallucination. The narrator, we decide, is very ill. And in his extreme illness, all his secret fears are rushing to break through the surface. He is saying things that he would not allow himself to say if he were well and in control.

The paradox, then, is this: Rushdie uses his finely tuned control of sentence patterns, of rhythm, of the representational power of his language, to represent a total loss of control. And in all this, Rushdie, the writer, is "off-stage," invisible; he does not appear, does not offer us any explanation. If he did so, the power of his representation of fever would be much reduced. "Oh," we would murmur, "it's a feverish hallucination that he's talking about." Whereas, our uncertainty and confusion as readers is part of the effect of his text at this point. We feel it all.

After the feverish text dries up and disappears from the page, the next part of Rushdie's text is as unlike the fever passage as it is possible to imagine. The first sentence of the next paragraph is only four words long. Can you guess what it is? In its meaning and its language it is the opposite of what you read on page 134. See if you can collaborate to work out a plausible and acceptable guess. (The answer is at the back of the book.)

The basic foundation of a text such as Rushdie's fever text is the simple *fiction* that it is possible for someone to write about an experience even while he/she is going through it. The text represents that experience so closely, with so much immediacy, in so much intimate inside detail that the reader feels the illusion of the experience as intensely *as if* he/she were actually going through it. (In some cases when scientists test drugs on *themselves,* or in some other way subject their bodies to abnormal states, this kind of *simultaneous* text is actually produced. It is then both reflective and very useful.)

WHAT NOW?

Using the same technique as that used by Rushdie, represent your experience of one of the following. Don't forget to use the present tense; keep it all in the "now."

A nightmare

An experience of (almost) drowning

The experience of being born

Severe intoxication

Panic

Being run down by a drunken driver

Trying to concentrate and being distracted by thoughts of all you have to do

A fit of anxiety

Daydreaming about past pleasures

What Are Participant Texts Good For?

TWO EXAMPLES

Here, now, are texts from two of our students who were trying their hand at writing participant texts for the first time.

> —— Damn!! they're paying by check—I hope the idiots have their card—Good, they do—now she'll ask me for the pen, right—of course—naturally she has to balance her checkbook while I wait here—Oh good—she's giving me back my pen—Now I had better take out my check sheet and write her number down, then her name, and then the amount of the check—great, she remembered to sign her check. Now I punch in 147, her account number, the amount of check, put the check under the printer, press "check tender," and wait for a beep—Why do I always act at the sound of the beep? I pull the check out, the drawer will hopefully open—good, it did—and I put the check away. I better hand her the receipt—she looks like the type who checks—Wow—her hair is really greasy—Anyway—have a nice day—(and wash your hair)—NEXT!
>
> —*Stacey Silverman*

Oh, no! Swim 16 laps! Is he crazy? Can't swim 16 laps. Haven't gone swimming for so long. Well, maybe . . . have to do it, anyway. Gonna look like a fool if I drown. Won't drown . . . do the backstroke. Lucky I learned how yesterday. Tread water—without hands? Wait a minute. O.K. Go! Damn wave. Wish he'd stop kicking me. Going under. Kick faster. Please let this end. Thank God! Five minutes with hands . . . relax . . . much better. Over? Could have kept it up longer. Now what? Dive for a brick? Oh, sure! Ha, ha! Couldn't find it, could he? Me next? So soon?

—Barbara Schmitt

On the basis of those two texts, let us see if we can begin to discern what participant texts are good for—what it is they can be expected to do, to offer, to represent—and, conversely, what their limitations are.

They can represent the dynamic energy of someone's inner life.

They offer particularities—physicists would probably call these fragments of particularity, *quanta*—things that have both mass and energy; that come at the reader, pow, pow, pow, in sequence but disconnectedly. They have the effect of being represented, voiced, spoken, even as they are occurring. In a word, they establish a sense of simultaneity or concurrence.

The text is like a direct transcript of inner speech.

The text withholds explanation; the reader has to build up her/his own sense of the meaning.

The readers of such a text can feel very close, in time and space, to the person whose voice they are hearing.

The writer/speaker seems completely unaware of the existence of readers/listeners and does not attend to their needs at all. The effect is of someone speaking in the sure knowledge that no one else can hear—which is what happens when we produce inner speech when talking to ourselves.

Every participant text must be either (a) a fiction, that is, invented, or (b) a reconstruction of what the writer "said" when he/she was still having the experience, a running commentary on each moment, each fragment of the experience.

Notes   Look, now, at Claire Windsor-Shapiro's text about drowning (almost) on page 309, and locate those parts of her text where she uses participant text to gain an effect of immediacy (of it happening here and now).

ANOTHER EXAMPLE

Let us now look at another of Barbara Schmitt's texts, again an experiment in writing a participant text. See if you can decide what it represents.

> Cows, cow highway, Ha! Stupid people walking dumb cows. . . . leaving shit all over the street. . . . stepping in it. . . . Hot here feet are burning. . . . better slide down this railing. . . . railing's too hot too. . . . better than walking. . . . Wait! Not stopping. . . . dark too long. . . . Ouch! Shit! Where am I? Big house there, misty, spooky, not going there. . . . a car. Pop?! Good going home, not right—don't know this place—stop! Wrong way. . . . I don't live here. . . . let me out. . . . wrong, wrong. . . . .

Again, you will have noticed how the participant text withholds any explanation of context—of why, when, where. You, the reader, are left to find your own way, and you experience a degree of confusion and uncertainty. And that experience, that strange mixture of knowing and not knowing, is precisely the characteristic effect of such texts, providing a strangely provocative, arousing, pleasurably puzzling experience for the reader. As a reader you can relish the sharp illusion of sensation and also recognize to some degree the dominant emotion of such texts *without having to be told*, just as you can recognize the meaning of a certain tone of voice in your friends and members of your family. How would you characterize the emotion that is implicit in this second text of Barbara's? Disgust? Fear? Nervousness? Nausea? Disapproval? A mixture of two or more of these?

WHAT NOW?

Write a participant text that represents your inner speech as you were reading (with interest? confusion? exasperation?) the last three texts.

LOSING PARTICULARITY, GAINING ECONOMY

Let us now substitute generalized statements for each of the texts you have met so far in this chapter. Then we can decide what is lost in the substitution.

RUSHDIE: I had a bad fever and hallucinated.

STACEY: I was feeling exasperated.

BARBARA: (swimming) I felt inadequate to meet the challenge.

BARBARA: (cows . . .) I was nauseated and confused.

The purpose of these types of statements is to convey information as quickly as possible—presumably because the situations in which they would/might be used call for an economic statement of fact. In such cases, the richness of detail that the participant texts offer would be neither required nor appropriate.

"Get to the point," someone says, and we produce those kinds of lean, matter-of-fact statements.

Notice that the four statements are perfectly explicit. They name states of mind, leaving no work for the reader to do. And they offer no sense of how the participants felt as they went through those experiences, moment by moment. In the original texts, we readers experienced the illusion of "felt life," of being inside other people's minds, of feeling the pulse not only of their heartbeats but also of their minds, their fears, their sensations. Our perceptions enjoy the privilege and vividness, the intensity and immediacy of being very intimate, and from the inside.

EUDORA WELTY'S RACE: A SPECTATOR / PARTICIPANT MIX

Eudora Welty is here looking back over many decades at her early school experiences:

> Every school week, visiting teachers came on their days for special lessons. On Mondays, the singing teacher blew into the room fresh from the early outdoors, singing in her high soprano "How do you do?" to do-mi-sol-do, and we responded in chorus from our desks, "I'm ve-ry well" to do-sol-mi-do. Miss Johnson taught us rounds—"Row row row your boat gently down the stream"—and "Little Sir Echo," with half the room singing the words and the other half being the echo, a competition. She was from the North, and she was the one who wanted us all to stop the Christmas carols and see snow. The snow falling that morning outside the window was the first most of us had ever seen, and Miss Johnson threw up the window and held out wide her own black cape and caught flakes on it and ran, as fast as she could go, up and down the aisles to show us the real thing before it melted.
>
> Thursday was Miss Eyrich and Miss Eyrich was Thursday. She came to give us physical training. She wasted no time on nonsense. Without greeting, we were marched straight outside and summarily divided into teams (no choosing sides), put on the mark, and ordered to get set for a relay race. Miss Eyrich cracked out "Go!" Dread rose in my throat. My head swam. Here was my turn, nearly upon me. (Wait, have I been touched—was that slap the touch? Go on! Do I go on without our passing a word? What word? Now am I racing too fast to turn around? Now I'm nearly home, but where is the hand waiting for mine to touch? Am I too late? Have I lost the whole race for our side?) I lost the relay race for our side before I started, through living ahead of myself, dreading to make my start, feeling too late prematurely, and standing transfixed by emergency, trying to think of a password. Thursdays still can make me hear Miss Eyrich's voice. "On your mark—get set—GO!"
>
> —Eudora Welty, *One Writer's Beginnings*

Reading Welty   Did you notice the remarkable little participant text inside that passage? Even if you were not yet absolutely confident of recognizing a participant text, we imagine the parentheses would have revealed it to you.

Let us look more closely at the shift from one kind of writing to another—from spectator to participant text.

How does Welty control the effects of her prose?

First she makes a generalization: "Every school week ... lessons." In other words, that is what generally, typically happened.

Next she provides examples: first Miss Johnson, then Miss Eyrich. Even though Welty is writing from a distance, she deftly and quickly characterizes each of these formidable women, so that we can grasp some of their salient features. In Welty's text, each woman is highlighted by the presence of the other. They come across as complementary.

Miss Eyrich comes over especially strongly. The first sentence of the second paragraph is shaped as a fact that cannot be altered, from which there is no escape. You can almost hear a key turning in the cell door. Gradually the sense of Welty's remembered fear increases in intensity: "Miss Eyrich *cracked out* ... Dread rose in my throat. My head swam." So far, then, some powerful statements of fact, of unavoidable, painful fact. But how is Welty to build further on what she has already stated? Can she go on merely stating facts?

With the assurance of a seasoned writer, she switches into a participant text. Jumping over the fence of the parenthesis, she moves into the present tense and offers us her inner speech as it might have occurred then: a series of breathless, tense, anxious questions and exclamations. As a participant she cannot know whether or not she has won the race. It is only when once more outside that fence of parentheses that she can know that then, so many years ago, she lost. And now, as a spectator of that remembered incident, she can even analyze *why* she lost.

The Nature of Participant Texts

A SERIES OF DISCONNECTED MOMENTS

What kinds of sentences, then, do participant texts tend to consist of? This is an interesting question, even if you are not especially interested in grammar. We are tempted to leave you to work it out for yourself but cannot resist the temptation to do some explaining and showing.

Let us compare two participant texts and see if they have anything in common. We will choose two very dissimilar texts, so as to reinforce our point.

Earhart in Flight

First, here is a short extract from a text you have already met:

> Instrument flying. Slow descent, first. Going down fast. It takes a lot to make my ears hurt. 5000 now. Awfully wet. Water dripping in window. Port motor coughing. Sounds as if all motors were cutting. Bill opens her wide to try to clear. Sounds rotten on the right.

3000 ft. Ears not so painful. Fog awful.
Motors better, but not so good.

Now the second text. (Notice how the first line is rather like a frame
round a picture, or like the beginning of a story in a conversation: "You
want to hear something amazing?")

Ted Hughes
at His Table

The Thought Fox

I imagine this midnight moment's forest:
Something else is alive
Beside the clock's loneliness
And this blank page where my fingers move,

Through the window I see no star:
Something more near
Though deeper within darkness
Is entering the loneliness:

Cold, delicately as the dark snow,
A fox's nose touches twig, leaf;
Two eyes serve a movement, that now
And again now, and now, and now

Sets neat prints into the snow
Between trees, and warily a lame
Shadow lags by stump and in hollow
Of a body that is bold to come

Across clearings, an eye,
A widening deepening greenness,
Brilliantly, concentratedly,
Coming about its own business

Till, with a sudden sharp hot stink of fox
It enters the dark hole of the head.
The window is starless still; the clock ticks,
The page is printed.

—Ted Hughes

Those two texts are about as unalike as one could possibly imagine.
The first is part of Amelia Earhart's logbook, which was primarily a
practical text but also offered room for some reflections. The second is
a poem. They could hardly be less alike. But both are participant texts.
Earhart's is literally so, having been written in the midst of an activity.
Hughes's creates a strong illusion of an utterance spoken from within
an experience.

If they are both participant texts, what features do they have in common despite their obvious differences?

Notice how, in Earhart's text, as she writes any one sentence or word, she *cannot* know—she literally, actually, is unable to know—what will happen next.

In Hughes's text we experience a powerful illusion that exactly the same is true for the narrator in the poem.

If, then, the text is being composed in the midst of the action it is representing, the way in which any two or more parts of the text can be connected will be severely limited. Most parts of the text can represent only "this moment." They cannot connect "this moment" to either the past or the future. So they cannot offer connections that express cause and effect, the reason why, the conditions necessary, or the consequences. *The writer of a participant text is either literally or apparently trapped within the present moment represented by each small disconnected segment of the text.* As the narrator moves through time, each moment simply adds another bit of text.

This explains the strong sense of disjointedness that we feel when reading a participant text. It is powerful, vivid, strong on sensation; but it is broken, fragmented, almost incoherent.

EXPRESSIVENESS VERSUS INTELLIGIBILITY

What do we have to do when producing a text-for-others that is intended to represent our inner speech?

At the outset, we have to admit that it is impossible actually to "record" one's inner speech—even if one tries to catch it by listening to it in a way that resembles trying to see how one looks to others by snatching a glimpse of oneself out of the corner of one's eye in a mirror set at an angle. But one can build up a sense of what it is like and of the ways in which it differs from vocalized social speech.

If one can reconstruct it in a reasonably "authentic" way, what must one do to it so that it will make sense to others?

In the first place, readers will expect it to look and sound different from a text that represents social talk—dialogue. Everyone has an intuitive grasp of such differences.

Let us take the example of Eudora Welty's inner speech:

> (Wait, have I been touched—was that slap the touch? Go on! Do I go on without passing a word? What word? Now am I racing too fast to turn around? Now I'm nearly home, but where is the hand waiting for mine to touch? Am I too late? Have I lost the whole race for our side?)

That is what Welty *chose* to write, as she balanced the claims of expressiveness and the claims of intelligibility. She could have stayed closer to expressiveness and written something like this:

(Wait! Touched? Slap a touch? On! Not pass word? Which . . . ? Too fast turn round? Nearly . . . Hand! Where touch? Too late? Lost—me? I? Our side?)

Our version is less intelligible, more of a riddle, but it is arguably closer to a representation of the frantic verbalizing of urgent inner speech. What do you think?

PARATAXIS

"There's this fella, and he's kind of scary, and he's coming over, and I back away, and he keeps coming, and I don't know what to do, and he's getting closer, and my mind's kinda numb, and . . ."

That is an example of **parataxis**. So was most of Earhart's logbook and Sei Shōnagon's *Pillow Book* and Ted Hughes's "Thought Fox"—and this sentence itself.

So what is parataxis? And why do we mention it?

If two things are of equal importance or value, they are said to be on a *par*. Perhaps you can apply that clue to making an intelligent guess.

One of the main characteristics of participant texts is that they are mostly paratactic. They consist of a series of relatively disjointed parts and do not offer the reader any very clear sense of the relationships between the parts. The only conjunction they tend to use is "and." And "and" tells the reader virtually nothing about *how* one part connects with another.

Why is this so? Because when we are participants in an experience, we do not know what is going to happen next, and the function of a participant text is to express through words what the experience feels like from the inside, even as it is happening.

Such texts tell the reader nothing about which part is—or may be—more important than another; every fragment of the experience is on a par with every other.

> Typewriter humming. Sunny morning. Garbage men. Bang, crash. Barking. Barking and yapping. Those neighbors' dogs . . . Shopping later. Finish this chapter first. Harbor Cafe for lunch? Liver and bacon . . . joke with waitress. Great smile . . . always cheerful. Very dark lipstick, though. Startling at first. Concentrate . . . almost end of page. . . .

In a word, participant texts are short on those elements that make a text coherent, that help it to hang together in a meaningful, clarifying way. They tend to offer only the "raw material" of thinking—the images, the sensations, the rapid shifting of the mind. They do not take the next steps that would offer the reader clear answers to such questions as: "But how does all this hang together? And what's the point?" For that, we have to turn to spectator texts, which are discussed in Chapter 8.

Four Student Texts

We now wish to share with you texts by four of our students who grasped something of this distinctive power of the participant text. These were among the earliest participant texts that any students ever wrote with us, and we were as pleased as they were with their results. It was from them that we began to appreciate the qualities of intensity, concentratedness, and vividness—not to mention the teasing mystery—that such texts can offer.

Read each text twice. First read *through* it, and concentrate on what the text represents. Then read it again, more slowly, concentrating more on the language. Notice how the text moves forward step by step, sentence by sentence, in a rather disjointed, disconnected, fragmentary fashion, both offering you information and withholding it, failing to give explanations because the mind represented in the text is indifferent to the needs of an audience.

> I don't know. I think. I think I saw it. I think I saw it the other day. It is over there. Don't ask me any more questions about it! I already told you what I know! Last time. Last time I saw it, it was over there. Maybe. Maybe, somebody moved it. Can it be? Since it is no longer there. Perhaps. Perhaps, she took it with her. Could be. But. But why? Why would she do that? She doesn't. She doesn't have a need for it. I don't think. I don't think she took it. Could it have been? Could it have been moved? To where? To where has it been moved? Somebody could have hid it. Hid it behind there. Why hide it? Why hide it over there. Maybe they didn't want. Want anyone else to use it. Why? I don't know. Leave me. Leave me alone.
>
> —*Lynn Horn*

> Jesus, I am so cold. I can't believe it's morning already. Just went to sleep, damn it. This is the hardest time of the day, and look at these hands tremble, like an old man's. Another chance not to make good. At least John dragged his butt out of here already, I can get in a little wallowing before breakfast. I can't think, that test is going to be a disaster, a humiliation, and it's so fucking easy, what would you have done with this garbage in your better years, ace that shit in a coma, that's right. I got an hour, come on, try and read that book. I really don't want to, don't know if I can, don't know why I can't. God, am I grim, I feel badly most all the time now and I don't know why. Probably fed up with my own laziness. Delancey St. here I come, come hell or high water, there'll always be windshields to clean, be my own boss, go as far as my squeegee can take me. Wonder how I'd look in dreadlocks. Hmm!!
>
> My eyes betray me, I can't read this, I itch all over. I mean I'd like to concentrate, but when I make an effort, every cell in my body clamors for attention, first one, then they all pick up the chorus, and my heart starts to resound like Methodist bells. Only an hour, that's enough. Christ, I didn't even realize I was raising my voice. Feel pretty good as a matter of fact. Aristotle, the theory of the household, all right let's start this brain up.

This stuff is so dry, but I'm getting there. Does the boy still have it? Could be, though it's a pale reminder of the past. Yes, it does differ from political authority, old Aristotle's quite right; of course, it wouldn't buy lunch at Chock Full O' Nuts but a valid point just the same.

What do you know, all done, and in thirty minutes, not bad even by my old standards. God no, it just hit me, somehow I hoped it wouldn't. I can't go, don't torture yourself, you know you're not going, if I'm going to ruin my life I'd rather be decisive about it. I feel that pressure seeping away. I won't be unhappy, I'll pull out of this soon, that will be so sweet. Now I've got the whole day, alone, I think I'll try to sleep now, though I know better.

—Marc Kieselstein

Ouch! Feel like I'm gonna pass out . . . legs feel weak. Going up these stairs NEVER tired me out before—I'm almost winded! I *must* be sick! Hope I make it home today. Maybe if I eat a little something I won't feel so lousy—where's my orange? Let the car warm up while I'm peeling it—that's all I'd need now, have the car stall out and get rear-ended by someone then bye-bye license.

On the road again . . . stop being silly now and drive! So many trucks on the LIE all the time! Back off! Don't hit me—just because you're bigger gives you no right to pick on me—besides I'm new at this. Exit here. Only sixteen more miles. Why the hell are my palms sweating? Oh yea—the fever. Southern State—hate this curve. Oh, no! Not the buzzing again! There go the legs! Quit shaking! Wow! Feels like I'm on an amusement park ride! Yes, here I am playing with my life on the Southern State—world's largest bumper car ride! Should I get off here and go to the shop! No, they'll only ask questions. If he finds out I drove the car like this he'd get another nervous attack—I don't want to (and can't) deal with that now. I should find out what they want for dinner . . . why'd she have to go now!? Renate doesn't need her there to have a kid anyway! To hell with them, they're big boys now—they can fend for themselves—I'm going to bed! That guy behind me must hate me—I practically cut him off—too bad.

Home. Throw this junk inside and relax. Smells nice, tulips are all out, hyacinths are dying—get outside dog! When will they learn to wash dishes?! TEA!!—peppermint—save that one, Earl Grey—yuck! camomile—tonight, mellow-mint—makes me nauseous . . . don't need help in that department. Get rid of this damn fever with peppermint tea—sweat it out!

It's so nice out, hate to sit around inside. Walk the dog—get fresh air. Can't make it, hate to turn back though. I'm beat—getting that jittery feeling again. Wish Chris were here—feel better when he's around—probably wouldn't do him a hell of a lot of good to see me moping around. Feel like I'm melting from inside out . . . tired too. Why not?! So stupid! Eyes are almost asleep, brain's dead too, hand's next . . . beautiful clouds. . . .

—Barbara Schmitt

Wow! Imagine right here . . . check it out. . . . It's only us three . . . nice beach. . . . No one else but us three. Is it real? So many, I never saw so many, well actually I never saw any before. But real battleships. It's weird. They're so nice and big and only us three. No one else left. . . . It's like a

World War II movie. How can it be? So real! All of them. . . . Wow this is some trip, it feels so real . . . I want to tell them will they know what I mean? What are they thinking of ? Is it my eyes? Am I seeing things? Why are there so many right here in the Atlantic Beach Bay? There's the bridge: everything, so desolate, only us three left, what will we do for women? What a trip! It can't be for real! But imagine if it was. Only us three. . . . They don't even know what I'm thinking, they'll think I'm crazy if I tell them. . . . But they're there, right there. (Said slow). How long have I been like this? Haven't said a word for hours . . . was it hours? What time is it? How long have I been here? It started at Joe's house at about nine. I couldn't believe those Snoopys. I never knew it would look like that, just a stamp. Amazing! They think I've freaked. . . . Haven't spoken for so long. I know how my face looks, it must be a face with no expression. Why? They keep asking me what's wrong. . . . How should I know? But I don't know what to say. . . . So I say nothing. . . . Why am I so confused?

Look at them, look at the bugs . . . I can't keep my eyes off them. . . . They are so many . . . all over . . . so many all over. . . . I feel disgusted. . . . So many under my feet. Everywhere I look, bugs — so many — get them away — you can't even kill them. Stop looking . . . I can't. They're there, all over. I told Joe and Stu. . . . They agree, but why? Are they being nice. . . . They seem to be with me, but somehow it's as though I'm in it alone. Did they take their Snoopys . . . or do they only want to see my reactions. . . .

Taking LSD never done that before. . . . Only once . . . should I have? Got to try everything once. Hey! Freud took it. . . . It opens the mind. I wonder what a shrink would say about my thoughts. . . . What does it all mean? Will these things come back to me in a few years? On TV. . . . In the Movie with the boy and his father. . . . It never left him. . . . The kid always had his trips even though he stopped taking LSD. . . . I hope that won't happen to me. . . . I never seen battleships before. . . . They were there, I know it. It'll be funny when I tell people. . . . They really were there. . . . It really wasn't my bad eyes. . . . Don't forget the aircraft carrier. . . . Are the battleships still in the bay? I can't see from here, in this forest. . . . You can only see trees and all those very ugly bugs. . . .

Where to? following the tread marks . . . where to? Just follow the high-tops. . . . His feet will direct his body. . . . He doesn't even know it. . . . His feet move while he goes, it carries him . . . just follow Stu's feet. Where to? Why here? Wow! what's he doing? Playing golf. . . . Now four. . . . He's old. . . . But Joe keeps faking it. . . . Speak up. . . . Why not? Why don't I say anything? What can I say . . . ?

So boxed in will I ever get out . . . ?

In my hand. . . . It's been through a lot. From the fields, to a factory, to a distributor, and then a local store, where I bought him. . . . Imagine all the places he's been and seen. . . . Even after he will be burnt up, after I've used him, there will still be a part of him left. It's seen what I've seen, it's been with me, close to me while I've tripped. Where is its destiny? He's traveled a lot and when I throw him away, where will he go? Who else will know him? Maybe he will stay here, maybe he will be taken away, without even a word said, no explanation given. All the way from Virginia to N.Y. (via highway 95), and of course, into my hands. He's been through a lot, and his trip is still going. What will be of my cigarette? Will he stay? How many people will know him? . . . Bye. . . . All boxed in like my cigarette was, at least here there are no bugs. . . . Only grass, glorious, beautiful grass, long beautiful hills of grass leading to water. I love water. . . . Should I jump in? . . . It's too far. . . . Everything is too far. . . .

   Still the Dead. . . . Okay I can handle it, but, I can't tell one song from the next. . . . It just goes on and on. . . . Wait!!! The music stopped. . . . So has my mind. . . . It's no longer drifting, it also stopped with the music. . . . Music stops trips. . . . The music's back, same Dead, but no trips. . . . Why did the music have to stop? That feels stupid. . . . I can't go back to the way it was, for it isn't the way it was. . . . It is now side II, not side I. . . .

—Don Winter

   In the next chapter we will show you how each of these writers became a spectator, recalling the experience from a safe distance, and so producing a very different kind of text.

WHAT NOW?

   "Become" one of the people in one of the photographs below. Write a text that represents that person's concurrent inner speech.

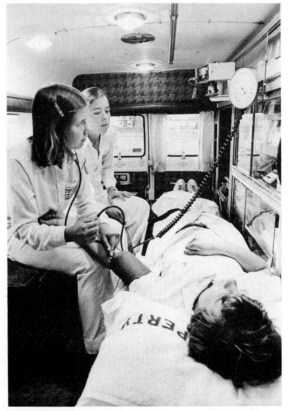

Jo's Message   To end this chapter, here is a strange participant text; don't take it too seriously.

Dear folks, folks,,
   you must be wondering what happened to me. I hope you are anyway, because it's good to be missed. What could be worse than to be away from home without an address, travelling heaven knows where, and have nobody back home asking, "Hey, where's Jo?"
   Anyway, as far as where I am at the moment is concerned, I'm completely in the dark. As a matter of fact, I'm actually writing in the dark. So if this letter ever reaches you and you find it illegible, that's the explanation. that's the explanation. And if I repeat repeat myself, that's because I can't see see what I've already writtenen down down. I think I just wrote down twicee.
   I've no idea how long I've been here. I thinkink I fell overboard, and sank beneath the briney. Then I don't remember much at all. Everything went dark, with a kind of red hazeaze. Finally I woke up, and I was here. But where here is, heaven only knows! It's dark and quiet cross that out! quite noisy, a kind of blubbering sound like very bad indigestion. And there's a bad leak somewhere. It's so darkark I can't find the source of the leak. So Im soaked to the skin but fortunately very warm, so there's no risk of catching pneueumoniaia.ia. Fortunately I had a bottlottle in my pocket. Almost empty. So I emptied it out and it's almost dry as far as I

can tellell. I'll put this letter inside the bootttlee and try to throw it out. If somebody findss it I hope they'll send it on to you. I'm still feeling seasick from all the vibrations of this this place. Maybe it's an earthquake. I seem to rememberber some of the prophets talking about an earthquake coming. Or was it an astrologer? I mean an astrologer talking, not coming, if you see what I mean. I'm sleeping pretty well. I suppopose that's because it's dark. But I can't find much toeat in this place. It could be a cave, but I can't get out to see the entrance from the outside. And the walls which keep moving feel a bit like a camel's stomachskin, when you first strip it off, warm and soft but tough as old sandals. I've triedied to cut a hole through for an exexit with my knife, but the whole place starting shaking violently so I decidicded to stop. It's all very strange, fishy, you might say. I wonder if I'll everer see you allall again. Sometimes I just feel like having a good cry, and crawling into a corner. But I recall what Mother used to say. "Don't let me catch you blubbering. Big boys don't cry." And, anyway, there's no corner in this place. It's more like the inside of a great leather ball. You must think I'm out of my mind but I'm not. I just wonder what I'veve gotten myself into.

Must stop now. I'm running out of clay tablets. Hope you can read my writining. Must stop now. Ever yours,

Jo

Notes   Who do you think wrote that letter? Where was he? What could he know about where he was? What was it impossible for him to know?

8 | Seeing Whole: Spectator Texts

Seeing Whole and Sizing Up

In his witty book about human beings and our place in the universe, *Lost in the Cosmos*, Walker Percy writes this:

> A stranger approaching you in the street will in a second's glance see you whole, size you up, place you,* in a way in which you cannot and never will, even though you have spent a lifetime with yourself, live in the Century of the Self, and therefore ought to know yourself best of all.
>
> The question is: Why is it that in your entire lifetime you will never be able to size yourself up as you can size up somebody else—or size up [the planet] Saturn—in a ten-second look?

WHAT NOW? SIZING YOURSELF UP

Choose three types of strangers, and imagine yourself as each of them in turn. From within those roles, write a brief sizing up of yourself as you appear to each of them casually on the street.

MAXIM GORKY AS SPECTATOR

Here now is Maxim Gorky writing of what he has learned from "spying"—either deliberately or accidentally—on other people.

> Today while I was watching a fair little lady in cream-coloured stockings, with the immature features of a child, who stood on the Troitzki bridge, holding on to the balustrade with her grey-gloved hands as though preparing to jump into the Neva, I saw her stick out a sharp, pink little tongue at the moon.
>
> The old man in the moon, the sly fox of the skies, was stealthily making his way through a cloud of dirty smoke. He was very large and his cheeks were crimson, as though he had had too much to drink. The young lady was teasing him very earnestly and even revengefully—so it seemed to me at least.

---

*"Place" here means to characterize, to assign someone to a category.

She recalled to my mind the memory of certain "peculiarities" which had puzzled me for a long time. Whenever I watch how a man behaves when he is alone, I always conclude that he is "insane"—I can find no other word for it.

I first noticed this when I was still a boy: a clown named Rondale, an Englishman, who was walking along the dark and deserted passages of a circus, took off his top hat to a mirror and bowed respectfully to his own reflection. There was no one in the passage but himself. I was sitting on a cistern over his head and so was invisible to him, and had thrust out my head just at the moment when he made his respectful bow. This action of the clown plunged me into dark and unpleasant speculations. He was a clown, and what is more, an Englishman, whose profession—or art—lay in his eccentricity.

Then I noticed how A. Chekhov, sitting in his garden, tried unsuccessfully to catch a sunbeam with his hat and to place both on his head. I could see that his failure annoyed the sunbeam-hunter; his face grew redder and redder, and he ended by slapping his hat on his knee, putting it on his head with a quick movement and impatiently pushing his dog away. . . .

Leo Tolstoy once said to a lizard in a low whisper: "Are you happy, eh?"

The lizard was warming itself on a stone among the shrubs that grew on the road to Dulber, while he stood watching it, his hands thrust inside his leather belt. Then, cautiously looking round, the great man confided to the lizard: "As for me—I'm not!"

Professor Tikhvinsky, the chemist, sitting in my dining-room, addressed his own reflection on the copper tea-tray: "Well, old boy, how is life?"

The image made no reply; so Tikhvinsky sighed deeply and began carefully rubbing it off with his palm, puckering his brows and twitching his nose, which resembled the trunk of an embryo elephant.

I was told that someone once found N. S. Leskoff occupying himself by sitting at the table and lifting a tuft of cotton-wool into the air, then letting it fall into a china bowl and stooping over it, listening, evidently expecting that the wool would produce a sound as it fell on the china.

The priest F. Vladimirsky once placed a boot in front of him, and said to it impressively: "Now then—go!" Then, "Ah, you can't?" Then, with dignity and conviction, he added: "You see! You can't go anywhere without me!"

"What are you doing, Father?" I asked, entering the room at this moment.

He looked at me attentively and explained: "It's this boot. It's all worn down at the heel. Nowadays they make such poor boots!"

I have often noticed how people laugh and cry when they are by themselves. A writer, a perfectly sober man who rarely indulged in drink, used to cry when he was alone, and whistle the old hurdy-gurdy tune, "As I come out alone on the road!" He whistled badly, like a woman, and his lips trembled: tears rolled slowly out of his eyes, and hid in his dark whiskers and beard. Once he cried in the room of an hotel, standing with his back to the window, spreading out his arms and going through the movements of swimming; but this was not for the sake of exercise, for the movements were slow and neither powerful nor rhythmical.

To see a child trying to remove a picture from the page of a book with his fingers is not very unusual; but to see a scientist, a professor, trying to do it and turning round and listening as though afraid of being caught in the act, is strange indeed.

The professor in question evidently was convinced that the printed drawing could be removed from the paper and hidden in the pocket of his waistcoat. Once or twice he thought he had succeeded. He took up something from the page and, lifting it between two fingers like a coin, tried to slip it into his pocket; but then, looking at his fingers, he frowned, held the picture up to the light, and again started to rub the printed impression persistently. Finally, seeing that this had no result, he threw the book aside and strode out of the room, stamping angrily. I examined the book very carefully. It was a technical work in German, illustrated with reproductions of different electric motors and their parts. There was not a single picture that was glued to the page, and it is obvious that anything printed cannot be removed from a page and slipped into the pocket! Probably the professor knew this too....

Women often talk to themselves while playing a game of patience or when they are busy at their toilet, but one day for five whole minutes I watched a well-educated woman eating sweets in solitude and addressing each of the candies, which she held up in the air with a small pair of pincers:

"Ah, I'll eat you up!" Then she would eat it up and ask, "One wondered whom?"

"Well, didn't I?"

Then again: "I'll eat you up!"

"Didn't I?"

She was sitting at the time in an arm-chair at the window, at five o'clock on a summer's evening, and from the street the muffled noise of the big town filled the room. The face of the woman was serious, her greyish eyes were fixed earnestly on the box of sweets in her lap...

Our Private Versus Social Selves

The texts by Percy and Gorky have this in common: They both represent the spectator's point of view. In Gorky's text, we see people participating in their own solitary private lives, thinking themselves unobserved. Alone, they are no longer playing their various social roles, and their minds and hearts are therefore naked, exposed.

Gorky concludes that our private conduct, what we do when alone, is "insane." Isn't he failing to recognize, to take into account, the remarkable differences between our social selves and our private selves? Failing to acknowledge that when we are alone, we can allow ourselves to do things that would be inappropriate in company?

WHAT NEXT?

You have probably had the same kinds of experiences as Gorky. What did you observe? Anything that would justify the claim that someone was insane?

What sorts of actions do you perform only when alone? What sorts of things do you say only when alone?

Note: the word "private" derives from the same root as "deprived." In what sense is private experience deprived?

A SPECTATOR IN RANDOLPH, MASSACHUSETTS

In 1984, the *New York Times* gave David Margolick an interesting assignment. Here is what he made of it.

Taking a stand against standing for the Pledge of Allegiance

RANDOLPH, Mass., Nov. 29—The morning began typically at Randolph High School. At 7:45 o'clock, the assistant principal, Richard Power, played a battered 45-r.p.m. record of the Philadelphia Orchestra playing "The Star Spangled Banner" over the public address system and recited the Pledge of Allegiance to the Flag.

As usual, all of the school's 1,400 students stood up for the ceremony, all, that is, except for one senior in Jean Noblin's homeroom, Susan Shapiro.

Miss Shapiro's decision to remain seated Wednesday was nothing new; she began to sit during the pledge last year. But her appearance Wednesday marked only the fourth time she felt safe enough to go to school in the last three weeks.

Barely an hour later, when a Randolph policeman refused to accompany her between classes, she went home. And today she did not go to school at all.

Her fear stems from a rash of abusive telephone calls and hate mail she and her family have received since a local newspaper reported over Veterans Day weekend her dispute with Mrs. Noblin. "Dirty Jew bastards, too bad you weren't put in the ovens," the Shapiros said one anonymous caller told them. The hate mail, which fills a plastic grocery bag, contains messages such as: "It can happen here! Think about it!—Jew!" and "People don't say 'never again' but 'one more time.' "

Miss Shapiro, who is 17 years old and hopes to go to beauty school next year, is crossing well-traveled constitutional territory. Forty years ago, in a case brought by Jehovah's Witnesses in West Virginia, the United States Supreme Court held that compulsory salutes to the flag violated the free speech guarantees of the First Amendment.

That decision may have settled the question legally, but the Shapiro case is still boiling over here, fueled by a complex blend of patriotism, prejudice, paranoia and the emotional power of two resonant symbols: the American flag and the Star of David. It continues to torment this quiet bedroom community.

Many members of the supporting cast are familiar participants in such dramas. In one corner are the local veterans' groups, which have called Miss Shapiro an ingrate and a Communist, among other things. In the other are the Massachusetts Civil Liberties Union; Alan Dershowitz, professor at the Harvard Law School, and the folk singer Joan Baez, who stopped by Miss Shapiro's house on Wednesday to offer her support.

The stereotypes stop here, however. As the personalities of the principles make clear, what has happened in Randolph is not a simple allegory about youth and old age, idealism and jingoism.

Miss Shapiro has little in common on the surface with the resisters of a generation ago. Her bedroom is filled with stuffed animals and posters of punk rock stars; she admits to being far more passionate about Motley Crue and Twisted Sister than politics, although she says she would probably have voted for President Reagan had she been old enough to.

Her precise reasons for remaining

seated seem to lie somewhere in the area bounded by contrariness, independence and indifference.

"The flag don't mean nothing," she said. "It's important to some people but not to me." Asked how she felt about being an American, she said, "I love it. I wouldn't want to be anything else."

Miss Shapiro's antagonist, the 63-year old Miss Noblin, is respected, almost revered, in this community. She is the kind of person who went to Dachau, the former Nazi concentration camp, on vacation so she could better empathize with her many Jewish students.

"The Shapiros, the Civil Liberties Union and Professor Dershowitz picked on the wrong person," said Mrs. Noblin's lawyer, Norman Silk, who is Jewish. "Jean Noblin is a Christian in the best sense of the word."

The dispute began on the second day of classes this fall, when Miss Shapiro remained seated on her desk, her back to the flag, as the morning exercises began.

The next week, Miss Shapiro again refused to rise, telling Mrs. Noblin that the flag was only "a symbol."

"Yes, it's a symbol, but so is the cross and the Star of David," replied Mrs. Noblin, the daughter of a brigadier general, wife and mother of a veteran and a one-time WAC. "You are spitting on the flag."

Miss Shapiro contends that Mrs. Noblin went on to say, "How would you feel if someone spit on the cross or the Star of David?" Mrs. Noblin denies the charge. "It's just been a nightmare," she said. "It's hard to believe that in one week a 30-year reputation could be so badly damaged."

In late September, Mrs. Shapiro wrote to the civil liberties union and to the Massachusetts Attorney General, demanding that a civil rights action be filed against Mrs. Noblin and the Randolph school system for "child abuse, harassment, humiliation and mental anguish."

The civil liberties group accepted the case, and on Oct. 17 it threatened to sue Mrs. Noblin and the town unless the teacher apologized and disciplinary action was taken against her.

Miss Shapiro and her parents, Gerald and Harriet Shapiro, say she will remain home until the school and the police department can guarantee her safety. They are afraid, they say, not of Miss Shapiro's fellow students, some of whom have taken to taunts and mock salutes, but of outsiders, perhaps those who have made threats.

"The teachers aren't with me and more than half the kids aren't with me," said Miss Shapiro, "so if anything happens to me no one is going to help."

John Zoino, the superintendent of schools, disputed the charge that security for Miss Shapiro was inadequate.

The Shapiros, along with nearly half of Randolph's 28,000 residents, are Jewish, and like them came here 20 years ago or so from the formerly Jewish neighborhoods of Boston: Dorchester, Roxbury and Mattapan, in part to give their children something more polyglot than their own provincial pasts.

Unlike many of the other Jews in Randolph, however, the Shapiros say that from their earliest days here they found something else, anti-Semitism. They contend it cropped up anew the day their daughter refused to rise, telling Mrs. Noblin that the flag was only "a symbol."

Out of town, Miss Shapiro has become a heroine of sorts; one of many admiring letter writers compared her to Mahatma Gandhi, Moses and Martin Luther King. But there appears to be little sympathy for the Shapiros here, particularly among Jews, who seem anxious to prove that Miss Shapiro speaks only for herself. Randolph, they say, is the most tolerant of towns, where Jews have succeeded in many spheres. Paul Alpert is moderator of the Randolph town meeting. And Jimmy Tandler and Art Cohen were the quarterback and fullback of the Randolph Blue Devils last year.

"This whole thing was fomented by the Shapiro family to some extent," said Mr. Silk. "They appeared awfully fast on all the talk shows, and were on two national programs the same day; they were saying the school was unsafe."

"The Jews in this town have crawled under a rock," countered Mrs. Shapiro. "They're ashamed of being Jewish."

Concerned for his family's safety, Mr. Shapiro, who sells equipment to garment manufacturers, has not gone to work in two weeks. The Jewish Defense League has provided security around the Shapiro house and Mr. and Mrs. Shapiro are seeking gun permits for themselves and for their daughter.

"That's nice, isn't it?" Mr. Shapiro, a veteran of the Korean War, said bitterly. "Susan was a very young sixteen. Now she's an old seventeen."

—David Margolick, *New York Times*

Problems of
the Spectator

An outsider visits a small community in which many of the inhabitants are caught up to some degree in a controversy that generates more heat—anger, dismay, indignation—than light. What does the outsider desire? To report on the matter as fairly as possible. ("Fairly" to whom? Who will suffer most keenly if the outsider misrepresents matters? Should the matter be reported at all, or be allowed simply to drift away?)

What does the community desire? What does the spectator desire? Are their desires irreconcilable?

Is the reporter's first duty to offer his readers an account of the matter as offered by the most directly and intensely involved participants? Would there be any justification for representing one participant's point of view and not the other's? Is it possible to represent them both with equal concern, in equal depth?

What can the spectator know of the inner mind of the major participants? How can he come to know?

The temptation for any spectator is to rush to make a judgment, in ignorance of the "facts." As a writer, his or her greatest pitfall is to oversimplify very subtle and complicated issues; to see it all from the outside, from a safe distance, clinically, in a detached way, remote from what is being felt.

Is it an advantage to be so detached? to stand at a safe distance, and view the scene as a whole, tidily?

What are the inherent strengths and weaknesses of being a spectator?

Use Margolick's report as an occasion for reflecting on these issues. They are important issues for they have to do with that very elusive commodity, disinterestedness. And you will meet them again whenever you take a course in social science.

YOURSELF AS SPECTATOR: THE TIME SHIFT

In relation to any event, you are a spectator when you are removed from the event in time or space. It is easy to think of this in terms of space. You read in the newspaper of an earthquake in South America. You are a spectator, safely removed from the event. You watch two friends having an argument. You are only two feet away from them, but as long as you don't intervene, you can claim the impartiality of the spectator. The moment you get involved you take on all the burdens of being a participant.

For our purposes, however, the more important shift is the one that occurs in the dimension of time. In your life of yesterday, or of even a minute ago, you are no longer a participant but are now "outside" it, a spectator.

What is it that we are spectators of when we look at our own past? It cannot be the events themselves, because they have been swept away by time. They no longer are. We must be spectators of something else; and that something else is the representation that survives in our memory and reflections.

What, then, is it that we can see as spectators of our past that we couldn't see at the time? What does the spectator see that the participant cannot? Think about the most important events of your recent past—yesterday or last week or a few months ago—and apply those last questions to them. We think you will find it interesting to do so.

Here are some typical answers to those questions:

> "At the time, I didn't know what to think, but now that I've slept on it, it's all become clear."
>
> "I now realize that I was very silly to let my temper get the better of me."
>
> "That movie? Well, there were some mildly amusing moments, but on the whole I think it was a waste of time."
>
> "The day of the picnic, the weather was terrible. But we had a great time—one of the best days of the summer."
>
> "Well, at the time I thought he was being unreasonable. Now I've come to the conclusion he was not only unreasonable but absolutely impossible!"

Those various brief statements are characteristic of what we do when we think *back* over an event and discover what we think about it. In other words, the spectator is able to reach an *evaluation*.

Like us, you are relatively remote spectators of the events in Randolph, Mass. And like us, you probably did what Walker Percy speaks of: a quick act of sizing up, of forming snap judgments—both of the issue and of the individuals involved. Like us, you probably formed a fairly quick impression of both Susan Shapiro and Mrs. Noblin from their own words. But having the luxury, the freedom of inaction—you don't have to participate—you can reflect again, think further, listen to other points of view, other evaluations. You can even change your mind.

Notes   On the basis of your present evaluations, what do you think the Shapiros should do next? Mrs. Noblin? Leaders of the community?

Psychological Distance: Points on the Spectrum

When we are spectators of other peoples' lives, we are either intensely involved, absolutely detached, or at some intermediate point between those two extremes. How we feel about the people in question—indifferent (detached), concerned (involved), or whatever—clearly determines the kind of report we offer as spectators.

The factor of psychological distance clearly affects the kind of report of an event that a spectator offers.

Here is a sequence of short texts representing six points of view, six points on the proximity/distance scale, from in-deep to out-far. See if you can determine the place of each text.

1. The patient appears to have been suffering a chronic series of faintings. He claims that he is always aware of when he might faint. He was observed at first as trying to prevent himself from fainting by the standard procedure of bending his head down between his legs and pressing his thumbs against his eyes, in order to bring the bloodflow back into his head. He showed no signs of consciousness when he fell on the floor, and, except for a few slight sounds and twitches in the eyes, remained perfectly still. No negative side effects have been found in the patient. His recovery period is very fast.

2. I had not been feeling very well that day. I didn't have much for breakfast and felt pangs of hunger throughout the day. I also felt rather lethargic. Perhaps it was due to the hot weather, for the event occurred on a hot day in June. As with all my fainting spells, I lost all recognition of where I was. To my dismay, when I woke up, I did indeed find myself on the floor of the classroom. The entire ordeal led to a somewhat embarrassing situation. I am now glad the event is over with.

3. He was sitting there in his seat at his desk, when all of a sudden his head began to drop. He had a long and pale look about his face. He started wobbling in his seat, and, before I knew it, he fell to the ground altogether. At first, I didn't take him seriously. I thought this was all some sort of bizarre joke, for he had been known at times to kid around in class. I watched him lying on the floor. His eyes began to move in a peculiar way. Strange grunting sounds came out of his mouth, almost as though he had been choking on some food. Finally, some of us had to help him back to his seat. That was the only time I had ever seen him do that.

4. Feel weak. My head is ringing. Am unstable. Must try to prevent it from happening again. Oh no! Going to happen! Too late. . . . Where am I? At my house. Oh . . . look! There are my parents. I am riding my bicycle. Talking to my friends. Happy. Not with my friends. I am . . . Where am I? I am, wait! Am I back? Oh yes, I am back . . . oh no! Now know where I am. C'mon . . . what is taking so long? Just a matter of time, now. As soon as I can open my eyes. Be rid of this dilemma. Can't wait! Feel the blood rushing back to my head. Can now open my eyes. Can see. Oh yes, the teacher's looking at me. Am lying on the floor. Now fully conscious, though I do feel dizzy. Some students are helping me back to my seat.

—Peter Mazzola

5. Oh, by the way, a student fainted in my class this morning. I know my lectures are sometimes boring, but I hadn't realized they were that bad! It was all a terrible nuisance—completely disrupted my chain of thought—and after he'd recovered and left the room it was almost impossible to get the students to concentrate properly.

6. I'm really worried about Peter. We were in class today, and he fainted again. That's about the fifth time this semester. I suspect he doesn't eat properly, so I'm going to lend him that book on nutrition

and try to persuade him to see a doctor. It was terrible to see him just lunge over and fall out of his seat. I thought for a minute he had banged his head but, mercifully, he recovered quite quickly and I took him outside to get some fresh air. Those classrooms are so stuffy, I wonder we don't all collapse!

Notes

See how your findings compare with these observations.

1. A fairly clinical report, using the evidence of eyewitnesses. No sign of any emotional involvement. The victim is classified as "the patient," and the data are what we would expect to find in the early stages of a diagnosis.

2. The erstwhile participant looks back as a spectator, and acknowledges both his embarrassment and his relief.

3. A friendly peer acknowledges that at first he misinterpreted the victim's behavior but then realized his fainting spell was genuine. There is no evidence of either extreme detachment or intense involvement.

4. This is the inner speech of the participant in the moment-by-moment confusion of the experience.

5. Here a spectator offers a very detached and unsympathetic evaluation of the event. The speaker is more interested in him/herself than in the victim of the fainting spell.

6. This is the report of a close friend, sincerely interested in Peter's well-being.

WHAT NOW?

Attempt a similar group of texts, representing different points on the near-distant spectrum. Choose an event in which you were yourself a participant.

The Components of a Spectator's Report

A spectator's account of an event in which the person him/herself is not involved usually depends on three elements:

1. What is observed

2. What is inferrred

3. Evaluation (e.g., Gorky's "insane!")

INFERRING FROM THE RICHNESS OF PARTICULARITY

On page 136, you encountered Stacey Silverman's inner speech expressing her state of exasperation. This is how a spectator might have
put it:

> It was a frantically busy day, and by two o'clock she was beginning to
> feel rather exasperated.

That account would be possible only in a text offered by an *omniscient**
narrator—one who has access to the inner life of other people's minds.
And does that abstract word "exasperated" help the reader to see Stacey
and to empathize?

If the reader is to be aroused, there must be more to the text than an
abstract statement of mood; as readers we are involved and aroused more
by particulars which we are left to interpret than by inferences offered
as fact by the writer.

What, then, would a spectator observe? Voice? Facial expressions? Gestures? Posture? For example:

> Her lips were clamped tight, but the corner of her mouth was
> twitching. She brushed her hair out of her eyes with a sharp flick of
> her left hand and slammed her drawer shut....

That text offers us the satisfying illusion of observation and enables us
to draw our own conclusions, to make our own **inferences**. A reader is
unlikely to infer that Stacey was feeling cheerful. The irresistible implicit
message is that Stacey is exasperated, impatient, or irritated. If you represent your observations to create a coherent set of impressions, then your
reader will make the appropriate inferences, which can then come to the
support of a concluding **evaluation**:

> Working as a cashier was a waste of Stacey's intelligence.

or

> Stacey didn't have the kind of temperament required for that kind
> of work.

WHAT NOW?

Select a moment of rage, anger, panic, or confusion from your childhood. Represent it as a simultaneous participant text, using inner speech.
Then present it as if written ten years later, with the benefit of hindsight,

---

*omni-scient: all-knowing.

as a spectator of your own past experience. Include sufficient contextu-
alization to help readers get their bearings.

Then write an unsympathetic *other* person's spectator text that offers a
negative evaluation.

Refer back to Eudora Welty's account of the race, page 139. Then read
the following translation, in which we have rendered Welty's participant
text as a first-person spectator text. Complete this text by adding an
evaluation.

> I hesitated, and as I did so, wondered if I had been touched. I was sure
> that someone had slapped me, but was that slap *the touch*? I urged
> myself to run, but I wondered if I should dare to start to run until I had
> heard some word from the previous runner in my relay-team. But I
> couldn't remember at that moment what the word was supposed to be. In
> any case, I ran and ran, but then I began to wonder if I was running too
> fast to be able to turn around....

What effects, present in the original, have been lost?

EVALUATING: DISTANCE LENDS PERSPECTIVE TO THE VIEW

Whenever we are spectators of any event, our habitual need and tendency are to "make sense of it." We do this by generalizing, that is, by
perceiving it as *typical*—for example, "That was a *silly thing* to do" or
"I shouldn't have been so *impatient*" or "Just *like an adolescent*." At lightning speed, we place the event within the context of our system of values
and attitudes, convictions and opinions. Once we have evaluated it, we get
on with our own lives. If we "don't know what to think about it," then "it"
stays with us, sometimes obsessively, until we have reached some kind
of resolution. The greater our psychological distance from the event, the
more easily we can make our evaluation.

Eudora Welty has written: "Getting my distance, a prerequisite of my
understanding of human events, is the way I begin work. Just as, of course,
it was an initial step when, in my first journalism job, I stumbled into
making pictures with a camera. Frame, proportion, perspective, the values
of light and shade, all are determined by the distance of the observing eye."

From a distance, we can see not only individual objects or people, but
also the larger context within which they are placed. The relationship of
light and shade cannot be appreciated from very close up; we need to
stand back to see the larger pattern.

Look at these images and try to make some kind of coherent sense
of them.

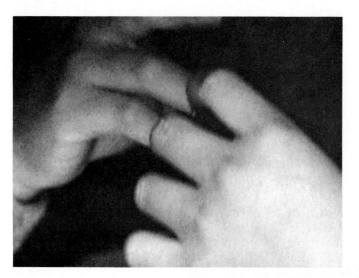

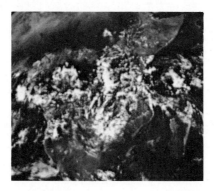

162

Back and Forth

TRANSLATIONS I

Here are two participant texts by students. We hope you will read them with pleasure, deriving the satisfaction from them that such texts can give, especially the pleasant, even intense illusion of "being inside" an experience.

So warm and dark. I feel so comfortable. No need for anything. Just dark warmthness. There are walls. Suspended between them, I stay here dark and warm. What is this sound in the walls and up above as if something moves through the wall and pounds overhead. What could it be? Are there others like me through the walls? I try to break the wall, but it yields to my force, then rebounds back in place. What is out there? I'll stay dark and warm, forever? What? Moving now? Turning and turning. Pressure all around. Am I to be crushed? Greater and greater, the pressure builds. The floor is now the ceiling or is it the walls? What is happening? Pressure building. New sounds. Sounds of fear and pain. Pressure building now, four fold building, crushing, building, crushing, then gone, as my atmosphere drains away from me through a hole in the ceiling or floor or is it one of the walls? I feel I shall never know. The walls moving now, getting closer, pressing against me, crushing, squeezing. The hole now opens and begins to engulf me, the walls crushing me, pushing into this hole, into the throat of some great beast. Being swallowed whole. What will I find at the end of this throat? Moving, crushing, why? Then I break free. The light, painful and blinding—am I to be burned by this light? No, too cold, so very cold—am I to freeze? But then comes the pain and I gasp for air and I AM ALIVE!

—*Eric Capponi*

Deer are invisible in a forest covered with snow. The glowing eyes are piercing the night as a pearl. The night is a night of a dancing ball in the forest. The ball is draped with white lace. The deer's masks are invisible in the silent night. The snow is falling silently on the forest encroaching a narrow road. The road becomes a road vanishing at the end of the forest covered with snow. The snow is brightening the cold night. The forest is a breathing creature hiding the invisible deer. The snow is dancing a waltz with an audible rhythm—un, deux, trois, un, deux, trois. The forest orchestrates the waltz echoing in the crisp air—un, deux, trois, un, deux, trois. The deer are dancing the waltz in the forest covered with snow. The deer are merrymakers of the merrymaking in the forest covered with snow. The night is a merriment full of snow. The deer become visible in the forest covered with snow. The snow is falling, falling in the night. The night is glowing in the brightened night. The deer become invisible again. Again the deer are invisible in a forest covered with snow: falling, falling, and falling. . . .

—*Masaru Matsumoto*

Masaru's intention was to create a not-too-obvious effect of someone walking in a snowstorm, slowly being affected by exposure, and beginning to hallucinate in an increasingly delirious state. How do you rate his success? (Masaru's first language is Japanese, and he was very nervous about writing English. If he had told you of his nervousness and lack of confidence, how would your response to his text have been different from what it was?)

WHAT NOW?

Stand back and "see" Eric's and Masaru's events as a spectator would. In each case, *become a spectator* and produce an appropriate text for each event.

TRANSLATIONS II

In Chapter 7, on page 144, you read a participant text by Lynn Horn. Here now is her spectator's account of the person who spoke in her previous text:

> He was always somewhat slow in learning. By now we thought he had made some progress. However, it was those drugs he had purchased on the street which set back all the progress we had made. From the next room I observed him in a conversation with his mother. All that she wanted to know was if he knew where her calculator was. He couldn't give her a clear response. He was hopeless. When she asked him additional questions, his answers, if any, were quite curt. There was no way to reach him. It was as if he was in another world. He strained for the sentences to come out of his mouth. Every sentence was a struggle for him. It was such a sad sight. I wanted to kill those men who had sold him those drugs. They had ruined all the progress we had made through the years.

In what ways is this text more explicit than Lynn's first one? How does it help you to contextualize the first text? What evidence is there in this second text that it was produced by a mature person?

On page 138, you read Barbara Schmitt's participant text representing a confusing dream. Here now is her text that offers the dreamer's later account of that dream. What differences do you notice?

> It all started in India. There were so many people on the highway walking their cows. Everyone was wearing white, it was a hot day, and there was cow shit everywhere. I was walking on an overpass and to avoid stepping in cow chips on the hot ground I decided to slide down the railing. I reached the bottom of the overpass, but didn't stop. Suddenly, everything went black and I was still falling—it felt like forever.

Then I came crashing to the ground—right into a nightmare. There was a big, eerie-looking house surrounded by mist—something out of "Dark Shadows." A black car—I think it was a Rolls Royce—stopped to pick me up. My father was in the car and I thought that he was going to take me home. We drove around, but the neighborhood didn't seem familiar, although I felt that my house was around the next corner. I knew something was wrong, but couldn't quite figure out exactly what it was. The light faded and I found myself being taken to that house again and I didn't want to go.

WHAT NOW?

1. Write a spectator's view of Don (p. 145). Make it *implicitly* favorable or condemnatory.
2. Read Marc's text again (p. 144), and write one of the following spectator texts as Marc's roommate:
   a. Marc's parents are very worried about him and have written to you for reassurance. Using the evidence of Marc's text, write a reassuring account of his condition.
   b. You are very anxious about Marc's state of mind and write confidentially to the university psychiatric center asking them to keep an eye on your friend. Use only the evidence in Marc's own text.
3. For each of these texts—Don, page 145; Marc, page 144; and Barbara, page 145—generate one and only one sentence that adequately generalizes it.

Another Case of Fever

In the following text, the narrator is an elderly man who is living in exile. He has annoyed the powers that be, and they have sent him to a remote and bleak corner of the country, where the natives, poor illiterate people, speak a different language. He has to live with a family, and he knows that the man of the house is keeping an eye on him and may even have been given orders to kill him at a convenient moment.

He is forced to go hunting with the men and boys of the village, and one day they capture a wild child who has grown up with the animals of the forest. The exile is given the task of trying to tame or train the wild child. Many people are afraid of the child, for they believe he is possessed by animal spirits. Now read on.

Looking at him on occasions, I have a clear glimpse of what he is doing. He is dreaming himself out into the winter countryside. I see him, briefly, moving over the soft snow among the birch trees, chewing strips of bark, kneeling to tear up lichen. I touch his shoulder, and he feels nothing. The black eyes, sunk deep in their sockets, stare through me, to dazzling fields of ice under the wind. When he quickens to a change of weather, it is, I realize now, to the change that comes over a landscape he is moving through in his head. If I thought we might find him again in the spring, I would let him go. But that is impossible. Having brought him in among us there is no way back. Already, in the warmth of the room, he is losing his capacity to withstand cold. For weeks now he has wrapped himself, like the rest of us, in a blanket of hide. Out there he would freeze. Whatever his secret was, I have taken it from him. He is as vulnerable now as anyone of us, and in that at least—even if the old woman does not see it—he shows himself human at last.

As if to prove what I have just perceived, the Child has a fever. Sitting as he does with his knees drawn up, staring, he suddenly pitches over and lies in a faint, but when I move to cover him, he wakes, and almost immediately begins shivering. Huge beads of sweat break out on his brow, his hair drips with it, his whole body streams. And in between the periods of burning, he freezes. I think he has never known before what it is to be cold. His whole body clenches on it, this new feeling, this discovery within himself of what winter means, what it is to be snow and ice, to feel oneself enter the realm of absolute cold, that polar world at the body's limits. He draws his knees up, closing upon himself. Every muscle in his limbs, his shoulders, his neck, goes rigid, his fists clench, his jaws tighten. He looks terrified, and when the convulsions begin I have to hold him, forcing a knife handle between his teeth, while he jerks, stiffens, goes through a whole series of spasms, and then sinks exhausted into a kind of nerveless sleep. Then again, the sweating. As I raise him in my arms and try to force a few drops of water between his lips, I am reminded of my brother, and realize what he means to me this Child, what it might mean to lose him.

The old woman watches from across the room. I know what she is thinking. This is no ordinary fever. The Child is wrestling with his demon, the animal spirit who protected him out there in the forest, and is fighting now to get back. When I appeal to her for some sort of medicine, some of the herbs she gathers and makes potions of, she shakes her head and turns her thumb down, spitting. I have to watch the Child day and night. If she thought for even a moment that the spirit might triumph and enter the Child's body again, she would cut his throat. I know it.

But the younger woman, who has a child of her own and is softhearted, cannot bear to see the boy writhe as he does, and sweat, and shiver, and jerk about under the rugs. Secretly she brings me food for him and a bowl of clean water.

I hear the old woman arguing with her, and I know what she is saying. What if the Child gave up the struggle, and we found ourselves shut up here with the giant white wolf who is his familiar, and who might at any moment succeed in filling the Child's body and then breaking out of it. The fever, she believes, is part of the painful transformation. The Child's blood boils and freezes, as drop by drop it is being changed. The Child's belly cringes for the raw meat that is the wolf's diet. His limbs strain to

The wild child in François Truffaut's *L'Enfant Sauvage*

grow claws. His jaw clenches against the growing there of fangs. And what if it isn't a wolf after all? But some other beast? Larger, more terrible than even she can imagine.

The young woman quails. And I see a new doubt has been sown in her mind. What if the beast, finding the Child too difficult to conquer, chose the body of her own son instead? It would be so easy. While we are all sleeping, our bodies empty in the dark, the Child's spirit slips out, crosses the room, enters her son's body—and there, it is done!

For two whole days the young woman refuses to come near us. She watches the Child, she watches her son, she keeps the boy as far from our corner of the room as possible, while the old woman whispers and flaps about between us.

But in the dead of night, when the Child's fever is at its crisis, and I am forced to call for help, it is the younger woman who stirs in the dark, wraps herself in her cloak, and comes with water. I am desperately tired and through sheer exhaustion, after nearly five days of watching, seem always on the edge of tears. My hand shakes so much that I cannot lift the bowl to the Child's lips.

She takes it from me. Kneels. Lifts the boy's head, letting him gulp at the coolness, and when she has laid his head back on the pile of rags I have contrived for a pillow, sits fanning him, while I rest for a moment against the wall and sleep. When I start awake again she is still there, her face just visible in the folds of the cloak. She sits perfectly upright, her hand moving back and forth to make a breeze. She nods, indicating that I may sleep again, and immediately I fall back into my body's depths.

In the early morning light that seeps in through the window cracks, I wake to find her holding the Child in one of his fits. She looks frightened, and I know that this is the real moment of crisis. I know too what it is she fears.

The Child's body jerks, loosens, his limbs fly about. . . .

—David Malouf, *An Imaginary Life*

REFLECTIONS ON MALOUF: A STUDENT'S NOTEBOOK

It's an event in the remote past. I'd have expected it to be written in the past tense—"I had . . . he was," rather than "I have . . . he is." What difference does it make? The present tense brings it into "now"—so the reader feels closer, more involved. And the storyteller doesn't know what's going to happen next, so there's more suspense, uncertainty for him, and so for the reader. That's probably why/how it kept me worried.

I don't think the narrator is just a spectator, just watching, because he's also involved in the action. He's participating in trying to keep the child alive. So he must be two things at once. . . . I've had this kind of double role. When my brother was very sick I watched him, and I did things for him. I certainly wasn't detached or cool or distant. So it must be possible to be a spectator and a participant. Both at the same time. Wait. I've just realized. When you're with your friends, you can do it. Everybody's talking, me included. Then whatever it is we're talking about gets less interesting or I suddenly feel tired. And I switch off, and just listen and watch. I'm no longer participating. And this notebook. When I'm writing, I'm a participant in its making. But when I flip back to last week or last month, what I wrote then, I'm a spectator. I'm sort of looking at myself. Not myself now. Myself then.

The narrator knows more than the other people in the room. He knows about what fever is like. So he can put it all together . . . the child's fever, and the old woman's crazy superstitions, and the young woman's fear for her own child. So he's making connections all the time, making sense of the situation. That's what we do when we're spectators. And he's really evaluating. We know from him that some things are better for the child than others. And the narrator explains things very clearly. He represents individual moments very vividly and he also helps the reader to grasp the connections. "*When* the convulsions begin I have to hold him, *forcing* a knife handle between his teeth, *while* he jerks, stiffens, goes through a *whole series* of spasms, and *then* sinks exhausted into a kind of nerveless sleep." With that kind of writing he lets us look over his shoulder, and we don't have to struggle through a lot of confusion because he organizes it for us. "I think . . . I know . . . I realize. . . ." He's interpreting what happens for us; so we too "realize."

States of Mind

A NERVOUS BREAKDOWN

Read this, Donald Burnham's account of the playwright August Strind-berg as he suffered a severe nervous breakdown.

> He attempted to gather and to sustain himself by lonely walks through the streets of the Montparnasse section. In the course of these walks he found meaning everywhere. To repeat his words, "Things that would pre-viously have lacked significance now attracted my attention." Flowers in the Luxembourg Gardens seemed to nod at him, sometimes in greeting, sometimes in warning. Clouds in the shape of animals foretold ominous events. Statues looked at him trying to tell him something. Scraps of paper in the gutter carried words that he tried to piece together into a message. Books which he found in sidewalk bookstalls seemed to have been specially "placed" there for him. The design of a leather cover of one seemed to contain a prophecy for him and when he opened the book a sliver of wood pointed to a particular sentence. Twigs on the ground took the shape of the initials of a man who he feared was pursuing him intent on murder. Seemingly unrelated items in the newspaper were connected to his inner preoccupations. Urgent personal meanings were everywhere.

WHAT NOW?

Put yourself in Strindberg's mind, and write (the text of) your inner speech as *you* participate in these experiences. Are you talking to yourself or to an internalized other—someone who may understand and help, or someone who angers you because he/she fails to understand?

Remember that you are "I" and in the present. The first four-and-a-half lines of Burnham's text, like the last two-and-a-half, will not be included. (Why not?)

BEING IN TWO MINDS I

Helen Vendler has written of "the ultimate familiarity of the dialogue of the mind with itself." Here now are two texts by students representing a "dialogue of the mind with itself":

— So?? What do you think??

* I think I like him.

— He's too old.

* No he's not.

— Thirty-one!? Come on, that's twelve years!!

* He's nice.

— *Nice??* What's "nice"? That's a stupid word. Besides, you know a lot of "nice" guys.

* No I don't.—He's different, there's something about him. He isn't like every other guy—he's different.

— You mean *strange!!*

* No!! Different.—He has a wonderful mind.

— Ha!!! Don't make me laugh!!

* Mmm, that does sound stupid, but I can listen to him all day.

— So what is he?—Your counselor?

* Well *he* listens to me.

— So does everyone else.

* No they don't. They think I'm funny—always joking—but they don't *really* listen.

— *He* just wants to go to bed with you.

* No, that's not true!!!

— Don't be so naïve, he said it himself.

* I told him how I felt.

— You don't really know *how* you feel.

* —You're right, I don't.

— *There!!! Told you!*

* *Shut up!!!*

— You're saying that because I'm right!—What about when Mom and Dad asked how old he was? You said—"I don't know."—*Liar!!*

* I didn't know what to say!!

— You *know* they won't approve.

* Oh *guilt,* oh *guilt!!*

— See! He's already causing problems.

Stop!!!

Stop thinking.
Shut off mind.
Go to sleep.
Warm cozy bed.
Tired limbs.
Soft pillow.
Rest.
Rest.

—Laura Ferronato

BEING IN TWO MINDS II

Oh please, not again tonight. I can't. I'm too tired. Please! Let me sleep tonight, and we'll do it tomorrow night. Please . . .

No way! You don't need to sleep: besides, those bags under your eyes are very becoming. Anyway, I'm not tired. There are millions of things on my side of the mind that we should think about tonight.

Very important things, I'm sure! If maybe we could solve some major problems, such as world hunger, the economic crisis, or nuclear annihilation, I'd be more than willing to miss a night's sleep. But deciding on what I should wear tomorrow is not enough of a problem to keep me up all night.

Oh! Excuuuuuse me! Our problems are not interesting or intellectual enough for you to miss a few zzzzz's, uh? How's this? . . . What are we gonna do about school next year? Are we going back to Florida or are we staying in New York? What are we gonna say to your father if he calls? And how are we going to bring up your grades before the semester ends? Eh? There! Sleep on that!

Ouch! Unfair! You really are nasty. And how come it's solving *my* problems, when your side is the one that causes all the trouble? Now, please! I'm tired. I have to sleep.

O.K. You want to sleep. I'll let you, but . . . I get a free day.

No, absolutely not! No. Remember what happened last time I let you loose? We wound up in the Hamptons at four in the morning. I still haven't recovered. No way!

Fine. Then what shall we think about, huh? Your love life? School? Dieting? School? You choose.

Enough! Enough! Let me sleep. You got it—a free day. But first promise me we won't do anything illegal, disgusting, or fattening.

I promise. No, go to sleep. Sweet dreams and all. Good night.
ZZZ....ZZZZZ.....ZZZ
        ZZ...
          ZZZZ....
            ZZZZ...
              ZZ....
                ZZZ....
                  ZZ...

—Lisa Portnoy

WHAT NOW?

1. Choose a question, a controversy, an issue on which you are "of two minds." Let your inner dialogue go to work on it, pro and con, then retrieve it as accurately as possible, writing it down in a text that is as close as possible to the inner utterances, i.e., don't write "text," write "utterance." Don't consider any other audience.

2. Try your hand, now, at writing two *extremely contrasting* texts, as unlike each other as possible. Make one a representation of a happening, in the private inner speech of the participant. Make the other a spectator's representation of the event. (Note the difference between a *happening* — "It happened to me" — and an *event* — "It happened to her.")

   You can choose to represent any of the following:

   a. A tired boxer in the last round of a 15-round contest.
   b. A nervous person in the dentist's chair.
   c. A motorist driving a car in dense fog.
   d. A parachutist making her/his first jump.
   e. A person being interviewed for a first important job.
   f. A person at his or her first elegant dinner in a fancy restaurant.

   Note: The spectator may be either the former participant looking back or another person.

THE TWILIGHT BEFORE SLEEP

When we go to bed, most of us spend some time thinking over the past day, more or less coherently. As we slide toward sleep, however, our thinking changes, blurs, becomes fragmentary and disconnected. It is an extremely difficult state of mind to capture, since if we try to pay attention to it, it is nudged out of our minds by the act of paying attention. Here is one student's attempt to represent that state of mind as naturalistically as possible.

> Is lunch made? Did you put your glasses in the bag? Your books? The red, the yellow, accounting book? The problem for accounting—catch the bus on time tomorrow, can't be late again. Will you shut up! Breathe deeply. In out, In out, In out, In out inoutinout. Leslie feeling better, I'm glad—makes me nervous. School so much more work. Accounting—no second test. Psych and Criminology—have to get an A on final. Finals after Christmas—work need money buy things, presents. Dad and Mom—birthdays, anniversaries, don't have time. Time to wake up? Can't be. Dancing—take more classes—no time. Time to study—nervous—might fail —need As—drop school—lottery—Europe—Leslie, Randi, Gwen, Beth, Mom, Dad, Robert come with me. Take everyone. Beth not appreciate, Leslie has to work Work 20 hours, 15 credits, need time to think, go away —Bahamas. Leslie—has to work. January—California—canceled—Uncle Murray died—wanted to meet him. Ring, necklace, diamond earrings—

gifts—Rather have met him. Uncle Kenny dead. Hard year—poor Grandma— have to see her—miss her, love her. Go to bookstore—suffocate—hard to breathe—watch pocketbook—get fruit—study—eyes hurt—close—go schluffy.

—*Sharon Fishbein*

SOMEONE ELSE'S NIGHTMARE

Nightmare

When you're lying awake with a dismal headache, and repose is
   taboo'd by anxiety,
I conceive you may use any language you choose to indulge in, without
   impropriety;
For your brain is on fire—the bedclothes conspire of usual slumber to
   plunder you:
First your counterpane goes, and uncovers your toes, and your sheet
   slips demurely from under you;
Then the blanketing tickles—you feel like mixed pickles, so terribly
   sharp is the pricking,
And you're hot, and you're cross, and you tumble and toss till there's
   nothing 'twixt you and the ticking.
Then the bedclothes all creep to the ground in a heap, and you pick 'em
   all up in a tangle;
Next your pillow resigns and politely declines to remain at its usual
   angle!
Well, you get some repose in the form of a doze, with hot eyeballs and
   head ever aching.
But your slumbering teems with such horrible dreams that you'd very
   much better be waking. . . .
You're a regular wreck, with a crick in your neck, and no wonder you
   snore, for your head's on the floor, and you've needles and pins from
   your soles to your shins, and your flesh is a-creep; for your left leg's
   asleep, and you've cramp in your toes, and a fly on your nose, and some
   fluff in your lung, and a feverish tongue, and a thirst that's intense, and
   a general sense that you haven't been sleeping in clover;
But the darkness has passed, and it's daylight at last, and the night has
   been long—ditto ditto my song—and thank goodness they're both of
   them over!

—W. S. Gilbert, *Iolanthe*

WHAT NOW?

Place yourself as a participant in that experience and write a text that expresses your inner speech.

A Familiar Story?

Police Report, Precinct XVI

Regarding the prisoner, John Dove (illegal immigrant?):

The prisoner was apprehended on the beach at approx. 1030 hours, apparently in a state of shock.

His presence there had been reported at 0930 by Diana Hunter, who had been exercising her dogs and was approached by the prisoner who proceeded to make a nuisance of himself. Ms. Hunter testified that, had it not been for the protection of her wolf hounds, she would have feared for her safety. Dove was shouting hysterically: "Leviathan! Leviathan!" and pointing at the sea, on which no ships or boats were at that time to be seen. According to Ms. Hunter, the prisoner stank offensively; in her words, "to high heaven."

Officer No. 999, who went to the scene and apprehended the prisoner, took down the following statement from the prisoner, immediately, first taking all due measures to protect him from the wolf hounds, which were by this time extremely excited. The prisoner said: "Where am I? What happened? Who are you? Why are these dogs trying to get me? It's not possible! I drowned and now here I am! It's impossible. I must be going out of my mind!"

Dove was then escorted to the cells at the Precinct (1130), and was immediately hosed down and fed. He then made the following statement: "I think I must have been swallowed up. God only knows why! Must be some kind of judgment. Imagine that! Swallowed by a sea monster! I was as good as dead. One great wave over the deck, and there I was, in the water, up to my eyes in drowning. And now here I am, large as life!" Throughout his statement Dove continually rubbed his eyes and sniffed.

At 1900 hours, at his own request, Dove made a third statement:

> I've been thinking about it, and I've come to the conclusion that I must recently have spent several days inside a whale, even though such a claim may well sound preposterous. While I was on board a ship, bound for Nineveh, a violent storm blew up, gigantic waves swept over the deck, I lost my grip, and was swept overboard. I plunged into the raging waters, felt myself to be drowning, said my final prayers, and then, to my surprise, it seems that I was swallowed by a whale.
>
> It was an extremely odd and disturbing experience, for I was plunged into total darkness, enveloped in a mass of heaving rubbery objects, and subjected to an extraordinary range of noises, most of which reminded me of the sounds that my own inside sometimes makes during severe bouts of indigestion.
>
> During my time inside the whale, I survived on a limited diet of water, body fluids—the whale's, not my own—and small organisms. At some stage, I must have lapsed into some kind of feverish delirium, for I became convinced that I was in prison, and attempted to

break out of my "cell" by carving at the wall with my knife, which amazingly I still retained. When I began to cut, however, the whale — as I realize now it must have been — protested vigorously, and I therefore desisted.

I appreciate that my story may well strike the authorities as most improbable, and I therefore request permission to dispatch a letter to my family, in the belief that they will corroborate my identity and at least part of my statement.

I respectfully request another shower.

(signed) J. Dove

WHAT NOW?

1. Using whatever you have learned so far from reading this book, try to characterize each of Dove's three statements, and account for the differences between them.
2. What connection is there between this text and the text on page 150?

Here are the complete versions of the pictures on page 162. Are you surprised when you compare them to the incomplete pictures?

part 3 | Reports, Reflections, and Transformations

9 | Only Connect . . . Hypotaxis

What Writing Makes Possible

The most important moment in the development of any language occurs when a system of writing is invented.

Think for a few mintues about a society without writing, what is called an oral society or oral culture. Everything is spoken and heard by talkers and listeners. Nothing is ever written down. Can you imagine such a state of affairs? And can you imagine the states of mind that such a situation gives rise to? How, would you assume, do such societies ensure that

Storyteller in Botswana, 1946

important knowledge such as laws or social rules will not be forgotten? Do they train and employ professional rememberers, people who are selected because they show signs of having specially retentive memories?

REAL TALK VERSUS TEXT TALK

Now turn your attention to yourself and to the ways in which you produce language. Make a tape recording of two or three minutes' informal conversation, and transcribe it very carefully, keeping all the *um*'s and *ah*'s, the *you know*'s and the *kind of*'s. Now look at your transcription. Does it look like writing, like text? How does it differ from the kinds of text-representing-talk that you read in novels—that is, dialogue? You will immediately see that although a novel's dialogue may sound very natural, it is not a direct imitation or unmodified representation of real talking. If it were, most readers would very quickly get tired and throw the book down.

Thus talk in a text is talk with much of the reality of actual talk ruthlessly removed—removed so that the dialogue will be readable text. When we hear real conversation, our brains filter out most of the real stuff of talking—all those hesitations and repetitions, *um*'s and *ah*'s. When someone talks without these features, we feel slightly suspicious of him/her. "Too smooth," we murmur. (Talking from a prepared script is another thing entirely; but good speech writers work hard to make a prepared script sound "natural.")

When we start to talk, our main task is simply to keep talking until we have produced what our listeners will recognize as a complete segment of talk. If we say, "Well, he was kind of er, sort of er, you know, like, weird!" in a friendly relaxed situation, our listeners will accept that as a completed contribution. If, on the other hand, we say, "I'm absolutely convinced he was a . . . ," that will be heard as incomplete, and our listeners will look at us expectantly, waiting for completion.

In many situations we have to talk "on our feet"—talk even as we are thinking, nudging our thoughts into that place in our consciousness from which we take them into our talking. We have to talk without benefit of premeditation. And what we say comes out bit by bit, additively. Hence the high frequency of "and" and "then" in talking. In other words, the structure of much talking is inevitably paratactic: 1 and 2 and 3 and 4. . . .

When we write, however, our minds can work in quite different ways. We are free of the pressure of having to keep talking. We can take our time completing a segment. We can look again at what we have just said; it is there on the page, independent of us, an object outside us, visible and reviewable. We can compose our thoughts in a variety of ways. Even as we write, we can change our minds and immediately rewrite. Above all, we can represent the relationships between the parts of our text—the words, phrases, sentences—in an almost unlimited variety of ways. In writing we have a far greater range of choice than in talking.

Hypotaxis: Creating a Hierarchy

Consider this sentence:

Although on the whole the behavior of whales is rather mysterious, nevertheless, as a result of some remarkable modern developments in electronic surveillance techniques, and a miniaturization that makes the handling of equipment so much easier, especially under water, we are now in a position to claim that we already know far more than we believed possible even ten years ago.

Does that sound like talk or like text? If you had produced that sentence as part of an informal conversation, wouldn't others have raised their eyebrows in surprise and given you some strange looks? Our oral memories, holding on to the words spoken and holding them together, can deal with only short segments, and this limitation in listening/holding on is another reason why talking tends to consist of short paratactic segments. But our eyes and therefore our pens are under no such limitation. Even as you were reading that sentence about the whales, your eye was flicking back and forth at a speed of which you were perfectly unconscious, pulling the parts together, making them cohere, so that you could construct a coherent meaning in your mind.

What, then, is the main point, or focus, of that long sentence about whales? How can you isolate it? How do you know which part of the sentence to foreground, which to hold off as background? What in the text signals the arrival of the main point?

The first clue you registered was the word *although*. From the fact that you speak the English language, you knew immediately that the sentence was first going to offer you some "although stuff," and that the main point could be expected some time after the "although stuff" had been dealt with. And when your eyes read "as a result," you recognized that there was going to be some "as a result of stuff," that is, causes. (For more on the various kinds of "stuff," see the appendix to this chapter.) So again you knew that the destination of the sentence had not yet arrived. By this time, your eye had already been flicking both back and forth, and you caught a microsecond glimpse of the white space at the end of the sentence. You knew that the sentence was winding down (up?) and that the point could not be withheld much longer.

The preceding paragraph is a very crude account of some of your mind's activity when reading that whale of a sentence. And turning the coin over, it is a clue to what we can do as writers that we can't do as talkers. The most useful shorthand term for what we can do as writers is **hypotaxis** (from the Greek: *hypo* means "under"; *taxis*, to put in order—thus placing some parts below others).

In other words, whereas in simple writing—as in most talk—we move forward in a paratactic way, in more formal writing we can produce a kind of verbal hierarchy: we can push some parts down and bring others up. Or, to change the plane of the metaphor, we can relegate some parts to the background and bring one or more other parts to the foreground.

Flipping back through this book, isolate some hypotactic sentences and see how they work, how one part is raised and others are lowered. Better still, read them with your ear, and hear how the shaping of an effective hypotactic sentence is like a kind of music, often saving the climax until last. Or you might imagine it as a wave—rising and falling, then rising to crest on the final period.

SHAPING HYPOTACTIC TEXT

The shaping of such satisfying structures and complex melodies/ rhythms, with a forward-driving impulse that feels as naturally irresistible as a wave, is one of the pleasures that awaits any writer—not only the satisfaction of getting something said but the extra pleasure that lies in the making itself, the very act of saying.

But surely, we hear you interject, it isn't as simple as falling off a wave! For the experienced writer it is. But what help can we offer the inexperienced writer? At the risk of overgeneralizing, here are a few guidelines:

1. When first getting your words on paper for any text, we suggest you rehearse the act of writing inside your head—anywhere, at any time.

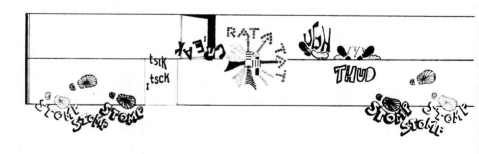

Listen in to your own thinking, and feel free to fantasize as an ideal self; enjoy the illusion of eloquence.

2. Let yourself be possessed by that which demands expression. If your subject excites you, don't resist it. Let it assume control, and just hold the pen, getting the words down as fast as possible. If you and the right subject have come together at the right moment, you may even feel "feverish." At this stage, control is the last thing with which to concern your mind. Simply let the words get into your notebook. Our guess is that this kind of text will be paratactic, rather like many of the texts in the first chapter of this book.

3. When your energy runs out, or your ideas dry up, or you feel that you have an ending, walk away from your text. Let's call that text 1.

4. Return to your text when you feel the need (pressure of time) or the inclination. Now become the spectator, the first reader of text 1. Read it aloud, or at least with your inner ear. Whatever you do, *hear* it. How does it sound? Repetitious? Disjointed? Childish? Immature? Corny? Flabby? Floppy? Stiff? If you are like us, you will find a lot of elementary things to put right in that text 1. Put them right. Then move on to the next stage.

5. Is the whole text reasonably coherent? Does it hold together? Are the parts in the right order? Is the language appropriate to your purposes and your audience? Too formal? Too familiar?

6. Tune your tone and redistribute any parts that are out of place. Let's call this text 2. Now walk away from it.

7. When you come back for a final reading, you will also be ready to revise for the last time. At this point, look at the shaping of your sentences. In each paragraph see if you can find at least one sequence of paratactic parts that can be organized into a strong, well-integrated hypotactic structure. Don't be inhibited by the discovery or realization that you are writing a kind of language that you would never *speak*. As the writer-spectator, you have the control and overall view that allow you to shape, reshape, and make choices at every stage in the fine-tuning of your writing.

EEK & MEEK by Howie Schneider

Premeditated and Unpremeditated Text and Talk

As you will have gathered, hypotactic text is the complete opposite of spontaneous, paratactic talk. The essence of hypotactic text is that it is premeditated. The word "premeditated" has an unfortunate reputation because it most commonly occurs in the following context: "It was a brutal and premeditated murder." Some words occur so persistently in the company of others, that we can easily fall into the trap of assuming that their only appropriate use is in that recurring context. Say "premeditated," and most people will say "murder."

To get some idea of what premeditated means in relation to talk/text, think of the various ways in which the wild child's fever (p. 168) could be represented:

1. Someone could *talk* about it as it is happening, provide an ongoing commentary.

2. Someone who had witnessed it could *talk* about it—two hours later, two days later, ten years later.

3. Someone could *write* about it as it is happening—by watching and making notes in his/her notebook.

4. Someone could *write* about it later—hours, days, or years later—in a variety of ways. (This is what Malouf did—even though he used the present tense.)

Versions 1 and 3 would be **unpremeditated**. The mind would not have turned the scene over, considered it, reflected on it, interpreted it before producing a record, either spoken or written. The representation would be raw, off the top of the head.

Versions 2 and 4 would be **premeditated**; they would have lost some of the immediate detail perhaps, but they would enjoy the benefit that comes when the mind has had time to reflect on an event, to make sense of it, to determine its significance. The speaker or writer would no longer be pressured by what was taking place; it would be over and at a safe remove.

Look again at Malouf's narrator's account of the child's fever, which we will call version A:

Version A (Malouf's)

He looks terrified, and when the convulsions begin I have to hold him, forcing a knife handle between his teeth, while he jerks, stiffens, goes through a whole series of spasms, and then sinks exhausted into a kind of nerveless sleep.

Compare that with this:

Version B

He, he looks kinda scared, scared stiff . . . and then he, he starts to con . . . conv . . . starts to go into convulsions, and I have to get hold of him, and I get this knife, and I . . . the handle, I force it in, in between his teeth, and all this time, all the time, he's . . . he's sort of jerking, and he's all stiff, and then, then he gets tired, sort of exhausted, and he falls asleep, like as if he's, oh, er, dead, you know.

Now compare A and B with this:

Version C

Child terrified. Convulsions start. Hold him down. Force knife handle between teeth. Much jerking. Spasms, one after another. Many spasms. Stiffens. Spasms, a series. Now exhausted. Sleeping. Like death.

Now compare those three versions with this one:

Version D

He looked terrified to me, and when he started the convulsions I had to get a tight grip on him and force a knife handle between his teeth, so he wouldn't bite his tongue. But all the time he was jerking, jerking, and stiffening, going through a whole series of spasms, till finally he just dropped off into a deep sleep.

Version A is, as we have already indicated, premeditated text. As for B, C, and D, one is an unpremeditated text, a noting of an event as it happens; one is unpremeditated talk; and one is premeditated talk. We do not believe that you will have any difficulty in deciding which is which.

Premeditated talk (version D) is much closer to text than is talk (version B). Version C—notes for a text—has dropped many of the features of normal text simply to economize effort and keep pace with the events as they occur.

In version A (Malouf's premeditated text) and in version D (premeditated talk), the nature of the relationships between the parts is much more clearly and explicitly offered, and there is a move beyond simple parataxis—"1 and 2 and 3 and 4" or "1 then 2 then 3. . . ." This connectedness, hypotaxis, is the hallmark of premeditated text/talk.

WHAT NOW? A COMPARATIVE EXPERIMENT

1. While you are observing someone doing something that is unfamiliar to you, talk your observations into a tape recorder.

2. Next day, tape yourself while you tell someone about what you observed.
3. Observe someone doing something that is unfamiliar to you, and make brief notes of your observations.
4. A day later write up your observations in a text that will demonstrate that since the action occurred you have made sense of it, you understand it, and you have evaluated it—that is, you have decided whether it was well or badly performed, appealing or unappealing.

It is texts of the fourth type that this chapter is primarily interested in. It is in such texts that you will be able to represent to the fullest extent your understanding of anything.

EXAMPLE OF A SWITCH FROM PREMEDITATED TO UNPREMEDITATED TALK

At 7:20 P.M. on May 6, 1937, the largest airship in the world, Germany's *Hindenburg*, was coming to rest at Lakehurst, New Jersey. Herb Morrison was covering the arrival for a local radio station. Here are his words:

> Here it comes, ladies and gentlemen. What a sight it is, a thrilling one, a marvelous sight! The sun is striking the windows of the observation deck on the westward side and sparkling like glittering jewels on the background of black velvet. Oh! Oh! Oh! It's burst into flames! Get out of the way, please! Oh my, this is terrible . . . it is burning . . . it's falling. This is one of the worst catastrophes in the world . . . it's a terrific crash . . . it's smoke and it's flames . . . I don't believe it . . . I'm going to have to stop for a minute . . . This is the worst thing I have ever witnessed. Oh! . . . and all the humanity!

Notes   What are the most striking differences between Morrison's rehearsed and unrehearsed talking?

WHAT NOW?

Take a passage of text from any page so far in this book, and translate it into (a) unpremeditated talk, and (b) premeditated talk.

Four Ways to Appreciate Gorky's Hypotactic Talents

Read again Gorky's opening sentence at the beginning of Chapter 8:

> Today while I was watching a fair little lady in cream-coloured stockings, with the immature features of a child, who stood on the Troitzki bridge,

holding on to the balustrade with her grey-gloved hands as though preparing to jump into the Neva, I saw her stick out a sharp, pink little tongue at the moon.

Do you imagine that sentence sprang, fully formed, ready-made, into Gorky's consciousness, and that all he had to do was catch it in writing before it evaporated? It seems unlikely, doesn't it?

Let us speculate about what qualities Gorky had that enabled him to form that delectable sentence.

1. An attentive interest in people, and good powers of observation.

2. Much previous experience of writing.

3. A well-developed intuitive grasp of the effects that hypotaxis can achieve. This would have been nurtured by his previous experiences of reading, which would have given him a repertoire of patterns, constructs, structures, templets, each working on him as a reader in a particular way. These patterns were available to him as the fruits of all his previous activity as a reader of both his own texts and the texts of others.

Let us now look at the pattern of his sentence. We will explore four different ways of representing the pattern. Each has a particular kind of usefulness, and some limitations; by using all four, we may get closer to an adequate appreciation of Gorky's words.

THE FIRST WAY

Diagram 1

Today
    (context: time)

while I was watching a fair little lady in cream-coloured stockings, with the immature features of a child,
    (context: time, particularized, and situation)

who stood on the Troitzki bridge,
    (specifying action of "lady" and offering context: place)

holding on to the balustrade with her grey-gloved hands as though preparing to jump into the Neva,
    (specifying narrator's expectation of what will happen next, therefore arousing or provoking reader's expectations)

I saw her stick out a sharp, pink little tongue at the moon.
    (final arrival of focal act, which arrives none too soon, as relief / surprise / anti-climactic climax / comical or absurd conclusion to this segment. It leaves the reader still wondering about her reasons, her state of mind, and therefore eager to inspect the next sentence.)

Diagram 1 best recognizes the fact that when we read a text, we move forward through time. Simplifying, we can claim that in general, sentences move through time in one of three ways: (a) They offer their emphasized point first, and that is followed by a trail of supplementary details and modifications; (b) they offer contextual information and supporting detail first and move finally into their major emphasis; or (c) they balance, with the focus in the middle.

Gorky's sentence, as you can see, proceeds as in (b). The text up to "I saw her" offers a cluster of contextual items and the evidence of an intense interest in one particular woman; the detailing of her appearance is a sign that she is interesting; and the reader's aroused curiosity is finally rewarded with her tongue, which is not only withheld to the end but is wickedly preceded by Gorky's clever trick of almost misleading us with that "as though," which seems about to tell of a suicidal leap.

THE SECOND WAY

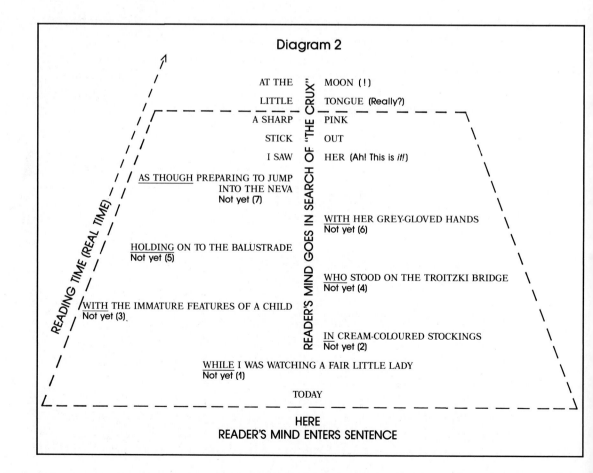

Diagram 2

Diagram 2 is a spatial variation of diagram 1, a perspective reconstruction of the sentence, transforming it into something like a theater stage, a hologram, or a picture with strong recession. The focal point of a sentence may be at the front of the space, or it may be cunningly almost hidden at the back, so that we have to peer and move through a lot of subsidiary detail in order to reach the prima donna.

If we encounter the important focal point first as we move into a sentence, we may not have much inclination to go all the way to the back of the stage, the end of the sentence. If, on the other hand, the writer withholds the "crux," as Gorky does, then we move forward, on and on, acquiring all manner of ancillary information—some of which may even mislead us for a moment or give us an injection of momentary excitement—before reaching the focal point. (Such sentences are like a detective story.)

THE THIRD WAY

A third way of viewing a sentence is to translate its elements into a diagram in a vertical plane, with the important element at the top and the subsidiary elements at various levels below. The eye then perceives a clear hierarchy, as depicted in diagram 3.

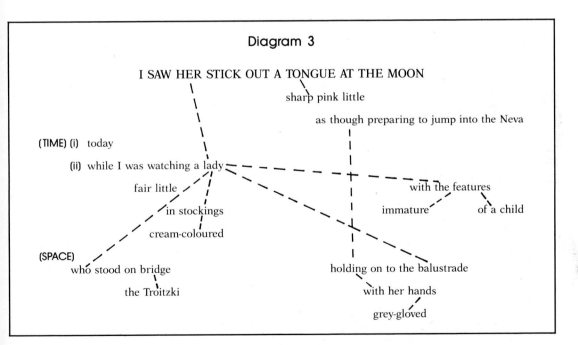

Diagram 3

I SAW HER STICK OUT A TONGUE AT THE MOON

sharp pink little

as though preparing to jump into the Neva

(TIME) (i) today

(ii) while I was watching a lady

fair little

with the features

in stockings

immature   of a child

cream-coloured

(SPACE)

who stood on bridge

holding on to the balustrade

the Troitzki

with her hands

grey-gloved

What this diagram stresses or highlights, on even a casual glance, is that most of the text is committed to the "lady"—that is, the text is committed to an act of particularization: this lady, not any lady.

The work of the sentence is committed not to the "I," the grammatical subject, but to someone else, the object. The narrator's involvement is that of a very curious spectator.

THE FOURTH WAY

The fourth metaphor/diagram best recognizes that a reader is involved in a dynamic relationship with the text (the author). It's a game for two players. The text arouses desires and expectations in the reader; then it either satisfies those desires, postpones their satisfaction, or frustrates them. For the writer, the pleasure of writing is in controlling, teasing, misleading, and finally perhaps pleasing the reader. Gorky's focal point is an anticlimactic climax; the possibility of high drama gives way to strange farce; our being denied tragedy is compensated for by a sense of relief and a sense of the absurd.

Diagram 4 depicts the dialogue between the reader and Gorky.

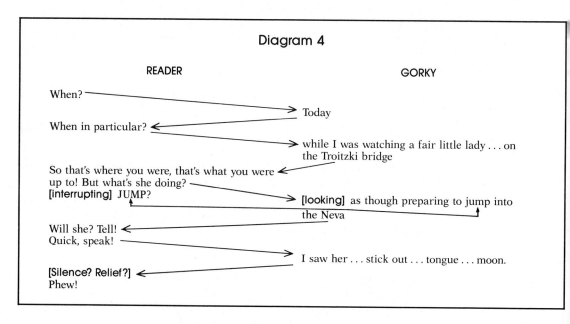

Diagram 4

As you can see, then, a sentence of any complexity is an arena in which the writer can play games with the reader. When you compose complex sentences, you can decide how you want to affect your readers—whether you want to make everything easy for them, or whether you want to tease them, lead them up the garden path, surprise them, or disconcert them.

The Reader as Asker of Questions

If the role of the reader is asker of questions and the role of the writer is answerer or withholder of answers, what kinds of questions does a reader ask?

Any and every reader asks certain questions of any and every text.

1. Who or What? The writer has to identify the topic, to answer the question, what are these words going to be about? The first need of the reader is identification of what is to be represented.

2. Next the reader wants the writer to predicate—that is, to say something about the who or the what. This second part may well include many of the answers to such context questions as when? where? and why? And some of the answers to such questions may attach to or even precede identification of the topic (e.g., Gorky's "Today").

3. As it proceeds, each text arouses or provokes its own distinctive set of questions; it sets up distinctive expectations in the reader. At the end of Gorky's first sentence, for example, most readers will probably ask, "But what does she think she's doing, sticking her tongue out at the moon?" Gorky's eventual answer will be: She is probably insane—which we find rather facile and disappointing.

In a recent class, a group (conspiracy?) of three students found 32 questions to ask of Gorky's sentence. They claimed that their score was a world record!

Our Students Go Hypotactic

We would like you now to read a collection of texts written by our students. They had enjoyed Gorky's classic sentence and had discussed the way it worked. They agreed that the energy the sentence aroused in them was due in large part to the various ways in which it affected them: a gradual increase in interest, partly due to the idea of "spying" on someone; a spurt of uncertainty and anxiety as it came to seem likely that the young woman would throw herself in the river; and then the final letdown, with its odd mix of comedy and incongruity—a "lady" sticking out her tongue! and at whom? the moon!—mixed with relief at her survival.

They had then confirmed their sense that it was a **left-branching sentence**—that is, a sentence that holds back its main clause until the end, unlike a **right-branching sentence**, which has its main point up front and then a series of lesser details trailing along behind. (For a detailed discussion of left- and right-branching sentences, see the appendix at the end of this chapter.) Left-branchers tend to be less easily grasped at first reading than right-branchers; but they have the capacity, the power, to set up suspense and uncertainty in a reader, which is finally resolved by the terminal main clause.

We then asked them to try their hand at a left-brancher and suggested they should play for high stakes and attempt a sentence of at least 75 words! Like us, they were very pleased with the results, and we want to pose this question for you to consider: Do their sentences strike you as boring textbook-exercise answers, or do they seem to give evidence of a genuine relish, a sense of pleasure in writing? We hope they give you pleasure.

> The two lovers lay writhing on the slick satin sheets of the queen-size canopied bed, their limbs intertwined, droplets of sweat glistening on their bodies, lust blazing in their eyes, too preoccupied with each other to notice the door across the room slowly, silently opening, providing entrance for their uninvited guest, who stealthily crept across the carpeted floor toward them, readying himself for the attack all the while, only to have his presence revealed by the soft mischievous purr which he could no longer suppress.
>
> —*Barbara Schmitt*

Version 1

> Not having noticed the truck speeding toward her when she had started to cross the street, now she knew the huge black menacing bulk of the International Harvester, the name *Valerie* emblazoned in deep scarlet red on the hood just above the grill, was looming toward her, no longer able to slow down or swerve to avoid hitting the small, auburn-haired child, who stood rooted in terror to the ground, her eyes and mouth wide open but mute from intense fear, then suddenly falling to the ground in a dead faint, allowing the truck to drive safely over her.

Version 2

> The child, not having noticed the truck speeding toward her when she started to cross the street, casually turned her head to the left to see HER—the huge, black, menacing figure of the International Harvester, the name *Valerie* emblazoned in deep scarlet on the hood just above the grill— looming toward her, brakes screaming wildly as her driver slammed them to the floor, trying in vain to slow down or swerve to avoid hitting the frail, petite, auburn-haired child who stood rooted in terror to the ground, her eyes and mouth wide open, but mute from intense fear, then suddenly fell limply to the ground in a dead faint, allowing the truck to drive over her—without harming a hair.
>
> —*Barbara Schmitt*

> As I look at myself in the mirror, wondering if this is the same little girl who had her bright dreams for the future, who wanted to paint and show her vivid, joyful colors to the world, who wanted to work with disturbed children, who wanted to improve the world and just make everyone happy, I wonder not only why it is that with all my wonderful goals all I see staring back at me are blank, empty eyes devoid of feeling but also what it was that broke me, numbed me, caused me to lose myself, and whether I will ever see me again.
>
> —*Ilana Lederberger*

The airplane was full to the limit, not a seat left, when suddenly a man in a trench coat, wearing an Indiana Jones hat with dark Carrera sunglasses came on to the plane, where he innocently sat in the seat next to mine, stretching his arms, relaxing with a glass of Scotch in one of his hands, while his other hand was reaching into his trench coat, shuffling around, until he suddenly pulled out a big black Colt Forty-Five revolver so that he could attempt to hijack the plane.

—Steven Epstein

Last week three of my neighborhood friends and I were driving home from school during a particularly congested and rainy rush hour, when, having headaches from the long day of classes, we all unexpectedly started acting crazy in unison, jumping around in the back seat, until my friend Steven pointed out that the distinguished-looking fat man in the next car—a Lincoln Continental—was sitting alone in the driver's seat with one chubby hand, big shiny rings on his fingers, on the steering wheel, while the index finger of his other hand was lost halfway up his nose.

—Elana Wilen

It was a cold winter's night, when the moon was full, shining on the heavy shutters which hammered against the red-brick exterior of the house, that the tall ugly stranger was lurking awkwardly on the short artificial green grass leading up to the split-level house, when all of a sudden strange noises could be heard above the ferocious roar of the frosty wind—none of which scared me because it was only a TV horror show.

—David Reich

I was driving alone in my brand-new sports car late one warm summer's night, remembering how my father had persistently warned me about staying within the legal speed limit, when, noticing that I had unconsciously picked up considerable speed, as if the accelerator was in tune with the tempo of the rock song on the stereo cassette deck, I quickly stepped on the brakes to slow my car down—just in time, because at the very next corner sat a state trooper with a radar gun aimed at the road, ready to pull speeders over.

—David Reich

I was walking along the street yesterday at about one o'clock, when I saw a familiar face on a bus going toward Manhattan, so I decided to get on the bus as well, but it began to drive away, holding in it the handsome man who, I knew, held a few pages of my past in his possession, although I could not remember his name or how I knew him, remembering only that his favorite color was blue, just like the suit and tie he had on.

—Sharon Fishbein

As I walked down New York City's Avenue of the Americas last Sunday night at approximately 2 A.M., I was keeping up quite a quick pace, such as is perfectly normal in this situation, especially since the wind-chill factor was ten below that night, not to mention the fact that a very heavy pair of footsteps had been at a close and constant distance behind me for nearly half a mile, and those footsteps were now beginning to quicken and steadily gain on me.

—Gail Ghingo

Seeing the look of sheer happiness on my dear old great-grandmother's wrinkled but still young face, the bright twinkle in her light blue eyes, the rosy color in her still round cheeks, and her wide grin that stretched almost from one side of her face to the other, greatly relieved my entire family last night at about nine o'clock, when we saw Granny passing through the huge metal customs gate at Kennedy Airport in Queens, New York City.

—Gail Ghingo

This morning, when I woke up, I saw two little green men hovering over my bed, speaking to one another in a language that sounded like accelerated Spanish slang, which I reacted to in English or, more appropriately, New York slang, thus overwhelming the two small aliens, causing them to scamper throughout the house, yelling in a language which now sounded like childish English—as if they were in fact overwhelmed by fear of me—and finally revealing themselves from behind my sister as my two nieces with their Halloween costumes on.

—Frank Cuttita

Today as I was driving to school I saw a young woman at the side of the highway, standing as if she were lost, her perfect complexion accented by her silky white dress blowing in the wind, her image confusing me and arousing my curiosity to such a pitch that I raced back to the tall slender blonde to try to confirm that I had met her before, even though, when I stopped in front of her and opened the car door, I realized that she was the very woman who had been plaguing my dreams for the past two and a half years, and who would now insist, as I embraced her, that I had already exceeded my limit of seventy-five words!

—Frank Cuttita

READING ILANA'S SENTENCE

At the risk of spoiling your pleasure, we want to make a few observations on the sentence composed by Ilana Lederberger.

Ilana becomes a spectator of herself—both of her past self and of her present self—and explores some of the contradictions and tensions between the two. She literally looks at herself in the mirror, but she also scrutinizes her inner self. The mirror is a perfect metaphor for her inner reflections. As a spectator, she stands outside her active life, her doings, and reflects on her development. In the process, she evaluates herself. Because she is a spectator, she can, in reflecting on her two selves, bring them into relationship with each other.

In sum, her text represents very well the possibilities that are available to us when we become spectators. It is also a very good example of what a spectator text can be: *connected,* a pattern of relationships that can be both perceived and represented by a spectator. Her sentence demonstrates what can be done through the use of hypotaxis. The very connectedness of the sentence is itself a sign that she is engaging in relational or connecting thought. Her use of the present tense—"I look" rather than "I looked"—brings her close to the reader. But there is no denying the fact that the intertwined form of her thinking could be available only after the event. In that sense, her present self is also a past self—the self of yesterday, of the last six months, of an hour ago.

WHAT NOW? REVERTING TO THE PARATACTIC

1. Reconstruct Gorky's inner speech, moment by moment, as he watched the woman on the bridge.
2. Reconstruct the woman's inner speech as she stood on the bridge, thinking herself unobserved.
3. Imagine that the woman spotted Gorky watching her. Reconstruct the resulting inner speech that then might have formed in her mind.
4. Reconstruct Steven Epstein's inner speech from the moment the stranger boarded the plane. Use a dialogue form, between the Steven that is calm and sensible and the Steven that is prone to panic.
5. The fat man in Elana's text sees the students staring at him. Reconstruct his inner speech from the moment he notices them.
6. Imagine that the man in Sharon's text actually spotted Sharon. Construct his inner speech.
7. Place yourself in the same self-examining position as Ilana, and construct your inner speech. Use the form of a dialogue between your earlier idealistic self and your more recent disappointing self.
8. Barbara offers two versions of her sentence. Which do you think is the more effective? Why?

WHAT NEXT?

1. Our students did not claim that their sentences were yet perfectly shaped; they would have been happy to go on modifying them and reshaping them, their patterns and rhythms, if we had had more time together. Choose three or four that you think could be improved on, and try to write them more effectively.
2. Take one of our students' left-branching sentences and put the main point in the middle, with branches to both left and right. What differences in effect does this create? You will find it helpful to read the sentences aloud so that you can *hear* them.

Informative Hypotaxis

Let us now turn to an example of a kind of prose with a different intention: not to tell an amusing little story but to convey a body of information. In such prose, many of the parts are interdependent; they therefore need to be closely related in the text, which must be read as more than a mere heap of bits and pieces.

How would the cat make its appearance in a popular scientific text? Let us assume that the purpose of this text is not to specify details of the behavior of a particular cat but to offer a general statement whereby we can understand cats as a species in the natural world.

Here is a quotation from the *Encyclopedia Britannica*—part of an article intended for the general reader. Notice how it is organized into a sequence of related parts (we have italicized the words that signal relationships):

> *Even though* all cats are similar in appearance, it is difficult to trace the ancestry of individual breeds. *Since* tabby-like markings appear in the drawings and mummies of ancient Egyptian cats, present-day tabbies may be descendants of the sacred cats of Egypt. The Abyssinian *also* resembles pictures and statues of Egyptian cats. The Persian, *whose* coloring is often the same as that of mixed breeds (*although* the length of hair and the body conformation are distinctive), was probably crossed at various times with other breeds; the tailless, or Manx cat, may be derived from another species *or* may be a mutation.

In that text, with its relatively straightforward and modest use of hypotaxis, you will see that at five points the writer has clearly used the kinds of words that signal connection.

WHAT NOW?

Attempt a similar kind of text, as if for inclusion in an encyclopedia, on one of the following topics:

Cosmetics

Automobiles

Tape recorders

Dogs

Horses

Shoes

Birds as pets

If you feel that your knowledge is insufficient, invent appropriate "facts." The task is to produce an "authentic forgery."

A SEIZED MOMENT

It was the last five minutes of an afternoon class. We asked our students to seize the moment, hold it in one sentence. Here is Marina's:

> As I am sitting here, trying to seize a moment, my eyes wandering around the classroom from one to another and back into myself, I realize that all of us—tall and short, dark and light, happy or sad, willingly or not—are united here in this room by the power of our English professor to move our pens rapidly, under pressure, stopping the time, looking for an instantaneous event of our past or present that is already lost in the, even to us, unknown virgin woods of our memories.
>
> —*Marina Berkovich*

Appendix
Left- and Right-Branching Sentences

A Tree as Metaphor for a Sentence

Here is a simple sentence:

(1) The cat chased the rat.

Let us plant that sapling in the soil of our invention and have it take root (diagram 1).

Diagram 1

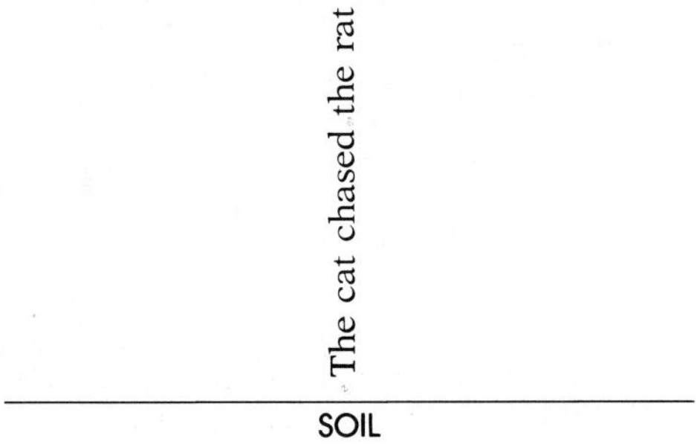

The cat chased the rat

SOIL

Now watch as it begins to sprout small twigs:

Diagram 2

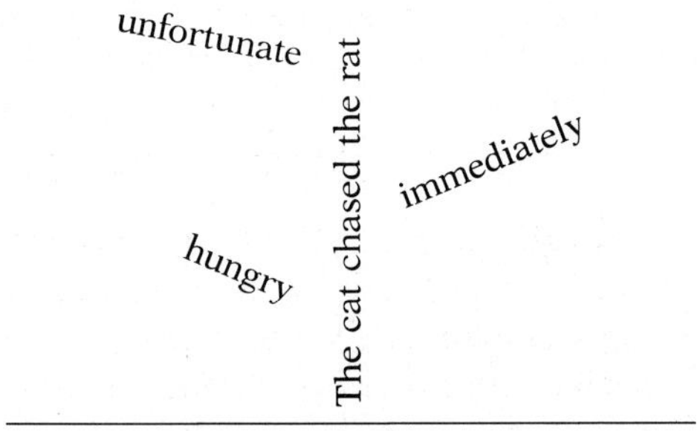

unfortunate

The cat chased the rat

immediately

hungry

(2) The hungry cat immediately chased the unfortunate rat.

Diagram 2 offers a clear picture of these facts:

1. *Hungry* is to *cat* as *unfortunate* is to *rat*.

2. *Hungry* particularizes *cat*.

3. *Unfortunate* particularizes *rat*.

4. *Immediately* particularizes *chased*.

5. Remove the twigs, and you still have a sentence.

6. Keep the twigs and remove the trunk, and you have no tree, no sentence.

Let us now watch the tree grow, with more and more branches (branches are more substantial than twigs).

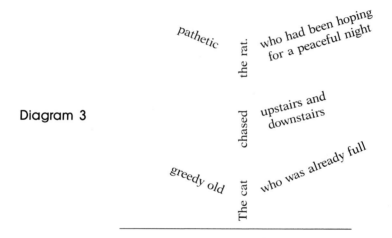

Diagram 3

When we translate the odd-looking tree in diagram 3 into a horizontal sentence, we find this (not the only possible form):

(3) The greedy old cat, who was already full, chased upstairs and downstairs the pathetic rat, who had been hoping for a peaceful night.

CONTEXTUALIZING BRANCHES

All the branches in (3) are particularizing the cat, the rat, or the chase. But branches can also be used to provide various kinds of contexts or settings in which the trunk takes place. Examine the following sentences, and decide what the branch does for the trunk in each case:

(4) a. As soon as we had gone to bed, the cat chased the rat.
    b. Although she had been bitten by the rat, the cat chased it.

c. If she felt sufficiently aroused, the cat chased the rat.
d. Wherever the rat dared to show his whiskers, the cat chased it.
e. Because she was a slave to instinct, the cat chased the rat.
f. The cat chased the rat, because she wanted to avenge past injuries.

We think you will agree that the respective branches answer these questions:

a. When?

b. Despite what?

c. Under what conditions?

d. Where?

e. Why? (For what reason?)

f. Why? (For what purpose?)

When these contextualizing branches occur *before* the trunk, the sentence is said to be left-branching—literally on the left as your eye scans the page [e.g., (4a) and (4e) above]. Here is another left-branching example:

(5) Even though I'd never done it before, when it came time to dive, *I quickly took the plunge.*

Note that the words underlined are the trunk; if you remove them you no longer have a sentence. Note also that in this sentence, the trunk is preceded by two left branches.

Now compare (5) with this:

(6) *I took the plunge* because, even though I was very nervous, I didn't want to be ridiculed by the more confident divers.

Like (4f) above, (6) is right-branching—that is, in each, the trunk comes first and to its right lie the branches.

Choosing Between Left- and Right-Branchers

How can you decide whether to shape a sentence so that it branches to the left or to the right? What factors should influence your decision? If you think you need to put the reader in the picture by offering the context of time and place, or by referring to a general question that you are going to examine in detail, it is effective to present this information as early as possible, that is, to go for a left-brancher. This shows proper consideration of your reader's needs and frees you to go on to concentrate on the trunk, the main point of your sentence. For example:

(7) After I had waited for an hour in a dark doorway on a fog-bound street corner in Fredericktown, my accomplice finally turned up.

The branching here is the same as in Gorky's first sentence. Both examples contextualize, and both gain some effect of suspense through delaying the disclosure of the trunk. But according to reliable tests, right-branching sentences are more quickly and easily understood by most readers. Compare (7) and (8), and you will probably see why this is likely to be the case:

(8) My accomplice finally turned up, much to my relief, after I had spent an hour waiting rather impatiently for him, in an inconspicuous doorway on a fog-bound street corner in Fredericktown.

Experts tell us that the mind processes the information offered in a hypotactic sentence by first storing away the essential data of the trunk and then adding on the branches one by one. It can clearly perform this task more easily with a right-brancher such as (8), because that is the sequence in which the sentence itself unrolls.

The disadvantage of a right-brancher, however, is that the opening words let the cat out of the bag. Knowing that the trunk of the present sentence is already in the bag, the reader's eye may well yield to the temptation to skim its branches in order to reach the trunk of the next sentence as quickly as possible. A simple experiment will illustrate the point. Let us convert Gorky's sentence into a right-brancher and feel the difference in effect. It will go something like this:

I saw a fair little lady stick out a sharp, pink little tongue at the moon, today, while I was watching her as she stood on the Troitzki bridge, dressed in cream-coloured stockings, holding on to the balustrade with her grey-gloved hands as though preparing to jump into the Neva.

Do you agree that this version is relatively flat, lacking the power to arouse expectation and wagging too long a tail? Once you know that she is safe and sound up there making rude gestures at the moon, do you really want to hear all about her gloves and the color of her stockings?

By contrast, in the left-brancher all the branches come first and the mind of the reader does not yet have a trunk to attach them to! So the mind has to hold on to a bundle of branches pending disclosure of the delayed trunk. When the trunk finally arrives, the reader's mind has to work very fast to attach all the branches almost simultaneously. But it is possible that this very experience is itself a source of pleasurable panic, which may help to account for the fact that most of our students find left-branchers more interesting, more arousing, though sometimes more difficult to grasp, especially at a single reading, than right-branchers. The beauty of left-branching hypotactic sentences is that they offer a field in which the writer can play games with the reader, and also a field in which the reader is drawn into playing games with the writer. What games are these? The writer sets down little cues and clues, little nudges and direction signs, little forecasts, little arousals, little promises. The reader construes them and builds up a set of anticipations about the rest of the sentence, expectations that are either totally frustrated, partly fulfilled, or totally fulfilled—though perhaps later than the reader had expected.

Read the following branches, and hold your expectations in your mind:

> Although she had always loved her mother, and indeed respected her, whenever she allowed herself to think hard about the women's movement, she . . .

What next?
Here now is the trunk:

> she had to admit to a twinge of disappointment that her mother had never carved out an independent life, never had a career, never really thought about her life except in domestic terms.

When you reached the point where the branches led into the trunk, what did you expect? We believe that, in one sense, you *could not know,* and that in another sense you *did know* what was coming, and knew fairly confidently. (Is this a ridiculous contradiction?) Because "although" was your point of departure, you knew intuitively that what the trunk would eventually disclose would be *a statement of a certain kind.* Even if you were not able to define the relationship between the meaning of the branches and the finally delivered meaning of the trunk, you nevertheless rightly expected—because of that one word "although"—that what the trunk finally delivered would run counter to what the branches had conceded. The eventual disclosure of the trunk therefore gave you the satisfaction of finding (a) the kind of statement that you had expected, thereby satisfying your expectations, and (b) something that you did not yet specifically know, a new disclosure. And we believe that it is in the interplay of (a) and (b) that both writer and reader can find satisfactions.

WHAT NOW?

Provide appropriate trunks for the following left branches:

1. When I itch, . . .
2. Since I'm desperately short of time, . . .
3. Although I'm desperately short of time, . . .
4. Whenever I'm desperately short of time, . . .

5. If you'll lend me your scarf, . . .
6. If ever I catch you bathing the cat again, . . .
7. When she finally returned home, even though she had often felt rather nervous about how her parents would receive her after her long and unexplained absence, . . .
8. Should you find that the engine overheats even though the dial reads "Normal," . . .
9. As she stood and looked at the model firetruck which she had worked on for so long and had finally completed, . . .
10. Whenever the plant shows signs of drooping, . . .

When you have provided trunks for those sentences, turn each one round so that the trunk precedes the branch(es), and consider the change in effect: What has been gained? What lost?

BALANCE

For an effect of balance, we can write a sentence that branches both to the left and to the right, with the trunk set firmly in the middle, so that the whole tree feels very steady. Here is an example of that kind of equilibrium:

> Although I hadn't seen him for many years and knew he had lost his hair and grown a beard, I recognized him immediately, for as he came down from the plane he walked with the limp that he had often been teased for in childhood.

CHECK

Whenever you produce an ambitious left-brancher, try to make sure that your sentence is not left-heavy—so overloaded with branches that your reader may be tempted to give up or, on finally reaching your long-delayed trunk wonder if all the effort was really worth it. Conversely, when you produce a longish right-brancher and put your cards on the table straightaway, try to avoid a floppy, loose, anticlimactic trail of branches.

Notes   Some experts claim the normal way to begin a sentence is with the subject and its main clause. But our advice is this: Experiment with various ways of fine-tuning. And read your own sentences with not only your eye but with your ear.

Let us share with you one of our own experiments, in which we gave an account of the same experience in two diametrically opposed ways. Which do you prefer? Why?

> Whenever I decided to trim the trees in the back yard, however carefully I placed the ladder with its rather slippery feet, which had lost their rubber caps, and however delicately I balanced the weight of my body, leaning

against the support of a branch whenever possible, the ladder invariably slid and slipped to throw me off.

I usually fell off the ladder when I tried to trim the trees in the back yard, because although I placed the ladder carefully on its slippery feet and I leaned against the support of a branch whenever possible to balance the weight of my body, the ladder, which had lost its rubber feet, invariably slid, slipped, and threw me off.

A CAVEAT

If we construct a sentence mechanically or by some rule book, adding branches in a mindless way to our trunk, then we shall end up with a sentence that sounds like a machine-made imitation of human language. For example, if we start with the trunk "The cat chased the rat," then merely add branches to each part of it, thus: "The cat, which was very greedy, chased with great ferocity the rat, which retreated in panic," the result sounds like a demonstration sentence from a grammar book. But real human language never resembles the artificial, dead language of grammar textbooks or workbooks. Doesn't the following sound more natural—more like the voice of someone genuinely interested in the chase?

> Whenever we dared forget to feed the old cat, who had a well-developed sense of natural justice, she would start to produce strange growling noises deep in her throat, sharpen her claws on the best sofa, lick her whiskers, stretch, and suddenly leap out at the poor old tame white rat, who for too long had been the apple of my mother's eye.

Is the rat overloaded with adjectives? Does the sentence's rhythm capture the slow cunning arousal of the cat, followed hotfoot by its sudden leap into action? We are still not sure. But the important point is this: As this sentence sits in a notebook, we have a text to look at, to reconsider, to play with, to retune. It will not evaporate. It is always there for when we are ready to perform a little delicate verbal surgery.

What Happened?
Representing Actions

Fillers: The Ordinary Become Extraordinary

> ### Getting out of the rain almost ruined the wedding
>
> Frank Collins wanted his girlfriend to look skyward during her college graduation in Waltham, Mass., and see his marriage proposal, so he chartered a plane with a banner and got ready to pop out the ring.
>
> One thing went wrong: The Bentley College commencement was held inside a huge tent because of rain, preventing his intended from seeing his message:
>
> "Sharon Fitzgerald, will you marry me?"
>
> "I can't believe this," Collins, of Weymouth, said Saturday after paying $160 to rent the plane. "I had no idea about this thing."
>
> He pulled the red-faced Miss Fitzgerald out of the tent, showed her the circling airplane, then produced the ring.
>
> She said yes.
>
> —*Daily Times* (Mamaroneck, New York), May 23, 1983

What do you first turn to when you pick up a newspaper? Front page headlines? Television listings? Sports? Obituaries? Editorials? Movie reviews? Stock market returns? The Op-Ed page? Classified ads? Are you looking for an apartment, a used car, a job? Or are you trying to find out what's new—in the world, the nation, your state, or your local community? If you're looking for any of these items, the table of contents on page 1 of any newspaper will direct you to the right spot. But if you're looking for "fillers"—as we so often are—you won't find them listed at all; they're spread through various pages in various sections of a newspaper. But what, you might ask, are fillers?

When make-up editors paste together the final layout of a daily newspaper, whether it's the *Los Angeles Times*, the *Washington Post*, the *New York Times*, or your local newspaper, they are left with small spaces to fill up. In newspaper talk, the pieces they choose, from wire services across the country and across the world, are called **fillers**—precisely because they are used to fill up empty spaces. We have discovered that many of our students regularly search out and read these bits of news about ordinary people—people like Frank Collins and Sharon Fitzgerald, like you and us. We read fillers for the same reason that we listen to gossip—because, as people, we're interested in what happens to other people; we want to know about their lives and loves, their wins and losses, their ups and downs, their adventures and mishaps. From the relative security of our living rooms or our back yards, we *watch*; we observe the ways others are or are not getting on in the world. We are *spectators*.

Fillers are, first of all, condensed stories: *something happened*. The "something" that "happened" represents a disruption in the way things usually are. There has been a jolt, a break, a hole in the floor of everyday life, an extraordinary moment in the ordinary ebb and flow of daily living or in our hopes or plans for the future. Frank Collins couldn't hold back the rain, and for a moment it didn't look as if his plan would work. But in the end Sharon said yes, and presumably Frank and Sharon will "live happily ever after."

EVALUATIONS: WHAT DO YOU THINK ABOUT IT?

"Did you hear what happened to Frank Collins?" we ask people, and then we tell them what happened. But we also mean more than we may say, because we never simply tell what happened. We also tell what we think about what happened. We **evaluate**—because we all have values. Whatever we do or say reflects our system of values. When we open a door or read a book or play the piano or take a walk or go to the movies or pound a nail, we are performing activities that involve our values. In the same way, when we perform verbal acts—talking and writing—these expressions, either implicitly or explicitly, involve our values.

We never tell a story without letting it be known, in some way, what we think of the events we are representing. By our mere selection of *what* we tell, we are in fact shedding light on what interests us and what matters to us. We are always asking or answering the unstated question: So what?

And so, what do *you* think of Frank Collins's escapade, his madcap adventure (note the evaluation in those words: *escapade, madcap adventure*)? Here are some of our students' responses:

So What?

—Ridiculous!
—Bizarre!
—What a waste of money!
—What a shame it rained!
—Sharon must have been mortified.
—What a romantic expression of love!
—Proposals should be private—what *is* the world coming to?
—What an egomaniac!

—Brilliant idea!
—That's something they'll always remember.
—That's something to tell their grandchildren about.
—How trivial!

Some of these are very brief judgments, short and sharp. All are evaluations, positive or negative; they either share/endorse/support the values implicit in Frank's action, or they reject/deny/negate those values. They either identify with Frank, or they stand back and judge him unsympathetically. Even apparently neutral observations—"that's something to tell their grandchildren about"—possess a distinct and recognizable tone—in this case, of approval. (You can't *hear* the original utterance, unfortunately, but you know very well that tone of voice often carries the evaluation.)

Other evaluations are not so quick, sharp, or easy because the events they represent are not so trivial. Things do not go well. In someone's life, the world has been rocked, jolted, perhaps irrevocably altered. And we may feel shaken. The ending is not a happy one, and we are reminded that the world is often unpredictable, hazardous, inexplicable. Consider the filler below about Bruce Lee:

Basketball player dies

OKLAHOMA CITY, May 14 (AP)—Bruce Lee, a reserve forward on the University of Oklahoma basketball team, died today of complications after a routine tonsillectomy, hospital officials said. Margaret Barett, a nursing supervisor at Deaconess Hospital, said that the cause of death had not been determined, but that Lee, 21 years old, had died after the operation, not during it.

—*New York Times*, May 15, 1983

We are told what happened: a 21-year-old basketball player died after a "routine tonsillectomy." But the evaluation is left implicit. What can we say about the event? How can we evaluate it? That it was unfortunate, untimely, yes ... But what else? This kind of filler evokes not our opinions but our puzzlement: What are we to make of it?

Evaluations: What Do You Make of It?

We continually try to make sense of our worlds, to *understand*. We recognize the trivial event and we recognize the serious event. We recognize Frank Collins and Bruce Lee. We know both good and bad endings; we know that's the way life is, filled with oppositions and contradictions: good and bad, birth and death, permanence and impermanence. We watch—we are spectators of others' lives—but our capacities for feeling nudge us to slip into others' shoes. So we find ourselves wondering about Bruce Lee's parents and about his friends. We wonder what went wrong in that "routine" operation.

Some of these daily turns of fortune move us, unsettle us, stay with us, long after we have closed the newspaper. We think about them, talk about them. And in talking—or in writing—we are attempting to make meaning, to figure things out, "to extend our control over a world that is not naturally disposed to serve our interests."* That is what evaluation is all about.

Because the filler is a condensed narrative, a strip, a slice that has been "cut from a stream of ongoing activity,"† we are often left *wondering:*

What else happened that was not reported?

What was the order of events?

How did the participants involved react?

What were the causes? The effects?

MAKING SENSE OF IT: THE CASE OF LAURA ETHEL CLARK

Newspaper space is limited. The make-up editor trims rough edges to tailor the goods. We are given a little information about the *who, what, when,* and *where*. But the *why* is usually left unanswered. And so, with a minimum of clues, we try to make sense of the event, to see the point of the story. Consider the following filler:

Garden invite

An 83-year-old great-grandmother convicted last year of growing marijuana in her Houston backyard thanked a judge for ending her probation last week, and invited him to see her garden. But Laura Ethel Clark told State Court District Judge Michael McSpadden that one plant—the marijuana she said she used to relieve her arthritis—would not be there. "There won't ever be any more of that," Mrs. Clark said.

—*Daily Times* (Mamaroneck, New York), May 15, 1983

What are we told? What are we left to wonder about?

THE FACTS	SPECULATION
WHO	
An 83-year-old great-grandmother	How many children, grandchildren, great-grandchildren does she have? What did they know

---

*Barbara Herrnstein Smith, *On the Margins of Discourse* (Chicago: University of Chicago Press, 1978), p. 85.
†Erving Goffman, *Frame Analysis* (New York: Harper & Row, 1974), p. 10.

THE FACTS   SPECULATION

about the "crime"? Did one of
them, perhaps, introduce her to
marijuana? Were they embarrassed, shocked, amazed, when
they found out, or is this action
characteristic of Mrs. Clark? Is
she something of a character?
Who did turn her on? Maybe a
doctor, whom she all this time
has been concealing? Maybe an
enlightened doctor who knew that
marijuana does suppress the pain
of severe arthritis? Is Mrs. Clark
suffering now? Is she really off
the stuff? How long had she
been using it? Can we believe
her when she says she won't grow
any more?

WHEN   How long have these laws been in
In 1982   effect? Are they being challenged?
Should they be challenged? Was
there a time when people could
grow whatever they wanted in
their back yards? When was that?

WHERE   What are the laws in Houston
In Houston   regarding marijuana? She had
been convicted and served probation for a year: is that typical for
Houston? Did she also pay a fine?
Did she attend drug rehabilitation
classes? Are these local, state, or
federal laws (possibly state laws,
because Judge McSpadden is a
State District Judge)? (Mexico is
close by. . . .)

WHAT   How was the crime discovered?
A crime: growing marijuana in the   Did one of her neighbors squeal
back yard   on her? (Surmise: She sent some
freshly grown vegetables—string
beans, carrots, lettuce—to a
friend; the friend cooked up a

THE FACTS	SPECULATION
	batch of string beans that were inadvertently mixed with marijuana; the friend ended up having a massive trip; an ambulance was called; the friend was diagnosed as "potted," etc.)
She had been convicted and served probation for a year	What are the laws in Houston regarding marijuana? Was her sentence typical? Did she also have to pay a fine? Did she have to attend drug rehabilitation classes?
WHY She was growing it to relieve her painful arthritis.	Why do events like these happen? What questions, issues about contemporary life can we infer from this case? (We argue: When the laws of a state prohibit an 83-year-old woman from finding relief from pain, isn't there something wrong? Why shouldn't she have that right? She presumably wasn't hurting anyone. She was affording herself relief that no one else could offer her. Isn't the law going too far? Shouldn't there be exceptions to the rule? Shouldn't the law be changed? But, we hear another voice: If they let her grow it, they'll have to let others. When will it stop?)

As we try to make sense of the event, the story arouses in us various frames of mind: observing, inferring, speculating, wondering, questioning, probing, surmising, imagining—particularly as we explore the *why*. We might imagine an editor in a Houston local newspaper taking up the issues:

> It is about time marijuana laws in this state were revised. What has happened to the rights of the individual when so-called laws of this state prevent one from gaining relief from pain? Particularly if that one is elderly and ailing? The laws should serve to protect rather than harm the well-being of others. But the opposition will protest: one never knows, particularly in this state of ours that is so often infiltrated by foreign drug traffic,

who is beyond suspicion. How do we know that Mrs. Laura Ethel Clark, an 83-year-old Houston great-grandmother, is not a drug pusher?
   Let us be reasonable. . . .

The story insists that we evaluate, that we become participants as well as spectators, that we "enter" it as concerned participant-observers who have comments to make about the issues raised—in this case, about the implicit values of a society where the elderly, the ill, must abide by rules that run counter to their needs. Mrs. Clark's case then, affords us an opportunity—as all stories do—to move the *particular* into a larger, more *general* context, to reflect upon the values, questions, and issues that push this case beyond the individual and evaluate the issues that are called forth by the case.

Transformations

A story invites us, as well, to enter, to identify with the characters and issues involved through **transformations**. By recasting a story into another form, we often come to see what we had not seen before as mere spectators. As writers, we can become participants—we can *understand* (literally, "step under")—and from the inside, we can *comprehend* (literally, "seize" or "grasp")—the meaning. As we enter the story, it enters us, and we make it our own.

MRS. CLARK'S LETTER

Here is one of our students, Karen Dyrbala, taking on the role of Mrs. Clark writing to her great-granddaughter:

> To my Great-granddaughter,
>   I'm writing to you to explain my reasons for growing marijuana. I hope that you will think of me as you always have and not as a criminal. Someday when the neighbors who turned me in get old I hope they never have to deal with the pain of arthritis. I feel I must explain to you that I did not mean to cause you any embarrassment. Sometimes when a person is in pain, as I am, they resort to any method that will relieve that pain. That is why I was growing the marijuana. I must tell you though that I have learned my lesson. Judge McSpadden will not see any more marijuana growing in my garden. My only problem now is making sure he doesn't go in the spare bedroom.
>
> Your loving Great-grandmother,
Laura Ethel Clark

In fictions, more than in real life, we have the power, the possibilities, the options, to make things turn out the way we want them to. We remember the class where "Mrs. Clark's letter" was read: We were listening to the voice of a woman who was trying to explain herself, who was distressed that she might be thought a criminal, who suffered from a disabling illness, who wanted her great-granddaughter to understand and be reassured that "I have learned my lesson." And then, in the last line, we heard her give Judge McSpadden a sharp, swift kick! Perhaps we feel amused, relieved, delighted, that the old woman (in Karen's fiction) has the last word. We remember the students' gasp after Karen read the last line and then their laughter—and, yes, applause. (Karen, by the way, discovered that she could make others laugh!)

WHAT NOW?

1. Reply to Mrs. Clark as her great-granddaughter. You will have to decide whether you approve or disapprove of your great-grandmother's subversive activities, or whether you are of two minds, seeing both sides and trying to resolve them.
2. Write as an editor for your local newspaper supporting or criticizing Judge McSpadden's handling of the Clark case.

WHY DID SHE SHOOT HER HUSBAND?

Bobby Thorn came to Copenhagen from her home in Bath, England, and shot her husband Tuesday—out of a cannon.

Roy Thorn, 46, took it all rather well.

Dressed in a white jump suit with a white-starred red stripe down the side, he climbed a ladder to the business end of a 28-foot-long cannon, gave a rather hesitant wave and slipped down the tube.

Seconds later he was flying through the air, his wife Bobby standing with her finger on the firing button.

"It was great fun, but I wouldn't want to do it every day for a living," he said afterward.

The stunt at Bakken, the world's oldest amusement park, came about through a competition in Britain's national newspapers called the "Great Dreams Contest."

—*Daily Times* (Mamaroneck, New York), May 4, 1983

A friend of ours, Joyce Kinkead, slipped into the shoes of Roy Thorn—just as he was to be shot out of that cannon by his wife. Here is her transformation.

Great Dreams

Jump-suited,
Red stars blazing down my side,
I watched the park crowd,
Smiled confidently.

When I saw the long black tube,
I strode toward it with her—
the woman with the finger.
Climbed the ladder to its mouth,
Hesitantly waved,
Let it swallow me.

Just as the drum beat bore the blast,
As that finger flirted with the cannon's firing button,
I wondered if she remembered, now,
Last night's spat.

—Joyce Kinkead

WHAT NEXT?

1. Speculate on the case of Bobby and Roy Thorn. Whose dream was it? If it was Bobby Thorn's dream, why, do you suppose, a woman had as her "great dream" the desire to shoot her husband out of a cannon? Where do you suppose the dream came from? If it was his dream, why do you suppose he wanted to be "shot"?
2. What do you imagine Bobby Thorn was thinking as she pressed the firing button?
3. How do you—as a spectator, one who has read this text—evaluate Bobby Thorn's stunt? Do you find this a worthy dream? Ridiculous? Amusing? Are you tempted to judge her or him—if so, in what way?
4. What are *your* great dreams? Can they be realized, enacted publicly? Are they private? How might they be evaluated by another, by a spectator?

CHARLES'S JOY RIDE

Here is a filler—one of our favorites. In fact, Charles has become a real presence in several of our classes.

6-year-old boy quite a driver

Six-year-old Charles Boyd wanted to visit his father at work Monday morning in Kings Mountain, N.C., so he hopped into his mother's car and started driving.

One-half hour and five miles later, just as he was getting ready to turn onto Interstate 85, the car rolled off a road and bumped to a stop.

Charles opened the door and climbed out, startling the man who had been driving behind him.

"He thought he was following a drunk, but he never saw the driver," Kings Mountain police dispatcher Roy Dyer said.

A little lost, Charles rode with the man to Garlock Industries in Gastonia, where his father works. That's about 20 miles from his home.

Dyer said an officer asked Charles how he worked the brakes and the accelerator, "and he said he looked through the windshield until it was clear, and then he'd get down and push the gas. Then he'd jump back up and steer until the car slowed down."

—*Daily Times* (Mamaroneck, New York), May 10, 1983

Notes

1. What are the *facts* of this account: who, what, when, and where? (For the *what*, relate what happened first, second, third, etc.; for the *who*, recount who the participants were, who the spectators.)

2. Do you consider Charles's mother a participant, a spectator, or both?

3. Is the man driving behind Charles a participant, a spectator, or both?

4. How do you *evaluate* this event? Is it surprising, alarming, humorous, or what?

5. If you were telling or writing of this event, what point might you want to make?

WHAT NOW?

Try writing the transformations suggested below *before* you go on to read how some of our students responded to Charles's adventure.

1. As one of the participants, represent the event as *it is happening*.
2. As one of the participants now removed in time from the event—it has already happened—imagine that you are recounting the event to someone who was not involved.
3. As a spectator—one who was in no way involved in the event—represent the event to a particular audience:
   a. As an editor of a local newspaper writing an editorial about today's children
   b. As a friend of Charles's parents writing to another friend about the incident
   c. As a child psychologist writing a clinical report about Charles's behavior
   d. As a teacher writing to a friend about this child in her class.

Our Students
as Participants
and Spectators

PARTICIPANTS

Charles (Neil)

The driver behind (Roberta)

Charles's mother (Lisa)

SPECTATORS

Charles (Lisa)

Charles's father (Fillmore)

A local newspaper editor (Neil)

Charles (During the Event)

Shoot, I wish I could visit my pa, but ma's not here and there ain't no one to drive me there. I know I could get there myself, but they won't let me. The car's right over there and . . . Oooh, mama left the keys here. Gee, I could drive to pa's myself. I seen ma do it and I know I could do it myself. Right, I got nothin' to lose and it'd be fun. Let's see, first ma puts the keys in here and turns them. . . . Awright, the thing's started. O.K., no what, um, yeah, they pull this thing and start drivin'. Sheeoot, I can't see outa the window and still reach the gas pedal. Oh boy, I gotta find a way. Waitaminnit! If I look out the window, jump on the pedal, then let her coast while I steer . . . ? Let's see. . . . Hot dog, it works. . . . It's goin' slow but at least it's movin'. Momma goes this way for a while then turns near the park. Here we go! O.K. Made it. Now I go straight till I hit the highway. I hope I'm goin' the right way . . . wait . . . yeah there it is . . . the highway. This is a harder turn than the other one. I hope I can . . . Shoot! . . . missed the road, now what, I ain't figured out how to back up yet. Geez, I hope the car ain't messed up. I better go see. Whew. Looks O.K. Maybe that man in the other car knows how to back up.

"Hey mister, you know how to back this up?"

"I drove it out here. . . ."

"I'm gonna visit my dad. . . ."

". . . at Garlock in Gastonia. . . ."

"You'll take me there? Gee thanks."

I knew I'd figure out a way to get to see my dad.

—Neil Frederickson

The Driver Behind (During the Event)

"Put that book down and look. I tell you what Mildred, that's the damnedest thing I ever seen in my life."

"What's that, Billy Jack?"

"Well, that car up yonder. D'you ever in your life see anything weave so bad? Hell, he's got more moves than a box of Exlax. I just don't dare git close enough to see who or *what* is drivin'."

"They're probably just drunk, Billy Jack. When we get over to Ersel's station, we maybe oughta call the police. They can check them out before they hurt somebody."

"Shoot. If we even make it that far. Geez, Mildred, now just take a look at that sign on the back of that thing. 'DRINKIN AND DRIVIN' DON'T MIX' . . . now ain't that something. You reckon that's one of them midgets from over to Rahliegh?"

"Lordy, I wouldn't know. But that intersection's comin' up and they'll never make that turn. Now you just mark my words."

"Jesus Christ! Look at that, Mildred. They've drove clean off the damn road."

"Now what did I tell you. You reckon we ought to stop to see if anybody's hurt or anything?"

"Yeah, we'd better check it out. But Mildred honey, you know what they always say . . . The Lord looks after drunks and kids."

—Roberta Meacham

Charles's Mother (During the Event)

"Charlie, Charlie, where are you?" Damn kid, I hate playing hide and seek.

"Charlie, you get in here right now or you're gonna get it." He wants another one. The hell with that. I can't even handle this one. No more babies for me.

"Charlie, Charlie!" I'll bet he's hiding outside. Damn kid.

"Charlie! Charlie!" Oh my god, where's my car?

"CHARLIE!"

"Oh no, oh no, oh no. Help, my baby's been stolen, my car's been kidnapped. Help."

Calm. Be calm. Breathe. O.K. Breathe some more. Go back inside. Call police. Be calm. Breathe. Pick up phone. Dial. Very good. Calm. Take deep breath. Oh, why the hell aren't they answering?

"Oh, help, someone has stolen my baby and my car. Yes, he's six. Blonde hair, blue eyes. Yes, about 40 lbs. Omigod. Have you found him? Is he dead? Is my baby O.K.? Where is my baby?"

"What, no. No! He . . . what? No! My husband is bringing him home? Could you explain this to me again? Yeah. O.K. Thank you."

I'm gonna kill him.

—Lisa Portnoy

Charles (After the Event)

Mommy's mad still. Daddy's not. Everybody got so loud. Yelling. Mommy yells loudest. I just wanted to see Daddy at work. Driving's easy. Wasn't even scared. Uh uh. Not me. I didn't hurt the car. I did what Daddy always does. Pushed on the pedal to go, the other pedal when I wanted to stop. Said shit when the light went red like Daddy does. I didn't hurt nothin'. The car fell off the road when I was drivin'. I got out and a nice man took me to Gastonia. To the cops. That was fun. I'm gonna be a cop when I grow up. Got to ride in the cop car to where Daddy works. He was so surprised. Daddy's funny. They let me turn on the screamer in the cop car. It was fun. Daddy and me and the cops went to get Mommy's car. They all pushed and pushed to put the car back on the road. Daddy and me got in. He drove. Daddy explained how I was real lucky to be alive and how I was supposed to tell Mommy from now on when I wanted to go somewhere. Mommy was cryin' when I got home. She was real mad though. I got a spankin'. Didn't hurt none but Mom always stops after I cry. I'm gonna have a baby. A brother or sister. I can't wait till it's as old as me so I can teach it how to drive!

—Lisa Portnoy

Charles's Father (After the Event)

Charlie is one hell of a kid. You know, he is my only kid, and I really like him. You know, we are very close buddies when we are together. In fact, two months ago, Charlie risked his life just to visit me.

My wife, as usual, wouldn't drive him down (we've been divorced for about three years now) and no one else was around. And do you know what Charlie boy did? He drove Martha's car, pushing the gas and looking up to see if all was clear. I was at Seven Sisters having a jug with the lads and the officer comes in and tells me Charlie is at the station. I really panicked. I thought something had happened. He said Charlie had had an accident and was well, but the stranger he had it with was pretty mad. Charlie, old boy, cried a bit, but he was fine. I rang up Martha and gave her an ear full. The stranger wanted to sue, but we never heard from him again. Charlie is the greatest kid. I should have had more kids like him.

—Fillmore Apeadu

The Hazards of Leaving Children Unattended: An Editorial

Unwatched children are becoming more and more frequent in today's society. Witness the case of Charles Boyd, a six-year-old, who, while left unattended, decided to drive to his father's place of employment 20 miles away, on his own. Finding the car keys, which had carelessly been left lying around, young Charles started the car and managed to drive five miles before running off the road.

Charles showed great imagination in driving the car, but this does not change the fact that he is only six years old and could have caused an accident on the highway. It was sheer luck that no one was hurt and Charles was stopped before an accident occurred. Even so, when he stopped, he was far from home and could have fallen victim to any number of hazards, not the least of which was possible kidnapping. Luck was again with Charles, that a kind man was in the car behind him and was able to help him.

Not all children would be so lucky. There are many cases where such situations end in disaster. But what can be done about the problem? Certainly, the first thing is to try not to leave such young children unattended. Have a neighbor look in on the child once in a while. But if it is necessary to leave the child alone, make sure he knows what he can and can't do. Also, don't leave any hazardous or tempting things (like car keys) lying around. Educate the child well and try not to leave him unattended for too long a period. Remember, the safety of your child is your responsibility, whether you are there all the time or not.

—*Neil Frederickson*

A Classroom Discussion

J.S.: So, what do you see as the differences between the participant accounts and the spectator accounts?

ROSEMARY: The participants' texts are more interesting; you have the feeling that you're really there, at the moment.

MARK: You're right there in Charles's mind when he decides he can get the car going; you see him figuring things out—he's a smart kid! The event hasn't happened yet—so you feel suspense: Is he going to make it? What's going to happen? Even though you know already. . . .

JOE: Same thing with the driver. He really doesn't know what's going on. Can you imagine driving behind a six-year-old? You would have thought the guy was crazy or drunk or asleep—or very short! You might have thought you were going crazy yourself. "Billy Jack" doesn't know what the heck is happening. And we really feel it, in the dialogue between those two people.

TAMMY: Billy Jack and Mildred! That text is one of the funniest things I've ever read. I didn't even think about *where* the event took place, but Roberta made the whole thing sound Southern, just because she was a careful reader; she noticed the reference to North Carolina. Terrific!

J.S.: And what about Charles's mother? How does she represent the story—to herself—she's all alone in the house.

MARK: It's a dialogue, too—between her inner self and her outer self (I almost said inself and outself—I like that!). Anyway, all the while she's trying to figure out what's going on, we hear her talking. She calls out to Charles and then she mutters to herself. We even know that she feels fed up with kids and doesn't want another one—even though her husband does.

SALLY: We feel all the things she's going through—she's irritated, annoyed, puzzled, exasperated, breathless, anxious—all in a few moments.

J.S.: Right—how does she do it?

ROSEMARY: The sentences are all paratactic—in fact, all the participants' texts are paratactic because the participant is *in* it—he can't see the forest for the trees, and so we *feel* the language capturing the immediacy. Hey, that's probably why I like these texts better. The parataxis—the verbs are mostly in the present. The language is doing all this work!

J.S.: And what about evaluation? Do the participants evaluate their experiences?

JOE: No, because they're *in* it—like Rosemary said—and not only haven't they figured out what's going on, but they don't know what it means. The driver behind is trying like mad to put the pieces together—so is Charlie's mother—but they can't.

SALLY: But, right at the end, when Charlie's mother knows where Charles is and knows that he's safe and knows what he's done, then she . . .

MARK: Becomes a spectator!

J.S.: And evaluates?

JOE: In a sense, wait . . . Sure she does. She makes a resolution based on her values; she says, "I'm gonna kill him."

J.S.: Right—she steps out of the moment and plans for the future. Once she knows he hasn't been kidnapped or harmed, once she knows that her car's O.K., she instantaneously becomes a spectator preparing for the future. The present gives way to the past as she plans the future out of her own system of values.

ROSEMARY: And that's what the spectators are all doing, they've all stepped back—they've got the distance now, so they can put things in order and make some sense out of them, from the outside.

TAMMY: Even Charles. All the time he's talking about Mommy being mad, he's patting himself on the back about his accomplishments! I can imagine him telling about this event all through his life, bragging about what he was able to do when he was six years old.

MARK: And Charles's father—he tells the story to *fit* his view: Charles was a smart kid whose mother kept him from seeing his father—and he found a way.

JOE: But look at the editor's account—look what happens to the story now. All the immediacy is lost, and there's a moralistic voice pointing a finger at neglectful parents. He's doing a lot of presuming— he says the mother was careless.

J.S.:   What else happens to the story?

ROSEMARY: The general truth is made more important than the story.

SALLY: The story becomes a case.

J.S.:   Brilliant! The event becomes subordinate to the message; the present and the past give way to the future—to a warning to all parents: Don't leave your child alone. Don't leave your keys lying around. Educate your child well. And so on. The particular gives way to the general. Charles isn't even Charles anymore (or Charlie); he becomes "the child."

WHAT NOW? TEXTS TO TRANSFORM

Here, now, are some other fillers for you to work on, by transforming them into other texts, as participants and as spectators. Try to unearth the questions buried within the given facts, and to speculate on and evaluate the issues implied within the events.

'Mother Superior' becomes nun at 68

Ruth Reilly, a widow who raised 11 children, was surrounded by 10 of them as she was professed a Roman Catholic nun, and said she never had second thoughts about joining the Ursuline Order at age 68.

"I don't feel self-conscious about my age at all. It has never been a factor in my life," Sister Ruth said after taking her vows at Mount Saint Ursula Chapel on East 198th Street in the Bronx.

When asked to join the Ursuline Order, "I sold my house and got rid of my furniture with absolutely no second thoughts. It's where God wants me."

Her husband, Newark attorney Walter Reilly, died of a heart attack in 1957 after 24 years of marriage.

The Reillys had eight sons, three daughters and 23 grandchildren. Ten of her children and some friends were present for "a big celebration" after she took her vows Saturday.

After raising her family, Mrs. Reilly attended Kean College in Union, N.J., graduating summa cum laude.

She also did social work in Montclair, N.J., specializing in the care of retarded children. Her oldest son, Walter, is mentally retarded and lives in a home in Woodbridge, N.J.

—*Daily Times* (Mamaroneck, New York), May 23, 1983

Woman awakes at her funeral

ADDIS ABABA—An Ethiopian woman, believed to have died in childbirth, suddenly regained consciousness during her funeral procession.

The Amharic-language daily, Addis Zemen, reported yesterday that Seida

Mohammed was thought to have died in labor.

But when her body was being taken for burial, she suddenly moved.

She was rushed to a nearby army hospital where she delivered a stillborn child.

The newspaper said the woman is now recovering at the hospital.

—New York Post, May 21, 1984*

Cabby doesn't want to feel left out

A whimsical departure from the myriad signs telling riders what not to do in taxicabs is a hand-lettered one, in a childlike scrawl:

PLEASE!

NO KISSING IN BACK SEAT OF TAXI

(unless driver included)

—New York Times, May 11, 1984

Vandals hit Stonehenge

SALISBURY, England (AP)—Vandals on Saturday sprayed soccer slogans in blue paint on five of the ancient monoliths at Stonehenge, a mysterious prehistoric circle of altar-like stones that is one of Britain's top tourist attractions. Two men were being questioned by police in connection with the incident at the monuments on Salisbury plain in Wiltshire. The slogans, in six-inch high letters, say "PFC," the initials of Portsmouth Football Club, "Pom-pey," the club's nickname, and "Kick to Kill Pompey." A custodian at the monuments, which date back to 2100 B.C. and which archeologists believe may have been built by ancient astronomers, said only time will tell whether the paint could be removed. He noted that a slogan painted 15 years ago was still visible on wet days and that another painted four years ago had also resisted chemical removers.

—Daily Times (Mamaroneck, New York), May 15, 1983

Ruttman gets pole spot

DOVER, Del., May 14 (AP)—A day after his father's death from a heart attack, Joe Ruttman won the pole position today for Sunday's Mason-Dixon 500 Grand National stock-car race in a record time of 139.616 miles per hour.

—New York Times, May 15, 1983

*See Edwin Morgan's instamatic poem, page 229.

Chimney gets him into jam

A 24-year-old man who got stuck in the chimney of a country club in Middleton, Ohio, said he was only trying to make a delivery. But police didn't believe him, and charged him with burglary.

"We read him his rights when he was standing on the damper inside the fire-place," said police Capt. Earl Smith after Michael Linton was arrested Tuesday.

Linton was found by Forest Hills Country Club custodian Bill Steele, who said he heard a voice from the fireplace asking, "Hey, give me a cigarette before they take me to jail."

—Daily Times (Mamaroneck, New York), May 15, 1983

200 cheer as grocery collapses into ground

BELLE VERNON, Pa., May 14 (AP)—A supermarket built over an abandoned coal mine sank into shifting ground and broke apart Friday as about 200 spectators cheered.

"You wouldn't believe how morbid people are," Police Chief Chris Kircher said of the collapse of the Red & White grocery.

"They were all cheering while the place was falling apart."

The building, worth an estimated $100,000, was built on concrete pilings over the old mine shafts. The store's nine employees and a number of customers were evacuated earlier Friday when cracks were discovered in the walls.

—New York Times, May 15, 1983

Pep talk

The Coalinga, Calif., City Council scheduled a town meeting in a park today to give hardy residents a "pep talk" to help their recovery from the recent devastating earthquake.

—Daily Times
(Mamaroneck, New York), May 15, 1983

Class by himself

BRADFORD, Pa. (UPI)—D. Edgar Cohn took all the door prizes at his 75th high school reunion—he was the only member of the class able to attend.

There are two other survivors from Cohn's class, but one was too ill to attend and the other couldn't be located, school officials said.

Being the lone classmate at the reunion didn't bother him too much, he said.

—Herald Journal (Logan, Utah), June 12, 1983

Goose is cooked

PITTSBURGH (UPI)—Charles Wood, Jr. found out what a pet goose is worth in court—at least $140.

Wood, 18, of Pittsburgh, was found guilty of criminal mischief Friday, fined $40 plus court costs and directed to pay $100 restitution to Gary and Andrea Simpson, who owned the pet goose, Pebbles, which disappeared May 27.

Acting on a tip, Mrs. Simpson said she and a Humane Society officer found goose feathers in the basement of Wood's home down the street shortly after Pebbles disappeared from their back yard May 27.

— *Herald Journal* (Logan, Utah), June 12, 1983

WHAT NEXT? ECONOMY VERSUS SUFFICIENCY

To appreciate the skills of the journalists who write effective fillers, all you need to do is (a) take an odd episode from your own life and (b) translate it into a filler. Part of the task is to provide contextual information that is sufficient but controlled: enough to forestall a lot of questions, but not so much that it squeezes the story dry.

When you introduce the people in your filler, you'll have to consider what information a reader will absolutely need to know in order to make sense of the story. The story of Charles, for example, would have been pointless if he had been fifteen: his age is of central significance to the story.

11

Who/What Matters?
Representing Reactions
and Evaluations

What Matters? To Whom?

The names of people who appear in fillers are unknown to the world at large. They are not household names as are Marilyn Monroe or John Lennon or Marvin Gaye or Michael Jackson or Ronald Reagan, who are so much in the public eye (at this moment in our histories) that, dead or alive, they make news.

But nothing is inherently trivial. Events that to the world may seem trivial, touch someone, mean something to someone. It is what our minds do with and make of an event that matters, that infuses it with values.

DEATH OF A LOCAL LIBRARIAN

Consider this: a local librarian dies, leaving her books to the library; the event could become a filler like this:

Local Librarian Leaves Own Books

Bess Smith left her extensive private collection of nineteenth- and twentieth-century children's books to the Ogden Public Library, with this stipulation: children, as well as scholars and researchers, be permitted to handle the books. "I want to know my books will be used by those whom they were written for," she is reported to have said.

To the poet William Stafford, Bess Smith matters in ways that cannot be captured in a news item; she is more significant to him than the "great national events," about which he is ironic. Of her death—to the question "So what?"—he answers with a poem: she mattered. Her life and death move him to celebration and remembrance.

Bess

Ours are the streets where Bess first met her
cancer. She went to work every day past the
secure houses. At her job in the library
she arranged better and better flowers, and when
students asked for books her hand went out
to help. In the last year of her life
she had to keep her friends from knowing
how happy they were. She listened while they
complained about food or work or the weather.
And the great national events danced
their grotesque, fake importance. Always.

Pain moved where she moved. She walked
ahead; it came. She hid; it found her.
No one ever served another so truly;
no enemy ever meant so strong a hate.
It was almost as if there was no room
left for her on earth. But she remembered
where joy used to live. She straightened its flowers;
she did not weep when she passed its houses;
and when finally she pulled into a tiny corner
and slipped from pain, her hand opened
again, and the streets opened, and she wished all well.

—Stories That Could Be True

DEATH OF A SUPERSTAR

"Others die and yet by this death we are a little shaken, we feel it, America." Edwin Morgan, the Scottish writer, is here lamenting the death of a public figure, a household name—Marilyn Monroe. More than twenty years after her death, she still makes news. Her address book was recently sold at auction for several thousand dollars. Biographies abound; a Broadway musical, *Marilyn*, was based on her life; and her death in August 1962 in Los Angeles is still shrouded in mystery.

Whose fault? Who is to blame? Where were the men, the husbands, the photographers, the fans, the relentless, peering spectators of Monroe—when she needed them? And how are we to evaluate the event—this is what Morgan wants to know:

The Death of Marilyn Monroe

What innocence? Whose guilt? What eyes? Whose breast?
Crumpled orphan, nembutal bed,
white hearse, Los Angeles,
DiMaggio! Los Angeles! Miller! Los Angeles! America!
That Death should seem the only protector—

That all arms should have faded, and the great cameras and lights
    become an inquisition and a torment—
That the many acquaintances, the autograph-hunters, the
    inflexible directors, the drive-in admirers should become
    a blur of incomprehension and pain—
That lonely Uncertainty should limp up, grinning, with
    bewildering barbiturates, and watch her undress and lie
    down and in her anguish
call for him! call for him to strengthen her with what could
    only dissolve her! A method
of dying, we are shaken, we see it. Strasberg!
Los Angeles! Olivier! Los Angeles! Others die
and yet by this death we are a little shaken, we feel it,
America.
Let no one say communication is a cantword.
They had to lift her hand from the bedside telephone.
But what she had not been able to say
perhaps she had said. 'All I had was my life.
I have no regrets, because if I made
any mistakes, I was responsible.
There is now—and there is the future.
What has happened is behind. So
it follows you around? So what?'—This
to a friend, ten days before.
And so she was responsible.
And if she was not responsible, not wholly responsible, Los Angeles?
    Los Angeles? Will it follow you around? Will the slow
    white hearse of the child of America follow you around?

—Poems of Thirty Years

Instamatic Texts

Fillers are usually *verbal,* that is, they are represented in/by words; but they can also be visual—news photographs, images.

Edwin Morgan is aroused by both and has written a series of *Instamatic Poems,* in which he represents an event *as it is happening*—the very instant. It's as if he is a news photographer who just happened to be on the spot when something odd, bizarre, extraordinary occurred, and clicked his camera at that very moment. But instead of a photograph, he offers words.

Does he let the event speak for itself? Does he evaluate? Does he nudge us toward evaluation? If so, how? Implicitly or explicitly?

Innsbruck July 1971

A furious baker with wasps in his pastry
has sucked a swarm of them into the bag

of a vacuum-cleaner and fixed the bag
to a gas-pipe. But in this picture
the bag has just burst, and the man is falling
backwards black with clouds of stings.
The furious wasps have a baker in their pastry.

London June 1971

The manager of a jeweller's shop
has with difficulty climbed onto the sill
and is measuring the window-breadth
against his wings.
He is eager to fly out over the traffic.
His secretary, Miss Bagge,
whom he sacked that morning for pocketing four rings,
is standing behind him. She fails to see the wings.
Having laced his afternoon tea with LSD
she watches his shoulders heave, and grins.

Naples February 1972

In the dead centre of this solemn picture
the corpse of an 84-year-old butcher
is laid out. Candles all round the bed
throw shifting shadows over his large family
and neighbours, properly wailing and praying
or properly stolid and silent.
But what the lens has seized
is the indescribable change
in faces on the very threshold
of ludicrous shock
as the old man crustily brushing aside
his death certificate and extreme unction
has opened his mouth wide
and calls for bread and salami.

WHAT NOW?

Look closely at the photographs on the next two pages. Then select any
of them, and write an instamatic text that captures the event in a neutral
way in all its particularity, as if your pen were a camera.

Now write a second version that expresses an evaluation.

Reactions to Inaction

A CRY FOR HELP IGNORED I

Death screams ignored

CHICAGO (AP)—Neighbors had ignored screams from a South Side apartment where a woman, her two daughters and a niece were found stabbed to death Wednesday, police said. There was one survivor, the woman's 19-month-old daughter. She may have been spared because she is too young to identify the killer, said police Cmdr. Thomas Faragoi. Relatives will take care of the child. Police identified the victims as Terri Dunning, 28; her daughters Kimberley, 5, and Michelle, 9, and niece Tiffany, 9. All died of stab wounds, Faragoi said. The woman was found in a corridor and the children in a bedroom. A door to the apartment was forced open, and the victims fought their attacker, Faragoi said. A blood-stained knife was found at the scene and a trail of blood led to the sidewalk.

—*Daily Times* (Mamaroneck, New York), May 19, 1983

This is a news story we all, most likely, have read in one form or another: a cry for help ignored, followed by a death. Linda Thorn read of such an event in a newspaper and subsequently took up her pen to lash out at those who refuse to become participants.

"Death Screams Ignored"

My ears covered
I writhe
Waiting, pleading
For God's sake stop the screams
Whatever it is, I don't want to hear any more
—*The Anonymous Citizen*

So many editorials have been written about the apathy of American society—the bar flies who stood around and watched, cheered, and applauded as a woman was raped on a barroom pool table; the upstanding citizens who walk by the old man who is being savagely beaten in the streets by a gang of hoodlums. This is certainly not a new reflection in that mirror called America. Yet, each time I read an article about people who are brutally murdered while others listen and refuse to act, I am re-reminded of the horror of that reflecting pool.

Four lives were snuffed out on Wednesday by a vicious murderer—four lives that could have been saved. One can only imagine what the neighbors were thinking as they overheard the screams.

"Probably just a hysterical, drunk woman."
"There's nothing I can do about it anyway."

"If I call the police, he (it) will come back for me."
"Thank God it isn't me."

Whatever the source of the ambivalence, it was enough to dissuade at least ten other families from calling the police, to ignore the desperation of a fellow human being, to walk away.

Deep in the heart of the civilized American is a darkness that cannot be talked about, cannot be reasoned with, cannot be comprehended. It simply is "the horror, the horror."

Linda, calling up the words of Joseph Conrad's *Heart of Darkness,* "Oh, the horror, the horror . . . ," reflects upon the "So what?" of this event. She searches after the causes, which she calls "the source of the ambivalence," that stopped others from becoming involved, from even calling the police. She wonders about the "heart of civilized America," which "cannot be talked about, cannot be reasoned with, cannot be comprehended," and she leaves us, as readers, with her evaluation: "It simply is 'the horror, the horror.' "

The event has aroused her, enraged, provoked, ignited her to speak her concerns about America, civilization, the nature of the human heart; about the nature of nonparticipation, about our unwillingness to become involved. The story, then, starts as someone else's, but she makes it her own. She becomes engrossed in it, and through her engrossment, she discovers her own passion and commitment.

This story, we presume, would have made headlines in the Chicago newspapers, where the event took place (we read it in New York); we hope that it did make headlines, for if we take such events for granted, if they are hidden in fillers, we worry that we, the public out there who read the "news," have come to accept such events as normal and ordinary: the everyday. We are reminded, as well, of a similar case in 1964.

A CRY FOR HELP IGNORED II

The News Item

> # Queens woman is stabbed to death in front of home
>
> A 28-year-old Queens woman was stabbed to death early yesterday morning outside her apartment house in Kew Gardens.
>
> Neighbors who were awakened by her screams found the woman, Miss Catherine Genovese of 82–70 Austin Street, shortly after 3 A.M. in front of a building three doors from her home.
>
> The police said that Miss Genovese had been attacked in front of her building and had run to where she fell. She had parked her car in a nearby lot, the police said, after having driven it from the Hollis bar where she was day manager.
>
> The police, who spent the day searching for the murder weapon, interviewing witnesses and checking automobiles that had been seen in the neighborhood, said last night they had no clues.

—*New York Times,* March 14, 1964

An Editorial

Seldom has The Times published a more horrifying story than its account of how 38 respectable, law-abiding, middle-class Queens citizens watched a killer stalk his young woman victim in a parking lot in Kew Gardens over a half-hour period, without one of them making a call to the Police Department that might have saved her life. They would not have been exposed to any danger themselves; a simple telephone call in the privacy of their own homes was all that was needed. How incredible it is that such motivations as "I didn't want to get involved" deterred them from this act of simple humanity. Does residence in a great city destroy all sense of personal responsibility for one's neighbors? Who can explain such shocking indifference on the part of a cross section of our fellow New Yorkers? We regretfully admit that we do not know the answers.

—*New York Times*, March 28, 1964

A Comment by
Two Psychologists

. . . We must distinguish between the facts of the murder as finally known and reported in the press, and the events of the evening as they were experienced by the Kew Gardens residents. We can now say that if the police had been called after the first attack, the woman's life might have been saved, and we tend to judge the inaction of the Kew Gardens residents in the light of this lost possibility. That is natural, perhaps, but it is unrealistic. If those men and women had had as clear a grasp of the situation as we have now, the chances are that many of them would have acted to save Miss Genovese's life. What they had, instead, were fragments of an ambiguous, confusing and doubtless frightening episode—one, moreover, that seemed totally incongruous in a respectable neighborhood. The very lack of correspondence between the violence of the crime and the character of the neighborhood must have created a sense of unreality which inhibited rational action. A lesser crime, one in character with the locale—say, after-hours rowdiness from a group of college students— might have led more readily to a call for the police.

—Stanley Milgram and Paul Hollander, "The Murder They Heard," *The Nation*

A Generalization
by a Philosopher

The spectator's judgment is sure to miss the root of the matter, and to possess no truth. The subject judged knows a part of the world of reality which the judging spectator fails to see, knows more while the spectator knows less; and wherever there is conflict of opinion and difference of vision, we are bound to believe that the truer side is the side that feels the more, and not the side that feels the less.

—William James, "On a Certain Blindness in Human Beings," *Talks to Teachers*

WHAT NOW?

Read those four texts together, and consider the various roles of the writers and the ways in which they reinforce or modify your understanding of the terms "spectator" and "participant."

Does William James, for example, contradict the views of Milgram and Hollander? Do the views of Milgram and Hollander modify your response to the editorial? Does any spectator possess a clearer grasp of a situation than a participant can hope to achieve?

The Particular Evokes the General

DALTON TRUMBO'S LIST

> What discoveries I've made in the course of writing stories all begin with the particular, never the general.
>
> —Eudora Welty, *One Writer's Beginnings*

We live in a world of particularities, the specific events that happen to us and that happen to others—that we read about in newspapers, magazines, books; that we watch on television; that we engage in as participants and observe as spectators; and that often lead us—as thinkers, as writers, as citizens—to become involved. Dalton Trumbo here lists for Carey McWilliams, editor of the *Nation,* those "specific incidents" in which he uncovers, or discovers, issues of *general* importance, matters of social/political significance, questions of values that are always implicit in events. He demonstrates that, for all of us, every *particular* experience only makes sense in relation to our general frames, our culture's values, our sense of what makes sense. Every particularity is an individual occasion (or location) for the operation of general significances.

Los Angeles, California
October 26, 1959

Dear Carey:

Here are some thoughts I've been having:*

1. About two years ago, a young woman ran through a crowded N.Y. street, crying, "Please help me! He's going to kill me!" Her pursuer finally caught her, and killed her, and no one helped at all. In several cities crowds have chanted "Jump!" to crazed persons atop skyscrapers. In Los Angeles the other day an elderly man, gasping and weaving, staggered through a downtown street. Finally he fell to the sidewalk. No one offered him help. An hour later, when picked up by the authorities, he was dead. Diagnosis: heart attack. Two days later a middle-aged woman guided her stalled car to a side-island of the freeway. For five and a half hours she signalled for help. No one helped. From one, or a sequence, of such appalling daily events, I could develop an article on our fear of each other (and hence perhaps our hatred), and the horrible lack of love in our lives.

---

*McWilliams had asked Trumbo for a list of topics to be used in a possible *Nation* series of Trumbo articles.

2. Again: every month or so a troubled parent murders his entire family—wife (or husband), children, everyone—and then commits suicide. From this I should like to take a good look at the American family. How many times in these past twelve years have I been cautioned, "You must think of your family; the home is your first obligation; what of your children?" This fragmentation of a nation into separate dens of animals is the worst kind of moral anarchy, as deadly to our own souls as it is to the nation and the world.

3. Again: based on a proper news item, such as a tragic abortion, a consideration of the absolute idiocy of teaching children all about sex, and then announcing to them that their knowledge may be neither used nor tested for truth until they are properly licensed. The romantic idea of love so carefully nurtured: does one fall in love, or does one learn to love? . . .

8. Again: from experiences I have had right here in Highland Park with the public schools, I am absolutely persuaded that lower middle-class and working-class neighborhoods are serviced by schools—and particularly high schools—which are specifically designed to provide industry with manual labor, just as schools in richer neighborhoods (and most universities) are designed to provide industry with technical and intellectual personnel.

9. Again: there is a local TV show which I'm going to take a look at. It involves jousting with cars, ten cars per joust, and ten jousts per show. A joust is not completed until all but one car has been hopelessly smashed. Thus a hundred are smashed a night. Moral obvious. . . .

29. Once more, please; the June rash of honorary degrees. This is a real absurdity, and could be nice clean riotous fun.

30. And again: in the same vein as above, the giving of prizes for all kinds of merit; the endless sequences of testimonial dinners generally organized by the guest of honor; the hundreds, perhaps thousands, of awards, plaques, shields, cups, bowls, parchments, etc.

I'm going to number the above, so we can refer to them in future correspondence without stating the thesis of each. Maybe they're bad, or, more likely, some are bad and some are good. It would be my idea, if you agree, to use some item from the press pertinent and dramatic, as a springboard for each piece. Thus I shall seem to have drifted into my general point from a specific incident. All this, of course, in addition to your suggestions.

Best,
Dalton
—*Additional Dialogue*

WHAT NOW?

Our lives are full of the kinds of issues and questions that Trumbo raises. Make a list of your own particular experiences and observations that seem to involve a general issue—moral, political, social.

ANNA QUINDLEN PARTICULARIZES

Like all great journalists, Anna Quindlen is moved by the force of what actually *is*, even when it is unsensational, unspectacular, and unglamorous. We invite you, first, to read some of her articles for pleasure, and then to reread, more closely, using our questions that follow her texts as guidelines for looking at what her texts do. Afterward, we will try to give you a sense of what we learned from talking with her.

Meet the Flash, who fixes trains in a flash

No one at work calls him by his proper name. Once his family was looking for him. "Jim Staveley," they said on the phone, but nobody in the stuffy little stationmaster's office at Penn Station knew whom they were talking about. "He fixes the trains," a family member explained. "Oh, you mean the Flash," said one of the stationmasters.

Flash was found, underneath a train somewhere. Everybody at work knows him, but everybody knows him as Flash. Conductors who speak highly of him, engineers who put their equipment in his hands, have no idea of his last name, or even his real first one.

He got the name Flash when he was an electrician on the Long Island Rail Road, but it fits just fine now that he is something called an equipment supervisor. That's a stiff, formal kind of name for what Flash really does, which is to make the railroad run. When a train pulls into Penn Station with a problem, Flash has some time to see how bad the damage is and to fix it.

At rush hour, some time is generally around five minutes. By 5 o'clock on any given evening, Flash is as warm and wet as a summer thunderstorm. "If I hold one train up, even a couple minutes, I'm holding a lot of other trains up," he says. The answer, says Flash, is not to hold anything up.

"Flash, you got an MA on Track 9," says one of the stationmasters.

"That's no lights," says Flash as he grabs his orange flashlight, his screwdriver and his wrench and looks up at the monitor to see how much time he has to try to make repairs. Flash comes down the stairs amid a rush of commuters and jumps onto the dark car. He opens a door on the side facing away from the platform, leaps onto the track and disappears under the train.

"I've never seen a rat yet," he says. "We got a family of cats that live under the platform." Then he uses his walkie-talkie. "How many minutes on 19?" he asks the stationmaster, to see if he's holding things up, and "Flash to 862 engineer," he radios up front, because he doesn't want the engineer to take the train to Babylon with his body under the wheels.

Flash climbs back onto the platform, grabs two fuses from a box attached to a pillar and climbs back down to the tracks. As he is working, a voice from the walkie-talkie tells him of another problem. Two women standing at the edge look down to see his gray sideburns and high forehead glistening with sweat in that narrow strip of darkness between the platform and the train. "Aaah," cries one of the women, pointing down. Flash comes up again and throws the light switch. The lights come on.

"He did it!" cries the woman, triumphant and relieved. Flash jogs across the platform, opens the doors, runs through the train on Track 18 and enters the train on Track 17 to install a speed control seal. The first train was due to leave at 4:40, the second at 4:42. Both are on time.

"That Flash," says an engineer leaning against one of the pillars, waiting for his own train to pull in so he could take it back to Long Island. "He's everywhere. He's an unsung hero."

At a time when union and management, particularly on railroads, seem to have serious signal problems, and when commuters seem to think no one does anything right, the Flash is an odd anachronism, a management man, once a union electrician, beloved on both sides of the fence and devoted to his work. He is supposed to work from around 2 P.M. until midnight on weekdays, but he often stays around much longer, and he is almost always in on Sundays.

"I try to take Saturdays off," he says. "However, if I receive a call of a particular incident requiring equipment, I'll come in, of course."

Flash is a diffident man, but he gets bright-eyed at certain scenarios: the idea, for example, of going in after a train broken down in one of the tunnels leading to Penn Station, or of finally getting a particularly troublesome car up in the yards at Jamaica and taking a look at it.

"Many times on the way home there'll be problems elsewhere on the railroad, West Hempstead or whatever, and I'll stop off and take care of that," he says.

"That Flash," cracked one of the men in the stationmaster's office, "we're going to bronze his sneakers."

Then Flash peers out the grimy window, whirls and runs out to Track 18. He does something at one of the doors and returns, out of breath. "That's called a commuter with an arm in the door," he says. "Very common problem. Took his arm out and off they went."

Flash lives in his own world on the Long Island Rail Road. He spends some time standing around the stationmaster's office, a tiny room positioned between and just above Tracks 18 and 19 that is filled with people and machines and painted a disconcerting electric blue. He spends a lot of time down on the tracks, where the silver and blue of the trains and the platforms give way to the mud browns of the trestles below and the dark ceilings above, and to the shadows where the tunnels and the tracks dissolve into one.

It's his world, and he makes it work most of the time, as though the Long Island Rail Road was just so much sophisticated equipment made by Lionel. The commuters are just a blur, their faces covered by newspapers, their bodies parts of an impatient whole. Still, they are his job.

"You got to keep the people moving," says Flash. "That's what it all comes down to. You can't hold things up. You got to work fast." A train pulls into the station with a problem with the lever called the dead man's control, which automatically applies the train's brakes. "Beat the clock," says the Flash, as he grabs his flashlight and heads down onto the platform again.

—Anna Quindlen, *New York Times*, April 20, 1983

A tireless search for one lost soul

Alice Scheller met Alma Siegel just over a year ago in a coffee shop in the Port Authority Bus Terminal. Alice was just passing through, on her way to Harlem to do volunteer work, but Alma lived there, at least part of the time, one of these elderly women who shelter themselves within the public places of New York City and become dirty and disconnected and sometimes mad.

Alice wanted to buy Alma something to eat, but Alma suspected that Alice was really among the shadowy contingents of "theys" who were out to get her. Besides, she said, the food was not kosher. Alice convinced her that orange juice would not be tainted, and Alma agreed.

On this unlikely foundation, a relationship was built. Alice came into the bus terminal from New Jersey twice a week, Tuesdays and Thursdays, and Alma was generally waiting for her, wearing house slippers and a cotton dress.

In the beginning, Alice told Alma she was from the Red Cross, bearing food from a kosher delicatessen, and that seemed to soothe her. Alice brought homemade chicken soup and kasha, a down coat and clean clothes. She clipped Alice's toenails, curved like claws. Once, when Alice could not come in because of bad weather, Alma went to an attendant in the women's room and cried, "Alice didn't come, Alice didn't come."

But she was just as likely to decide suddenly that Alice was one of them.

"I tried to get her home with me, just for

the winter," Alice said, "but then at the last moment she was afraid to get on the bus. She was so afraid that someone would put her away."

Once Alice had made the mistake of asking to see where she slept, and Alma had flown into a rage.

"Sleep! Sleep!" she shrieked. "Who sleeps in a telephone booth?"

That was where they went the last time Alice saw Alma, to the booth near the back of a long line of booths in Penn Station, which Alma would wipe out with a tissue every night and in which she would rest. While they were there, two young men began to make fun of Alma, with her wild white hair and her ulcerated legs, and, suspecting that Alice was in league with them, Alma fled.

This is how the search for Alma Siegel began. Perhaps it is odd to be looking for one lost soul in a city where it seems that there is a bundle of bags, and a pile of clothing, and a human being underneath all, on every corner in midtown Manhattan. No one knows how many homeless people live in New York; the city has abandoned the idea of counting them all. But Alice wants to find Alma, and she is trying to get other people to look for her, too.

The other night, Amy Haus, who is program coordinator for the Coalition for the Homeless, went to Penn Station and the Port Authority to seek news of Alma.

Alice had importuned her to join the search, and while this is not exactly what her job is all about, Miss Haus ventured into the fluorescent anonymity of these buildings carrying snapshots of Alma, an aged twig of a woman sitting on a plastic milk carton and talking on a pay phone, her upper back curved like the bowl of a spoon.

Alma used to call 911 at the slightest opportunity to let the police know that they were after her again. Alice took the pictures.

There were two remarkable things about the events of that evening. One was that almost everyone shown Alma's picture recognized it. In the women's room, one of the attendants looked at the pictures and said: "A white lady? Very old, can hardly walk? She was in last night. She said, 'Help me, help me.' "

In the coffee shop where Alma would sometimes buy a takeout container, the cashier said in a soft drawl: "Yes, I know this lady. This lady would never take nothing from nobody. She always wanted to pay for her coffee. When I got back from vacation, one of the girls told me a policeman had been in and said she got very bad and they took her to the hospital and she passed away."

One of the waitresses interrupted: "Your best bet is Wally the cop. Tell him I sent you."

"Yeah, I know her," the police officer said. "I saw her in the waiting room the other night."

All of this sounded encouraging, except that the other unusual thing about the search for Alma was how many women there were like her: the tiny old woman asleep in a waiting room, her shoulder blades, slip straps and sores revealed by the armholes of her too-large dress; the white-haired woman in the women's room, dressing and undressing from a large shopping bag, rubbing her skin with a wet towel until it was red; the two sisters, one sweet-faced, one fiercely protective, both wearing neat khaki balmacaans, good shoes, nice blouses, with months and months' worth of dirt ground into the good quality cotton. Alma could be one of a hundred women.

"I know this woman," said a police officer in the Port Authority. "This is the woman I had sent to Bellevue. Family in New Jersey, right? Some money in it?" But then he looked closely at the picture and saw that it was someone else he meant.

Alice Scheller is 62 years old. Her husband is sick, and she has been ill in recent months. She has written to agency after agency, but what she asks is off the beaten bureaucratic path. She wants only to know that Alma is alive and well.

"I was born in New York City," she said. "There was nine of us in three rooms. I used to sit and wonder with money what life would be like. I don't have money, but I got heat in the winter and clean clothes, and to me, walking by somebody like this is like watching someone bleed to death."

Alice is worried about Alma with winter coming on. She hopes that she has simply found another hiding place and is not dead, or put away someplace. She hopes that they, whoever they were, did not finally get her.

—Anna Quindlen, *New York Times*, September 15, 1982

A sunny world in a window

Mary Frances Carpenter lives in a ground-floor window on West 48th Street. Like New York's luckiest hanging plants, she gets sunshine all day long. From the street, there is just her moon face in the window, with its half-moon grin, and the shadowy edges of the chairs and tables inside her railroad flat.

This is how almost everyone knows Miss Carpenter—from the street. The brick painted tan on the outside of her building is rubbed raw to the natural brown just below her window, where dozens of people every day stop to talk to her.

On either side of the window are mirrored panels, once the doors of a bathroom cabinet that belonged to a man who lives down the street. Now Miss Carpenter uses them to see those hard-to-get-at spots. "There are certain people I like to watch, and certain buildings," she says. "I don't miss much."

New York is not really a city; it is more a series of neighborhoods, and they are more a collection of blocks, and those are more an amalgam of small institutions. Miss Carpenter is a small institution. She reclines day and night on a single bed pushed flush against the two windows at the front of her building, her head propped up on a pillow, a flowered nightgown slipping over one round white shoulder. She never moves. Each day Pauline, a homecare aide, comes in to cook and clean for her.

Miss Carpenter is 67 years old and she has not walked since she was 8, when she began to feel poorly and her mother put her to bed. Something with a long name had attacked the nerves in her back, and from then on she was paralyzed from the waist down and became a permanent observer of the human condition.

It was almost as if all of her was frozen at that time when her lower half was, for she has the clear blue eyes and the pink cheeks of a baby, the ebullience of a child, as if in living in the window she has never grown old. She is a gay personality estranged from its physical moorings, like a helium balloon on a string.

"I'm an old thing here," said Miss Carpenter, framed by the window frame. "I'm here 45 years, not this house, but this block, and I love it here. I was raised on 52d Street, three months in Brooklyn, then back to 52d Street, then here, first across the street, then in this building. It was a very nice block, all children, all families.

"It ran down but now it's coming back again. We have the nicest men on the block, all bachelors. I adore it with my whole heart. They're renovating the building next door. One family bought it and four families are going to live in it. They fixed up that building across the street. They're charging $650 for a studio apartment. Oh, hello, honey, howya doing? Good? I'm good."

This is what it is like to come to Miss Carpenter's window, a mélange of reminiscences, comments on current affairs and chance encounters with those who know her or those who feel compelled to respond to the greetings that emanate from the window. Miss Carpenter is a testimonial to something that was supposed to have died a horrible death long ago in New York, a kind of open-handed trust and a belief in the essential good of human nature.

Richie, who is 29 and lives upstairs, goes to the corner every morning and brings her a container of takeout coffee. Terry, who is 34, lifts her into her wheelchair on those rare occasions when she goes out. A priest from Sacred Heart Church comes on Sunday mornings to give her communion through the window. The paths within the community garden just across the street were made wide enough for her wheelchair. The tenants' meetings in her building are held in her living room.

It is common knowledge on the block that she lives alone and that she is helpless, and yet she has no fear. Her trust was betrayed only once, last December, when two young women came to the window pretending to be nurses. A man with them broke down the door and the three stole all the money Miss Carpenter had in the house.

"Oh, you poor thing, we feel so sorry for you," one of the women had the gall to say. "You don't have to feel sorry for me," Miss Carpenter told her. "I'm the happiest woman in the world."

The experience did not sour Miss Carpenter. "You have to trust people because if you didn't you wouldn't have a friend," she said. "I'd just be sitting here all alone and then where would I be?"

Where she is now is a busy place; there are always people passing by, raising their hands in greeting, women stopping their baby carriages so Miss Carpenter can take a look. A little girl on the other side of the street carrying a teddy bear blows kisses; a patrol car slows, and the two officers wave.

"Hello, Vinnie," Miss Carpenter calls to a man across the street. "Hi, sweetheart," he says.

"I had Mayor Koch one day at the window," said Miss Carpenter. "He was very nice."

She says she has no regrets. "I would have liked it if I had got married and had children 'cause I would have had about 10," she said. "I like kids. But I never once regretted the way things turned out. When I had an operation they said maybe feeling would return, and I said, 'Gee, I wouldn't know what to do if it happened; I think I'd better just stay this way.' "

On Saturday Miss Carpenter hopes to go to the Ninth Avenue Festival. Terry will hoist her into her chair and someone will roll her down the avenue. It is getting harder and harder for her to take these trips, but Miss Carpenter says that spending the day in the window is almost as nice.

"I don't drink, I don't smoke, I don't gamble," she said. "I have no vices except looking out the window. I want to live until the next century because we're going to have a big party. That's all."

—Anna Quindlen, *New York Times*, May 11, 1983

Toys as a serious business

In one of the showrooms, with its wall-to-wall carpeting and designer plants, there was a big sign: "We Have Seen the Future and It Is Smurfs."

Outside, ordinary people sloshed along Fifth Avenue. They didn't know. They hadn't heard. They passed right by the trailer in which the Chipmunks rest between appearances. For them, the Chipmunks meant nothing. For Barry Schwartz, they mean everything. Mr. Schwartz has seen the future, and it is Chipmunks.

"This is definitely the year of the Chipmunks," said Mr. Schwartz, a spokesman for Ideal Toys.

The Toy Fair is in town, bringing with it Smurfs, Chipmunks, Care Bears, Dream Date Barbie, video software for children, dolls for adults and 12,000 buyers from all over the United States and the world.

There was one child in evidence yesterday. Her name was Julie Jones, and she is 10 years old. Her parents are opening a store in Charleston, S.C., called Julie's Doll House. Julie fit right in at the Toy Fair. She takes dolls very seriously.

"Ideal has made some good changes in their line," she said, quiet and self-possessed. "They have a lot more collecti-bles." Julie is doing a lot of the merchandising for Julie's Doll House.

"She's gotten the red carpet treatment here," said her father, Theron.

"We rely on her opinion quite a bit," said her mother, Barbara.

"I like the soft-bodied dolls," said Julie seriously.

The Toy Fair comes to New York every winter, to the Toy Center North at 1107 Broadway, the Toy Center South at 200 Fifth Avenue, and several other exhibit and showroom locations around Manhattan.

Don't think it's child's play. This is serious business, choosing between the Bi-Tread Defense Tank and the Star Wars Millenium Falcon. The buyers take it very seriously. They refer to Betsy Wetsy, who still does, as "the merchandise."

They want to know what the Smurfs are stuffed with. They wear name tags and they watch, expressionless, as moving parts are moved for them and commercials are played on little television screens. They talk about toys like grown-ups, not children.

They say things like this:

"It's clever, but it's not representative of what I see as the trend in video games."

"As a doll, it's fine. As a sales item, I can't see it."

"I don't care what Coleco has. Just tell me this: Should I buy the stock?"

They say these things as they are watching a thin young woman with long blond hair twirl three peppermint-striped Wham-O Hula Hoops around her midriff in a display window.

Don't be fooled by the fact that these are grown men and women with Smurfette decals on their briefcases; the people who sell toys are not much different from the people who sell insurance. In fact, Eugene Rinaman of Pittsburgh, who is the road man for Mr. Hobby Wholesale, conceded that before he sold toys, he did sell insurance.

Lost of buyers are thinking bulk, deciding the potential of Care Bears—"Each bear captures and expresses a human emotion and personality which is illustrated by a symbol on its tummy," said the release—and whether Twirly Curls Barbie will do better than Angel Face Barbie, Dream Date Barbie, Horse Lovin' Barbie, Pink and Pretty Barbie or Fashion Jeans Barbie.

Instead of children playing with the toys at the Toy Fair, there are actors and actresses between jobs, like Jenise Parris. This year she demonstrated Manglor, a bilious green scaly guy made out of some compound that can be ripped apart and put right back together. While a bevy of buyers surrounded her, Miss Parris held Manglor aloft.

"You can crush him," she said with a smile, crushing Manglor into a ball. "You can stretch him," she said, stretching him. "You can tear him apart," she said, pulling off Manglor's left leg and attaching it to the side of his head. "The child can rip off any part to create his own fantasy monster."

"What's the point?" said a buyer in a tan and a blue suit to one of the salesmen.

"It can go up against G. I. Joes and Star Wars," the salesman said.

"Naaah, it's different."

"Sure, it's different, it's unique," said the salesman.

"Forget unique," said the buyer, walking away. "It's weird."

Miss Parris continued with her presentation. Manglor has two dinosaur friends, Manglosaurus and Manglodactyl. He lives in something called the Manglor Mountain, surrounded by slime.

"The slime is nonstaining and nontoxic," she said. She is sort of enjoying Manglor, who is billed as "maybe the most revolting creature ever created." Last year she demonstrated Flowerific. The paper used to make the flowers was scented, and by the end of the week she smelled like a florist's shop. Manglor has no odor.

All over the Toy Fair, there are toys like this. There are people that can be torn apart and put back together; there are dolls more beautiful and better dressed than most people. There are video games that think faster, and are more interesting, than some of the people who purchase them.

This may be the only merchandise exhibition all year in New York in which three small people dressed as the Chipmunks—Alvin, Theodore and Simon, for those who have long forgotten their adenoidal recordings of a generation ago—can walk through a room filled with business people and nonchalantly shake hands. The Chipmunks are back this year, stuffed, in plastic and on a board game.

So is Groucho Marx, as a doll, the third in something called the Legend Series. So is Shirley Temple, in porcelain, a signed collectors' edition that will retail for around $400. Around them eddied the human beings who apparently can tell which of them will sell.

As two men left the Toy Center South for lunch, one said solemnly to the other, "I think Smurfs will continue to do well."

—Anna Quindlen, *New York Times*, February 9, 1983

Notes

1. As you reread Quindlen's texts, judge the degree to which she remains a spectator, placing herself at an appropriate distance from her subject. Does she seem to allow herself any deep or intense emotional involvement?

2. Would you consider her a participant as well? How so?

3. Since reporters are not writing history but reporting on life in the here and now, they use techniques that allow us to experience the illusion of being present. How does Quindlen bring us, her readers, into the here and now? Point to places in the texts that capture a sense of immediacy, of presence.

4. What "defamiliarizing" techniques (see Chapter 13) does Quindlen use to represent her subject, so that we can see the ordinary, the daily, the things we take for granted, in a new light?

5. Every one of her representations contains an implicit evaluation—an answer to the question "So what?" Like all good journalists, Quindlen is a compulsive evaluator—*this* matters, or *that* is worth considering; *this* is admirable, *that* is deplorable. But she doesn't force her values down our throats. Rather, they are felt to emerge gradually and persuasively from the particular bit of life she has chosen to represent. How does the evaluation seep through? Consider the titles of her articles, the selected detail, the dialogue, the ways in which she represents a moment, an event, a place, a person.

A Conversation with Anna Quindlen

An Anna Quindlen article always made us sit up straighter and take better note of the people around us—the bus driver, the toll collector, the newsstand owner, the woman across the street who rarely left her house. (Was she another Mary Frances Carpenter, we wondered, surveying the world through her window?) We looked forward to the days when Quindlen's column would appear. And then, one day, we wondered if we might try for an interview. "Of course," she wrote back. And one afternoon we spent several hours with her—a young, vivacious journalist, who is now deputy metropolitan editor of the *New York Times*.

We were curious about her reasons for choosing journalism as a career. Quindlen describes herself as "nosy," a "real gossip," who asks "incredibly weird questions and gets away with them." An "insatiable reader," a "lover of fiction," she eventually decided that she might be able to make a living out of reporting on others' lives. And so she has—relying on her own method of taking "copious notes," committing to paper what people say and how they say it, attending to their physical appearance, their gestures, their surroundings. "If it's important enough to write it down," she says, "then it's important enough to quote." Her attentiveness, her keen observations, her involvement in a real conversation with a real person in a particular time and place—all that would be impeded by reliance on a tape recorder; *she* has to be there, participating in a genuine meeting, as one person to another.

The person-to-person encounter is always brief. In fact, Quindlen describes herself as an "emotional hit-and-run driver": she is in and out; she goes in, collects her notes, and then "escapes." She invades a private life and makes it public, knowing full well that a column in the *New York Times* can change a life. (Mary Carpenter received a letter from the President!)

Since Quindlen chooses her own assignments—a person or issue that arouses her in some significant way—the responsibilities are awesome: "Is it fair?" "Is it accurate?" "Did I get it right?" "The unimportant people," she says, "always need more protection" when their lives are suddenly brought into the public eye.

When she first began to write—as a child—she would read her words aloud to hear the way they sounded, to listen to the music they made. Now that she is an experienced writer, she reads aloud silently and revises the word or phrase that goes "clunk" to her trained inner ear. This is what she would recommend to novice writers, she says, to read aloud, to hear the language of the written text, to keep the energy of the voice in the writing. You get so used to writing, she suggests, that it becomes just like "talking on paper." And read, she advises, read, read, and read; that's how you get a writer's sensibility, by reading. Her favorite writers? Dickens, Faulkner, Jane Austen, Tolstoy. For her, the characters in these books are real; they make her feel as if she were participating in their lives and not looking in from a distance. Perhaps that's why she represents real people so vividly, so that her readers feel as if she's brought them right into their living rooms, their minds, and their hearts.

WHAT NOW?

1. Represent someone you admire or respect: observe that person "in context" (at home or at work), conduct an interview, and then write about him/her from the role of a spectator. Allow the reader to "hear" the voice of the person you are representing. Let the evaluation be implicit; *show* rather than *tell*.
2. Explore some social issue by presenting it in a portrait of one person: *one* case shows how it *is*, what it means to live daily in a particular environment.
3. Represent something—cars, stereo equipment, computers, jogging, etc.—that others take seriously but that you find in some way ridiculous. You are a cool spectator, viewing this "cultural phenomenon" with ironic detachment.

The Paralysis of the Spectator

For the final selection in this chapter, we offer you a short extract from an essay by Ted Hughes. As you will see, it deals very passionately with issues raised earlier in this chapter.

Some years ago in an American picture magazine I saw a collection of photographs which showed the process of a tiger killing a woman. The story behind this was as follows. The tiger, a tame tiger, belonged to the woman. A professional photographer had wanted to take photographs of her strolling with her tiger. Something—maybe his incessant camera—had upset the tiger, the woman had tried to pacify it, whereupon it attacked her and started to kill her. So what did that hero of the objective attitude do then? Among Jim Corbett's wonderful stories about man-eating tigers and leopards there are occasions when some man-eater, with a terrifying reputation, was driven off its victim by some other person. On one occasion by a girl who beat the animal over the head with a digging stick. But this photographer—we can easily understand him because we all belong to this modern world—had become his camera. What were his thoughts? "Now that the tiger has started in on her it would be cruelty to save her and prolong her sufferings," or "If I just stand here making the minimum noise it might leave her, whereas if I interfere it will certainly give her the death bite, just as a cat does when you try to rescue its mouse," or "If I get involved, who knows what will happen, then I might miss my plane," or "I can't affect the outcome of this in any way. And who am I to interfere with the cycles of nature? This has happened countless millions of times and always will happen while there are tigers and women," or did he just think "Oh my God, Oh my God, what a chance!"? Whatever his thoughts were he went on taking photographs of the whole procedure while the tiger killed the woman, because the pictures were there in the magazine. And the story was told as if the photographer had indeed been absent. As if the camera had simply gone on doing what any camera would be expected to do, being a mere mechanical device for registering outer appearances. I may be doing the photographer an injustice. It may be I have forgotten some mention that eventually when he had enough pictures he ran in and hit the tiger with his camera or something else. Or maybe he was just wisely cowardly as many another of us might be. Whatever it was, he got his pictures.

The same paralysis comes to many of us when we watch television. After the interesting bit is over, what keeps us mesmerized by that bright little eye? It can't be the horrors and inanities and killings that jog along there between the curtains and the mantelpiece after supper. Why can't we move? Reality has been removed beyond our participation, behind that very tough screen, and into another dimension. Our inner world, of natural impulsive response, is safely in neutral. Like broiler killers, we are reduced to a state of pure observation. Everything that passes in front of our eyes is equally important, equally unimportant. As far as what we see is concerned, and in a truly practical way, we are paralyzed. Even people who profess to dislike television fall under the same spell of passivity. They can only free themselves by a convulsive effort of will. The precious tool of objective imagination has taken control of us there. Materialized in the camera, it has imprisoned us in the lens.

—Myth and Education

WHAT NEXT?

Ted Hughes offers us two situations: one of a particular photographer witnessing a killing, the other of "most of us" watching television. Do you agree that both these situations involve the "same paralysis"? Or do you find his equation unconvincing?

Even though he strongly disapproves of the photographer's conduct, it is worth noting that he takes care not to assume a position of moral superiority. Similarly, in his second paragraph, he uses the pronoun "we," thereby including himself as one who is likewise a prey to passivity or paralysis.

Think over your recent past and choose a situation in which you remained a spectator, refusing to participate or seeing participation as not your responsibility. Write two accounts of the experience. In the first, use the third person singular—he or she—and report it as if by a spectator. In the second, use the first person singular—I—and include a representation of your inner speech, so as to allow the reader to "read" your mind.

12 | Take a Look at This! Representations that Familiarize

Two of the most important functions of texts are

1. To represent a particular object so accurately and clearly that the reader (spectator) will be able to construct an appropriate and clear image of it, even though he/she cannot perceive it directly;

2. To produce a universal description of something, so that if, for example, the text offers a description of a dog, the reader will be able to recognize all dogs as corresponding to, or fulfilling, the description.

The first kind of description often occurs in our social lives, when we wish to share our knowledge of a specific object or person with a friend. The second kind occurs most frequently in reference and instructional texts, and tries to ensure that when a reader encounters a case of the phenomenon in question he/she will recognize it (for example, descriptions of illnesses in a medical dictionary).

In the hands of an accomplished writer, the second kind of description can be so effective, vivid, and pleasurable that it is possible to enjoy it as much as the first kind, even though it is performing a task with very strict rules, namely to be true for all cases.

In the texts that follow, you will see writers producing both kinds of descriptions.

Enabling the Reader to Share that Which Is Not Present

AGEE'S REPRESENTATION

The Lamp

It is late in a summer night, in a room of a house set deep and solitary in the country; all in this house save myself are sleeping; I sit at a table, facing a partition wall; and I am looking at a lighted coal-oil lamp which stands on the table close to the wall, and just beyond the sleeping of my relaxed left hand; with my right hand I am from time to time writing, with a soft pencil, into a school-child's composition book; but just now, I am entirely focused on the lamp, and light.

It is of glass, light metal colored gold, and cloth of heavy thread.

The glass was poured into a mold, I guess, that made the base and bowl, which are in one piece; the glass is thick and clean, with icy lights in it. The base is a simply fluted, hollow skirt; stands on the table; is solidified in a narrowing, a round inch of pure thick glass, then hollows again, a globe about half flattened, the globe-glass thick, too; and this holds oil, whose silver line I see, a little less than half down the globe, its level a very little—for the base is not quite true—tilted against the axis of the base.

This 'oil' is not at all oleaginous, but thin, brittle, rusty feeling, and sharp; taken and rubbed between forefinger and thumb, it so cleanses their grain that it sharpens their mutual touch to a new coin edge, or the russet nipple of a breast erected in cold; and the odor is clean, cheerful and humble, less alive by far than that of gasoline, even a shade watery:

William Michael Harnett, *Mr. Huling's Rack Picture,* 1888

and a subtle sweating of this oil is on the upward surface of the globe, as if it stood through the glass, and as if the glass were a pitcher of cool water in a hot room. I do not understand nor try to deduce this, but I like it; I run my thumb upon it and smell of my thumb, and smooth away its streaked print on the glass; and I wipe my thumb and forefinger dry against my pants, and keep on looking.

In this globe, and in this oil that is clear and light as water, and reminding me of creatures and things once alive which I have seen suspended in jars in a frightening smell of alcohol—serpents, tapeworms, toads, embryons, all drained one tan pallor of absolute death; and also of the serene, scarved flowers in untroubled wombs (and pale-tanned too, flaccid, and in the stench of exhibited death, those children of fury, patience and love which stand in the dishonors of accepted fame, and of the murdering of museum staring); in this globe like a thought, a dream, the future, slumbers the stout-weft strap of wick, and up this wick is drawn the oil, toward heat; through a tight, flat tube of tin, and through a little slotted smile of golden tin, and there ends fledged with flame, in the flue; the flame, a clean, fanged fan.

—James Agee, *Let Us Now Praise Famous Men*

Reflecting on Agee's Representation

What evidence do you find in that text to support the view that Agee was a writer who was very easily sidetracked? Let us assume that in the passage, he did not entirely keep to the point. Did you mind? Did it matter? If not, why not? What is the "use" of Agee's text?

Do you regard Agee as a participant? If so, what is he participating in? Or is he a spectator, observing? Or is he a mixture of both?

If good writing gives the reader pleasurable and effective surprises, what in Agee's text surprised you?

Does Agee try to relate the parts systematically to the whole? Or does he not need to?

What evidence could you offer to support the view that even though he could be sidetracked, Agee has remarkable powers of attention?

Try to draw Agee's lamp. Which parts of Agee's representation cannot be translated into visual terms?

WHAT NOW?

Translate Agee's text into a universal description that would be true of all oil lamps.

Agee Presents His Frames of Mind

That moment, when Agee sat writing about the lamp, must have been for him one of those "moments of being," of arousal, of intensified awareness that Virginia Woolf wrote about (see page 328). He felt at that moment that he could do anything and that he could share that sense of unlimited power with his audience. Here is his account of how he felt:

The light in this room is of a lamp. Its flame in the glass is of the dry, silent and famished delicateness of the latest lateness of the night, and of such ultimate, such holiness of silence and peace that all on earth and within extremest remembrance seems suspended upon it in perfection as upon reflective water: and I feel that if I can by utter quietness succeed in not disturbing this silence, in not so much as touching this plain of water, I can tell you anything within realm of God, whatsoever it may be, that I wish to tell you, and that what so ever it may be, you will not be able to help but understand it.

It is the middle and pure height and whole of summer and a summer night, the held breath, of a planet's year; high shored sleeps the crested tide: what day of the month I do not know, which day of the week I am not sure, far less what hour of the night. The dollar watch I bought a few days ago, as also from time to time I buy a ten cent automatic pencil, and use it little before I lose all track of it, ran out at seventeen minutes past ten the day before yesterday morning, and time by machine measure was over for me at that hour, and is a monument. I know of the lateness and full height by the quietly starved brightness of my senses, which some while ago made the transition past any need for sleep without taking much notice of it, as, in the late darkness, the long accustomed liner loses the last black headland, and quietly commends her forehead upon the long open home of the sea.

WHAT NOW?

1. Choose something from your world that you enjoy looking at *in a concentrated way, with close attention,* and represent it.
2. Recall a moment when you enjoyed the feeling of having the ability to do anything, or a moment of extraordinary well-being, and write an account of it—either as a participant or as a spectator looking back. (Do you look back with nostalgia, a sense of loss, or with renewed pleasure?)

SHARING SACRED OBJECTS: OUR STUDENTS' OFFERINGS

"Sacred objects" was W. H. Auden's name for those things that we treasure for their value to us, though they may have no monetary value.

Here are some of our students' representations of their sacred objects. They will probably serve to remind you of your sacred objects and, we hope, encourage you to share your representations of them.

Rare are the times that I leave the house for any length of time that the faded, blue-gray, ratty old rucksack is not with me. It is my security blanket. My thumb to suck when I must face the world. More often than not it is my friend and companion, a confidant that is always there and rarely gets sassy. I am quite certain that if my neurotic Labrador did not accompany me on my frequent forays into the hills and fields, I should find myself talking to it. Perhaps even patting it on the head and searching for eyes to look into.

That canvas rucksack, from England, fits my needs and wants most perfectly. It came to me as a present from an understanding wife when I graduated from college: A replacement for another, which, no longer structurally sound, hangs in honor in my most private basement corner. In its barrel-shaped form less than two feet high and a foot wide, I can carry all that I need to enter a vicarious world of simplicity that seems to be more elusive each year. No flashy, high-tech indestructible nylon with whistles, bells, toggles, and pockets for toilet paper rolls, it is made of honest cotton duck that ages, that takes on character, and that, like me, will some day wear out.

The straps are simple and stout, and are beginning to wear. A simple top with one strap provides almost water-proofness to the contents and the ice axe loop on the back has carried ice axes, shovels, ski-poles, and rifles. The recent addition of a bright red strap to the crampon rings on the lid was a deliberate wish to add a bit of color to a saddening face, worn with time and distance.

No stay-at-home, this sack has been throughout the United States, including Alaska. It has been up many mountains and served in many ways. I once left it for a grizzly—hoping he would find it more appetizing than the painfully mortal flesh of a scared Utahnian far from home. A walrus once rolled on it, to my horror, and I knew it was lost forever.

Far more important than the exterior, which exists only to give shape to the memories within, is the wonderful interior. For it is here that I have carried the finest books that I have read, the finest wines that I have drunk, the finest fishing flies that I have tied, and the journals that have guided my recollections of times and places long ago and far away.

At any given moment a stranger should hesitate to put their hand into this cavern. The bottom is usually littered with the foil wrappers of ski-wax tins, stale pipe tobacco, dried-up mustard, sardines that somehow dropped in and were forgotten, and rolls of film that I meant to develop months ago. I washed it once, perhaps twice, but have put that foolishness behind me now. No, this is not for looking pretty or for carrying a truckload of hardware up some mountain. I have three other rucksacks for that. This is for carrying my memories and expectations, and the key to myself.

—David Foxley

This leather belt with holster is twenty-eight years old. It was made for a five-year-old waist by my father, a leather tooler. Now the leather is dark brown, curled at the edges and more brittle and shiny than when it was first made. My name, LYLE, is tooled on the back of this two-inch wide belt so as to make it stand out. Also on the belt are riveted glass stones, green, red, and white, set in silver caps. The belt is buckled by a silver, flower-stamped buckle, untarnished.

From this belt hangs only one holster. The other has torn off and left a ragged piece of leather hanging on that side. The remaining holster hangs by a loop inserted through a slot in the belt. Similar to other holsters, it has a silver, flowered circle in the middle, from which hang two leather straps cut in a slant point at the end. There is a hole at the bottom of the holster. A thong used to thread through it and around the leg. The thong is gone, the hole has narrowed, and the edge has curled.

—*Lyle Wakefield*

I was born in a family of women, three older sisters who influenced what I thought, said, and wanted. My sisters loved dolls. I never owned a doll, but I longed for something of my own to which I could give affection. At four years of age I found the object: Casper the Friendly Ghost. I had been a fan of the cartoon, and now, courtesy of Mattel toys, Casper became a real companion. That Christmas morning I woke with anticipation. As I rushed into the living room, I was elated to find the twenty-inch ghost waiting with a green bow around his neck.

Casper had a hard, shiny, white plastic face. The eyes were ovals which stood on end with two small black circles covering the bottom of the ovals. The features of the face were formed in plastic, the small nose and lips much like my sisters' dolls, the cheeks puffed like a chipmunk's with a mouth full of nuts. The lips, slightly smiling, were painted a brilliant red. The back of the head was covered with a white terry cloth material. This white towel-like cloth also formed the body. Casper's head was proportionally bigger than his body, the body about two or three heads long. A squeezable cottony material formed the stuffing of the body. Across the chest was written "Casper" in red cursive script, similar to the cartoon logo.

Casper and I became inseparable. He accompanied me for naps and to the sandpile while I played with my Tonka bulldozer, and he sat perched on the edge of the tub while I bathed. My mother won out, however, when I wanted to take Casper to church; perhaps she figured we would get the "spirit" in other ways.

Casper's body was about the size of a newborn baby. Before long I discovered Casper could wear the clothes I had worn as an infant. Casper still wears a white and yellow one-piece cotton outfit I wore as a baby.

To my delight Casper also spoke. This was no ordinary ghost. A hard plastic ring, about the circumference of a nickel, was attached to a twelve-inch string at his neck. When the string was pulled it would return slowly while a recorded message sounded: "I'm Casper the Friendly Ghost"; "I like you"; "I'm co-o-o-ld"; "Will you be my friend?" Indeed, Casper was a friend. A brother I never had? An object of affection? A companion that never went away angry? Casper still sits on my closet shelf. Though the white terry has dirtied and the red lips are chipped, he still asks, now somewhat garbled, "Will you be my friend?"

—*Karl Smart*

My night table is the oldest piece of furniture in my room. It is approximately thirty-six inches high, sixteen inches wide, and eighteen inches in length. It is made out of oak, stained a dark brown with a high gloss finish.

It has certain characteristics, which have developed with age, that make it unique: for example, one of the front legs is removable; I knocked it off by accident while I was vacuuming—at least, that's what I told my mom. Actually it was on one of those rare occasions when my younger brother dared me to a wrestling match and of course I won. While I was busy trying to rearrange his face I rearranged the design of my night table. The opposite back leg is missing. It must have gotten lost somewhere along the way from my great-grandmother's bedroom to mine. If you lean on it the wrong way, everything comes tumbling down with a loud crash. I position the night table against the wall for support to try to prevent this from happening.

The top of the table is a complete mess. I have two nail-polish-remover stains in the middle. I also have red and pink streaks alongside the stains. I never could get the knack of painting only on the nail segment of my finger. I tried soaking the stains with furniture polish, which only aggravated the situation by discoloring the wood even more.

There are two shelves and one bottom drawer. The left-hand corner of the drawer is chipped so the whiteness of the wood is visible. This is offset by the black ink stain on the right-hand corner. That's from when I used to practice calligraphy. I finally gave that up after the bottle spilled over onto the drawer.

In the center of the drawer I inscribed my initials, for I consider this night table as my work of art since it has survived and is still hanging in there: with its crippled legs, stains, and all. It will probably last for another lifetime.

—Stephanie Kushner

Yellowstone Park

I needed to think today, so I returned to the place where I do most of my heavy thinking. As I sit on the hill, I look down and see my life before me. After all, I've practically grown up here, on a spot once named Devil's Hill, now known as Yellowstone Park. No, it's not in Yosemite Park, and no, it's not National, but it's most definitely important. There is so much meaning to me in this place. It is my favorite spot, and not one of my friends, new or old, has not experienced some of its magic with me.

When I was young, the rules were laid down for me: the lower area is for kids; the basketball courts for the older teens. God, how afraid I was to enter those basketball courts; but that didn't really matter, because all I wanted was down here.

The swings were my thing; through the years I've mastered them. I can soar into the trees, shake the chains, and swing around like a wild animal. When I was not swinging solo or taking someone up (two on a swing at once), there were some pretty awesome games of manhunt and ringolevio. All the girls and guys would play for hours. Spring and summer used to allow us to have extra time after dinner.

The first time I ever kissed a boy was under the bridge—the very same one I once fell off, nearly cracking my head open. I watched them take away the big blue slide because some kid almost died on it, and after many complaints it was gone. They later removed the merry-go-round, too. I remember begging my father thousands of times: "Spin me faster!" because I liked how it felt when my tummy tickled.

I could never forget the water-balloon fights we used to have in the summer when it wasn't hot enough for them to turn on the sprinklers; and I'm so glad I was never shake-and-baked: that was when a wet person was rolled in the sandbox.

Then I got older. New people were coming to hang out in the park, *my* park. I felt violated. But eventually my hostility faded and friendship took over. Soon we were hanging out at night, to drink when we weren't allowed anywhere else, or to smoke because no one's parents would know. We used to have parties—everyone would come—and we used to talk about how those older kids in the courts were smoking pot.

Last day of school filled the park with kids exchanging summer addresses and tears. How many crushes did I go through, while hanging out here? Too many to name. Oceans of tears I've shed in this place. And I can't even measure the amount of laughter. *Never* a bad memory.

The time eventually came when I was hanging out in the basketball courts. Where had all the time gone? How had I gotten here so fast? It was only yesterday that Kevin was pushing me on the swings; and now I'm watching the guys play basketball!

Romantic nights alone with a heart's desire have been spent here. It's so nice and peaceful. A lot like home (maybe not). And the graffiti on the walls tell millions of stories: like the day Yogi threw his ice cream stick and it landed right in a crack in the wall. It has never been removed. By the way, his real name is Neal, but every Yellowstone Park needs a Yogi Bear. You just didn't grow up in Forest Hills and not be a part of Yellowstone history. The saddest day was when everyone gathered to sign high school yearbooks and say our beginning goodbyes. I've never outgrown the basketball courts.

Well, as I slowly come back to reality, I think of how truly sad it is that no one hangs out anymore. Except for me. I've had too many good times and too many more to come to ever give it up. This is my sanctuary. If one can have a love affair with a park, I guess that I have. On the wall around the sprinkler, my name is engraved, and I suppose that as long as that is there, we'll always be a part of each other.

—*Randi Adelman*

Enabling the Reader to Recognize That Which Is Unfamiliar

Our second function for representative texts was to enable readers to recognize something when it comes their way.

It arrives. "What is it?" we cry. And we rush to find out, to identify it, as quickly as possible. It is also important to get it right.

AGASSIZ'S REPRESENTATION

Seen floating in the water Cyanea Arctica exhibits a large circular disk, of a substance not unlike jelly, thick in the centre, and suddenly thinning out towards the edge, which presents several indentations. The centre of that disk is of a dark purplish-brown color, while the edge is much lighter, almost white and transparent. This disk is constantly heaving and falling, at regular intervals; the margin is especially active, so much so, that, at times, it is stretched on a level with the whole surface of the disk, which, in such a condition, is almost flat, while, at other times, it is so fully arched that it assumes the appearance of a hemisphere. These motions recall so strongly those of an umbrella, alternately opened and shut, that writers, who have described similar animals, have generally called this gelatinous disk the umbrella. From the lower surface of this disk hang, conspicuously, three kinds of appendages. Near the margin there are eight bunches of long tentacles, moving in every direction, sometimes extending to an enormous length, sometimes shortened to a mere coil of entangled threads, constantly rising and falling, stretching now in one direction and then in another, but generally spreading slant-ingly in a direction opposite to that of the onward movement of the animal. These streamers may be compared to floating tresses of hair, encircling organs which are farther inward upon the lower surface of the disk. Of these organs, there are also eight bunches, which alternate with the eight bunches of tentacles, but they are of two kinds; four are elegant sacks, adorned, as it were, with waving ruffles projecting in large clusters, which are alternately pressed forward and withdrawn, and might also be compared to bunches of grapes, by turns inflated and collapsed. These four bunches alternate with four masses of folds, hanging like rich cur-tains, loosely waving to and fro, and as they wave, extending downwards, or shortening rapidly, recalling, to those who have had an opportunity of witnessing the phenomenon, the play of the streamers of an aurora borealis. All these parts have their fixed position; they are held together by a sort of horizontal curtain, which is suspended from the lower sur-face of the gelatinous disk. The horizontal curtain is itself connected with the disk, fastened to it as it were by ornamental stitches, which divide the whole field into a number of areas, alternately larger and smaller, now concentric, now radiating, between which the organs already described are inserted.

—Louis Agassiz, *Contributions to the Natural History of the United States*

Reflecting on Agassiz's Representation

What is the role of the writer in making that text? He is obviously a biologist—how do we know? He is also writing rather than working in his laboratory, so he is also a teacher or explainer. What is he explaining?

Do you think he is writing for an audience of experienced biologists or for lay readers interested in biology and wishing to know more? What is the evidence for your deduction?

How many similes (x is like y) does he use? What is the effect of his similes?

Everything can be broken down into a whole and its parts. Do you think Agassiz succeeds in making the parts fit neatly into a coherent whole? (No explanation should leave a reader with an untidy heap of bits and pieces; they must all be fitted into place in such a way that the reader can see how the whole thing hangs together.)

WHAT NOW?

Try to draw a picture of Cyanea Arctica, using Agassiz's text.

WHAT NEXT?

Choose something from your own world and using the same kind of universal procedure as Agassiz, represent it so that your reader will be enabled to compose a coherent mental image of it, the various parts fitting into the whole. Although such texts invariably name the object, omit the name in yours, and see if a reader can deduce it.

MAKING FEVER RECOGNIZABLE

FEVER is the condition of the body characterized by an increase in temperature. It is one of the most common accompaniments of diseases in general, and serves to make the distinction between *febrile* and *non-febrile* ailments.

Symptoms—The onset of a fever is usually marked by a rigor or shivering, which may exist only as a slight but persistent feeling of chilliness, or, on the other hand, be of a violent character, and, as occasionally happens with children, find expression in the form of well-marked convulsions. Although termed the *cold stage* of fever, in this condition the temperature of the body is really increased. There are, besides, various accompanying feelings of illness, such as pain in the back, headache, sickness, thirst, and great lassitude. In all cases of febrile complaints it is of importance for the physician to note the first occurrence of shivering, which in general fixes the beginning of the attack. This stage is soon followed by the full development of the febrile condition, the *hot stage*. The skin now feels hot and dry, and the temperature, always elevated above the normal standard, will often be found to show daily variations corresponding to those observed in health—namely, a rise toward evening, and a fall in the morning. There is a relative increase in the rate of the pulse and quickness of breathing. The tongue is dry and furred; the thirst is intense, while the appetite is gone; the urine is scanty, of high specific gravity, containing a large quantity of solid matter, particular urea, the excretion of which . . . is increased in fever; while, on the other hand, certain of the saline ingredients, such as chlorides, are often diminished. The bowels are in general constipated, but they may be relaxed, especially if the gut is the primary site of infection, as in typhoid fever. The nervous system participates in the general disturbance, and sleeplessness and disquietude are common accompaniments, and there may be delirium. The wasting of the muscles, and corresponding loss of strength, may be marked, and continue even although considerable quantities of nutriment may be taken.

The decline of the fever takes place either by the occurrence of a *crisis* . . . i.e. a sudden termination of the symptoms, often accompanied with some discharge from the body, such as profuse perspiration, copious flow of thick urine, and occasionally diarrhea, or by a more gradual subsidence of the temperature, technically termed a *lysis*. If death ensues, this is due to failure of the vital centres in the brain or of the heart, as a result of either the infection or hyperpyrexia.

—Black's Medical Dictionary

Differences   If you compare that fever text with Rushdie's (p. 134) and Malouf's (p. 167), what striking differences do you notice?

The following terms may help you to focus:

once

unique

narrative

participant

proximity/distance

reflective/practical

particularization/generalization

clinical

function

What difficulties did you experience with the language of that last text? Could the writer have prevented them by using other, more familiar language?

Specialized Work, Specialized Language   Every society contains pockets of specialists who, when they work together, may use a language that no outsider will understand. If you wish to become an effective member of any such group (e.g., computer programmers, surgeons, lawyers, fishermen, farmers) you will have to master the language of the group. You will need to know the language in order to participate not only in the specialized activity itself but also in the talking that both precedes and follows and that often is an integral part of the activity. (What does a lawyer do, other than read, write, talk, and listen?)

The work, discoveries, conventions, do's and don't's, traditions of every such group are to be observed in both its doings and its language. The transmission of skills and competences depends on transmission of the language.

Notes   Which working or recreational group's language have you already mastered? Which languages are you at present learning? In what ways can such language (and the knowledge it represents) be abused (used in such a way as to exploit or take advantage of those not in the know)?

WRITING DEFINITIONS AND UNIVERSALLY VALID DESCRIPTIONS

The task that faces those who write definitions for dictionaries or descriptions for encyclopedias is this: whatever they write must be true for all cases, all instances, all examples of their given subject. We would be unlikely to turn to someone suffering from a fever for any such definition or description. Why not?

WHAT NOW?

Attempt both a definition and a universally valid description of some of the following:

typewriter	common cold	headache
depression	depression	nostalgia
(meteorological)	(psychological)	hangover
dieting	writer's block	writing
infatuation	obsession	gluttony
talking	sneezing	laughter
death	comedy	

In doing this assignment, you may discover that writers for encyclopedias walk a tightrope: on the one side lies the vagueness of ordinary everyday language, on the other lies the "secret" language of the experts. How do you keep your balance between these two, falling neither into loose approximations nor into the linguistic elitism of the initiated?

*Mis*representations

Our perceptions are *never neutral*; Sally encounters a frog, and is delighted by the delicate patterning, the subtle colors, the bright eyes, the powerful leaps; Sarah shudders and looks away. If she always looks away, she will never have an opportunity to change her mind. To give in to a feeling of revulsion or disgust, often learned from parents who should have known better, is to deny oneself many possible pleasures. Matters are even more problematic when it is a question of how we perceive other human beings, because we all carry around a bundle of prejudices, many of which are rooted in ignorance.

WILLIAM JAMES MISUNDERSTANDS

When the American philosopher William James was traveling in North Carolina in the 1890s, he fell prey to a misunderstanding, and if it had not been corrected, he would have carried a misrepresentation back inside his mind to Boston.

Some years ago, while journeying in the mountains of North Carolina, I passed by a large number of "coves," as they call them there, or heads of small valleys between the hills, which had been newly cleared and planted. The impression on my mind was one of unmitigated squalor. The settler had in every case cut down the more manageable trees, and left their charred stumps standing. The larger trees he had girdled and killed, in order that their foliage should not cast a shade. He had then built a log cabin, plastering its chinks with clay, and had set up a tall zigzag rail fence around the scene of his havoc to keep the pigs and cattle out. Finally, he had irregularly planted the intervals between the stumps and trees with Indian corn, which grew among the chips; and there he dwelt with his wife and babes—an axe, a gun, a few utensils, and some pigs and chickens feeding in the woods, being the sum total of his possessions.

The forest had been destroyed; and what had "improved" it out of existence was hideous, a sort of ulcer, without a single element of artificial grace to make up for the loss of Nature's beauty. Ugly, indeed, seemed the life of the squatter, scudding, as the sailors say, under bare poles, beginning again away back where our first ancestors started, and by hardly a single item the better off for all the achievements of the intervening generations.

Talk about going back to nature! I said to myself, oppressed by the dreariness, as I drove by. Talk of a country life for one's old age and for one's children! Never thus, with nothing but the bare ground and one's bare hands to fight the battle! Never, without the best spoils of culture woven in! The beauties and commodities gained by the centuries are sacred. They are our heritage and birthright. No modern person ought to be willing to live a day in such a state of rudimentariness and denudation.

Then I said to the mountaineer who was driving me, "What sort of people are they who have to make these new clearings?" "All of us," he replied. "Why, we ain't happy here unless we are getting one of these coves under cultivation." I instantly felt that I had been losing the whole inward significance of the situation. Because to me the clearings spoke of naught but denudation, I thought that to those whose sturdy arms and obedient axes had made them they could tell no other story. But, when *they* looked on the hideous stumps, what they thought of was personal victory. The chips, the girdled trees, and the vile split rails spoke of honest sweat, persistent toil and final reward. The cabin was a warrant of safety for self and wife and babes. In short, the clearing, which to me was a mere ugly picture on the retina, was to them a symbol redolent with moral memories and sang a very paean of duty, struggle, and success.

I had been as blind to the peculiar ideality of their conditions as they certainly would also have been to the ideality of mine, had they had a peep at my strange indoor academic ways of life at Cambridge.

Wherever a process of life communicates an eagerness to him who lives it, there the life becomes genuinely significant. Sometimes the eagerness is more knit up with the motor activities, sometimes with the perceptions, sometimes with the imagination, sometimes with reflective thought. But, wherever it is found, there is the zest, the tingle, the excitement of reality; and there *is* "importance" in the only real and positive sense in which importance ever anywhere can be.

The spectator-stranger saw nothing but "unmitigated squalor," whereas the participants saw the shaping of a better future. Elsewhere in the same essay, James asserts: "The spectator's judgment is sure to miss the root of the matter, and to possess no truth." An exaggeration? James goes on: "The subject judged knows a part of the world of reality which the judging spectator fails to see, knows more while the spectator knows less." Does that make your head spin? We hope so.

WHAT NOW?

Select some experiences from your own life to illustrate your own position either agreeing or disagreeing (partly or wholly) with James's argument.

WHAT NEXT?

Carpenters and joiners from North Carolina travel to Boston in search of work. They are employed by William James to renovate his floorboards. Assume the role of one of these men, and write a letter home to your wife: the first half to misrepresent James because you can't see the point of sitting pointing your eyes at a page all day, the second half to correct or modify the first half as a result of a conversation over coffee with James, in which he has helped you to see the point of his work.

(MIS)REPRESENTING STRANGERS

Here are four short texts in which the writer is giving an account of a stranger or strangers.

To each act of observing-describing, we all bring a bundle of assumptions—attitudes, preconceptions, prejudices, points of view—which we have learned from our parents, our social group, our culture.

See if you can identify the color of skin of each writer; and locate those assumptions that are likely to cause at least misunderstanding and at worst war.

Here are two clues: the location of each encounter is Africa; the time, late nineteenth or early twentieth century.

A Pink Cheek man came one day to our Council. . . . He came from far, from where many of their people lived in houses made of stone and where they had their own Council. He sat in our midst and he told us of the King of the Pink Cheek who was a great king and lived in a land over the seas. "This great king is now your king," he said, "and this land is all his land, though he has said you may live on it as you are his people and he is your father and you are his sons." This was strange news. For this land was ours. . . . We had no king, we elected our Councils and they made our laws. . . . With patience, our leading Elders tried to tell this to the Pink Cheek, and he listened. But at the end he said, "This we know, but in spite of this what I have told you is a fact. You have now a king . . . and in the town called Nairobi is a Council or government that acts for the king. And his laws are your laws. . . ."

The hunters return, and their friends run out to greet them as if they had been gone for years, murmuring to them in a kind of baby language, calling them by their names of love, shaking their right hands, caressing their faces, patting them upon their breasts. . . . And so they toy and babble and laugh with one another till the sun turns red, and the air turns dusky, and the giant trees cast deep shadows across the street. . . . A European Government ought perhaps to introduce compulsory labour among the barbarous races that acknowledge its sovereignty. . . . Children are ruled and schooled by force, and it is not an empty metaphor to say that savages are children.

. . . They are just like children . . . always laughing or quarrelling. They are good-natured and passionate, indolent, but will work hard for a time; clever up to a certain point, densely stupid beyond. The intelligence of an average Negro is about equal to that of a European child of ten years old. A few, a very few, go beyond this, but these are exceptions, just as Shakespeare was an exception to the ordinary intellect of an Englishman. They are fluent talkers but their ideas are borrowed. They are absolutely without inventive power. Living among white men their imitative faculties enable them to attain a considerable amount of civilization. Left alone to their own devices they retrograde into a state little above their native savagery.

When we heard that the man with the white flesh was journeying down the Lualaba we were open-mouthed with astonishment. . . . That man, we said to ourselves, has a white skin. He must have got it from the river-kingdom. He will be one of our brothers who was drowned in the river. . . . Now he is coming back to us, he is coming home. . . .

We will prepare a feast, I ordered, we will go to meet our brother and escort him into our village with rejoicing! We donned our ceremonial garb. We assembled the great canoes. . . . We swept forward, my canoe leading, the others following, with songs of joy and with dancing, to meet the first white man our eyes had beheld, and to do him honour.

But as we drew near his canoes there were loud reports, bang! bang! and fire-staves spat bits of iron at us. We were paralysed with fright; our mouths hung wide open and we could not shut them. Things such as we had never seen, never heard of, never dreamed of—they were the work of evil spirits! Several of my men plunged into the water. . . . What for? Did they fly to safety? No—for others fell down silent—they were dead, and blood flowed from little holes in their bodies. "War! that is war!" I yelled. "Go back!" The canoes sped back to our village with all the strength our spirits could impart to our arms.

That was no brother! That was the worst enemy our country had ever seen.

—David Killingray, *A Plague of Europeans*

Notes

Which of those texts strikes you as most emphatically *racist* in its attitudes/assumptions? Which phrases/words strike you as especially expressive of racist attitudes?

Our Commentary

When the white explorers/invaders (choose, according to your point of view) encountered native Africans, the white men carried guns and ammunition. Inside their minds, they carried "ancient opinions and rules of life," and they failed to realize that the Africans too had their own equally valid "ancient opinions and rules of life." Most white men failed to value African cultures for a variety of reasons. One was that they were unable and/or unwilling to examine their own prejudices toward anyone unlike themselves. Instead of "hesitating in the moment of decision, sceptical, puzzled and unresolved," they rushed in with damning judgments, absolute certainties, and bullets.

WHAT NOW?

Dig into your memory and write of an occasion when you deliberately or unwittingly misrepresented someone so that you would feel more comfortable about the way you treated them. Or, turn the tables and recount an occasion when you were the victim of such misrepresentation.

WHAT NEXT?

Can you illustrate the following generalizations with examples from your own experience or from your knowledge of the contemporary world? Consider, for example, prejudice and propaganda.

Human beings do not live in the objective world alone, nor alone in the world of social activity as ordinarily understood, but are very much at the mercy of the particular language which has become the medium for their society. . . . The fact of the matter is that the "real world" is to a large extent built up on the language habits of the group. No two languages are ever sufficiently similar to be considered as representing the same social reality. The worlds in which different societies live are distinct worlds, not merely the same world with different labels attached.

—Edward Sapir, *Culture, Language, and Personality*

13 | "Eh?" Representations that Defamiliarize

Familiarity and Contempt

When we are spectators, as was William James in North Carolina, it is very easy for us to miss the point, to misunderstand and so misrepresent. But what of the problem of overfamiliarity? What happens when our world is so familiar to us that we despise it? Or no longer give it any attention? When we suffer from not unfamiliarity but overfamiliarity? How then do we represent the object of our scorn and weariness? How do we represent our derision, our boredom?

An easy, quick, and unsatisfactory answer is: Just generalize. Say, "It stinks." If your listener is yourself alone, and the purpose of your utterance is no more than to relieve your feelings, that kind of generalized cliché is perhaps enough. But what if you wish to represent it adequately to someone else?

WATT'S NEW?

Let us see how Samuel Beckett does it in his novel *Watt*. Perhaps you will want to try his way too.

Personally of course I regret everything. Not a word, not a deed, not a thought, not a need, not a grief, not a joy, not a girl, not a boy, not a doubt, nor a trust, not a scorn, not a lust, not a hope, not a fear, not a smile, not a tear, not a name, not a face, no time, no place, that I do not regret, exceedingly. An ordure, from beginning to end. And yet, when I sat for Fellowship, but for the boil on my bottom . . . The rest, an ordure. The Tuesday scowls, the Wednesday growls, the Thursday curses, the Friday howls, the Saturday snores, the Sunday yawns, the Monday morns, the Monday morns. The whacks, the moans, the cracks, the groans, the welts, the squeaks, the belts, the shrieks, the pricks, the prayers, the kicks, the tears, the skelps, and the yelps. And the poor old lousy old earth, my earth and my father's and my mother's and my father's father's and my mother's mother's and my father's mother's and my mother's father's and my father's mother's father's and my mother's father's mother's and my father's mother's mother's and my mother's father's father's and my father's father's mother's and my mother's mother's father's and my father's father's father's and my mother's mother's mother's and other people's fathers' and mothers' and fathers' fathers' and mothers' mothers' and fathers' mothers' and mothers' fathers' and fathers' mothers' fathers' and mothers' fathers' mothers' and fathers' mothers' mothers' and mothers' fathers' fathers' and fathers' fathers' mothers' and mothers' mothers' fathers' and fathers' fathers' fathers' and mothers' mothers' mothers'. An excrement. The crocuses and the larch turning green every year a week before the others and the pastures red with uneaten sheep's placentas and the long summer days and the newmown hay and the wood-pigeon in the morning and the cuckoo in the afternoon and the corncrake in the evening and the wasps in the jam and the smell of the gorse and the look of the gorse and the apples falling and the children walking in the dead leaves and the larch turning brown a week before the others and the chestnuts falling and the howling winds and the sea breaking over the pier and the first fires and the hooves on the road and the consumptive postman whistling *The Roses Are Blooming in Picardy* and the standard oillamp and of course the snow and to be sure the sleet and bless your heart the slush and every fourth year the February débacle and the endless April showers and the crocuses and then the whole bloody business starting all over again. A turd. And if I could begin it all over again, knowing what I know now, the result would be the same. And if I could begin again a third time, knowing what I would know then, the result would be the same. And if I could begin it all over again a hundred times, knowing each time a little more than the time before, the result would always be the same, and the hundredth life as the first, and the hundred lives as one. A cat's flux. But at this rate we shall be here all night.

Reading *Watt*
(Beckett)

We hope you didn't read that passage with your eye alone. Of all the texts in this book, it is the one that depends most on the ear. But what, you may ask, is the ear supposed to hear? The voice of a disenchanted spectator looking back over his years and the cycle of the year, and going on and on and on? What is the main pattern of the prose? It is simply and repetitively paratactic. 1 and 2 and 3 and 4 and 5 . . . and so on. Or the 1, the 2, the 3, the 4, the 5. . . . But what is the implicit effect of the energy of the "speaker"? How does his seemingly inexhaustible energy affect you? Is it depressing? Tedious? Wearying? Or is it that the explicit complaining is contradicted by the implicit glee of the extravagant cataloguing? Isn't he enjoying himself? Doesn't he love it? (He would never admit it, of course.) We are not being invited to laugh with him, but can we not reasonably laugh at him? At his humbug? At his self-indulgence?

WHAT NOW?

1. React to, answer, Beckett's complaint by writing your own "reply"– a cheerful or even ecstatic text that represents all the pleasures and delights of your life's years, your years' months, your months' days.

2. Using a form similar to Beckett's, assume one of the following roles:
   a. A surgeon, on the edge of a nervous breakdown from overwork, looking back on all the operations he/she has performed in the last month
   b. A guilty glutton recounting details of the meals he/she has recently indulged in
   c. A teacher, on the verge of burn-out, recalling all her/his troublesome students
   d. A "jock," telling of his injuries on the field or in the gym
   e. A radical feminist, enumerating all the offensive acts of men she knows
   f. A weary housewife, reeling off all the chores that make up her week's work

---

"THERE'S NOTHING OUT THERE": MOON LOOKS CLOSELY AT THE EARTH

Overfamiliarity produces not only scorn but also a kind of blindness; we have seen some things so often that we no longer see them at all, even when we look at them. William Least Heat Moon, who made a celebrated journey on the back roads of America a few years ago, was near Eldorado, Texas, when he was told by the locals: "There's nothing out there." Instead of accepting those dismissive words at their face value, he decided to put them to the test.

Straight as a chief's countenance, the road lay ahead, curves so long and gradual as to be imperceptible except on the map. For nearly a hundred miles due west of Eldorado, not a single town. It was the Texas some people see as barren waste when they cross it, the part they later describe at the motel bar as "nothing." They say, "There's nothing out there."

Driving through the miles of nothing, I decided to test the hypothesis and stopped somewhere in western Crockett County on the top of a broad mesa, just off Texas 29. At a distance, the land looked so rocky and dry, a religious man could believe that the First Hand never got around to the creation in here. Still, somebody had decided to string barbed wire around it.

No plant grew higher than my head. For a while, I heard only miles of wind against the Ghost; but after the ringing in my ears stopped, I heard myself breathing, then a bird note, an answering call, another kind of birdsong, and another: mockingbird, mourning dove, an enigma. I heard the high *zizz* of flies the color of gray flannel and the deep buzz of a blue bumblebee. I made a list of nothing in particular:

1. mockingbird
2. mourning dove
3. enigma bird (heard not saw)
4. gray flies
5. blue bumblebee
6. two circling buzzards (not yet, boys)

7. orange ants
8. black ants
9. orange-black ants (what's been going on?)
10. three species of spiders
11. opossum skull
12. jackrabbit (chewed on cactus)
13. deer (left scat)
14. coyote (left tracks)
15. small rodent (den full of seed hulls under rock)
16. snake (skin hooked on cactus spine)
17. prickly pear cactus (yellow blossoms)
18. hedgehog cactus (orange blossoms)
19. barrel cactus (red blossoms)
20. devil's pincushion (no blossoms)
21. catclaw (no better name)
22. two species of grass (neither green, both alive)
23. yellow flowers (blossoms smaller than peppercorns)
24. sage (indicates alkali-free soil)
25. mesquite (three-foot plants with eighty-foot roots to reach water that fell as rain two thousand years ago)
26. greasewood (oh, yes)
27. joint fir (steeped stems make Brigham Young tea)
28. earth
29. sky
30. wind (always)

That was all the nothing I could identify then, but had I waited until dark when the desert really comes to life, I could have done better. To say nothing is out here is incorrect; to say the desert is stingy with everything except space and light, stone and earth is closer to the truth.

—*Blue Highways*

WHAT NOW?

1. Choose a perfectly familiar scene—your kitchen, back yard, bus stop—and make a list of everything that you have stopped noticing or never noticed before.
2. Choose the most boring place you know, and describe it as if you were seeing it for the first time, through eyes energized by curiosity, inquisitiveness, or a sense of strangeness.

Rendering the Familiar Unfamiliar

A NEWSPAPER COLUMNIST DEFAMILIARIZES

Our aim, by the way, is to give complete satisfaction. If this column is not in good condition when you receive it, return it to this office and your money will be refunded. In addition, you will receive six stouts in a hand-some presentation cooper. When the column is written, it weighs exactly 0.03 grammes. Due to heat, evaporation or damp, the contents may become impaired or discoloured. In case of complaint, return it to this office with the rest of the newspaper and we will gladly replace it, or, at your option, return your money in full. Our aim is to make every cus-tomer a friend for life. We wish to give you complete satisfaction. We are your obsequious handwashing servants. We are very meek and humble. One frown from you and we feel that we have made a mess of our whole lives.

—Myles na Gopaleen, *The Best of Myles*

WHAT NOW?

Take an ordinary, familiar object or action and defamiliarize it by "changing the frame," i.e., deliberately misunderstand it as if you were a naïve or innocent stranger or alien. For example, write about

1. A car as a front-garden sculpture

2. Cosmetics as disguise

3. Dog treated as a child

4. Smoking as breast-feeding

5. Child treated as pet

6. Doing nothing as a keep-fit exercise

7. Reading as eye exercise

8. Teacher as silence-breaker

9. Statues as pigeon-rests

10. Shoes as weapons

RIDDLES: THEY WERE THE DEATH OF HOMER

When we were much younger, about 7 or 8, we used to spend much time in posing and solving riddles. You probably did the same, no matter where you grew up. It seems that there is no society in the world that does not use riddles. They are particularly popular with children, and you may have noticed that we grow out of them. Few adults that we know introduce them into conversation; they are much more likely to tell a joke or a story than to pose a riddle. (See if you can recall just one from your earlier years.) But perhaps this is not true of all societies; Homer is said to have died of vexation at failing to solve a riddle about a louse.

What exactly are we doing when we exchange riddles? See if you agree with the following account:

1. We are offering the other person(s) a description or a representation of a bit of the world.

2. This representation is built up of small hints, but the familiar frames are withheld—no name is given, no context is offered. (When we *name* an object, the other person recognizes what we are talking about. Similarly, when one sees garbage *in a trash can*, the fact that it is *there* and not on a kitchen shelf *confirms* one's belief that it really is garbage!)

3. We are testing someone's powers of observation and his/her ability to match words and things.

4. The game of exchanging riddles is mildly competitive.

5. When we pose a riddle, we cannot lose: If the other person solves our riddle, we are pleased because the riddle "worked," the accuracy of our hints, of our description, was recognized; if the other person fails to solve our riddle, we are pleased because then we can supply the answer.

6. The riddles of one society will probably not make sense to the people of another society.

7. Unlike certain games (solitaire in cards, certain video games), there's no point in playing by oneself. The satisfactions are *social*.

Solve These

Sharpen your wits on these riddles. Try them alone, then compare your solutions with those of others. (Answers on page 375.)

1. Something that devours without mouth or stomach,
   Trees and animals are food for it.
   If you feed it, it becomes vigorous and lives;
   But if you give it a drink of water, it dies.

2. I often murmur, but never weep;
   Lie in bed, but never sleep;
   My mouth is larger than my head,
   In spite of the fact I'm never fed;
   I have no feet, yet swiftly run;
   The more falls I get, move faster on.

3. Legs I have, but seldom walk;
   I backbite all, yet never talk.

4. Little Nancy Etticoat,
   With a white petticoat,
   And a red nose;
   She has no feet or hands,
   The longer she stands
   The shorter she grows.

5. Four stiff-standers,
   Four dilly-danders,
   Two lookers,
   Two crookers,
   And a wig-wag.

6. Around the rick, around the rick,
   And there I found my Uncle Dick.
   I screwed his neck,
   I sucked his blood,
   And left his body lying.

7. A shoemaker makes shoes without leather,
   With all the four elements put together,
   Fire, Water, Earth, Air,
   And every customer takes two pair.

A good riddle works because it invokes both the familiar and the unfamiliar. In other words, a riddle will work only if the solver is already familiar with the thing referred to, but it will not work well if the clues are so fully descriptive that they give it away. The clues must give the solver enough to work on, but in such a way that the object is partly hidden or disguised.

WHAT NOW?

The best way to test what you just read, is to apply it. So try composing a riddle that satisfies both rules: choose an object with which everyone is *familiar,* then observe the object's features closely, and express them in *unfamiliar* terms. Test your riddle on a chosen victim, and try to find out:

If he/she solved it, what produced the moment of enlightenment?

At what point did the solver first think he/she had found the solution?

If the victim failed to solve it, was this due mostly to the inadequacy of your clues, to a failure of observation on his/her part, or a bit of both?

Now Solve These

a. Thirty white horses
   Upon a red hill,
   Now they stamp,
   Now they champ,
   Now they stand still.

b. Black I am and much admired,
    Men seek for me until they're tired;
    When they find me, break my head,
    And take me from my resting bed.

c. Formed long ago, yet made today,
    Employed while others sleep;
    What few would like to give away,
    Nor any wish to keep.

d. Riddle me, riddle me,
    riddle me ree,
    I saw a nut cracker
    up in a tree.

By Morning

Some for everyone
  plenty

  and more coming

Fresh   dainty   airily arriving
  everywhere at once

Transparent at first
  each faint slice
  slow   soundlessly tumbling

  then quickly thickly a gracious fleece
  will spread like youth   like wheat
  over the city

Each building will be   a hill
  all sharps made round

  dark worn noisy narrows made still
  wide   flat   clean   spaces

Streets will be   fields
  cars be   fumbling sheep

A deep bright harvest will be seeded
  in a night

By morning we'll be   children
  feeding on manna

  a new loaf on every doorsill
                              —*May Swenson*

ELIZABETH BISHOP SEES WITH ALIEN EYES

It is midnight. The writer Elizabeth Bishop has turned down the dimmer to reduce the amount of light in her study. As she looks at all the familiar tools of her trade, she takes on the role of a very small alien visitor, whose task it is to make sense of each feature of this strange landscape. The familiar is defamiliarized, the old becomes new—hence the title.

12 O'Clock News

gooseneck lamp

As you all know, tonight is the night of the full moon, half the world over. But here the moon seems to hang motionless in the sky. It gives very little light; it could be dead. Visibility is poor. Nevertheless, we shall try to give you some idea of the lay of the land and the present situation.

typewriter

The escarpment that rises abruptly from the central plain is in heavy shadow, but the elaborate terracing of its southern glacis gleams faintly in the dim light, like fish scales. What endless labor those small, peculiarly shaped terraces represent! And yet, on them the welfare of this tiny principality depends.

pile of mss.

A slight landslide occurred in the northwest about an hour ago. The exposed soil appears to be of poor quality: almost white, calcareous, and shaly. There are believed to have been no casualties.

typed sheet

Almost due north, our aerial reconnaissance reports the discovery of a large rectangular "field," hitherto unknown to us, obviously man-made. It is dark-speckled. An airstrip? A cemetery?

envelopes

In this small, backward country, one of the most backward left in the world today, communications are crude and "industrialization" and its products almost nonexistent. Strange to say, however, signboards are on a truly gigantic scale.

ink-bottle

We have also received reports of a mysterious, oddly shaped, black structure, at an undisclosed distance to the east. Its presence was revealed only because its highly polished surface catches such feeble moonlight as prevails. The natural resources of the country being far from completely known to us, there is the possibility that this may be, or may contain, some powerful and terrifying "secret weapon." On the other hand, given what we *do* know, or have learned from our anthropologists and sociologists about this people, it may well be nothing more than a *numen*, or a great altar recently erected to one of their gods, to which, in their present historical state of superstition and helplessness, they attribute magical powers, and may even regard as a "savior," one last hope of rescue from their grave difficulties.

typewriter eraser

At last! One of the elusive natives has been spotted! He appears to be—rather, to have been—a unicyclist-courier, who may have met his end by falling from the height of the escarpment because of the deceptive illumination. Alive, he would have been small, but undoubtedly proud and erect, with the thick, bristling black hair typical of the indigenes.

ashtray

From our superior vantage point, we can clearly see into a sort of dug-out, possibly a shell crater, a "nest" of soldiers. They lie heaped together, wearing the camouflage "battle dress" intended for "winter warfare." They are in hideously contorted positions, all dead. We can make out at least eight bodies. These uniforms were designed to be used in guerrilla warfare on the country's one snow-covered mountain peak. The fact that these poor soldiers are wearing them *here*, on the plain, gives further proof, if proof were necessary, either of the childishness and hopeless impracticality of this inscrutable people, our opponents, or of the sad corruption of their leaders.

—Elizabeth Bishop, *Geography III*

Notes   What did Elizabeth Bishop do in order to defamiliarize a familiar set of objects? See if you agree with the following:

1. She withheld *names*.

2. She changed the *scale*: relatively small objects became very large, and the room became a landscape.

3. She made the aliens *assign* unfamiliar (alien) *meanings*, which were independent of and contrary to the meanings that the same objects have for us. First they misinterpret, then they misinform.

OUR STUDENTS MEET THE CHALLENGE OF DEFAMILIARIZATION

The art of effective defamiliarization is *not* to cheat. If you change the scale, then you must change the scale of everything. You must not distort objects but merely assign unfamiliar but plausible functions to them—as when the alien in the movie *Starman* deduces that the yellow traffic light at a crossing means "Drive very fast." (*Starman* was distinguished by some ingenious and delightful moments of defamiliarization.) If you invent new words, they must not deliberately mislead the reader.

Read the following texts by some of our students. You will find that they involve two very different kinds of reading: the first reading is a plunge into mystery, but gradually you find your bearings and realize what part of the familiar world it is that is being represented in alien ways. Once you have recognized the "reality" you can then reread the text and see how accurately the "aliens" have represented it, and how plausible, logical, and consistent their misreadings are.

1.

Marvelous! The world is marvelous. Oh, hell! Here it comes again. Up. Hoisted up, again up, again up I go. What a bore. Come on now—let me go. I'm going to get angry. Go ahead and howl. I am going to go my way.

Hmm. I wonder what that sound is. Maybe it is yummy. I'll sneak up and see. I smell it—it is yummy. Gonna get it. No way out for it. I'm going to get yummy . . . going to get yummy. Here I go slowly . . . slowly. Ha, cotcha! Bop it back and forth. Ha. Looks good, smells good. Yummy.

Oh, hell, here the big it comes. Hurts my tail. I'm going up and fast. Up and up and up. It might follow. Better climb out there. It is so big that it can't follow. Hang on. Everything is shaking. I'd better leap and get out of here. Run! Damn its. Such pests. The little it ups me and the big it won't leave me alone. Damn its.

I know—I'll get a little sleep. Under the color thing. Oh damn, here comes the it again. Oh, it didn't see me. Good! Ah, marvelous.

What! What's this. It-rain! Why can't the its leave me alone. It-rain! Out I go and fast fast fast. Damn its. Mash, and up, and rain. I'm leaving.

The black earth is always so hot and hard. I'll run. Good! Now I'm in belly-highs. Ah, I love belly-highs. They tickle my undersides. Maybe that it will tickle my belly. I love belly tickles.

Hey, it! I'll rub its lifters. Ah, wow, ecstasy. Belly tickles! Wow. This is a good it.

I think I'll go home. Damn it, quit! Can't you see I'm finished. Want to leave. Come on, I'm finished! I'm getting angry. Stop, it. Out go my stickers. Smart it! Thanks and bon voyage.

Hmm. I'm still tired. I think I'll find cool. Where? Oh right over there. That big color thing. No its. Soft belly-highs. Wow! Marvelous. Life is marvelous.

That was some little yummy I had there. I'll think about yummies. Easier to rest. Almost see one in the belly highs. Marvelous. What a life. I love belly-highs. I love yummies. I love big color things. I love cool. I love its that tickle my belly. Life is marvelous. Simply marvelous . . .*

—*Lonnie Kay*

2.

We have made a safe landing and our search crew has packed necessary supplies for the day's search. We have found the surface of the planet slick and shiny and of unusual design. It reminds us of our formal gardens at home, but is strangely two-dimensional. It provides very little traction for our vehicles. Our crew agronomists wonder how it is kept so neat and manicured. It seems that this unusual strain of vegetation has mass produced itself in a strikingly similar manner, and is now arrested in growth. We have detected no change in it since our landing two days ago.

From the vantage point of our spacecraft the structures to our west are cubical and rectangular. The buildings are devoid of habitation, at least we have not yet discovered any forms of life. Some of the structures appear hinged on the front allowing complete exposure to what's inside. Crew sociologists believe a "let it all hang out" attitude accompanies this

---

*Glossary: it, children; belly-highs, grass; color thing, bush; lifters, legs; it-rain, sprinkler; yummy, smaller animal/mouse.

exposure of one's living quarters to the community. Above us is a strange squarish orb with two bright spots emitting light, no doubt the sun of the planet.

Due east we come upon a cubical structure quite different from the row of hinged buildings. The surface is extremely slick, much slicker than the initial landing surface. Initial attempts at scaling the structure proved futile. Our men could not cling to the surface. The structure seems important to the life form of the planet, centrally located in our search area. An amount of heat is emitted from the structure, but not so much as to penetrate our space suits. A party to the northeast has found a long tubular piping running from near the bottom of the structure on the far side to the top. The tube, somehow connected to the white stone behind the structure, may be part of an intricate communication system. The piping is within our reach and we are able to use it to scale the structure. When reaching the top we find the pipe connected to an object monitoring something. There is a dial-like configuration surrounded by a strange alien alphabet. A quiet hum comes from the mechanism.

The top of the structure's surface is similar to the slick sides, but is interrupted by four circular platforms. These platforms seem to be a source of power. Three of them are dark in color and cool to touch. The fourth is a brilliant orange-red and emits a tremendous amount of heat. On the brilliant red platform is a metallic structure the same diameter as the platform. One can hear a strange gurgling sound from within and a vapory substance rising from the top of the metallic structure. Due to the heat, we are unable to scale the structure. However, our aerial observer indicates that some life form exists inside the metallic object. The life form is extremely active and able to withstand intense heat. The humans, if that is what they are called, are almost identical in size, shape, and color: tubular, hollow in the middle, half the size of one of our men, and a bland whitish, yellow color. They seem oblivious to our presence and engaged in a ritualistic orgy, the source of their energy and power. A dead specimen was found on the far side of the structure, but was completely lifeless and did not respond to us in any way. We conclude that the intense heat and the liquid surrounding these creatures give them some sort of life, and if they leave this environment or are exposed without protection, they die.

As evening approaches we take this specimen back to our mother ship. It is late, and the analysis of this strange life form will keep crew scientists busy for months. We shall explore further tomorrow.

—Karl Smart

3.

. . . . we flew near one of many for closer inspection. The head was supported by a long neck, brown at the bottom, and growing greener toward the top. This neck was bent and wavy with both horizontal and vertical lines visible in ordered patterns.

The very top or head of this structure was domed yet flat on top. Raised spots dotted this dome in concentric circles from a single center with lines linking dot to dot. It looked much like the eyes of our mounts only magnified tenfold.

From this pale green head streamed the hair downward, broad and in varying lengths. The color of this hair was a mixture of green, both pale and dark with red streaks. It looked scraggly and uncombed with some hair close to the neck and other projecting out away. This broad hair looked like chutes, narrower and darker at the bottom. Each chute was bumpy and veined inside and twisted and curled toward the bottom. A ride down one chute would send one through space to land on a carpet of analogous objects. We were tempted, but refrained.

—Lyle Wakefield

4.

Frank Martin and I have been walking this past hour through a jungle. We had to eject from our burning craft and landed here. The surface is smooth yet cavernous pits lurk everywhere. We must make our way carefully to avoid falling in. We are totally surrounded by trees. But these trees are different from any we have ever seen. They are tall but have no branches. As they grow taller, most of them bend to the south as if a strong wind, higher than us, is constantly blowing and bending them.

We have spotted a plain with no trees. Only smaller, lighter colored baby trees exist here. We can see in the distance a great terrace shelf rising perhaps a thousand feet high.

Suddenly the light source is cut off and we are in shade. A monstrous apparition has blocked the light and descends rapidly upon us. We lie flat on the edge of the forest hoping to be safe. This huge cylindrical object crashes north of us and scrapes through these trees, just missing us. Somehow the soil is not gouged and the trees spring back into their original shape. The huge object disappears from the sky and all is quiet. We were saved by being on the edge.

We fear this object's return and so set off over the plain toward the terraced shelf. We hope to gain a vantage height for reconnaissance.

Approaching from the west, we see a bluff with a valley on each side. We choose the south valley and proceed. A brown substance is sighted and Martin tests it. It is soft yet sticky and thick. We can and do cross it but it seems to stick to our shoes for a while until it wears off. Its source is a spiraling pit. Somehow this substance is forced out of that pit onto the lower plain.

We climb further. On a particularly high shelf Martin slips and falls into that terrible pit. I hear him cry and I shudder and shrink back. At that moment, as if signaled, the huge apparition before mentioned appears again and jams itself into that pit and turns forward and backward. Martin's cries are stifled and die out. He is killed. The monster leaves and I quickly climb higher, hoping for an escape route. Alone I top the highest ridge. I look over and my heart stops. Below me is a near vertical drop of one thousand feet. Away to the east lies more forest even denser with longer trees than before. I give up.

—Lyle Wakefield

5.

Why are they sitting there so long? Why are they so quiet, so somber? It must be punishment. But what strange punishment! It does not look particularly painful. How could it possibly hurt? None of them are crying. None of them scream. They are so quiet, so sad, so serious. I don't think it is punishment. It must be work. They are making something. But what? I have never seen anything like what they are making. It can't be food. And it is too small to wear or to use for shelter. What good could it be? And yet they keep at it so long and so seriously. It can't be a game. What pleasure could they get from sitting here inside this shelter filling white spaces with darkness. And yet they don't make it completely dark either. Why? It is so tedious and so methodical. Gradually their white fills up with dark shapes. What is the point? Yet they keep working at it.

Do they do this forever? How long does this go on? I could have caught a fish, cooked, and eaten it in the time they have spent on this foolish work.

There must be an answer. I will watch them longer. I am curious. Oh. Now one stops. He smiles. He is through. Now another. No more silence. They can speak. I do not understand their language.

Now one of them, who was not working but was watching the others, speaks. He must be the chief. The others are quiet. They listen. All of them are through with their curious work.

The chief points to one of them and tells him something. He looks away from the chief. He looks at the white that he holds in his hands. Then he holds it in front of his face and he speaks.

Perhaps the white things are magical. Perhaps it holds some sort of enchantment. As long as he holds the white in front of his face, he speaks, but when he puts it down, he is silent.

The chief points to another person. He does the same with his white thing.

This must be a religious ceremony. These must be holy men. Putting dark shapes on white must be a ritual. It seems serious business at first. But, once in a while, when speaking about their white-thing-made-dark, they laugh. Theirs is a strange religion.

—Lind Williams

6.

Radio Report #2

I have found it necessary to revise my hypothesis concerning the dominant life form on this planet. As I mentioned before, there were distinct signs of rational thought and complex behavior by certain thin-skinned, nearly hairless, upright bipeds. However, my observations of this evening have led me to believe that these creatures may instead be solar-powered robots.

I became suspicious when a large number of them moved at night into a large warehouse-type structure. As I followed them inside, I found that my premonition seemed to be correct. It was indeed some kind of warehouse or storage facility. In addition to a large number of motionless or nearly motionless robots, there were hundreds of rows of racks, each containing what appeared to me to be some kind of recharging units. The robots had apparently been programmed to come to this facility for recharging. The procedure was very intriguing. The robot would pick up a recharging unit and go sit beneath huge panels in the ceiling that transmitted stored daylight. The rays fell upon their recharging units. Each recharging unit contained somewhere between 100 and 500 solar plates which apparently converted the sunlight into usable energy which was absorbed by the robot through the two sensors in the robots' ball-like upper appendage.

The various sizes of the recharging units may have to do with the complexity of the robot in question and its particular energy needs. I observed some robots who had to use more than one recharging unit, whereas others could apparently get by on just a few solar plates out of a single unit.

Some robots had obviously not reached the facility in time. They appeared to have collapsed and were unable to move. Both their recharging units and their sensors were closed.

Radio Report #3

This morning I have observed other, more advanced robot models. These units are able to take their energy directly from the sun without the use of bulky recharging units to convert the light to energy. They are equipped with sensors but apparently do not even have to use them. Neither do they require the same amount of protective coverings that I observed on the more primitive models. They simply position themselves upon the ground exposing their entire surface area, or most of it, to the direct rays of the sun. As they take on the sun's energy and become fully charged their surface becomes noticeably darker, sometimes even taking on a reddish hue.

Again, let me repeat, these reports are extremely hypothetical. Much of what these robots have been programmed to do is very mysterious and hard to interpret. Please stay posted for a revised assessment.

—Lind Williams

"That Naive Naked Man Waving His Hand": How (Not) to Communicate with Aliens

EDWARD ROTHSTEIN'S COMMENT: THE INTENTION WAS GOOD

When Pioneer 10 was launched from Earth in 1972, it bore a plaque meant for extra-terrestrial beings. Scientists at the National Aeronautics and Space Administration wanted the imperishable gold-coated aluminum plate to be decipherable to any scientist, of any physiognomy, living anywhere in the universe.

The plaque contains a schematic drawing of a man and a woman drawn to scale in front of a sketch of the spacecraft; the man's hand is raised in greeting. A dumbbell figure pictures the hydrogen atom, to give a measure of time and space; it is the key to a star-figure, locating Earth relative to 14 radio-wave emitting pulsars. Circles below portray the solar system; a miniature Pioneer swerves between Jupiter and Saturn, soaring into the celestial beyond.

If ever some superior intelligence on some other world comes across this little picture, peering at it with whatever sensory apparatus it enjoys, the fact of the plaque will say more about humans than the message it presumably conveys. Why, after all, should an extra-terrestrial "scientist" even recognize the plaque as a message? Why would it translate a diagram into a three-dimensional object? Why would it organize lines to create a picture? Why would it ask the questions—like where does this come from and who built it—that the plaque presumes to an-swer? The plaque is based on implicit *human* assumptions; it is even bound to the particular culture that created it. Not everywhere on Earth would a hand be raised in greeting, would a man's hair part on the side, or a woman's hair drift down below her shoulders.

The plaque is interesting because it illustrates—on an interstellar level, perhaps—questions about every act of communication. *Signs* are used to convey meaning, but their interpretation is based upon unexamined, often hidden relations. There was a time when language was considered natural, linked directly to the world, the way the "species-proof" Pioneer language claims to be. But most linguistic signs are now viewed as arbitrary inventions. What assumptions then, does a language embody in its arbitrariness? How is language related to culture? How is it linked to the world? How, in a broader sense, is any information communicated?

—Edward Rothstein, *New York Times*, October 18, 1981

THE OFFICIAL EXPLANATION

Here is an official explanation of Pioneer 10's message:

> [The] primary goal is to send back to earth, some two years hence, close-up pictures and scientific observations of Jupiter, largest planet of the solar system. But a more exciting—albeit uncertain—mission is to announce to some distant civilization that we are here. It is the first official effort on the part of mankind to draw attention to itself. As the vehicle, Pioneer 10, passes Jupiter, the gravity of that planet will seize it and hurl it out of the solar system. It will sail indefinitely through the vast reaches of the Milky Way Galaxy, carrying a message in the form of a gold-coated aluminum plate, for any members of other planetary civilizations who may happen to encounter it. Scientists agree, however, that the chances are very slim indeed.
>
> The message is designed to be decipherable to any scientist, regardless of his physiognomy, history or location in space and time. The symbol, upper left, draws attention to the two states of the hydrogen atom as the unit of time (radio frequency) and distance (wavelength) to be used. The star-like diagram shows the position of the earth relative to fourteen pulsars. These are stars that emit radio pulses at regular (though in some cases slowly changing) rhythms. Solid lines indicate the relative distances of these pulsars. The dashed extensions of these lines are marked with tics indicating the rate at which that pulsar is pulsing. The rate could be used to identify each pulsar, much as each lighthouse has its characteristic rhythm. Since a few pulsars are slowing their rate, the message also indicates roughly the time of launch.

The long horizontal line extending to the right behind the two figures indicates the direction of the centre of the Milky Way Galaxy. The figures stand in front of a schematic diagram of the spacecraft with its dish-shaped antenna to give an idea of the dimensions and appearance of earth's inhabitants. The man's hand is raised in friendly salute. Below is a representation of the solar system with the sun at the left, showing that Pioneer 10 was launched from the third planet out from the sun and then was thrown out of the system by Jupiter's gravity.

—Walter Sullivan

HOW EFFECTIVE IS PIONEER 10'S MESSAGE?

If I nod my head in Greece, I may intend to mean yes, but Greeks will "read" my nod as no. How would aliens interpret a nod of the head? Or a wave of the hand?

Take a close look at the picture representing Pioneer 10's plaque, and try to read it as an alien might. How much information can you derive from it? How effective is it as a message?

NASA National Aeronautics and
      Space Administration

Headquarters
Washington. D

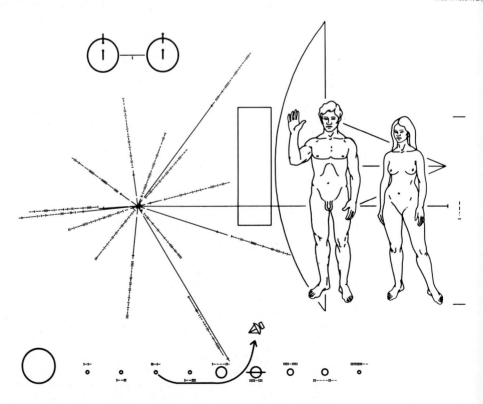

Dell Hymes defines a message as follows:

> The concept of message implies the sharing (real or imputed) of (1) a code or codes in terms of which the message is intelligible to (2) participants, minimally an addresser and addressee . . . , in (3) an event constituted by its transmission and characterized by (4) a channel or channels, (5) a setting or context, (6) a definite form or shape to the message, and (7) a topic and comment.*

In the light of that definition, is *any* extraterrestrial intelligence likely to decode the message of Pioneer 10's plaque?

Another way to test the effectiveness of a message is to see whether all the necessary elements of communication are present:

1. Someone sending the message

2. Someone receiving the message

3. A contact that joins them

4. The message

5. A context that makes sense of the message

6. A linguistic code that both sender and receiver, addresser and addressee can decode

Only two of these six elements are present in the Pioneer 10 project.

So, were the members of the team that composed the message to be carried by Pioneer 10 sending their message on a wild-goose chase? Barking up the wrong tree? Talking to the silence? Were they deliberately ignoring or side-stepping all the conditions that are necessary for effective communication?

EDWIN MORGAN'S COMMENT

Translunar Space March 1972

The interior of Pioneer-10
as it courses smoothly beyond the Moon
at 31,000 miles an hour,
is calm and full of instruments.
No crew for the two-year trip to Jupiter,
but in the middle of the picture
a gold plaque, six inches by nine,

---

*Dell Hymes, "Toward Ethnographies of Communication: The Analysis of Communicative Events," *American Anthropologist*, vol. 66, no. 6, part 2 (1964).

remedies the omission. Against a diagram
of the planets and pulsars of our solar system and galaxy,
and superimposed on an outline of the spacecraft
in which they are not travelling
(and would not be as they are shown
even if they were) two quaint nude figures
face the camera. A deodorized American man
with apologetic genitals and no pubic hair
holds up a banana-like right hand
in Indian greeting, at his side a woman,
smaller, and also with no pubic hair,
is not allowed to hold up her hand,
stands with one leg off-centre, and
is obviously an inferior sort
of the same species. However,
the male chauvinist pig
has a sullen expression, and the woman
is faintly smiling, so
interplanetary intelligences may still have homework.
Meanwhile, on to the Red Spot,
Pluto, and eternity.

WHAT NOW?

Design your own version of the plaque intended to give essential information about Earth and its people to extraterrestrials. If you can't draw, simply describe it in words.

part 4 | Representing Ourselves

14

"Well, As I Recall It, . . ." Autobiography I

Chapters 14 and 15 concentrate on writing about the past, including *your* past. We try to offer guidance and ideas to help you write about your past more effectively and with greater pleasure. But why write about the past? What do our minds do when we try to reconstruct the past? What frames of mind do we engage in when we try to put pieces of the past together and sort them out? Is it enough to say that all of us spend much of our waking (and dreaming) time *working over* our past lives — the events of yesterday, the day before, last month, last year, ten years ago — in order to prepare for the future? The reasons for exploring the why's and how's of recalling, recollecting, and reconstructing are numerous enough to fill several volumes. Let us encapsulate an answer in one word: *understanding*. We often recall in order to understand — to interpret, to make sense of, to learn. These chapters are based on a simple assumption: there is nothing more interesting than the way our minds work. We shall start with the curious activity of remembering.

Remembering

Q: What do you carry around inside your mind all the time?

A: Memories.

Q: What is strange/mysterious about memories?

A: Although they are there, inside the mind, tucked away somewhere, we are not, fortunately, aware of them all the time. Since they disappear or hide, we can attend to the present moment; the memories don't get in the way.

   (That's not entirely true. Consider this: You had a flaming row this morning. It left you shaken. Now you are sitting in a classroom. You find it *impossible* to concentrate because your memory of that quarrel is so powerful, intense, vivid, hot, that it drives everything else out of your mind.)

Q: When we say "I remember," what do we mean? What kind of mental act are we referring to?

A: Our students have provided us with hundreds of answers, and we have discovered that it helps to distinguish between these main forms of remembering:

- We have to remember facts for a test. In order to retain them, we memorize them, and hold on to them, in our short-term memory, just long enough for the test. Then many of them "evaporate."
- We are *not deliberately* remembering, when suddenly a memory "leaps" into our mind, with disconcerting speed and clarity. It's as if we have been swept back, at the speed of light, into our past life.
- A friend says, "Remember when we . . . ?" and we apply our mind to remembering.

Because we use our inner eye and inner ear, even our inner sense of smell or touch, when we remember, and because these mental "sensations" can be very vivid and clear, we sometimes confuse our memory of an experience with the experience itself. But the two are different. The event has been swept away: it was there, then. We are here, now. We cannot literally go back. Time always moves forward.

A STUDENT REMEMBERS

So what are we doing when we *remember* that day or that moment? Here is an answer provided by Charles Hyacinth, one of our students. Charles's first language is French—he was born in Haiti—and so he appropriately begins in French, the language of his earliest memories.

L'Avenue des Mémoires

L'Avenue des Mémoires is my favorite street in the whole city; it is so quiet and peaceful. The sidewalks are very clean, with trees on both sides of the street. One would never guess that inside each building on this seemingly quiet street there is so much going on.

I'm now walking down the Avenue; a feeling of serenity comes over me. The icy fingers of the cold December wind tug at my ears and nose, and yet I do not shiver. The smell of hot buttered popcorn warms me. I grin and continue to walk, stopping in front of each theater on the avenue to look at the posters displaying their present features in large line drawings in black and white. Each depicts a scene from the movie, usually its focal point. As I walk, I examine each poster, and finally I notice one that attracts my attention.

It depicts a young boy staring intensely at a beautiful girl with the look of love in his eyes; she does not notice him. For some reason I want to witness the experience captured in that one still.

I open the theater doors and walk inside—it's free. I walk up to the candy counter and ask for a medium-sized popcorn and a soda. The beautiful girl behind the counter hands them to me—they're free, too. She smiles and says, "How are you today, Charles?"

"Fine, thank you, Laura."

I turn around. As soon as I do so, she disappears. I walk down the center aisle of the empty theater and choose my favorite seat. I get comfortable and signal to Richard, the projectionist, to start the projector. He does so and vanishes.

The lights go off. I am all alone; privacy is very important. The movie starts. This is not just an ordinary movie. I identify very much with someone on the screen. Hey! That's me! I can't believe I'm wearing that shirt with those pants.

The movie continues. It is not always a perfect description of events as they happened.[1] Authors use the phrase "poetic license" to defend this distortion. Sometimes the details are faded by time. Sometimes by pain and anger.

That shirt again . . . it's ridiculous. It makes me look like a clown. No wonder Eileen resisted my advances. Stop! Mentally I summon Richard. He appears. I command him to rewind the film to the point where Eileen and I just got together. He does so. The picture is back on the screen. It is still. I change my shirt, comb my hair, and clean my shoes. Richard disappears. The movie continues, and I sit back confident that this substitution will enhance my chances.[2]

"Can I walk you to class, Eileen?"

"O.K."

"Thank you . . . your books—they seem heavy."

"Oh, not really."

"Let me carry them for you."

"That's not necessary."

"I don't mind."

"No, thank you."

Stop! Why is she being so cold? I changed my shirt. I look better now. What could it be?[3] She's playing hard to get, that's all. Don't give up, Chuck! Start!

"So what are you doing this weekend?"

"I don't know yet."

"Aren't you going to the school dance, Saturday?"

"I'd like to, but nobody nice enough has asked me."

"Well, maybe . . ."

"Yes, Charles?"

"Well, maybe . . . I was thinking . . ."

"Yes?"

"Well, you know, today is only Thursday. You'll find someone by Saturday."

"Thanks. I've got to go now."

---

[1]For footnote explanations (1–3), see "Reconsidering One's Text," p. 288.

"Wait! I'll walk you to the door."

"No thanks."

Stop! You did it again, Chuck. You blew it. The most beautiful girl in the school was almost throwing herself at you, and you did nothing.
Come on, kid. This is the moment you dreamed about so often. Don't let it go by.

Richard! He reappears. Rewind, please. Start!

"I'd like to, but nobody nice enough has asked me."

"Well, maybe . . ."

"Yes, Charles?"

"Well, maybe . . . I was thinking that . . . maybe we could go together."

"Really? I'd like that a lot."

"Wow! You mean that?"

"Sure I do . . . I've got to go now."

"Wait! I'll walk you to the door."

She turns around. The most beautiful face in the world is on the screen. I don't remember all the details. Therefore I make them up.

Kiss her, Chuck! He does.

The   End

Back in my seat, I am satisfied and grinning. Richard reappears to take care of the equipment. I get up and wave to him; he waves back. I walk past the candy counter. Laura is there. "Did you enjoy it?" she asks. I respond in the affirmative and wave good-bye.

I walk out of the theater. It disappears. I am back home, "on the throne," slowly regaining consciousness.

Reconsidering One's Text   Many texts are never absolutely finished inside the mind of the writer. The novelist John Fowles has confided in a personal communication that he would prefer not to publish his novels but leave them in a drawer and take one out, maybe ten years later, and work over it again. At the end of this, his "final" draft, Charles added these notes:

1. In my earlier version, you said not to generalize at this point, but I think that it might be O.K. here, since later on I particularize.

2. That should be a new paragraph, right?

3. I want a pause, a long pause, between these two sentences. Should the second one be on a separate line?

4. Any other suggestions?

Helping Your Instructor Read Your Mind   These questions were very useful for us, because they allowed us into Charles's mind and gave us a sharper, clearer sense of the kinds of choices that he was beginning to recognize as an interesting part of the act of writing. *The fact that he asks such questions is more important, much more important, than our answers could be.* He's now reflecting usefully, specifically, on his own text, as it moves onto the page. And many of his questions will be better answered by himself than by us. He has reached a state of "mature dependency"—a stage of development as a writer in which he can openly admit to uncertainties and questions, without feeling either threatened by us or terribly dependent on us. He can use us as consultants, encouragers, questioners, close readers (of his texts) and providers of critical feedback. We wondered whether we should suggest that he reconsider the last two words of his text: do they perhaps suggest that he has been *asleep*? But we decided that his little myth of the cinema clearly signifies *not* sleep but that strange interaction in the mind between memories and fantasy.

What gave us special pleasure in Charles's text, apart from the ingenuity of his metaphor and his successful exploitation of it, was the deft way in which he slipped between (a) being a spectator of his own memories and (b) acting as a participant in those memories to change the outcome of a scene that had in reality already gone into the past.

Notes   Students in a composition course can help their instructors learn what they, the students, need at any given stage in their development as writers. They can help their instructors learn how to be most effectively useful—as consultants, readers, and teachers. Good composition students use their intelligence and maturity to develop a productive relationship with the instructor—a relationship that may be very different from the one they had with their teacher(s) in high school.

Apply these generalizations to yourself and your writings.

The Memory Is Not the Event

Charles's metaphor of the cinema screen helps us recognize that memories are not events but *images* or *representations* of events—just as the cinema screen gives us an image of an event and not the event itself.

But you know as well as we do that when you become intensely involved in a film, it is *as if* you are no longer in the cinema—a *spectator*—but in the event, experiencing it as a *participant*. So your hands sweat, your heart thumps, your muscles tense up, just as they would if you were actually in the event. Similarly, some memories (mostly ones that we don't try or even wish to recall) leap up into our minds, uninvited, and it is as if we were back there participating in the experience. Many of us, for example, find that memories of moments of embarrassment do this: we find ourselves blushing again.

Because memories have this power to make us *feel* (both in terms of sensation and in terms of emotion) that we are actually participating, we can very easily confuse a memory of an experience with the experience itself (con-fuse: to run together, to meld).

One last word before we ask you to look at a text. When we write one of our memories down, we are making a representation (text) of a representation (memory) of an event. The event is twice-removed. Yet language is so powerful in its capacity to create an illusion that when we become really absorbed in someone's text, we can enjoy (or suffer) the illusion that we are experiencing the actuality—it's as if it is happening to us!

RICHARD WRIGHT REMEMBERS

Read this opening page of Richard Wright's autobiography, *Black Boy,* and then listen in on a class discussion.

> One winter morning in the long-ago, four-year-old days of my life I found myself standing before a fireplace, warming my hands over a mound of glowing coals, listening to the wind whistle past the house outside. All morning my mother had been scolding me, telling me to keep still, warning me that I must make no noise. And I was angry, fretful, and impatient. In the next room Granny lay ill and under the day and night care of a doctor and I knew that I would be punished if I did not obey. I crossed restlessly to the window and pushed back the long fluffy white curtains—which I had been forbidden to touch—and looked yearningly out into the empty street. I was dreaming of running and playing and shouting, but the vivid image of Granny's old, white, wrinkled, grim face, framed by a halo of tumbling black hair, lying upon a huge feather pillow, made me afraid.
>
> The house was quiet. Behind me my brother—a year younger than I— was playing placidly upon the floor with a toy. A bird wheeled past the window and I greeted it with a glad shout.
>
> "You better hush," my brother said.
>
> "You shut up," I said.
>
> My mother stepped briskly into the room and closed the door behind her. She came to me and shook her finger in my face.
>
> "You stop that yelling, you hear?" she whispered. "You know Granny's sick and you better keep quiet!"
>
> I hung my head and sulked. She left and I ached with boredom.
>
> "I told you so," my brother gloated.
>
> "You shut up," I told him again.
>
> I wandered listlessly about the room, trying to think of something to do, dreading the return of my mother, resentful of being neglected. The room held nothing of interest except the fire and finally I stood before the shimmering embers, fascinated by the quivering coals. An idea of a new kind of game grew and took root in my mind. Why not throw something into the fire and watch it burn? I looked about. . . .

A Classroom Discussion

MARK: Wright makes me really mad; he makes me so angry I feel like walking out of the room.

J.S.:   [Surprised] Why so?

MARK: Because he can remember back to when he was four! and my earliest memory—why, I don't think I can remember *anything* before I was twelve, and that was only six years ago.

MARIA: Yes, and how can he remember *so* much?

STANLEY: How can he remember that the wind was whistling and that the coals were glowing?

LIORA: And how can he remember what people said—I mean, *exactly* what they said?

J.S.:   Do you think that he *remembered* all that? Do you think he remembered *precisely* the way it was?

MARK: Yes! That's why he's a writer, because he has—what do you call it—a photographic memory—and that's why I'll never be a writer, because I can't remember *anything*.

JOE: Agreed. All the writers I've read can all remember that way—and that's the difference between them and us. They were born that way. Their brains are different.

J.S.:   Does that mean that when you're invited to write about your own lives, you're stumped—at the very beginning?

STANLEY: I hate writing about my life because I try and try to remember, and I can't.

BARBARA: Me, too. I've wanted to write about this scary thing that happened to me when I was ten—when I was stranded on this island in Cape Cod—Billingsgate Island. Well, you see, it's an island only at low tide, and then when the tide comes in, it disappears, the tide came in faster than I thought, and I was stranded and the Coast Guard came, but I can't remember what happened first, second, and third, and who said what. And what it *felt* like. I know that experience has a lot to do with how afraid I am of water and boats. I want to remember what the sky looked like. And I think there were lots of shells on the island that I was looking at, *before*. But, oh, it gets me angry, because I want to write about it.

J.S.:   But wait a minute, think for a minute. Say you got up this morning, and you had a dream—a very vivid dream—and you sit down at the breakfast table, and you tell your sister about it. Do you *remember* everything?

MARK: No, what you don't remember, you skip over.

JOE: But sometimes you discover as you're telling it that you remember more than you *thought* you had.

J.S.:   Right. The telling brings it back. Can you ever recapture the dream —as you dreamt it—can you ever recapture the whole dream, as it was during your sleep?

LIORA: No, that's an impossibility.

J.S.:   Why?

STANLEY: Because the dream and telling your sister about it are different.

J.S.:   Now, you're getting somewhere. How so? How are the dream and the telling different?

MARK: The dream really "happened," and the telling is words. You use words to try to tell about something that happened before. I mean, the telling comes after the dream.

J.S.:   Exactly. The dream is *mediated* or presented through language, and if you're really caught up in the telling—particularly if it was a dream with lots of action, with things happening, with people talking, with lots of detail—then your sister might have the illusion that she is right there with you in the dream. But the telling is not the dream. The dream has already occurred. It's the same with all experience: the experience and the representation are not the same. In the experience you were a participant; in telling, later, you are a spectator. And when you *present* your representation to someone, you will unconsciously shape it, bend it, in order to have some desired effect on your listeners.

MARK: Wait a minute. Are you saying that Wright didn't actually remember all that? Is that what you're getting at?

J.S.:   What do you think?

[Silence]

J.S.:   Here, let me diagram it for you. [She goes to the blackboard.]

1. The happening itself	Participant
2. Images in the head, mostly visual and aural	
3. Self-representation (You tell it to yourself)	
4. Representation (You shape it in order to tell it to someone else)	
5. Presentation (You tell it)	Spectator
6. Conversation (You and your listeners share its meaning)	
7. Evaluation (You agree on a "verdict"—"Yes, that was terrible!")	

The event happens; that's the first step. You don't reflect or meditate on it because you're *in* it. You're a *participant*.

Later—five minutes later or a day later or a week later—your mind works on the event or the dream; you start putting it together to make sense of it. Now you're removed from the dream— a *spectator.*

And then, yet later—five minutes later or a day later or whenever—you tell it to someone else. You're trying for a representation of the event. But it's not the event. That already happened. It's over, gone. You're talking *about* the event; you're representing it through words and you may present that representation to another—in talk or in writing.

BARBARA: That sounds like psychology or philosophy. . . .

J.S.: As a matter of fact, Sigmund Freud spent a lot of his later life thinking about this, talking about the gap of time between the event itself and the telling of it. The word he used to signify the gap was *belatedness.*

MARK: You mean, then, that to remember exactly what happened is really an impossibility? That trying to remember in that way is futile?

J.S.: Right.

MARK: You mean that Wright probably didn't remember all that he makes us think he did?

J.S.: Right.

MARK: But, the book is an autobiography—it's supposed to be the truth.

BARBARA: But what she's saying is that it's impossible to get things down exactly as they were—he didn't have a video machine hooked into his life when he was four years old. He filled in the gaps.

J.S.: That's what writers do. They write *texts*. They choose beginnings and endings. You see, we're *not* video machines. We might not be able to remember the exact words of conversation . . . excuse me, we *cannot* remember the exact words of conversation, but we can try to represent it, to recapture it, knowing all along that our tools are words, but that we have the power to realize a past moment so vividly that we—and others—can actually feel as if we were there.

MARK: Very interesting.

RECONSTRUCTION IS PARTLY INVENTION

Since we *can* recall exactly *some* words/phrases of conversations, we may be led to believe that we can really recall a whole conversation. But we can't. We don't even *notice* the whole conversation; even as we listen, we unconsciously edit and rewrite inside our minds. When we recall it, as inner speech, we recall the edited version or a paraphrase of the edited version. Even as we recall it, we're *shaping* it.

A simple example will illustrate the point. Take a transcript of an actual conversation:

A. But . . . er . . . this . . . um . . . whatever you call it . . . er . . . sure, surely it, it's not exactly like the, like a carnivorous plant.

B. Well . . . um . . . it . . . er . . . it's not exactly the same thing, but it is part of, a, symbiotic . . . er . . . system.

If you had been A or B (or C) in that conversation, your memory would *not* have stored those utterances exactly (how do you even represent an "um" or an "er"?). What your memory would hold would be an approximate, selective version, and in the longer run, you would probably hold only a summary of it (if it was important in some way) or quite possibly nothing at all beyond a sense of the tone, the feeling—pleasant/congenial or unpleasant/uncongenial.

Notes

We invite you to talk and write about what and how you remember, by using the following questions as tools for retrieving your past and making sense of it:

What are your earliest memories?

How far back in time can you go? Do you tend to remember people, places, events, or sensations most sharply?

Do you remember feelings rather than specific moments?

What people or places surface in these early memories?

What do you remember about yesterday, last week, last month?

Pick a day from your past—can you reconstruct it? If not, why do you suppose you can't?

Do you remember most vividly the ordinary or the extraordinary moments?

What memories or dreams or nightmares keep surfacing, keep insisting on being "replayed"? Do you wonder why?

If you were to single out, say, five of the memories that surface repeatedly, in waking or in dreaming, what would they be?

About some memories: do you wonder whether *you* remember them or whether they have been told to you, so that in fact you are remembering someone else's representation?

Which of your senses are stronger in remembering—sight, sound, hearing, smell, taste, touch?

When do you first remember having seen your face in a mirror? What do you recall about that moment, if anything?

Why do you suppose you forget so many things that, on reflection, seem to be worth remembering?

When you discover yourself remembering—perhaps in a daydream —do you also recognize that the memory has some bearing on your present life, on the present moment? that the memory helps you make sense of some past experience as it relates to the present and to the future?

Are some memories nagging or irritating—do they seem to call up unfinished business, a sense of something still unresolved?

Do you see any patterns to your memories: do you tend to remember moments of intense satisfaction or dissatisfaction, of enlightenment, of turning points?

If you were to write your memoirs or the story of your life, where would you begin? Think of three or four different beginnings.

WHAT NOW?

If possible, leaf through your family photograph album—going back as far as you can—and choose (1) the most cheerful photograph, (2) the saddest, (3) the most surprising, (4) the most embarrassing, (5) the most amusing, and (6) two or three that bring back particularly vivid memories. Write about any of these to help others understand why these photographs affect you as they do.

Using your notes, choose some aspects of memory and reconstruction, and write a reflective text about them.

An Area in Which We Are All Experts

There is one area of knowledge in which we are all experts, knowing more than anyone else. It is a knowledge derived not from reading books of any kind but from having been there, of having used our eyes and ears, sometimes as if our very lives depended on it—it is our own life. It is the life in which we have been the central character, the major participant; the life in which others have been spectators, and participants too—but not all the time, and not at center-stage.

Consider now your own past life, of which you have the most intimate, the most richly detailed knowledge, a knowledge that contains all that you have observed and experienced—not from a safe, comfortable distance, but from the very center, intimately.

Remember the feel of the inside of those shoes, the texture of those socks, the peculiar abstract patterns in that bedroom wallpaper, the sound of your breathing as you begin to fall asleep, the feel of your eyes as you stagger out of bed and rub the sleep away; that face in the bathroom mirror, the hair that frames it, and the characteristic sound of your mother's footsteps as she moves around her bedroom beyond that wall, the subtle vibrations of the floorboards, and a million other distinctive little sensations that made up your life, not to mention the secret center of your life— the never-ending life of your own inner consciousness inside your mind: a continuous process of language production that cannot be switched off except in sleep.

Even when we look back to an earlier moment in our life, we can reconstruct how it was; much of the detail comes back without our having to try to recapture it. And even as the scene returns to our inner ear and eye, we can observe it once again, on that strange inner cinema screen called memory. The eye can move, taking in and registering this or that detail—all the small elements that made that moment what it was, and not otherwise.

But what is remembered later is very much dependent on what is observed, noted, at the time. Writers, more than most people, need to be observant.

ON BEING OBSERVANT

The ability or capacity to observe well—this is not something that we either have or don't have. Powers of observation can be nurtured, developed, exercised. But effective observation is not indiscriminate. A keen observer doesn't try to notice (and remember) everything; she/he is selective. Good detective fiction—the novels of Ross MacDonald, for example— will quickly help you to realize that the eye and ear of the inquirer is usually sharply focused, concentrated on the search for significant detail— signs. And the experience of reading *The Zebra-Striped Hearse*, or any other of MacDonald's books, is also an occasion for you, the reader, to exercise your powers of observation and of deduction: seeing what counts, what signifies, and then drawing the most appropriate conclusions.

Just as you will change the lens of a camera for a particular kind of image, or use a portable tape recorder because what something sounds like is more important than how it looks, similarly you can select a particular aspect of the world around you to observe. Today it could be people's gestures, the way they use their hands, arms, and facial expressions; tomorrow you could home in on the variety of tones of voice that you hear people using; another day you might concentrate on people's clothes or their cars. You can start this very moment, by lifting your eyes from this book and looking around. Use your notebook, and jot down a note about anything that you have *never noticed before*.

A MASTER OBSERVER RECALLS HIS PAST

A few years ago, the internationally famous movie actor Dirk Bogarde set himself to writing down his memories. In his memoir, he acknowledges that, of all his gifts, the most important was the possession of well-trained powers of observation, for it was these that made the most valuable contribution to his work as an actor. As a child, he had learned to derive pleasure from observing by following the lead of his eccentric grandfather, who made a living by painting art forgeries.

I, of course, was mesmerised by him. I was happy to sit in a chair beside him in his smelly, crowded studio, looking at his stamp albums, his maps of the Amazon, faded and torn, his piles of old magazines and books, or just listen to him talking in his heavy accent about his journeys into the Andes on a mule or his astonishing voyage on a sailing ship from Lima to Valparaiso; but more than that he would not give away. And the stories had a vague not-quite-true-but-could-be quality about them which in no way diminished their delight.

He sat in a high carved oak armchair, his long bony fingers clasping the arms; his finger-nails were long like a Mandarin's, but always scrupulously clean which constantly amazed me. Sometimes in the middle of a story he would start to crack eggs and flour into a bowl and begin to cook something for his supper, a cake or biscuits: he told me that one of the wobbly tables which supported his gas-rings came from Versailles and probably belonged at one time to Marie Antoinette because there was an "A" worked into the chipped and crumbling gesso. Lifting the tattered American cloth he would make me peer at the fine carved legs and stretchers and ask me if I could see the "A", and sometimes I thought that I did. But I could never be sure. He said that all his Bits and Pieces came from junk shops and sale rooms when he was looking about for his work. The great red lacquer bed was from China and he felt sure that it was brought over after the Boxer Rebellion, and who was I to doubt him? All his Treasures, he said, had cost him nothing but a discerning eye, and he said that one must cultivate such a thing by watching, looking and listening, and also by always asking Why? and What? and Where? "You must be Observant, boy. Always Observe. If you do not understand what you see, ask someone to tell you what it is . . . if they don't know, you must take books and find out. Always seek, always question, always be Interested, otherwise you will perish."

This, strangely enough, was something which my father had inherited from him. We were always told to Look . . . to watch, to see and to listen. Even if it bored us to death at times; like Chamber Music which I hated but had to listen to very often in order to be able, later on I was told, to appreciate the great symphonies. Consequently we were curious children and delighted in finding things out for ourselves even though our frequent questioning must have seemed tremendously irritating to many of our friends. Although I detested any form of Games, and had always managed to avoid Children's Parties for fear that I should be forced to play them, I did enjoy, constantly, my father's Remember Games. In a tube train° look and see how many pairs of brown shoes there are on the people opposite.

°**tube train**: subway

How many bunions, which has a lace untied, who wears spats? And then look away at the faces above and try to fit each one out. This was a simple game to play and fun, but quite often caused offence to the unfortunate victims sitting facing one who twitched and fidgeted and stared about them under the implacable observing eyes of the child opposite.

Other games were looking in shop windows and counting the number of pots or pans with a black lid or a blue lid, how many milk jugs there were on a given row, or plates in a pile, then, making a mental list, one wandered away for a few minutes to return later and check. This caused one to give the impression that one was loitering; however it was all very good training and not easily forgotten. And although I was such a dunce at school, at these games I was more than outstanding, simply because I found detail fascinating. Of course there were never any rewards for being good at these games; it was just expected that you would be, and the reward was getting the lists as correct as possible. And it was rewarding in a strange way. Lastingly so I imagine.

Dirk Is Exiled

Dirk Bogarde's adolescent years were very unhappy. (So what else is new? we hear you cry.) When he was about 12, he was sent to a technical high school about 500 miles from home. To save money, he was lodged with an aunt and uncle who lived in a rather grim suburb of Glasgow city —Bishopbriggs. Many years later Bogarde wrote:

°**trams**: streetcars

Bishopbriggs was where the trams° from Glasgow ended. Clacketting, racketting, lurching their way from Renfield Street through the black canyons of faceless tenements in Springburn, trundling through acres of blighted wasteland, scabbed with wrecked cars, rubbish tips, blackened clumps of thistle and thorn, they coasted gently into the blank granite square of what once might have been a pleasant country village. Here the small gabled houses, empty-eyed windows, draped in white lace, secret with half drawn blinds, gleamed in misty rain. Beyond slate roofs, the pointed caps of the Tips, like my sister's spilly hills of sugar only black. Dead volcanoes spotting the ruined fields. "The Bingies," relics of a thriving pit closed since the start of the Depression.

From the terminus, the steel rails shining like swords in black granite cobbles, past a scatter of gas lit shops, up a brick alley, through a long dripping tunnel under the railway line, one arrived on "the other side" of the town. A straggling, cold, ugly housing estate, in Avenues, Crescents, Terraces, and Drives; no Streets or Roads for the new middle classes. Flat-faced pebble-dash houses; four windows up, four below, pink-grey asbestos tiled roofs, concrete paths, creosoted picket fences and washing dripping in every back garden. All about one there was nothing to see but row upon row upon row of roofs, backed here and there by the pointed nose of a Tip or a few wind-twisted trees high on an, as yet, untouched hillock. It rained gently.

24 Springburn Terrace was the same as all its neighbours. The only way I could distinguish it for the first few months was by the fact that it stood on a corner and had a slightly larger area of garden around it with a lamp-post at the front gate. The houses were not Houses at all. They

were flats. One up and one down. The down one had a front door in the
centre, the up one had a front door at the side up a flight of concrete
steps. Walls and the floors were made of cardboard. From the front door
a long narrow passage. To the right a sitting-room, beyond that a bedroom. At the top of the narrow passage a lavatory and bath together. To
the left a dining-room, beyond that the kitchen with a door leading out
into the pleasures of a wan garden. Yard more like. A hedge of Golden
Elder, a few neat flower-beds, a bit of grass in the middle and in the
centre of that a tall iron post for the laundry. A small world for three
ill-assorted people.

Dirk with his sister, 1927

Dirk with his mother, sister, and family friends, 1931

Dirk Bogarde, actor and author

Bogarde as Gustav von Aschenbach in *Death in Venice*

Aunt Belle, my mother's elder sister, was tall, kind looking, with a patrician face and soft auburn hair flecking with grey. Her husband, Uncle Duff, was slightly shorter than she was, with thin black hair parted in the middle and glued to his head with Yardley's Hair Cream. His small black moustache looked as if it had been smudged on with coal. They welcomed me to this unprepossessing house shyly and warmly with a crackling fire and high tea.

"All boys like to eat," said my aunt, "so I did a Baking for you especially!" There were five different sorts of biscuits, scones, and cup cakes, as well as a Madeira Cake with candy peel on top. Sandwiches, toast, anchovy paste, and strawberry jam.

Also a canary, Joey, who lived in the window in a cage with a yellow silk drill round the base to stop the seed from scattering. Afterwards, in the sitting-room across the hall, we sat by the fire, my aunt sewing, my uncle showing me his bound volumes of Bruce Bairnsfather's° cartoons. I wondered, vaguely, where I should sleep.

°**Bruce Bairnsfather**: famous cartoonist of World War I

About nine o'clock he went out to the kitchen to make the cocoa for supper. My aunt put aside her sewing and said I must be tired after such a long day and so many excitements. I was aware that she meant travelling, and trains and farewells and all that sort of thing. She explained gently that they had moved out of their bedroom next door so that I should have it, and that they would sleep on a Put-U-Up Settee in the dining-room.

°**Put-U-Up Settee**: sofa-bed

"This is a rather small house for the three of us, but I'm sure we'll manage very well," she said. "It's the Depression, you know. Uncle lost everything, I'm afraid, and so we just had to cut our cloth to suit the material. It is not the sort of place we like to live in. But it'll just have to do. I don't suppose you remember the other house, do you?"

I did. Gleaming mahogany furniture, heavy and sombre, shining brass jugs filled with flowers and leaves, a piano scattered with silver frames, high windows velvet-curtained, all looking out over a soft green wooded park. Not at all like this sad, apologetic, squashed little house.

Some of the old stuff had made the swift descent from gentility to near-poverty and looked defiantly out of place in such cramped quarters. The ladder-backed chairs in the dining room, a tall mahogany bookcase, some bold chintz armchairs with antimacassars pinned to them like maids caps, my grandfather's water-colours in thin gold frames, a set of Nashes Magazine Covers for 1918 framed in black passe-partout,° and the black marble mantel-clock which thinly struck the hours and quarters.

°**passe-partout**: adhesive strips

My bedroom was a square of pink distemper. Two windows over the bleak square of garden and the dead backs of the houses beyond the ragged hedge. A one-bar electric fire, a yellow oak wardrobe with an oval mirror which reflected the entire room, a dressing chest, a dressing table and a wide yellow oak bed spread with a shining pink satin cover. In the bed a scalding aluminum hot water bottle called a "pig" . . . and a hot brick wrapped in flannel.

I was told to use the bathroom first. A bath, a basin, a lavatory. His ivory brushes stuck together by their bristles, W.D. entwined in black on the back. The oval tin of Yardley's grease. Toothbrushes huddled in a tumbler like old men at a wedding. Izal on the lavatory paper. We said goodnight, and I lay in the dark of the wide yellow bed listening to them raking out the fire in the sitting-room and setting the china for breakfast. Then bathroom noises and the lavatory flushing twice. Pattering of feet down the corridor to the front door, a chain rattling, a bolt running home, the dining-room door closing. Silence and then the slow, low, murmur of worried conversation through the wall.

The clock struck a quarter. Ting Ting Ting. Light from the lamp-post flickered through leaf shadows on the buff paper blind. A draught waggled the cord and made the little acorn handle tap tap against the glass. In the house upstairs someone else pulled a chain and I heard a soft cataract of water and a pipe beside the wardrobe started to knock gently.

I turned into the pillows and tried to smother my blubbing.

Notes

Question: How does Bogarde get us to the bathroom?

Bogarde's choice of elements to compose a map of depressing, uninviting bleakness moves like a bird descending, homing in, or like a zoom lens on a helicopter, sweeping in from large-scale panorama to fine detail: landscape, townscape, district, street, garden, exterior of house, interior. After describing the inhabitants—aunt and uncle—he turns to scan more closely the contents of the house, its furniture and bric-a-brac. Finally, he shows us round his bedroom, and the bathroom with its "senile" toothbrushes.

Scale, then, has imperceptibly contracted from cityscape—five miles across—to toothbrush, six inches long. Carried on/by/through that journey of the eye, Bogarde's details do not overwhelm us. He is selective, and his selection seems to be shaped by the *expressive* power of his choices, each item chosen for its capacity to reinforce the overall effect—which is one of almost unrelieved gloom. *What expectations does Bogarde arouse?* Do you anticipate a cheerful story or a bleak one? Do you think Dirk is going to enjoy living in Bishopbriggs?

Life in
Bishopbriggs

Dirk was very unhappy at school, feeling like a fish out of water, because he felt like an exile and found technical subjects very uncongenial. Slowly he learned the full extent of his uncle's meanness.

> After a year in Bishopbriggs things gradually began to deteriorate. Inevitably, I returned back from one holiday to find that I was no longer sleeping in the pink bedroom but on the Put-U-Up which now occupied the place of the piano in the sitting-room. The piano was in the dining-room. My uncle explained nicely that I was, after a year's wear, starting to destroy the furniture in the bedroom, that the chest of drawers, his only remembrance of his mother, was creaking badly because of the weight of the things which I placed in the drawers. Books and writing materials, as well as all my clothes. Also, far worse, the foot of the yellow oak bed had been hopelessly scratched by my long toenails. So it was decided that they should move back to their own room and I should from there on sleep on the Put-U-Up.
>
> That the culprit, or culprits, of the scratched bed end were not my toe-nails, but instead the scalding aluminum "pig" or the hot brick in flannel splitting the veneer, were unacceptable excuses.
>
> "I have repeatedly told you about cutting your toenails," said my uncle, "every bath time. We are not made of money up here, you know, there's a Depression on."
>
> He had never ever mentioned my toenails, although he was frequently in the bathroom on Friday nights which was the allotted time of the week for my "ablutions" as he called them. At first I had been rather surprised that he seemed to wish to brush his hair at such an odd hour in the evening, and when I, once only, locked the door, I was firmly admonished not to do so again because how could they help if the geyser blew up or I had a fainting fit suddenly? They, after all, were responsible. So no locked doors. I only minded because it was the one place where I could sing away and feel totally private without being a "noise" either to them or the people who lived up in the house above and who, from time to time, did complain that my piano playing, pretty dreadful, by ear, and limited to a range of three melodies, "The Wedding of the Painted Doll," "Always" and "Over My Shoulder," all played very loudly with both pedals firmly down, disturbed their rest and also made it difficult to hear the Football Results on the Radio. The complaints were always very tactful and genteel. However, they *were* complaints and the piano stopped. So the bathroom seemed the next best thing musically. And also the mirror over the washbowl was useful for trying out expressions.

In the summer, his aunt and uncle paid weekly visits to the tennis club. The games were followed by "The Tea"—a ritual meal, for which Dirk's aunt baked her very best cakes.

After The Tea, at which I helped to serve, and later wash up, they sat, if the weather was fine, in deck-chairs knitting and sewing until their game came up. The time passed slowly enough and I was often allowed to go home before the final game was over, to open the house and set the table for supper. I was always eager for this excuse because it meant, if I was pretty quick, that I could get back in time to put on the brown bakelite radio and just catch the nightingale singing from a Surrey wood. If it sang. It was a delicate thing to do. On with the radio, lock the front door, hang out of the window, eyes glued to the road from the tennis courts, willing, pleading, aching, for the blasted bird to sing. All Surrey flooded into the cramped, beige-and-ladder-backed room. But, as I said, I had to be quick, for apart from prudery I had learned deceit. The radio was expressly forbidden to be touched. So it was only when I had the house to myself, and played it low so that Upstairs could not hear and give me away, that I dared to put it on. And then only with a wet towel standing by, because the machine had a habit of getting warm as time went on, and the moment my uncle came back from Tennis the first thing he did was to cross the room and caress the sleek bakelite sides. Just to see. I had once been caught—the room filled with nightingales and cellos, my eyes maudlin with tears. My uncle's anger was controlled; I was being deceitful and morbid. He was polite enough in a steely way and for a short time the radio was removed to their bedroom. But I managed.

"Why Not Post It?"

One day, a crisis occurs for Dirk, when his uncle tells him that he has come to the conclusion that Dirk is wasting his parents' money and his own time. By this time, the reader gets the impression that the uncle would be glad to get Dirk out of the house.

The fact that I never, at any time ever, saw my school reports—they were always addressed to him, correctly, as my Guardian and he sent them on to my parents—nor ever had any discussions with anyone about them didn't seem to occur to either of us at the time. I was simply struck dumb with shock. As far as I was aware, I had worked as hard as possible and had tried my best.

The next morning, after an anguished night watching the patterns flicker on the ceiling from the Valor Perfection Stove, my uncle and I parted company as usual at Queen Street Station. At the bookstall I bought a stamp and a picture postcard on which, leaning against a pile of magazines, I wrote in pencil, "I am very unhappy here. Please, please let me come home." A swift Burberry'd arm shot over my shoulder and lifted it up.

My uncle's face was expressionless, a nicotined finger brushed his little moustache.

"Well now, Sonny," he said kindly, "why not post it?" He flipped it on to the magazines and walked away.

Dismay and guilt gave way to rising desperation. I did exactly as he said and went on to school.

WHAT NOW?

Dirk's father knew exactly what he wanted—intended—his son to do in life: he was to train for a steady, sensible career. Dirk's mother, on the other hand, was very sympathetic to her son's passion for the stage. How would each of them react to Dirk's postcard? Remember that Dirk's father made all the decisions.

1. Compose Dirk's mother's reply. Consider: What effect does she want to have on her son?
2. Assume the role of Dirk's father, and compose his reply.

WHAT WE CAN LEARN ABOUT WRITING FROM REREADING BOGARDE'S TEXT

Context

Bogarde's first task is to put his readers in the picture. This means he has to give us a context within which we can find our feet or find our bearings, so that we don't cry out: "Where am I?" and "When was this?" **Context**, then, is a representation of time and place. Once these are given, we the readers can follow him, can place ourselves as invisible spectators of his life there and then.

Point of Departure

The level of generality or of particularity that any writer chooses as his point of departure, to get the text started, will depend on what she/he can reasonably expect the reader (a) will need to know in order to begin to make sense of the text, and (b) knows already. In the early paragraphs of any text, you can determine exactly what decisions the writer has made about the knowledge the reader is likely to bring to the reading of that text.

And those are the choices that you must make, either consciously or unconsciously—that is, by habit (the journalist who has worked for the same paper for the last 20 years, for example, makes such choices by habit)—as you begin to get your text moving from its beginning. Needless to say, some writers, for very special effects, will deliberately withhold some of this kind of contextualizing. A mystery story, for instance, may deliberately set out to make the reader feel confused or uncertain in order to achieve the kind of oddly pleasurable bewilderment for which one reads a "mystery."

Episodes— Unique and Routine

But what is it that we observe? We observe various episodes. They may be unique—this happened only once—or they may be events that occurred many times, a part of life's routine.

Try now to identify each of these kinds of episodes in Bogarde's text.

The tennis teas and his secret listening to the radio—these were repeated events, part of the continuing, repeating pattern of his life—the usual thing. The repeated events are the habitual, the recurring—how life normally is for all of us. And when we tell our story, it is against the background of the repeated, the usual, that we can offer something else. "That's how life generally was but one day . . ." What does that phrase "but one day" alert a reader to? What does a reader expect next? The "one day" is going to be—what? Unusual, different, odd, not typical but worse or better, a crisis, a special moment, a "once" that was different. What then do we do with that "once," that hole in the floor? Do we merely glance at it? What do we want our readers to do? As for all of us, Dirk's life consisted of routine and experiences that painfully or pleasurably jolted him out of the routine—crisis, shock, or surprise.

Consider the following simple case: "For months I was perfectly happy, but then . . ." The text moves fast, taking giant strides through time, then with "but then" the text warns us that it is going to slow down, that it is going to change the lens from wide-angle to one that will register detail, close-up. In a word, the *scale* changes. And, if we are effective readers, responding quickly to the little signals in the text, our reading changes—not so much the speed of our reading, but the kind of attention that we give it. We shift gear. We prepare our minds—in a split second—for attention to something in particular, for particularization.

When we as writers offer our reader(s) a "once," we invite them to observe our particularizing. For what makes a "once" interesting and significant is what *it is in particular*, what distinguishes it from the routine stuff.

You will have noticed that the sentence, "For months I was perfectly happy" gave you very little to go on: it generalized, sweeping past and over those months because they are the quick way of offering a time context within which the "once" will now be located. It is the difference between those typical months and the atypical "once" that counts. And the difference will be part of the meaning. Think of all the ballgames you have watched or played; think of all the conversations you have participated in. They are all typical of "life as usual." But one or two games, one or two conversations, will stand out, will stay with you vividly and powerfully, foregrounded in your memories. It is to these that you will pay special attention, it is these that you will get to know and reknow inside out, in every detail, every moment. The special, crucial meanings of those experiences that stand out in your memory will of course only gradually, later, yield themselves up and offer their particular significance as you relive them and examine them as a spectator of your own past. Only later will you be able to realize how important they were, and why.

Background or context provides the "field" within which you place your particular "once." This "once" then involves you in a change of level: you move from generalization to particularity, and the smallest detail may be of the greatest consequence. It is in the part of the text that offers the "once" that the reader will expect the greatest intensity or density of particular detail, specific elements, a view through a microscope.

When you write of a "once" you will have many such details swimming or crowding into your head. If one refuses to come you will have to invent it, make it up. And if your invention is plausible, your reader will be none the wiser.

Notes   Look again, now, at the particularity, the detail, the specifics, in Bogarde's text. Has he overloaded us, or has he judged well how much detail each episode can carry, how many details it needs in order for us, his readers, to *realize* it? By "realize," we mean experience the illusion of reality—a sense not of someone talking about it but of its being present, touchable, visible, audible, and effective in arousing our feelings. (Such writing is sometimes called concrete—as opposed to abstract—but the term is slightly misleading, because words are not things but signs of/for things.) Bogarde's text affects us. We dislike the uncle not because Dirk tells us to dislike him, but because the uncle as we *seem* to experience him directly, *is*, in himself, as he comes to us, mean, hateful, and so on.

BOGARDE'S HARVEST

Now, let's end this chapter by giving Dirk Bogarde the last word. Looking back over the decades, a spectator of his own past, he counts his blessings and explains how well all that observing served him, years later, in one of his most brilliant performances—in the film *Death in Venice*:

> But in those times of loneliness, in those solitary walks across the ruined fields, the dreadful Teas and Bakings, the reading of knitting patterns and endless games of Solitaire, I did not sit idle and let my mind float off into a vacuum. Instead I turned to my father's old teaching of the Remember Game and played it assiduously. I "pelmanised"° a million details which, one day, I felt would "come in handy." . . . I looked and I watched continually. Looking and watching, as one knows, are two very different things. I watched.
>
> My Grandfather Aimé had always said, "You must Observe. Always question." I started to become a professional, as it were, Observer. I was unable to question for I knew that I should not receive honest answers from people who thought questioning a lack of respect for one's elders.
>
> So I observed and from observation answered my own queries. Not always accurately, but satisfactorily enough for me at the time. At least my sluggish brain was working for itself.
>
> From this easy, silent game, which never intruded on anyone's conversation or alarmed them, I assembled a rag bag of trinkets into which I am still able to rummage. Aunt Teenie's dreadful twitch on her poor scarred face became the twitch on von Aschenbach's face at moments of stress, in *Death in Venice* for example; my own shyness and diffidence and loneliness at those Tennis Parties or Tea Parties became his when he arrived, alone, at the Grand Hotel des Bains. The games I played then, and the things I stole, gleaned, collected, observed, have remained with me, vividly, for the rest of my life.

°**Pelmanism**: a once popular system of mental self-improvement.

15

"Then Again, ..."
Autobiography II

About Autobiography

Q: What do we expect to find in an autobiography?

A: The satisfying illusion of observing someone move through his/her life.

Q: The whole of his/her life?

A: Yes and no. The writer will not leave gaps that would make us say: "But he/she's left something out!" But some months or even years will be passed over in a very general way, while other times will be reconstructed in great detail. A good autobiographical text does not try to tell everything. On many days of our lives, nothing specially noteworthy takes place.

Q: What then is the main difference between the parts of the life that are merely skimmed and those that receive very close attention?

A: You can answer that question by looking at how you yourself talk about last week or last month to your friends. You have decided, in the interim, what is "important" and what is not. You have very little difficulty in making that distinction. In fact, it is probably made for you by the operations of your memory: if it was important you remember it; if you remember it, it was probably important.

Q: What do we mean when we say of an experience, "It was important"?

A: We have various names for "important" experiences; depending on their particular quality—pleasant or unpleasant—we can call them crises, highlights, red-letter days, turning points, climaxes, tragedies, accidents, calamities, surprises, and so on. What they have in common is that they are all uncommon experiences.

Q: How do we recognize them?

A: By their extraordinary power to arouse. They aroused us when they happened, and they continue to arouse us when we recall them. And when we offer them socially in writing or telling, it is likely that our readers/listeners will experience a sense of arousal.

Q: In a state of arousal, what is it that is aroused?

A: Any of a thousand emotions, reactions, senses of joy and delight, senses of shock, dismay, amazement, horror, even sexual or spiritual excitement. And as soon as we begin to reflect, we are also moved to a moral response: we feel a sense of approval or disapproval. In Bogarde's case, disapproval of the uncle is certainly an important part of most readers' experience.

Q: Is there a convenient shorthand for referring to these various ways of being aroused?

A: Yes. We can borrow a phrase from Wittgenstein, the philosopher, and call them "forms of life." When we feel them inside ourselves, we know—we are reminded—that we are very much alive.

Q: So a text contains forms of life?

A: Exactly. And when we read, we indirectly experience those forms of life. It is rather like the situation in which friends recount to us a recent experience of, say, frustration leading to anger and an outburst of rude behavior—such as giving someone a really powerful telling-off. Even as they describe it, we enjoy (or suffer) the illusion of sharing in that rage; we internalize or echo or reflect that form of life. We rediscover it inside ourselves. We recognize it as ours.

Claire's Text

Let us now look at an autobiographical text by one of our students that is a powerful example of the intense arousal of forms of life: fear, panic, rage, relief, and many others. (We have numbered the paragraphs for the purpose of later discussion.)

(1)   There was nothing even remotely sinister about being on the same beach where Dr. No had attempted to discount 007 permanently. Perhaps it was the lack of ominous background music.

(2)   Love Beach, Nassau, the Bahamas, the site of scenes from the first James Bond movie, is lushly tropical, with high palm trees, cotton-soft bone-white sand, and Caribbean blue water running into greens as bright as an Irish meadow. The day was sunny, sleepy, and not quite real to a temporarily transplanted New Yorker who'd worn boots and a ski jacket thirty hours before.

(3)   Fifteen people were scattered at intervals along the beach worship-
ping the sun, serving as sacrificial offerings to be burnt or tanned, depending
on heredity and cosmetic chemistry. Waves no bigger than a foot flopped
lethargically on the shore and even the breeze was lazy, barely stirring
scents of coconut and hibiscus.

(4)   If I hadn't already rented the face mask and snorkel, nothing could
have induced me to move—not that the water wasn't inviting, but bodies
at rest tend to remain at rest when they're perfectly content to do so.

(5)   I contemplated moving for quite a while, but orders from my brain
to my body filtered through my muscles and seeped out my toes. "I'm
going . . . I'm going to move . . . I'm going to move! One . . . two . . . THREE!
. . . four, five, six." I sat up, yawned widely, and nearly fell back down. The
heat, the sun, or inertia held my eyelids to pencil-slim slits, which was
just as well since my mind was not prepared to deal with big scenes.
Nearby, in the shade of a scenically arched palm tree, my husband slept
peacefully, blissfully, intelligently. (He hadn't rented snorkeling gear.)

(6)   The sea temperature was so delightfully warm that nothing dis-
pelled the illusion that I was sleepwalking through a dream day, not
even the normally daunting, eye-opening step—the crotch-wetter. This
time it tickled and I smiled, enjoying several instant replays before
moving on.

(7)   Snorkeling in the tropics is akin to visiting an underwater fairy
land. Coral castles seemed to be inhabited by brightly colored knights in
fins courting unseen mermaids or blonde fish princesses. I followed a
bulging-eyed porkfish past several rock beauties before joining a school of
sea anemones. Like Cinderella at a ball with no clock, I was timelessly
enchanted.

(8)   Many images and unknown minutes later I lifted my head out of
the water to stare at the unbroken line of the Caribbean Sea. There was
nothing on the horizon except water and sky. I turned toward shore and
blinked. It wasn't there. I turned right again, looking at the sea and then
left where the island should have been. Disoriented, I tore off my face
mask and snorkel, swiveling in circles to get my bearings. If I hadn't had
a sharply lucid thought in hours, I more than made up for it in a dozen
split seconds. Where was the island? Who's playing games with me? Slam-
ming hard heartbeats punctuated each thought. I was a half-mile or more
from the beach. Was my husband still sleeping? Did he know I was swimming? Could he see me? Would anyone hear if I screamed? If I waved my
arms would they see me? Was there anyone on the shore who could swim
this far fast enough to help me? With a rapidity that rivaled that of a
computer, bad news registered. There was no lifeguard on the beach and
no row boats for emergencies. There were no boats behind me. The one
person in sight with the skill and training to rescue anybody was about
to drown.

(9)   Like a dybbuk taking possession, panic imploded. Machine gun
palpitations hammered my ribs, making breathing impossible. Muscles
twitched in spastic frenzy. I was strangling and suffocating and drowning.
I was going to die . . . here . . . on Love Beach. Me and James Bond.

(10)   In a childish terror tantrum I started to cry, furiously pumping
my legs to keep my head above water, gasping for air. I sobbed and choked,

shivering with fear. Lack of oxygen was a cloud covering the sun, and day became night. It was dark, literally dark. I couldn't breathe. I was gulping air but not breathing. On the verge of hyperventilating I pushed my head back and tried to float. Even then I couldn't draw a deep breath. I was hiccuping and whimpering. I couldn't breathe. I sank and swallowed water, or the water swallowed me. Nothing was clear except terror and a need to breathe. I fought my way back to the surface and forced myself to float.

(11)   Look at the clouds. The clouds look soft. Breathe. Breathe. Meditate on the clouds. Concentrate on the clouds. Breathebreathe . . . breathe. I'm floating further away from the shore! Oh God! Help! Somebody! Help me! Breathe . . . breathe . . . breabreathe . . . breathe. Look at the clouds and breathe. I needed the litany, the rhythm for breathing.

(12)   Fighting panic for possession of myself, for the life of me, I struggled to breathe. Each breath was a new battle. Panic rules reason. Let me breathe. Panic is the killer. On land, on sea, in the sea, in the air, panic is the enemy. Let me breathe. The mind views panic, and the brain releases chemicals into the bloodstream that cause people to self-destruct. The chemicals were killing me! Breathe! Don't panic. How dumb! As a swimming instructor I'd drummed the words into my students as they'd been drummed into me. Don't panic. The first, foremost, primary rule of lifesaving . . . the one they printed in capital letters, "DON'T PANIC!" So dumb! The rule should have read "FIGHT THE PANIC!" Breathebreathebreathe. Breabreathe. Breathe! Fight the panic. Float on your back and breathe. Breathe. Other rules flipped through my mind. Never swim alone. Never swim without a lifeguard present. Extraneous! Extraneous to breathing. Objection! Sustained! Breathe! Float on your back and breathe. Look at the clouds and breathe.

(13)   Gently, very gently, I pointed myself toward shore, trying to gauge the direction without seeing the distance. Now easy . . . easy . . . kick your legs just a bit. It was a game—a war game. Don't let the panic know what you're doing. It was alive in my chest, between my collar bones. I could feel it just below my throat. I could hear it. I didn't know you could hear panic.

(14)   Float on your back and breathe. Look at the clouds and breathe.

(15)   I was clutching my face mask and snorkel unconsciously, like a security blanket. If I threw them away it would be an admission that maybe I wasn't going to make it. I needed them. I had to return them. I'd only rented them. They had to be returned.

(16)   Float on your back and breathe. Look at the clouds and breathe.

(17)   Never have I disciplined my thoughts and movements with such rigid, concentrated, single-minded determination. I could have written books, built cities, and cured diseases with that telescoped intensity. And I needed it, all of it. I had the adrenaline for ten times the energy I required, but my body was dead without my mind. If the panic got my mind the adrenaline would be used against me. Why did the panic feel bigger and stronger than me? I had created a monster and it wouldn't let go.

(18)   Float on your back and breathe. Look at the clouds and breathe.

(19)   Again and again I repeated the sequence, over and over until I felt calm enough to swim. Swim slowly, easily, with effortless strokes. Two yards forward, one yard back. The current giveth and taketh away. It played leader as if I'd forgotten to say "May I?" Three kicks to each

arm stroke, roll your head, breathe when the right arm is raised. Don't look at the shore. Don't look! It was back! It hadn't left! The panic was growing again! Breathe breathe. Float on your back and breathebreathe breathe. Look at the clouds and breathe. Float on your back and breathe. Think of your training. Remember your training. Remember your training. . . .

(20)   I was the youngest in the lifesaving class, not yet thirteen, and the teacher was slightly sadistic. At least I'd thought so at the time. On the final lifesaving test she had played victim, yelling and thrashing about in the lake. Float . . . breathe . . . Look at the clouds and breathe. It was my turn to save the teacher. I jumped in—lifesavers don't dive. You can't lose sight of the victim. I swam until I was about 5 feet in front of her and then I did a surface dive. You have to. You can't give the victim a chance to grab you around the neck because victims have a tendency to panic. That's funny. Panic. Breathe . . . breathe . . . float on your back and . . . breathe. I approached her underwater, turning her legs, keeping my hands in contact with her body. I surfaced behind her, avoiding her clutches, and grabbed her securely in a lifesaving carry. Breathe . . . breathe. . . .

(21)   Using her far greater height and strength my teacher had flipped over and gotten me in a stranglehold, pulling us both underwater. She'd trained us so well that I had felt only minimal panic . . . breathe breathe . . . float on your back . . . look at the clouds. After all, she wouldn't really let me drown. Automatically I'd followed the lifesaving manual, forcibly subduing her—if need be knock her out or shove her head underwater until she is unconscious or stunned. Any lifesaver is a potential victim, so do what you must to save the victim, and if it's impossible then just save yourself. Breathe . . . breathe . . . I'd dragged my teacher to the shore eventually. She must have been black and blue and aching like crazy after testing 15 kids that day. I can't remember her name. That's sad. Breathe . . . She saved my life and I don't remember her name. Float . . . breathe. . . .

(22)   Totally hypnotized by the words, the rhythm, and the memories, I didn't know I had reached the shore until the snorkel scraped bottom. My legs buckled twice before I could stand and I staggered, whimpering, wounded.

(23)   "You idiot! What kind of moron swims out that far? You friggin' lunatic! You should have your head examined. You have less brains than a peapod. You scared me half to death. Do you know how easily you could have drowned?" My husband screamed at me nonstop until he ran out of words. I stared at him blankly, ankle deep in water with my teeth chattering. It made no sense. If he knew I was in trouble why hadn't he come to help me, or why hadn't he sent someone to help me? Or had he realized that with the distance between me and the shore no one could have helped me but myself? It didn't make sense, but I was too drained and much too tired to think sensibly. I even stopped shivering. I didn't have the strength for it. I walked, talked, dressed, ate, and functioned in a zombie-like state for at least twelve hours. When the shock hit and registered I cried uncontrollably, hysterically until I was cried out. Then I slept for a long, long time.

(24)   Having had more training than most people in water safety, how the hell do I forgive myself for breaking a dozen basic rules? How many times can I call myself stupid? Eventually, for the sake of my own self-respect,

I've had to put it out of my mind. But stupidity aside, there's got to be a way to teach people about panic so that they can save themselves. Somewhere in our school systems, in the early grades, someone should be teaching "Panic Survival." Parroting the words "Don't panic" is senseless because given a terrifying situation you can't prevent panic any more than you can prevent a knee-jerk reaction. How you *fight* that panic is a matter of life and death. To my knowledge no one has ever suggested a course or class in panic training. Is it possible that there are so few of us who have experienced panic and lived to tell about it?

—Claire Windsor-Shapiro

A FIRST AND SECOND READING OF CLAIRE'S TEXT

A strong and satisfying first reading is like living through the experience; it offers a vivid illusion. If of terror or panic, your hands may even sweat. Images, sensations, flood into your head. The movie moves! In a second reading, you can begin to appreciate how it is done.

WHAT NOW?

1. We imagine that you enjoyed Claire's text and that it aroused you. Putting it to one side now, jot down a page of notes on your first reading of it. Write quickly—just rough notes that you can talk from.
2. Now read the text again, more slowly. This time, look not at what the text represents—the experience—but at Claire's words, sentences, shifts, details. Look not *through* the text but *at* it. Make a page of notes on what you observed Claire doing to get her effects in that text.

One Student's Reflections

Here is one of our students writing about the differences between her first and second reading of Claire's text:

In my first reading, I wasn't able to concentrate on every word of the text, but in my second reading, I was able to give more thought to the text, about Claire and her almost drowning. I was more of a spectator than a participant in my second reading, because in my first reading, memories and associations kept popping into my mind, and I started remembering when I almost drowned, and I was so caught up in Claire's experience and couldn't wait to see what happened; I was a participant.

Going back to the text, I noticed things I hadn't the first time. I realized that there was a story within a story—when she goes back to learning how to be a lifesaver; and then I noticed the varieties of her sentences and the changes in verb tenses. I noticed that the beginning was like a fairy tale; everything was peaceful and even romantic. That made the change all the more intense. When I could sit back as a spectator—once I knew she was O.K.—I could read it another way, not less pleasurable, but a different kind of pleasure.

WHAT NEXT? ANOTHER COMPARISON

In the narrative of John Dove (p. 176), Dove makes three statements about his experience. Look again at those three statements. Do you find that they correspond to three stages in Claire Windsor-Shapiro's text? If so, how?

OUR APPRECIATION OF CLAIRE'S TEXT

Here now is part of our appreciation of Claire's text. Note that we use many of the terms that have already been introduced in this book.

> Claire begins by contextualizing—placing the events of her text both in time and place. She can do this because she is now—as she writes—a spectator of her own past experience.
>
> Line 3 of paragraph 1 and line 2 of paragraph 3 seem to foreshadow the calamity of the climax. As readers, we appreciate these only on a second reading.
>
> Paragraph 5 sustains the spectator frame but also marks a shift toward a participant text, by quoting and referring to very specific small details.
>
> Paragraph 7: Meanings are to be found in the differences; the fairy-tale, enchanted tone of this paragraph works effectively to lull the reader—as the writer herself had been lulled—into a state of euphoric relaxation.
>
> Paragraphs 8–10 nudge closer and closer toward a participant text, and paragraph 11 plunges us into participation, establishing a rhythm that becomes the recurring *motif* of her struggle to overcome panic. The last sentence of paragraph 11 and the first two sentences of paragraph 12 shift quickly back into spectator text (note the verb tenses) and represent her own explanatory commentary. They serve to distance us momentarily and allow us to catch our breath.
>
> Paragraphs 13–20 veer between participant and spectator, shifting out of an exclusively participant text as she escapes from her panic. But we as readers have, as it were, "felt" her panic precisely because of the effectiveness of her participant text.
>
> The last sentence of paragraph 19 prepares us for the shift in paragraph 20, the reminiscence of her experience of lifesaving, punctuated by her present litany "Float . . . breathe." The memory mostly reassures her, but it also occasionally scares/disconcerts her.
>
> Paragraph 22 demonstrates narrative economy as a means of avoiding a crudely chronological, moment-by-moment, narrative. Then paragraph 23 gives us a spectator within the text, her husband expostulating. And then her confused and tense questions "If . . . why?" But she's still too exhausted to "think sensibly"—that is, achieve a satisfactory evaluation. It is only with paragraph 24 that she represents a point in time from which she, as distanced spectator, can express a coherent, definitive, evaluation of those awful events.

WHAT NOW?

Compare your appreciation (your notes in the exercise on page 313) with those of others in your class and then with ours.

Themes

One of the most mysterious questions that English teachers ask is this: "What is it [the text] about?" Every text is about something. Perhaps we would do better to ask "What does this text do?"

Well, what does Claire make her text do? It offers a representation of an *episode*. She decided when and where that episode should begin and end. Life itself never tells us; the writer must decide what is a beginning and what an ending. In addition to giving us that representation, the text offers something else: Claire's evaluation of the experience and her conclusion about what should be.

If it is true that we learn from experience, then we could say that Claire not only gives us a case of herself learning from experience but also hopes that others will learn from it—otherwise, why mention it? We are now beginning to sense what we think that text of Claire's was "about." Or to put it another way, we are beginning to identify its **theme**.

What then is a theme? It's a general term denoting what all the particular elements of something add up to. Perhaps the theme of last weekend was chaos—in other words, everything we did seemed to add to the confusion and mess of the weekend. But perhaps Claire's text has more than one theme; perhaps it has two or three, neatly interwoven, so that they appear to be inseparable. What do you think?

Note that when we speak of the theme of someone's life, we have borrowed the idea from our reading of books and transferred it to real life. Usually, it is easier to identify the theme(s) of someone's life after they are dead and their "story" has ended. For similar reasons, we cannot identify the themes of our own immediate experience. But as we look back, spectators of our own past, we find it easier to see the main theme(s) of, say, our childhood or our adolescence. Themes then are what are perceived by spectators; the participant is too busy climbing the trees, or cutting them down, to see the wood clearly in outline.

NABOKOV'S "THEMATIC DESIGNS"

When Vladimir Nabokov, the Russian-American novelist, looked back at his early years, some stretches were very obscure or fragmentary; others had stayed with him, as fresh as if they had occurred yesterday. As he unravels and reconstructs, he discovers one of his major themes: the disintegration of the world of his childhood through wars and revolutions. And the image that he discovers to express, to encapsulate that theme is nothing more impressive than a handful of matches.

To fix correctly, in terms of time, some of my childhood recollections, I have to go by comets and eclipses, as historians do when they tackle the fragments of a saga. But in other cases there is no dearth of data. I see myself, for instance, clambering over wet black rocks at the seaside while Miss Norcott, a languid and melancholy governess, who thinks I am following her, strolls away along the curved beach with Sergey, my younger brother. I am wearing a toy bracelet. As I crawl over those rocks, I keep repeating, in a kind of zestful, copious, and deeply gratifying incantation, the English word "childhood," which sounds mysterious and new, and becomes stranger and stranger as it gets mixed up in my small, over-stocked, hectic mind, with Robin Hood and Little Red Riding Hood, and the brown hoods of old hunch-backed fairies. There are dimples in the rocks, full of tepid seawater, and my magic muttering accompanies certain spells I am weaving over the tiny sapphire pools.

The place is of course Abbazia, on the Adriatic. The thing around my wrist, looking like a fancy napkin ring, made of semitranslucent, pale-green and pink, celluloidish stuff, is the fruit of a Christmas tree, which Onya, a pretty cousin, my coeval, gave me in St. Petersburg a few months before. I sentimentally treasured it until it developed dark streaks inside which I decided as in a dream were my hair cuttings which somehow had got into the shiny substance together with my tears during a dreadful visit to a hated hairdresser in nearby Fiume. On the same day, at a water-side café, my father happened to notice, just as we were being served, two Japanese officers at a table near us, and we immediately left—not without my hastily snatching a whole *bombe* of lemon sherbet, which I carried away secreted in my aching mouth. The year was 1904. I was five. Russia was fighting Japan. With hearty relish, the English illustrated weekly Miss Norcott subscribed to reproduced war pictures by Japanese artists that showed how the Russian locomotives—made singularly toylike by the Japanese pictorial style—would drown if our Army tried to lay rails across the treacherous ice of Lake Baikal.

But let me see. I had an even earlier association with that war. One afternoon at the beginning of the same year, in our St. Petersburg house, I was led down from the nursery into my father's study to say how-do-you-do to a friend of the family, General Kuropatkin. His thickset, uniform-encased body creaking slightly, he spread out to amuse me a handful of matches, on the divan where he was sitting, placed ten of them end to end to make a horizontal line, and said, "This is the sea in calm weather." Then he tipped up each pair so as to turn the straight line into a zigzag—and that was "a stormy sea." He scrambled the matches and was about to do, I hoped, a better trick when we were interrupted. His aide-de-camp was shown in and said something to him. With a Russian, flustered grunt, Kuropatkin heavily rose from his seat, the loose matches jumping up on the divan as his weight left it. That day, he had been ordered to assume supreme command of the Russian Army in the Far East.

This incident had a special sequel fifteen years later, when at a certain point of my father's flight from Bolshevik-held St. Petersburg to southern Russia he was accosted while crossing a bridge, by an old man who looked like a gray bearded peasant in his sheepskin coat. He asked my father for a light. The next moment each recognized the other. I hope old Kuropatkin, in his rustic disguise, managed to evade Soviet imprisonment, but that is not the point. What pleases me is the evolution of the match theme, those magic ones he had shown me had been trifled with and mislaid, and his armies had also vanished, and everything had fallen through, like my toy trains that, in the winter of 1904–05, in Wiesbaden, I tried to run over the frozen puddles in the grounds of the Hotel Oranien. The following of such thematic designs through one's life should be, I think, the true purpose of autobiography.

When we write about our own past life, Nabokov suggests, we should be "following . . . such thematic designs." His word "following" is cunningly chosen, because it doesn't commit him to deciding whether those "designs" actually exist in the happenings of our lives or whether we invent them, imposing or teasing them out, choosing particular episodes to fit our theme. By using the word "following," he avoids that problem altogether. But it was a convenient and neat coincidence for Nabokov that the disarray of the matches served so well as an image of the disarray of the Russian army and navy.

Can you find themes in your own past that neatly and convincingly sum up your experiences? Or are you like the historian George Kennan, who insists that the remembered past bears little resemblance to the actual past?

The fact is that one moves through life like someone with a lantern in a dark wood. A bit of the path ahead is illuminated, and a bit of the path behind. But the darkness follows hard on one's footsteps and envelopes our trail as one proceeds. Were one to be able, as one never is, to retrace the steps by daylight, one would find that the terrain traversed bears, in reality, little relationship to what imagination and memory had pictured. We are, toward the end of our lives, such different people, so far removed from the childhood figures with whom our identity links us, that the bond to those figures, like that of nations to their obscure prehistoric origins, is almost irrelevant.

—Memoirs: 1925–1950

Or are you more like the great Roman emperor Hadrian?

HADRIAN'S "SHAPELESS MASS"

Marguerite Yourcenar, the French-American writer, spent about 30 years of her life, off and on, delving into the life of the emperor Hadrian (see p. 93). After many trials and crammed wastepaper baskets, she eventually decided that she would assume the role of Hadrian and write his "auto-biography" as he lies on his deathbed, dictating to a secretary. Looking back, Hadrian is distressed at the absence of clear direction in his life:

> When I consider my life, I am appalled to find it a shapeless mass. A hero's existence, such as is described to us, is simple; it goes straight to the mark, like an arrow. Most men like to reduce their lives to a formula, whether in boast or lament, but almost always in recrimination; their memories obligingly construct for them a clear and comprehensible past. My life has contours less firm. As is commonly the case, it is what I have not been which defines me, perhaps, most aptly: a good soldier, but not a great warrior; a lover of art, but not the artist which Nero thought himself to be at his death; capable of crime, but not laden with it. I have come to think that great men are characterized precisely by the extreme position which they take, and that their heroism consists in holding to that extremity throughout their lives. They are our poles, or our antipodes. I have occupied each of the extremes in turn, but have not kept to any one of them; life has always drawn me away. And nevertheless neither can I boast, like some plowman or worthy carter, of a middle-of-the-road existence.

Hadrian's assessment of his life swings like a pendulum. First he sees it as so ordinary (and therefore boring) that there is no good reason for assuming that anyone will be interested. Then he sees his life as so very odd and unusual that no one will be able to see any pattern to it or make sense of it.

> Sometimes my life seems to me so commonplace as to be unworthy even of careful contemplation, let alone writing about it, and is not at all more important, even in my own eyes, than the life of any other person. Sometimes it seems to me unique, and for that very reason of no value, and useless, because it cannot be reduced to the common experience of men. No one thing explains me: neither my vices nor my virtues serve for answer; my good fortune tells more, but only at intervals, without continuity, and above all, without logical reason. Still, the mind of man is reluctant to consider itself as the product of chance, or the passing result of destinies over which no god presides, least of all himself. A part of every life, even a life meriting very little regard, is spent in searching out the reasons for its existence, its starting point, and its source. My own failure to discover these things has sometimes inclined me toward magical explanations, and has led me to seek in the frenzies of the occult for what common sense has not taught me. When all the involved calculations prove false, and the philosophers themselves have nothing more to tell us, it is excusable to turn to the random twitter of birds, or toward the distant mechanism of the stars.

When we read a text such as that, we feel reassured that others have the same uncertainties about their lives as we have.

WHAT NOW?

Adolescence is generally regarded as the stage of greatest uncertainty, of the feeling that "No one understands me," of severe self-criticism and self-doubting, of bouts that sometimes feel weirdly close to some kind of insanity. What do you recall of the uncertainties of your adolescent years?

WHAT NEXT? THAT WHICH YOU HAVE NOT BEEN

"As is commonly the case, it is what I have not been which defines me," Hadrian ruefully admits. Write a "definition" of yourself in those terms. (Hint: Keep your sense of humor well tuned.)

The Theme of Happiness Remembered

In the two texts that follow, happiness remembered is the general theme. Each writer looks back in thankfulness for good things. Each writes implicitly of the pleasure of community, of doing things together with others. But the settings and time frames of the texts are very different.

JOHN NEIHARDT'S CHILDHOOD MEMORIES

First John Neihardt, writing in his late eighties, looks way back to his childhood in Kansas in the 1890s:

> Remembering the summers out on Uncle George's farm, I wonder what has happened to the human race since then! Can it be that we were wiser, knowing less? Or happier, with a little valued more? Or is it merely later than I think, and am I getting older than I know?
>
> Anyway, it is like a brief sojourn in Eden to recall the way it was out there that enchanted summer of '94.
>
> There is my Grandfather with his quiet, sobersided wit and the twinkle in his bright blue eyes; a bit slow-footed, maybe, and walking with a stoop reminiscent of uncounted horses shod, but still the old magician at his forge.
>
> There is my Grandmother, still patiently busy and always helping, still radiating the old sense of soft-bosomed, comforting goodness.
>
> There is my ageless Uncle George with his merry banter, a hero for his way with horses, and his knowing, easy way of doing whatever needed doing. And was he not once champion cornhusker of our county? Why, they say that when a husked ear struck the bangboard, he always had another in the air and already on the way! I was proud that I could sometimes beat him in our sweet-corn-eating contests, when each strove

Prairie family, c. 1890

manfully to produce the longer row of stripped-off corncobs to prove his prowess. How it delighted him to see a hungry boy eat!

And there is my worshiped Aunt, my Uncle George's wife, newly a mother and sweet with nursing, a born ally of boys, and pretty as Miss Field—almost! And there is the baby, Tommy, whom I often rocked to sleep. He and I became such buddies that he regarded my singing voice as perfectly magnificent—even though I deliberately committed vocal mayhem in a rusty-hinge soprano, out of tune. I am sure of this, because his loudest indictments of the cockeyed world ceased abruptly when I broke out in full song. Except for the way he smiled and gurgled with appreciation, it might have been amazement that he felt. I lived to know him as an old man, retired after a career as locomotive engineer on crack trains bound for the Coast and back—a boyhood dream come true.

Yes, I know the "Drouth of '94" was a weather classic such as old men recall to make a story. And I myself saw the corn blades curl in the searing gale, turn yellow, wither, blow away. Indeed, that wasn't Eden; it was more like Kansas.

But it's quite another picture that I see first when I remember and last when I forget. Merciful evening has come at long last. The booming wind has gone down with the heat-pale sun. A horizon-wide hush has fallen with the darkness. The stars look "old and full of sleep."

No use trying to sleep indoors. The house is like an old Dutch oven ready for the dough. Although the prairie seems to pant with heat left over from the day, it's easier breathing in the open air.

So we are all together there in the starlight, lounging on blankets spread out on the grass: Grandpa and Grandma, Aunt and Uncle with Tommy in his cradle; old Shep, all tongue and panting, stretched out in un-doglike abandonment to misery and unmindful of the cats that have come to share our unfamiliar doings and be people for a while. It's hot, breathless hot! But there's a lifting sense of holiday release about it all, of equality in sharing calamitous experience, a feel of perilous freedom from the humdrum tyrannies of common things.

Along the vague horizon north and west, heat lightning flares by fits—flash on flash of star-devouring brilliance. It should be a rainstorm working up. The big ones come from there; but there's no wisp of cloud. We watch the ghostly storms of light and listen hard for thunder far away.

There! There!

But only tremendous silence trails the flashes.

The ghostly storms grow more remote and dimmer, glimmer awhile beneath the prairie rim, and cease.

—Then, suddenly the cool white of early morning and the vacant sky.

That's what I remember first and last from the Drouth of '94—all of us together there, immortal in the starlight.

WHAT NOW?

As Neihardt looks back, years later, to the drought of 1894, he realizes that it was a gloriously happy moment in his long life. Represent a moment from your own life that you now realize was a moment of intense happiness.

IRIS ORIGO'S MEMORIES OF A NEW LIFE

Next, Iris Origo, who first appeared on page 8 of this book, takes us back to the 1920s—very busy years, when she and her husband were putting their farm on its feet. Notice that even though her text's underlying structure is a simple chronological list, she avoids the pitfall of the inexperienced or inconsiderate writer and never allows her text to lapse into a mere catalogue.

How can I recapture the flavour of our first year? After a place has become one's home, one's freshness of vision becomes dimmed; the dust of daily life, of plans and complications and disappointments, slowly and inexorably clogs the wheels. But sometimes, even now, some sudden trick of light or unexpected sound will wipe out the intervening years and take me back to those first months of expectation and hope, when each day brought with it some new small achievement, and when we were awaiting, too, the birth of our first child.

For the first time, in that year, I learned what every country child knows: what it is to live among people whose life is not regulated by artificial dates, but by the procession of the seasons: the early spring ploughing before sowing the Indian corn and clover; the lambs in March and April and then the making of the delicious sheep's-milk cheese, *pecorino*, which is a speciality of this region, partly because the pasture is rich in thyme, called *timo sermillo* or *popolino*. ("*Chi vuol buono il caciolino,*" goes a popular saying, "*mandi le pecore al sermolino.*")* Then came the hay-making in May, and in June the harvest and the threshing; the vintage in October, the autumn ploughing and sowing; and finally, to conclude the farmer's year, the gathering of the olives in December, and the making of the oil. The weather became something to be considered, not according to one's own convenience but the farmer's needs: each rain-cloud eagerly watched in April and May as it scudded across the sky and rarely fell, in the hope of a kindly wet day to swell the wheat and give a second crop of fodder for the cattle before the long summer's drought. The nip of late frosts in spring became a menace as great as that of the hot, dry summer wind, or, worse, of the summer hail-storm which would lay low the wheat and destroy the grapes. And in the autumn, after the sowing, our prayers were for soft sweet rain. "*Il gran freddo di gennaio,*" said an old proverb, "*il mal tempo di febbraio, il vento di marzo, le dolci acque di aprile, le guazze di maggio, il buon mietere di giugno, il buon battere di luglio, e le tre acque di agosto, con la buona stagione, valgon più che il tron di Salmone.*"†

Some of the farming methods which we saw in those first years became obsolete in Tuscany a long time ago. Then, the reaping was still done by hand and in the wheat-fields, from dawn to sunset, the long rows of reapers moved slowly forwards, chanting rhythmically to follow the rise and fall of the sickle, while behind the binders and gleaners followed, bending low in a gesture as old as Ruth's. The wine and water, with which at intervals the men freshened their parched throats, were kept in leather gourds in a shady ditch, and several times in the day, besides, the women brought down baskets of bread and cheese and home-cured ham (these snacks were called *spuntini*) from the farms, and at midday steaming dishes of *pastasciutta* and meat. A few weeks ago, one of the oldest *contadini* still left at La Foce, a man of ninety—*laudator temporis acti*—was reminiscing with my husband about those days. "We worked from dawn to dusk, and sang as we worked. Now the machines do the work—but who feels like singing?"

An even greater occasion than the reaping, was the threshing—the crowning feast-day of the farmer's year. Threshing, until very recently, had been done by hand with wooden flails on the grass or brick threshing-floor beside each farm, but in our time there was already a threshing-machine worked by steam, and all the neighbouring farmers came to lend a hand and to help in the fine art of building the tall straw ricks, so tightly packed that, later on, slices could be cut out of them, as from a piece of cake. The air was heavy with fine gold dust, shimmering in the sunlight, the wine-flasks were passed from mouth to mouth, the children climbed on to

---

*"The man who wants good cheese, will feed his sheep on thyme." [Origo's note]
†"Great cold in January, bad weather in February, March winds, sweet rain in April, showers in May, good reaping in June, good threshing in July, and the three rains of August—all with good weather—these are worth more than Solomon's throne." [Origo's note]

the carts and stacks, and at noon, beside the threshing-floor, there was a banquet. First came soup and smoke-cured hams, then piled-up dishes of spaghetti, then two kinds of meat—one of which was generally a great gander, *l'ocio*, fattened for weeks beforehand—and then platters of sheep's-cheese, made by the *massaia* herself, followed by the *dolce*, and an abundance of red wine. These were occasions I shall never forget—the handsome country girls bearing in the stacks of yellow *pasta* and flask upon flask of wine; the banter and the laughter; the hot sun beating down over the pale valley, now despoiled of its riches; the sense of fulfilment after the long year's toil.

Then came the vintage. The custom of treading the grapes beneath the peasants' bare feet—often pictured by northern writers, perhaps on the evidence of Etruscan frescoes, as a gay Bacchanalian scene—was already then a thing of the past. At that time, the bunches of grapes were brought by ox-cart to the *fattoria* in tall wooden tubs (called *bigonci*) in which they were vigorously squashed with stout wooden poles, and the mixture of stems, pulp and juice was left to ferment in open vats for a couple of weeks, before being put into barrels, to complete the fermentation during the winter. Now, the stems are separated from the grapes by a machine (called a *diraspatrice*), *before* the pressing, and then the juice flows directly into the vats, while for the pale white wine called 'virgin' the grapes are skinned before the fermentation (since it is the skin that gives the red wine its colour).

Last, in the farmer's calendar, came the making of the oil. Unlike Greece and Spain, and some parts of southern Italy, where the olives are allowed to ripen until they fall to the ground (thus producing a much fatter and more acid oil) olives in Tuscany are stripped by hand from the boughs as soon as they reach the right degree of ripeness. Then, when the olives have been brought in by ox-cart to the *fattoria* and placed on long flat trays, so as not to press upon each other, the oil-making takes place with feverish speed, going on all day and night. When first we arrived, we found that the olives were being ground by a large circular millstone, about two metres in diameter, which was worked by a patient blindfold donkey, walking round and round. The pulp which was left over was then placed into rope baskets and put beneath heavy presses, worked by four strong men pushing at a wooden bar. This produced the first oil, of the finest quality. Then again the whole process was repeated, with a second and stronger press, and the oil was then stored in huge earthenware jars, large enough to contain Ali Baba's thieves, while the pulp (for nothing is wasted on a Tuscan farm) was sold for the ten per cent of oil which it still contained. (During the war, we even used the kernels for fuel.) The men worked day and night, in shifts of eight hours, naked to the waist, glistening with sweat. At night, by the light of oil lamps, the scene—the men's dark glistening torsos, their taut muscles, the big grey millstone, the toiling beast, the smell of sweat and oil—had a primeval, Michelangelesque grandeur. Now, in a white-tiled room, electric presses and separators do the same work in a tenth of the time, with far greater efficiency and less human labour, and clients bring their olives to us to be pressed from all over the district. One can hardly deplore the change; yet it is perhaps at least worth while to record it.

Origo's Themes   What are the themes of Iris Origo's text? The pleasures, or at least
the satisfactions, of a job well done? The pleasures of improvement?
Change for better and worse? Do you agree that one of the successes of
her text is her control of thematic development, the whole text becoming
richer and richer, touching on more and more? Clearly, she had the skill
not to cram it all in too quickly, even though she ranges through all the
seasons in a relatively small space. Is her time scale consistent? Is her
level of particularity/generalization consistent?

WHAT NOW? A YEAR IN THE LIFE OF . . .

Compose a text that takes a reader through the seasonal changes of
a year in your early life, using about the same pace and scale as Iris Origo.
Did each season have its distinctive pleasures? games? pranks? Did you
change significantly over the course of that year? For better or for worse?

The Memories of Virginia Woolf

MAKING A BEGINNING

We suggest that you read the following text slowly, two or three times.
It is not difficult so much as subtle. If you read it quickly, you will miss
too much. Notice that the writer explores some of the questions we have
already raised in this chapter and the preceding one. (See pages 285, 308.)

The writer is Virginia Woolf, famous English novelist, author of *To the
Lighthouse, Mrs. Dalloway, The Waves,* and *The Years,* as well as numerous
essays and a voluminous diary. Though an avid reader of autobiography,
Woolf had never written one herself. Here, two years before her death, she
is writing not exactly autobiography but reflections, thinking about doing
so by *writing about it.* She recognized that she knew many different ways
of writing a memoir, but feared that if she stopped to analyze them and
their merits and faults, she would never begin. So she takes the plunge,
diving back into her first memory.

> Without stopping to choose my way, in the sure and certain knowledge that
> it will find itself—or if not it will not matter—I begin: the first memory.
>   This was of red and purple flowers on a black ground—my mother's
> dress; and she was sitting either in a train or in an omnibus, and I was
> on her lap. I therefore saw the flowers she was wearing very close; and
> can still see purple and red and blue, I think, against the black; they
> must have been anemones, I suppose. Perhaps we were going to St Ives;
> more probably, for from the light it must have been evening, we were
> coming back to London. But it is more convenient artistically to suppose

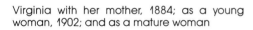

Virginia with her mother, 1884; as a young
woman, 1902; and as a mature woman

that we were going to St Ives, for that will lead to my other memory, which also seems to be my first memory, and in fact it is the most important of all my memories. If life has a base that it stands upon, if it is a bowl that one fills and fills and fills—then my bowl without a doubt stands upon this memory. It is of lying half asleep, half awake, in bed in the nursery at St Ives. It is of hearing the waves breaking, one, two, one, two, and sending a splash of water over the beach; and then breaking, one, two, one, two, behind a yellow blind. It is of hearing the blind draw its little acorn across the floor as the wind blew the blind out. It is of lying and hearing this splash and seeing this light, and feeling, it is almost impossible that I should be here; of feeling the purest ecstasy I can conceive.

I could spend hours trying to write that as it should be written, in order to give the feeling which is even at this moment very strong in me. But I should fail (unless I had some wonderful luck); I dare say I should only succeed in having the luck if I had begun by describing Virginia herself.

RECONSTRUCTING EARLY IMPRESSIONS

When Virginia does "describe" herself, she offers facts: her birthdate, birthplace, parents' names, the social world into which she was born and raised—in short, the context of time and place. All the while she describes herself, she insists that to say "This is what happened" is not nearly enough. *Who is the person* to whom events happen; and how does a mind remember, reconstruct, and reshape those events—these are the questions that intrigue her. In the next passage, she recalls sensations of color, sound, shape, and shading—all this she remembers and in so doing, she enjoys the illusion of being there again.

If I were a painter I should paint these first impressions in pale yellow, silver, and green. There was the pale yellow blind; the green sea; and the silver of the passion flowers. I should make a picture that was globular; semi-transparent. I should make a picture of curved petals; of shells; of things that were semi-transparent; I should make curved shapes, showing the light through, but not giving a clear outline. Everything would be large and dim; and what was seen would at the same time be heard; sounds would come through this petal or leaf—sounds indistinguishable from sights. Sound and sight seem to make equal parts of these first impressions. When I think of the early morning in bed I also hear the caw of rooks falling from a great height. The sound seems to fall through an elastic, gummy air; which holds it up; which prevents it from being sharp and distinct. The quality of the air above Talland House seemed to suspend sound, to let it sink down slowly, as if it were caught in a blue gummy veil. The rooks cawing is part of the waves breaking—one, two, one, two—and the splash as the wave drew back and then it gathered again, and I lay there half awake, half asleep, drawing in such ecstasy as I cannot describe.

The next memory—all these colour-and-sound memories hang together at St Ives—was much more robust; it was highly sensual. It was later. It still makes me feel warm; as if everything were ripe; humming; sunny; smelling so many smells at once; and all making a whole that even now makes me stop—as I stopped then going down to the beach; I stopped at the top to look down at the gardens. They were sunk beneath the road. The apples were on a level with one's head. The gardens gave off a murmur of bees; the apples were red and gold; there were also pink flowers; and grey and silver leaves. The buzz, the croon, the smell, all seemed to press voluptuously against some membrane; not to burst it; but to hum round one such a complete rapture of pleasure that I stopped, smelt; looked. But again I cannot describe that rapture. It was rapture rather than ecstasy.

The strength of these pictures—but sight was always then so much mixed with sound that picture is not the right word—the strength anyhow of these impressions makes me again digress. Those moments—in the nursery, on the road to the beach—can still be more real than the present moment. This I have just tested. For I got up and crossed the garden. Percy was digging the asparagus bed; Louie was shaking a mat in front of the bedroom door.* But I was seeing them through the sight I saw here— the nursery and the road to the beach. At times I can go back to St Ives more completely than I can this morning. I can reach a state where I seem to be watching things happen as if I were there. That is, I suppose, that my memory supplies what I had forgotten, so that it seems as if it were happening independently, though I am really making it happen. In certain favourable moods, memories—what one has forgotten—come to the top. . . .

There at the end of the avenue still, are the garden and the nursery. Instead of remembering here a scene and there a sound, I shall fit a plug into the wall; and listen in to the past. I shall turn up August 1890. I feel that strong emotion must leave its trace; and it is only a question of discovering how we can get ourselves again attached to it, so that we shall be able to live our lives through from the start.

But the peculiarity of these two strong memories is that each was very simple. I am hardly aware of myself, but only of the sensation. I am only the container of the feeling of ecstasy, of the feeling of rapture. Perhaps this is characteristic of all childhood memories; perhaps it accounts for their strength. Later we add to feelings much that makes them more complex; and therefore less strong; or if not less strong, less isolated, less complete.

MOMENTS OF BEING AND NON-BEING

Next Woolf distinguishes between ordinary, routine, everyday life—what she calls "moments of non-being"—and those moments of arousal that break the routine because they are moments of special intensity or awareness—"moments of being."

---

*The gardener and a domestic servant.

These then are some of my first memories. But of course as an account of my life they are misleading, because the things one does not remember are as important; perhaps they are more important. If I could remember one whole day I should be able to describe, superficially at least, what life was like as a child. Unfortunately, one only remembers what is exceptional. And there seems to be no reason why one thing is exceptional and another not. Why have I forgotten so many things that must have been, one would have thought, more memorable than what I do remember? Why remember the hum of bees in the garden going down to the beach, and forget completely being thrown naked by father into the sea? (Mrs Swanwick says she saw that happen.)

This leads to a digression, which perhaps may explain a little of my own psychology; even of other people's. Often when I have been writing one of my so-called novels I have been baffled by this same problem; that is, how to describe what I call in my private shorthand—"non-being." Every day includes much more non-being than being. Yesterday for example, Tuesday the 18th of April, was [as] it happened a good day; above the average in "being." It was fine; I enjoyed writing these first pages; my head was relieved of the pressure of writing about Roger; I walked over Mount

°**Mount Misery**: a local hill

Misery and along the river; and save that the tide was out, the country, which I notice very closely always, was coloured and shaded as I like— there were the willows, I remember, all plumy and soft green and purple against the blue. I also read Chaucer with pleasure; and began a book— the memoirs of Madame de la Fayette—which interested me. These separate moments of being were however embedded in many more moments of non-being. I have already forgotten what Leonard and I talked about at lunch; and at tea; although it was a good day the goodness was embedded

°**cotton wool**: absorbent cotton

in a kind of nondescript cotton wool.° This is always so. A great part of every day is not lived consciously. One walks, eats, sees things, deals with what has to be done; the broken vacuum cleaner; ordering dinner; writing orders to Mabel; washing; cooking dinner; bookbinding. When it is a bad day the proportion of non-being is much larger.

"Moments of being," for Woolf, are "sudden violent shocks" that jolt her out of the humdrum of non-being and force her to notice, question, speculate, wonder, evaluate. And it is only through writing, "by putting it into words," that things begin to make sense.

As a child then, my days, just as they do now, contained a large proportion of this cotton wool, this non-being. Week after week passed at St Ives and nothing made any dint upon me. Then, for no reason that I know about, there was a sudden violent shock; something happened so violently that I have remembered it all my life. I will give a few instances. The first: I was fighting with Thoby on the lawn. We were pommelling each other with our fists. Just as I raised my fist to hit him, I felt: why hurt another person? I dropped my hand instantly, and stood there, and let him beat me. I remember the feeling. It was a feeling of hopeless sadness. It was as if I became aware of something terrible; and of my own powerlessness. I slunk off alone, feeling horribly depressed. The

second instance was also in the garden at St Ives. I was looking at the
flower bed by the front door; "That is the whole", I said. I was looking at
a plant with a spread of leaves; and it seemed suddenly plain that the
flower itself was a part of the earth; that a ring enclosed what was the
flower; and that was the real flower; part earth; part flower. It was a
thought I put away as being likely to be very useful to me later. The third
case was also at St Ives. Some people called Valpy had been staying at St
Ives, and had left. We were waiting at dinner one night, when somehow I
overheard my father or my mother say that Mr Valpy had killed himself.
The next thing I remember is being in the garden at night and walking on
the path by the apple tree. It seemed to me that the apple tree was connected with the horror of Mr Valpy's suicide. I could not pass it. I stood
there looking at the grey-green creases of the bark—it was a moonlit
night—in a trance of horror. I seemed to be dragged down, hopelessly,
into some pit of absolute despair from which I could not escape. My body
seemed paralysed.

These are three instances of exceptional moments. I often tell them
over, or rather they come to the surface unexpectedly. But now that for
the first time I have written them down, I realise something that I have
never realised before. Two of these moments ended in a state of despair.
The other ended, on the contrary, in a state of satisfaction. When I said
about the flower "That is the whole," I felt that I had made a discovery. I
felt that I had put away in my mind something that I should go back [to],
to turn over and explore. It strikes me now that this was a profound difference. It was the difference in the first place between despair and satisfaction. This difference I think arose from the fact that I was quite unable
to deal with the pain of discovering that people hurt each other; that a
man I had seen had killed himself. The sense of horror held me powerless. But in the case of the flower I found a reason; and was thus able to
deal with the sensation. I was not powerless. I was conscious—if only at
a distance—that I should in time explain it. I do not know if I was older
when I saw the flower than I was when I had the other two experiences. I
only know that many of these exceptional moments brought with them a
peculiar horror and a physical collapse; they seemed dominant; myself
passive. This suggests that as one gets older one has a greater power
through reason to provide an explanation; and that this explanation
blunts the sledge-hammer force of the blow. I think this is true, because
though I still have the peculiarity that I receive these sudden shocks, they
are now always welcome; after the first surprise, I always feel instantly
that they are particularly valuable. And so I go on to suppose that the
shock-receiving capacity is what makes me a writer. I hazard the explanation that a shock is at once in my case followed by the desire to explain
it. I feel that I have had a blow; but it is not, as I thought as a child, simply a blow from an enemy hidden behind the cotton wool of daily life; it
is or will become a revelation of some order; it is a token of some real
thing behind appearances; and I make it real by putting it into words. It
is only by putting it into words that I make it whole; this wholeness
means that it has lost its power to hurt me; it gives me, perhaps because
by doing so I take away the pain, a great delight to put the severed parts
together. Perhaps this is the strongest pleasure known to me. It is the

rapture I get when in writing I seem to be discovering what belongs to what; making a scene come right; making a character come together. From this I reach what I might call a philosophy; at any rate it is a constant idea of mine; that behind the cotton wool is hidden a pattern; that we—I mean all human beings—are connected with this; that the whole world is a work of art; that we are parts of the work of art. *Hamlet* or a Beethoven quartet is the truth about this vast mass that we call the world. But there is no Shakespeare, there is no Beethoven; certainly and emphatically there is no God; we are the words; we are the music; we are the thing itself. And I see this when I have a shock.

This intuition of mine—it is so instinctive that it seems given to me, not made by me—has certainly given its scale to my life ever since I saw the flower in the bed by the front door at St Ives. If I were painting myself I should have to find some—rod, shall I say—something that would stand for the conception. It proves that one's life is not confined to one's body and what one says and does; one is living all the time in relation to certain background rods or conceptions. Mine is that there is a pattern hid behind the cotton wool. And this conception affects me every day. I prove this, now, by spending the morning writing, when I might be walking, running a shop, or learning to do something that will be useful if war comes. I feel that by writing I am doing what is far more necessary than anything else.

VIRGINIA WOOLF'S "PHILOSOPHY"

Here is an outline of Woolf's propositions about remembering and making sense of the past—what she terms her "philosophy." See whether or not *your* philosophy meshes with hers.

1. Days are made up primarily of "moments of nonbeing," stretches of time when we engage in ordinary, routine activities that she likens to "cotton wool"—eating, walking, talking, sleeping, working, taking the dog for a walk, cleaning house, etc. ("Do you ever reflect how you pass your life?" Sydney Smith once asked a girl. "If you live to 72, which I hope you may, your life is spent in the following manner: An hour a day is three years; this makes 27 years sleeping, 9 years dressing, 9 years at table, 6 years playing with children, 9 years walking, drawing and visiting, 6 years shopping, and 3 years quarreling.")

2. Within those stretches of non-being occur the occasional moments of being: *something happens* that jolts us into awareness. Woolf recalls three "shocks" from her childhood: (a) fighting with her brother, (b) looking at a flower in the garden, and (c) learning that a Mr. Valpy had committed suicide. She calls these events shocks because they shocked her when they happened and have lingered with her throughout her entire life. She relives these moments of being over and over; "they come to the surface unexpectedly."

3. These shocks are exceptional, extraordinary moments. They break the pattern of ordinary life; they break through the routine, habitual, daily things we do. They demand *explanation*. They force us to make sense of that moment.

4. The "sense" comes in the form of an *explanation*, an *evaluation*. For Woolf, two of her earliest shocks (fighting with her brother and Valpy's suicide) were distressing because they were unexplainable. The third (seeing the wholeness of the flower and the earth) she felt, even then, could be explained. Such moments represent her relationship with the world: In some situations she is powerless; over others she has control.

   The power, for her, comes from *putting it into words*, from discovering that the parts have fallen into place. "Oh, that's what it meant," she can now say—as a spectator.

5. As children, we are more impressionable, more susceptible to feeling these moments as disconcerting and distressing, because each one is new and we do not yet have the power of explanation to ward off the blows. As we grow older, as we accumulate experiences *and* explanations (cf. "funding," page 92), the shocks do not deal us such severe blows. We know what to expect. They become *moments of being*, in which we become aroused, moved, provoked, to understand.

6. For Woolf, writing things down helps her *see* how the parts fit together; she discovers "what belongs to what."

7. We always see that past from the present moment; the I now merges with the I then.

8. What we write today will not be written in the same way next week or in a year's time—because the I now is always changing.

9. How does Woolf's word "shock" sit with you? We have some difficulty with it, for we believe that those moments when we can and do come into awareness, when we are provoked to ask questions, to figure things out, are not necessarily negative. Woolf's word gives these experiences a slightly negative tinge. We much prefer "moments of being," and William Wordsworth's phrase "spots of time"—moments we remember in the same way as we remember important places, places that matter to us because of what happened *there*.

WHAT NEXT? YOUR MOMENTS OF BEING

1. List as many "moments of being" or "spots of time" from your own life as you can in ten or fifteen minutes of brainstorming. Each event will have cut through the ordinariness of daily life, will have stopped you

in your tracks, or made you cry out something like "Eureka!" *Something happened* that you recall over and over to yourself—and perhaps to others.

2. From the list you have made, choose one extraordinary event, one that has lingered in your mind for some time. Then
    a. Write of it, as you remember it happening *then*: for example, "When I was ten. . . ."
    b. Write of it as it appears to you now, looking back.
    c. What explanations did you come up with then?
    d. What explanations do you come up with now?
    e. Do (c) and (d) coincide or conflict?

part 5

An Extending Repertoire

16

When the Talking Has to Stop: Texts from Prison

The theme of this chapter is the prolonged imprisonment of prisoners of conscience, at times under conditions of solitary confinement. At the end of the chapter, we shall invite you to produce a variety of texts through assuming a variety of roles related to the experience of prolonged solitariness—roles that will involve you as participant, as participant-spectator, and as spectator.

The Case of Anatoly Shcharansky

JERUSALEM, June 28—Avital Shcharansky's tenth wedding anniversary is approaching, and with it comes the tenth anniversary of her last glimpse of her husband, Anatoly. It has, she says, been a decade of pain, of waiting, of uncommon devotion.

One day after they were married in Moscow July 4, 1974, she followed his urging and emigrated to Israel just before her hard-won exit visa expired. They were both confident he would be allowed to join her in a few months. But the months stretched into years, and the years saw a rising effort among Jews to emigrate and a tough crackdown by Soviet authorities. In 1977 Anatoly Shcharansky, one of the outspoken leaders of the emigration movement, was arrested on a charge of treason, then sentenced to 13 years in prison.

They were still new to adulthood in 1974, still fresh with joy and optimism. "When we married we felt like big winners," Mrs. Shcharansky recalled recently. "So excited. When we were separated we were so sure we were going to meet again very soon."

He is now 36 years old; she is 33. Parts of their lives have been lost. But to judge by his letters from prison and her constant travels and appeals on his behalf, they have lost none of their fervor for each other.

For the last decade, Mrs. Shcharansky has devoted her life almost exclusively to campaigning for her husband's release. She has traveled almost constantly throughout the Western world, meeting political leaders and heads of state, foreign ministers and private citizens. She has seen President Reagan and, during the previous administration, President Carter. She has talked with Prime Minister Margaret Thatcher of Britain, President François Mitterrand of France and, as she remarks with a smile, "three or four heads of state of Italy."

None of this seems to have hardened her with cynicism. "I have no doubt that he will come," she said. "Not too soon, but he will be here."

She credits her husband for her optimism. "Anatoly is so optimistic in his whole life that he makes people believe he will be free," she said.

Indeed, Mrs. Shcharansky's moods swing with his, as well as she can perceive them through the separation of prison and censored mail. "In the last six months I got two direct letters to me," she said. A third was apparently confiscated. But his mother, Ida Milgrom, who lives just outside Moscow, has been receiving the monthly letter that he is allowed to write. She speaks with Avital by telephone every week or so and reads his letters to her.

On the visits his mother is allowed every six months, he scolds her for not giving the details he craves about Mrs. Shcharansky's life, she said. This brings a glowing smile to her face.

Mr. Shcharansky's recent letters have been full of the romantic, witty philosophizing that his wife knew when they were together in Moscow. It buoys her own spirits. "When I see his letters, they make me really excited," she said. "It makes me see how the spirit of a human being can win everything.

"The K.G.B. try to kill him emotionally," she continued. "They try to break his soul and make him one of them. They came and said if Anatoly writes to the Supreme Soviet and says he's sick and asks for a pardon, they would release him after half his sentence. But he wouldn't do it. In an appeal for a pardon, you somehow say that you're guilty, and you play the game."

Mr. Shcharansky, who was pressed by the authorities to brand the Jewish emigration movement as having links with American intelligence, alluded to this in a letter a year ago, when he wrote:

"In addition to Newton's law on the universal gravity of objects, there is also a law of the universal gravity of souls, of the bond between them, and the influence of one soul on the other. And it operates in this manner, such that with each word that we speak, and with each step that we take, we touch other souls and have an impact upon them. So why should I put this sin on my soul? If I already succeeded once in tearing the spider web spun by the uncontrollable forces of life . . . how is it now possible to take even one step backwards toward the previous status?"

Last month, writing about his mental efforts to survive interrogation, he said he was compelled to summon up "pictures from my past, and thoughts concerning history and tradition; the Hebrew language and the books that I read; all that remained in my memory from my preoccupation with mathematics and chess; even visits to the theater, and of course, the ability to laugh—not at jokes or clever plays on words, but as if I were a spectator viewing the world from the sidelines, without undue melodramatics, discovering many interesting things, both comical and absurd."

In Israel, Mrs. Shcharansky has become an observant Jew, keeping the Sabbath, keeping kosher, binding her hair with a tight kerchief in the manner of religious married women. Three years ago she began studying Tanach, a Hebrew acronym for the holy scriptures of Judaism, and painting part-time at a religious women's college near Tel Aviv. But she has not really tried to make a life for herself outside her husband's cause.

And what has this done to her? Has she changed? What will Mr. Shcharansky find different about her if he is able to rejoin her?

"Age," she said, and laughed. "We are in close contact. Maybe outside we are changed, but not inside."

—David K. Shipler, *New York Times,* July 1, 1984

DON'T JUST SIT THERE, DO SOMETHING

You have just been a spectator of an extraordinary situation, the imprisonment of Anatoly Shcharansky, a man who hangs on to his sanity partly by imagining himself as "a spectator viewing the world from the sidelines . . . discovering many interesting things, both comical and absurd." If you believe that Shcharansky is a victim of injustice, what can you do about it? How can you become a participant in some kind of effort to make the world a less brutalized place?

We will not presume to advise you in such a matter but simply offer you a proverb: "It is better to light one candle than to curse the darkness."

Nazim Hikmet: A Poem from Prison

At this very moment as your eye is moving across this page, thousands of people are languishing in prisons—not because they have committed any crimes but because their political or religious beliefs run counter to those of their governments. One man who spent many years of his life in prison for his refusal to "toe the line" was Nazim Hikmet, a Turkish writer who won the World Peace Prize in 1950, the year he was released after spending 12 years in prison. How, through years of imprisonment, did he manage to cling to his sanity? By writing. By writing to and for his closest friends, Hikmet managed to hang on to a sense that he was still a member of a community, that he could still derive those profound fulfilments of desire, those satisfactions of deep needs, that we derive from our closest friendships. Here is one of Hikmet's texts.

Ninth Anniversary

One night of knee-deep snow
my adventure started—
pulled from the suppertable,
put into a police car,
sent off on a train,
and locked up in a room.
Its ninth year was over three days ago.

In the corridor, a man on a stretcher
is dying open-mouthed on his back,
the grief of long iron years in his face.

One thinks of isolation
       —sickening and total,
           like that of the mad and the dead—
first, seventy-six days
    in the silent hostility of the door that closed on me,
and then seven weeks in the steerage of a ship.
Still, we weren't defeated:
my head
      was a second person at my side.

I've completely forgotten most of their faces
—all I remember is a very long, very thin nose—
yet how many times they lined up before me.

When my sentence was read they had one worry:
                                    to looking imposing.
                                    They did not.
They looked more like things than people:
like wall clocks, stupid
                    and arrogant,
and sad and pitiful like handcuffs, chains, etc.

A city without houses or streets.
Tons of hope, tons of grief.

The distances microscopic.
Of the four-legged creatures, just cats.

I'm in a world of forbidden things!
To smell the lover's cheek:
                        forbidden.
To eat at the same table with your children:
                                    forbidden.
To talk with your brother or your mother
    without a wire screen and a guard standing between you:
                                            forbidden.
To seal the envelope of the letter you've written,
or to get a letter still sealed:
                        forbidden.
To turn off the light when you go to bed:
                                forbidden.

To play backgammon:
                forbidden.
And not that it isn't forbidden,
        but what you can hide in your heart and have in your hand
            is to love, to think, and to understand.

In the corridor, the man on the stretcher died.
They took him away.
Now no hope, no grief,
                no bread, no water,
                no freedom, no prison,
                no wanting women, no guards, no bedbugs,
                and no more cats to sit and stare at him.
                    This business is finished, over.

But ours goes on:
my head goes on loving, thinking, understanding,
the pitiless rage of not being able to fight keeps up,
and since morning the ache in my liver goes on . . .

                                                    (1946)
                            —Nazim Hikmet, *The Epic of Sheik Bedreddin*

"My head was a second person at my side" is one of the most interesting observations in Hikmet's text. He is writing about being in solitary

confinement for 76 days. Pause now in your reading, and try to imagine those 76 days—days on which you would talk to no one; days on which your prison food would be thrust at you by someone who did not say a word; 76 days with only yourself for company. But inside your head, Nikmet discovered, there is "a second person."

Notes
     Speculate for a few minutes about the identity of this "second person." Make notes in your notebook about the sense in which, when you are actually alone, you can still feel the presence of another. Where is that person? In what ways are you aware of his/her presence? In what ways does he/she talk to you, listen to you? In what sense can you see him/her?

Edith Bone's Seven Years in Solitary Confinement

YEARS BEFORE PRISON

Edith Bone was another prisoner of conscience for whom the "head was a second person." She grew up in a prosperous home in Hungary at the turn of the century. When she was an adolescent, her father asked her what she wanted to do with her life and offered to make anything possible for her. When she said she wanted to be a doctor, he told her flatly that doctoring was *not* for women.

Soon she asserted her independence and became a communist; she traveled widely in Europe and the Soviet Union, and became acquainted with the leaders of the new Soviet government. She found Stalin rather coarse and ignorant.

Subsequently she settled in England and married an English journalist; they both believed in the promises of communism. After World War II, they went to Hungary on assignment; there, without warning, they were arrested on a charge of spying and separated. The year was 1949; she was 60, and her sentence was 15 years' solitary confinement. As things turned out, her imprisonment lasted 7 years.

After her show trial was over, the threat of execution hung over Bone's head. But her many friends in England refused to allow her "disappearance" to be forgotten. Although she didn't know it, they directed a barrage of letters and phone calls at the British Foreign Office (State Department). The Foreign Office, therefore, made inquiries about her, and this interest probably influenced the way she was treated—for example, she was not tortured. Then, when the Hungarian uprising took place in 1956, she was suddenly released and returned to England. There her friends persuaded her that her story might be of interest to others.

Later, she admitted that her book, *Seven Years Solitary*, had been "written in haste and under great stress." But when it was reprinted she decided to leave it as it was rather than try to rewrite it in a more tranquil and detached mood.

Edith Bone

AN UNBREAKABLE SPIRIT

From the first day of her captivity, Bone made a clear decision: her captors were not going to "break" her:

> I made up my mind from the start that I would not let the position get me down. Apart from everything else, I did not want to give my captors the satisfaction of having "broken" me. One of them asked, "What's the point of this resistance? You will get broken, just like all the others. We've broken harder nuts than you."
>
> He was quite annoyed when I said: "I learned in primary school that you cannot compare two quantities unless you know them both. How do you know that those others whom you did 'break open' were harder nuts? Perhaps I am the harder one."

Two factors helped her to resist: one was her own temperament, the second was the nature of her guards.

It was, perhaps, also fortunate for me that my basic instincts do not prompt me to submission and obedience. I had always been a disobedient child, refractory at school and altogether by temperament a no-sayer, not a yes-sayer. It would be incorrect to say that I devised my tactics of disobedience and resistance deliberately or consciously. All I did was to obey my instinct. It was a lucky thing for me that this instinct proved correct. My jailers were like Hungarian farm-dogs, enormous shaggy creatures, Komondors, who rush out and threaten to demolish you if you so much as stop at the gate. If you run away or show terror, they will pull you down; but if you stand your ground, bend and pretend to pick up a stone, even if there is no stone handy, these dogs will run away.

LIFE IN PRISON—A BATTLE WITH THE GUARDS

Edith Bone quickly framed her captivity as a "battle": "My life in this prison I regarded as a battle I had to fight with these very inferior people. . . . I regarded the matter as a challenge, not only to myself but to that higher civilization of which I considered myself a product, however modest."

At mealtimes the food was now brought by the guards and put down on the ground beside the door. Prisoners were supposed to come to the door and take the food up off the floor. When my door was opened and the guard said, "Come and take your food," I made no move to do so. He came in and asked, "Why don't you take your food?"

"Because I am not a dog; I don't eat off the floor."

"Don't be a fool, come and take it."

"I am not a dog and I don't eat off the floor," I repeated.

At that the guard closed the door and went away. Presumably he reported what I had said; as I later found out, everything I said and did had to be reported.

Only a few minutes went by before the sergeant-major came and asked the same question: "Why don't you take your food?" and I gave him the same answer. He went away, and came back with the medical orderly, dressed all in white.

"What's the matter with you that you don't eat?" he asked.

"Nothing," I replied. "Leave me alone."

Nine Days
Underground

At first, for nine days, she was confined to a small underground cell with absolutely no light, either daylight or anything else.

As an act of self-defence, I had to avoid being sorry for myself and devise, out of my own resources—since I had no others—ways of passing the time that would not be entirely without profit to myself.

She began to recite poems that she remembered; then to translate poems (inside her head) from one language to another; finally, to compose her own. She called it "doggerel," meaning that she thought it was not very accomplished. But the important question is not "Is it good verse?" but "How did it help her to stay sane?" Here is part of one of her early efforts:

The Blanket of the Dark

Under the blanket of the dark I lie,
It is a warm blanket, soft as down.
It shields me from the jailers' spying eye,
And laps me in its folds as in a gown.

Strange how desire performance does outrun:
To punish me they took the light away,
They have no notion of what they have done,
What floodgates opened for my fancies gay.

No longer need I watch the concrete floor,
The rivet-studded door, the whitewashed wall;
Since grim reality intrudes no more
The queerest things me all the time befall.

Last night my cell turned to a Noah's ark.
The crew were mice; the captain, a white rat,
Hoisted for sail the blanket of the dark
And ran before the wind to Ararat.

I found a penny-farthing on the bed
And rode it, slap through all the bolts and bars,
Towards another planet—it was red,
The name, if I remember right, was Mars.

A brindle cow from Nowhere called today
The selfsame cow that jumped over the moon,
She took me on her back, brooked no delay,
And whisked me off to fairy Avalon.

So I go where I list, in arks, on cows,
On penny-farthings; or can, if I choose,
With regal crown bind my plebeian brows,
Or solve *Times* crosswords even without the clues.

The whole world's mine to do with as I please
Including Fairyland and points beyond.
I turn things into something else with ease
By one touch of my dark-born magic wand.

But hush! The jailers must not hear what great
Boon they conferred when they put out that light,
Or they'd switch on a thousand candles straight
And drive away my host of fancies bright.

(1951)

When, after nine days, she was moved to a dark cell on the first floor, she was just beginning to "get tired of a mental diet consisting entirely of poetry."

Imaginary Wanderings

Then she recalled a short story by Tolstoy in which a prisoner in solitary confinement had passed the time by taking imaginary walks in cities he had known. She decided to do the same. As a journalist, she had lived in many cities, so she was not short of places to revisit. And these journeys naturally led her to "visit" old friends, and to "have conversations" with them: since she admits that she often used to monopolize the conversation in her real social life, these imaginary conversations, in each of which she had to invent the other's contribution, were not so very dissimilar to the real thing!

Her new cell measured four-feet nine inches by ten feet, but the bed (three feet wide) took up most of the floor. Even so, she started to walk, literally—up and down—and also, in imagination, to walk back to England. In fact, she made that journey four times, using different routes, and moving slowly so as to explore every detail—and so *pass the time*.

Counting

After five months of total darkness, a 60-watt bulb was put into her cell, and her life was transformed: now she could be more genuinely active. For three years she lived almost entirely inside her head. But she made an abacus, out of dried bread pellets and broom stalks, on which to count, count, count. How many English words do I know? (She counted to 27,369.) How many birds can I name? How many trees? How many makes of cars?

Getting a Haircut

My very first battle with the administration of the prison had to do with hair. I had no comb and no brush, my hair had grown long in close on two years of captivity and I was allowed neither side-combs, hair-clips, nor so much as a short end of string to tie my hair back, so that it hung into my eyes. I asked for a hair-cut and was told that women were not entitled to them as they wore long hair. I remonstrated: "But I have always worn my hair short," to no effect.

I did not argue the matter, but proceeded to tear off my hair thread by thread, leaving only a stubble of about a hand's breadth on my head. It took me three weeks to get it done and the result was rather as if rats had gnawed my hair off. I had also cut my fingers on the hair, and small bits of hair had remained in the cuts, causing them to fester, but at least I had short hair again. During the three weeks I put a batch of grey hair in the dustpan every day, which excited comment among the guards.

Six months later I repeated the operation, this time with a better technique, so that I completed it in a fortnight and had no cuts on my fingers.

But when, another six months later, I started to shorten my hair for the third time, the sergeant on duty outside my door came in and said: "The governor sends you word not to tear off your hair. The barber will come and cut it for you tomorrow." Next day the barber turned up and cut my hair, asking how I wished it shaped, and remarking on its strange condition. "It looks as if the rats had gnawed it off," he said.

"So they did," I told him, not untruthfully, meaning, of course, the rats who had refused me such an elementary necessity.

Making a Printing Press

In three years Bone had composed a great number of verses in her head, which she repeated three times a day so as to remember them. But this was too time-consuming: she needed to write them down. But how? She had no pen, no ink, no pencil, no paper. How then could she do it?

She had already made an abacus out of bread and bits from the broom. Maybe she could make a printing press? Rather as in the little rubber printing sets that children play with, she fashioned individual letter-fonts out of bread. Masticated to a paste, and then shaped, the coarse dark bread would set very hard. So she began; by the time she was satisfied that she had enough, she had 4,000 letters and a compositor's case with 26 separate compartments. With these, she could set up 16 lines of verse at a time. For ink, she used saliva, blood, dust, and anything else that could offer color. So she managed to take all her writings out of her head, and see them with her own eyes! Toilet paper made regular little pages; thus, she printed her book of poems. The guards, she remarks, "were very surprised at my constant activity. I was always doing things that were not 'normal,' that is, not within their experience."

Making a Spy Hole

One of the things the staff made every effort to enforce was preventing me from knowing what was going on outside my cell. Why this should have been so is still a mystery to me, but they were certainly very much concerned about it. The natural result was that although I was only very mildly interested in what was going on outside my cell, I made up my mind to beat them at this game if possible. One of the main amusements in prison is to make fools of the screws.

I decided I would try to contrive a spy-hole in my door through which I could look out, just as they could look in through the regulation spy-hole which is a feature of every prison door. The door was made of two-inch solid oak, but of course its surface was not flush. It was built up of several beams and there were points where three of these joined; obviously these joints were weak spots, which could be attacked.

I had noticed long before that a nail, or rather the large head of a nail, projected from the door close to the floor. It stood to reason that it must be a large nail. I decided that the first thing to do was to pull it out and see whether it could be made into a bradawl.° It only projected about an eighth of an inch, but that was enough to get a purchase on it with a cord, and then pull. This is not, of course, the most efficient way of pulling out nails, but I had no other. From this a second problem arose; I needed a cord, a strong cord. Where could I get one? The jailers were sensitive about the smallest piece of string, presumably because of their inexplicable, unreasonable and inconsistent fear of suicides among the prisoners.

I decided that the best possible cord could be made of threads pulled out of the coarse linen towels which we were given. These linen threads were thick and strong. Of course, I could not tear strips from my towel—

°**bradawl**: pointed gadget for piercing holes in wood or leather that would have been noticed and my cell would have been searched and my precious cord discovered. But the towel had some lengthwise red stripes in it, two on each side, and I decided to draw threads on each side of these red stripes, since the absence of a thread would be much less noticeable there. This I did, with precautions; and it was not at all easy, because the guard looked in every now and then through the spy-hole, and one never knew when he was peeping in. One had to be very careful not to be caught in the act of pulling threads out of the towel.

The device which safeguarded me from this was a little spot of white which I put on the middle of the spy-hole cover. (By this time I possessed some white in the shape of toothpaste.) A mark of this sort had been made by one of my predecessors in the middle of the bottom edge of the spy-hole cover, and I followed his example, except that I put a little dab of white there instead, which proved a mistake because it was noticed. But when I put my spot of white on the edge of the spy-hole cover where it was hidden from sight unless the cover was moved, it was not discovered for months. So most of the time I knew when the screw was looking in, and could amuse myself by putting on some kind of mysterious act for his benefit while he thought I was unaware of being under observation. This amused me a great deal.

But to come back to the towels; these were only changed once a fortnight and so it took me about two months to get the required thirty-two threads from which to plait my cord.

Fortunately for myself, I had always been a fanatical lover of knots, and possessed that most remarkable publication, *The Ashley Book of Knots*, which I had studied assiduously and which, in addition to knots, also contained a number of sinnets.° I plaited a beautiful sinnet—a round one, the sort known as coach-whipping—out of thirty-two threads in groups of eight.

°**sinnet**: piece of macramé

This cord was strong enough to carry even my own weight, so there was no fear of its breaking. I put a strangler knot (this, too, out of the Ashley book) round the nail head, and, with my foot against the door, pulled for all I was worth; but the nail still resisted all my efforts. I realized that mere pulling was not enough. The nail would have to be loosened by joggling it up and down and right and left. For a long time I seemed to be making no headway, but I persevered until I felt a slight wobble. I loosened and pulled day after day, for many weeks, whenever I could be sure that none of the guards was loitering near my door, and in the end I got that nail out. This was triumph.

The nail was about an eighth of an inch thick and three inches long. I put an edge on the end of it instead of the existing point by the simple expedient of rubbing it on the concrete floor, which was exactly like a carborundum whetstone,° especially noticeable in its effects on the soles of one's shoes or boots. The result was a bradawl. With it I succeeded in boring a hole in my door at a point where three members of solid oak met. It was only a pinhole, of course, and it had to be very carefully concealed. It would not have done, for instance, for any wood-dust to have fallen outside, so I used my mouth as a pump and sucked out the little splinters of wood as my bradawl removed them.

°**carborundum whetstone**: a device for sharpening blades

By a dispensation of providence, the oak had been so blackened by age that it was exactly the colour of my black convict bread. Thus, the little hole could be stopped up by a tiny plug which matched the wood so perfectly that my spy-hole was never discovered. The plug was a necessity, as otherwise my little pin-point spy-hole would have showed up like a bright star whenever there was a light in the cell and none outside. I never took out the plug without taking care to block the light.

Until I was transferred to another prison, in Vác, which was in May 1954, I had the constant use of this spy-hole and it gave me more information on the routine of the prison than my jailers intended.

What was more interesting was that I could see all my fellow-prisoners. This again was a little triumph because the screws were most anxious to prevent me, not only from seeing them, but even from knowing how many there were in my section of the prison. I first ascertained the number of prisoners by counting the cell-doors with keys in the locks as I was taken along the passage into the exercise yard. After a time they realized that this was a give-away, and put keys in all the doors. But as the keys of the uninhabited cells were rusty, and the keys of the inhabited cells bright through constant turning, I scored once again.

My cell opened on to a large hall, in which, among other things, coals and wood were kept in two huge boxes. The tops of the boxes were used for serving out the food, and if by any chance I asked to go out while the mess-tins were still there, the guard always carefully screened them from my view; the idea being that by counting the mess-tins, I could deduce how many fellow-prisoners I had. Why this should have been a top secret I do not know to this day. I rather think their orders were to let no one see *me*, rather than for me to see no one.

SAVED BY LANGUAGE

Edith Bone's battle of wits with the prison officials and guards, her writing and printing, her busy inner life—all kept her so occupied that on many days she was surprised to discover that the time had passed so quickly. It is no exaggeration to claim that she was "saved" by language: it was by exploiting so many uses of language that she managed to create cheerfulness and the means of survival in a situation that might well have reduced her to a vegetable. She even welcomed the opportunity to be taken out of active *participation* in the life of the world and of work, and to think things over as a *spectator*:

> For many, many years this was the first opportunity I had to think over and digest all the things I had absorbed in more than sixty years of life, which I had never yet had time to absorb properly under the stress of circumstances, the necessity of making a living, and the pressure of new things cropping up all the time.*

---

*Cf. Marguerite Yourcenar's comment on her decision to write Hadrian's "autobiography" as memoirs rather than as a journal: "A man of action rarely keeps a journal; it is almost always later on, and in a period of prolonged inactivity, that he does his recollecting, makes his notations, and, very often, has cause for wonder at the course his life has taken" (*Memoirs of Hadrian*, p. 338).

SOME COMMENTS ON EDITH BONE'S TEXT

See *how far* you agree with the following comments on Edith Bone's text. We hope you will find several things on which to disagree.

1. She is placed in the role of prisoner, against her will. The only people she can communicate with directly are her jailers.

2. Within the role of prisoner, she uncovers the role of "free" woman, able to make many choices about how to use her well-stocked mind and what to do with her time.

3. She is confined within the frames of captivity and impotence, but within these she finds the contrary frames of freedom and power.

4. She is able to use her time to reflect on her past life and to reexamine her values, as a leisurely spectator of her own past.

5. It is by "placing" her captors within the evaluative frames of stupidity and slavishness, and treating them accordingly, that she is able to gain power over them.

6. By using her cunning, determination, and intelligence, she is able to nudge her captors into roles they did not choose.

7. In the solitude of her cell, she is able to enjoy an amazing variety of roles—rememberer, recapturer, friend, visitor, knot maker, spy, writer, printer, problem solver, resister, striker, reader. How many more can you uncover?

8. Some of those roles are actual, others are "virtual"—that is, imaginary or vicarious.

9. She wrests the frame of hope from the frame of despair; the frame of activity from the frame of enforced inactivity; the frame of cheerfulness from the frame of misery.

10. We can learn nothing from her example: hers was "a special case."

11. In her life, the personal and the public, the individual and the political, interpenetrate. Her story achieves its full meaning only if we see it as it is, within an ideological frame.

12. It is useful to see her story in terms of *contradictions:*
    a. **contra-dict** means "to speak (or write) *against.*"
    b. "Contradiction" is also a political, ideological term. Socioeconomic systems contradict themselves by acting in ways that, in effect, contradict or deny their propaganda's claims. The system that imprisoned Edith Bone was riddled with contradictions.

13. A show trial is a public ritual in which an innocent person is put in the role of a criminal. In order that the trial shall "succeed," it is

advisable to deprive the prisoner of a proper defense, to prevent her from being seen in the frame of "defensible."

WHAT NEXT? TEXTS IN A VARIETY OF ROLES

1. Imagine that you are a prisoner of conscience and that you have been placed in solitary confinement.

   You are allowed two sheets of paper and a pencil, and are given permission to write a letter to your family. You are informed that it may be the last letter you will be allowed to write. Before you write your letter, first consider this: Do you wish to say farewell? To reassure them? To prepare them for the worst? To express your hopes and fears? To ask for help? To warn?

2. Now take on the role of the prison's psychiatrist. You have been instructed to take the letter of a prisoner (another student), which has been intercepted by the jailers, and to use it as the basis for a diagnosis, prognosis, and recommendation.

   Note: The prison governor is very busy, so the report on the prisoner must not waste his time. It should clearly advise him on what action, if any, should be taken. Above all, the governor doesn't want the scandal of a suicide on his hands.

3. Take on the role of governor and respond in a brief memorandum to a psychiatric report (that of another student). Is it to the point? Is it useful? Does it sound professional, without being full of incomprehensible jargon? Are its recommendations clear?

4. The prison has many rules, but you, the prisoner, decide that you also will make rules. They will be your way of helping yourself to stay sane. You will write them on a small piece of paper that you can hide in your mattress. When you are desperate, you can take them out and read them.

5. You are allowed two sheets of paper that you can use for writing anything you wish. You now suspect that the prison guards intercept your letters, so you decide to write a letter that *may* have the effect of gaining you more privileges. But they must not suspect that you suspect. . . .

6. You are about to receive a letter. Decide who it is that you would most like to receive a letter from, and write that letter.

7. The government that imprisoned you has been overthrown; you are free to return to the United States, to your home. First, you must write to your family to tell them of your release and to prepare them for the ordeal of meeting you again after _____ years. (Make your choice: 3, 5, 10, 15, or 20 years.)

8. You have been back home for a month or two. Write to a friend to tell him/her of all the changes that have surprised you, of what is still

essentially the same, of your pleasures and difficulties in returning to normal life.

9. Write a reflective paper on the pleasures of being alone, as you experience them in your real life.

10. Write a letter to a friend who will have to spend much of his/her time alone for the next nine months, advising him/her on how to try to turn solitariness into a positive experience.

17 | Frames of Mind: Writing as a Member of an Academic Community

Tasks of the Student Writer

Your tasks as a student writer are far less momentous than those that faced Edith Bone: she wrote in order to hold on to her sanity, whereas you will presumably write in order to express the life of your mind—and to graduate. She wrote with only the community of those she remembered for company, support, and encouragement; you write as a member of an actual, available community.

Your privilege and opportunity, therefore, is to exploit all the resources of your community: to read, to discuss, to argue, to listen, to share and test your ideas, to obtain feedback, and to write for an actual audience. In this final chapter, we shall try to help you understand more fully your responsibilities and resources as a writer in college.

As a college student, you are doubtless required periodically to produce a paper or essay as evidence of your intellectual and academic progress. In what follows, we hope to provide some guidelines for you in the fulfillment of such assignments—in addition to the hints that you will already have garnered in working through the book to this point.

Guidelines for Writing Academic Papers

THE STAGES OF WRITING A PAPER

Framing
(Stages 1–3)

1. Think of your paper as a considered, premeditated answer to a question.

2. If necessary, find your question. (In many cases, the question will be provided by your instructor.)

3. Let your question "explode" into a set of constituent, more limited,

questions. These questions will provide lines of inquiry along which to probe the various aspects, or facets, of the total question. Each of these subquestions will have its own distinctive conceptual unity and, in many cases, these will derive from the particular methodology of the discipline within which you are writing your paper. Sociologists ask certain kinds of questions, economic historians different kinds of questions, political theorists yet other kinds of questions.

The nature of the topic itself, combined with the conventions of the discipline in which you are working—these will provide you with the necessary ways of formulating significant and appropriate questions.

Reading and Noting (Stages 4–7)

4. Read and reread your essential source materials.

5. Make notes of those elements in stage 4 that provide the raw material or data for stage 3.

6. Distribute stage 5's notes in the appropriate slots of stage 3 (3a, 3b, etc.). Locate any deficiencies in your data and repair the omission by selective reading. (Use a separate card/sheet for each individual question in 3. These will be the basis of your paragraphing.)

7. Place your parts in an appropriate sequence. If each part is on a separate card/sheet, you will find this relatively easy.

Writing (Stages 8–11)

8. Write a draft, converting your notes into a prose text; concentrate on *what* is to be presented.

9. Become a reader: read the draft you wrote in stage 8, and assess it. If in doubt, find another reader (a peer) and get his/her reactions.

10. In the light of 9, judge the strength/weaknesses of your draft. (Do you have a strong opening? Is your point of view consistent and clear? Do you avoid contradicting yourself?) Revise accordingly.

11. Edit and modify your revised text (10) in terms of its quality as a text. (Do your paragraphs tend to repeat the same structure—e.g., right branching—over and over, so as to sound tedious? Do you find you have repeated certain phrases and expressions too often? Do you hear awkward structures when you read your text aloud?)

PROCEDURES AND CHOICES IN WRITING A PAPER

Relationship with the Reader

Experienced writers have internalized a very versatile and comfortable sense of their readers. They have little or no difficulty in finding an appropriate tone—neither too distant (cool) nor too familiar (effusive).

If uncertainty about this is one of your problems, then give it some thought—but *not* at too early a stage in your writing. Tone is a feature of writing that can be adjusted and fine-tuned *after* the draft is on paper and holds all the information, content, data, facts, that are required.

Sequence and Coherence Within the Paper

In many kinds of texts, the sequence is self-evident. For example, in many history essays, a *chronological* sequence is evidently called for and may well provide the scaffolding on which you can build the more complex and significant sequences of cause and effect, of rising or falling fortunes, and so on.

Beginning and conclusion, even in a chronological treatment, offer scope for choice. You may choose how far back to go in tracing the causes of the American Revolution; similarly, its effects are presumably even now still resonating. You will, therefore, have to choose a cutoff point. This is a matter of judgment, approximation, and plausibility: you will have to exercise choice in distinguishing between the significant and the insignificant, the major and the minor, the proximate and the remote.

The appropriate sequence in a nonhistorical paper—for example, in sociology or philosophy—will depend on the nature of the question that you are trying to answer. If it is an *assigned* topic, read it carefully, word by word; for the wording of the topic may itself point you toward choosing the appropriate sequence.

Suppose, for example, you were assigned this sociology topic: "The decline of the extended family has exacted a considerable emotional price —discuss." First we would "explode" each of the constituents of the sentence, and brainstorm:

> "decline"—When did it start? accelerate? Any statistics? Best kind of evidence?
>
> "extended family"—Define it. What are its essential features? How did (does) it "work"? N.B. role of grandparents. Do children need grandparents? Aunts and uncles? Burden exclusively on parents? No spreading of the load—loss of sources of emotional satisfactions. Support-system—dealing with domestic crises, childbirths, deaths; sense of a *supportive* community (but also claustrophobic? Mother always breathing down your neck?).
>
> Disadvantages/price to be paid for/burdens of extended family: cf. "liberation" with distance from parents? "Live your own life."
>
> Causes of decline? Mobility. Divorce. Moving 3000 miles for new job. Inevitable? Breakdown of traditions—cf. loss of ethnic identity?
>
> Use: Generalizations? Particularities? *Personal* knowledge?

That is a fairly random set of notes; a paper that simply expanded each note into a paragraph would be rather short on **coherence**. (Coherence is a patterned sequence of parts, in which the parts are *related* in a convincing way.) So, where to start? Perhaps with a definition? Rather abstract? Why not start with a participant's voice—the voice of a grand-mother lamenting the dispersal of her large family: she doesn't get to see her grandchildren, etc. She feels a poignant sense of loss. O.K. Decision: start with a quotation from a grandmother, bewailing decline of extended family. Then lead into a definition. But how general, how common a phe-nomenon *is* it? Statistics and generalizations. Yes. Even before we have col-lected all our data, we have a sense of how we would like to kick off:

1. Participant voice. (No context.) Quote real person or fabricate it? (Role-text.)

2. Definition—*this* is what she's talking about.

3. The scale/scope of the phenomenon: generalizations and statistics (if we can find them). These will provide context for (1) and lead on to the next stage of the paper—that is, an attempt to characterize the blessings of the extended family. (That to be followed by its disadvan-tages.) Then we'll have to decide who in particular is paying the price for the decline of the extended family. Mothers? Children?

Questions of Generality/ Particularity

1. How "large" can generalizations be and still be dependable?

2. When does particularization burden the reader with an overkill of detail?

3. Should generalizations precede particularizations, or particulariza-tions precede generalizations?

1 and 2 are best answered when you examine your first draft (stage 9). If in doubt, ask someone else to read it: that person's judgment of pro-portions will be cooler than your own.

As for 3, there is no generally valid answer. When should the particu-larizations (or examples) come before (branch to the left of) the main generalization that they illustrate/validate/support? Certainly when one of your main purposes is to intrigue/arouse your reader. In general, the papers you write in college will be written for readers *who know more of the subject than you do.* Therefore, you are unlikely to make under-standing difficult for them by withholding your generalization, and their interest in your topic may well be stirred by your choice of interesting particulars. Left-branchers represent more *directly* the way in which much intelligent inquiry proceeds—that is, **inductively**.* In a left-brancher, your particulars (examples or cases) lead irresistibly to your summarizing generalization (for which all your particulars offer support). In many

---

*Inductive thinking occurs when a provisional general proposition is derived from a body of particular facts which have been observed. Conversely, *deductive* think-ing starts from a proposition or premise which has already been established.

inquiries, all we have to study, to observe, is a mass of particular bits of information, clues, specifics, and it is from them that we have to construct our conclusion—rather as Sherlock Holmes proceeds to unravel a mystery and, in so doing, makes sense of many apparently random, trivial, or incomprehensible fragments.

The left-brancher, then, simulates the way in which the inquiring mind works: it starts by *not* knowing the answer. The answer, at the end, is the reward.

If, however, a particular instructor prefers right-branching patterns because of their more explicit clarity—putting the big card on the table first—he/she will doubtless let you know.

Your Main Task

Your task is not to tell your instructors something they don't yet know but to show them that *you* know. This showing—if a bare enumeration of facts—can be tedious. Good instructors look for more: not merely a knowledge of the facts but an understanding of their significance, a consistent interpretation or criticism of the data. As for opinions, they are dirt cheap and not worth the paper they are written on.

What then can you offer? The best thing to offer is *evidence of having given the question some serious thought*. We cannot tell you how to think as a sociologist or as a biologist; that is something you will learn in other courses. But any paper that offers opinions that seem to have dropped too easily out of a casual glance is doomed to disappoint. Coherent papers give their conclusions (evaluations) a sense of responsibility; and the evidence for that responsible attitude is in all the irresistible support that inevitably leads the reader to draw the same conclusion as you, the writer, have. It should therefore be possible for the reader—having attended to your prior marshaling of evidence, data, examples, etc.—to arrive at your conclusion, or something very close to it.

How to Conduct an Argument

An argument is a brawl in a bar, a conflict of cats on a midnight roof, a descent into emotional violence or vituperation. In the academic community, however, it is an appeal to your reader's *intelligence and reason*—as opposed to his/her prejudices or preconceptions. How is the reasonable reader persuaded by argument to arrive at your conclusion?

The best guidance offered in this matter may well come from H. P. Grice in his William James lectures at Harvard in 1967. He suggested that when we communicate effectively with someone else it is because we adhere to the **cooperative principle**. In observing the cooperative principle, we comply with these four maxims:

(1) *Maxim of Quantity*. Make your contribution as informative as is required, but not more informative than is required.
(2) *Maxim of Quality*. Try to make your contribution one that is true. That is, do not say anything you believe to be false or lack adequate evidence for.
(3) *Maxim of Relation*. Make your contribution relevant to the aims of the ongoing conversation.

(4) *Maxim of Manner.* Be clear. Try to avoid obscurity, ambiguity, wordiness, and disorderliness in your use of language.

—Eve and Herbert Clark, *Psychology and Language*

Abstractions   Abstractions are among our worst enemies. All propagandists and demagogues exploit them to arouse mindless emotionalism. Yet we cannot do without them. How would we get through a week without using such words as depression, cheerfulness, tolerance, happiness, love, boredom?

If you have to produce papers in disciplines that depend heavily on abstractions—sociology, anthropology, philosophy, psychology—handle all abstract terms with great care. Check and double-check their uses by experts; and decide whether the experts' usage is or is not significantly different from the ordinary everyday usage. In law, especially, common words often carry a very specific technical meaning quite different from that which is intended in ordinary social use.

Relationships Between Segments   Paragraphing a text is a useful convention. Paragraphs help the writer to achieve a reasonable level of conceptual unity within segments; and a new paragraph signals to the reader that he/she is being invited to turn to another aspect or facet of the topic.

The problem for many inexperienced writers is not one of unifying a paragraph within itself, because a paragraph, for most purposes, can be thought of as an extended sentence. No, the problem is the **transition**— the move from one to another, the crossing of the gap in such a way that continuity is maintained. Discontinuity in a text gives the reader, as he/she travels forward through the text, an acute sense of zigzagging round hairpin bends and of finding no bridges where one road ends and another begins.

What, then, is a *transition*? (Note that transit means "traveling across.") It is *not* a piece of Scotch tape connecting two parts that in the absence of the tape don't seem to belong together in any recognizable way. Transitions are like the Roman god Janus—after whom January is named— who had a head with two faces, one looking back, the other forward. Thus on January 1, we too look both back (to last year) and forward (to the year ahead). Transitions, then, have a foot both in what precedes them and in what follows them; they straddle the gap between segments as do the hands of dancers in a ring. Without effective transitions, a text is disjointed; with overheavy transitions, it becomes clogged, swollen at the joints.

Academic Texts: Some Prime Exemplars

In the texts that follow, we will try to help you to observe very closely how three accomplished writers manage the various features of academic writing that we have mentioned so far. We shall *not*, however, try to do all your thinking for you. In many instances we will simply provide the question that will serve to help you focus on a crucial feature.

The texts we have chosen are not by writers. They are by people who have to use writing in order to get things done, people who write in order to disseminate ideas, pose questions, present new points of view—all aspects of the enterprise of intelligence—to get people to think about this or that and to think more effectively, more intelligently, more pleasurably.

We offer you their texts with pleasure and, in the first two, also provide some comments by way of highlighting how these writers respond to some of the main challenges that you will encounter when you try to make a contribution to the community of those who are pleased to exercise their minds.

We recommend that you first read straight through the Tuchman and Frith texts, ignoring our comments. Then, on a second reading, read our commentary/notes together with their texts.

BARBARA TUCHMAN

> The business of rewriting what is already well known holds no charm for me.
>
> —*Barbara Tuchman*

Barbara Tuchman is one of the most brilliant historians of her generation. She has not only achieved great distinction in the academic world but has also been recognized as one of the great popularizers, introducing thousands of people to the sheer pleasure of reading history. In 1978 she published *A Distant Mirror,* an account of Europe in the fourteenth century. The book's subtitle—*The Calamitous 14th Century*—highlights the fact that the Black Death (bubonic plague) wiped out one-third of the population of Europe. The word "mirror" in her title, therefore, suggests that we also live in a "calamitous" century, a period of similar disarray. In her foreword, Tuchman writes: "If our last decade or two of collapsing assumptions has been a period of unusual discomfort, it is reassuring to know that the human species has lived through worse before."

A few years ago, the Smithsonian Institution in Washington held a symposium on biography: eight biographers contributed papers, and the extract that follows is from the one presented by Barbara Tuchman. It offers us a chance to hear an accomplished historian talk about how she practices her craft.

Biography as a Prism of History

1.   In so far as I have used biography in my work, it has been less for the sake of the individual subject than as a vehicle[1] for exhibiting

---

1.   Here Tuchman states the theme of her paper: how, through portraying *one* individual, she can offer a picture of an epoch, an era, a society, a way of life.

an age, as in the case of Coucy in *A Distant Mirror*; or a country and its state of mind, as in the case of Speaker Reed and Richard Strauss in *The Proud Tower*; or an historic situation, as in the case of *Stilwell and the American Experience in China*. You might say that this somewhat roundabout approach does not qualify me for the title of biographer and you would be right.[2] I do not think of myself as a biographer; biography is just a form I have used once or twice to encapsulate history.[3]

2.   I believe it to be a valid method for a number of reasons, not the least of which is that it has distinguished precedents.[4] The National Portrait Gallery uses portraiture to exhibit history. Plutarch, the father of biography, used it for moral examples: to display the reward of duty performed, the traps of ambition, the fall of arrogance. His biographical facts and anecdotes, artistically arranged in *Parallel Lives*, were designed to delight and edify the reader while at the same time inculcating ethical principles. Every creative artist—among whom I include Plutarch and, if it is not too pretentious, myself—has the same two objects: to express his own vision and to communicate it to the reader, viewer, listener, or other consumer.[5] (I should add that as regards the practice of history and biography, "creative" does not mean, as some think, to invent; it means to give the product artistic shape.)

3.   A writer will normally wish to communicate in such a way as to please and interest, if not necessarily edify, the reader.[6] I do not think of edifying because in our epoch we tend to shy away from moral overtones, and yet I suppose I believe, if you were to pin me down, that esthetic pleasure in good writing or in any of the arts, and increased knowledge of human conduct, that is to say of history, both have the power to edify.[7]

---

2.   Strong sense of audience: she anticipates her readers' objection, presents it herself, and agrees with it.

3.   Repeating and emphasizing: biography can *encapsulate* history. She repeats the idea in (1) but in *new* words.

4.   Neat transition from paragraph 1 to paragraph 2, and the main statement for a right-branching paragraph: she will now move right from this statement, to offer example, support, illustration.

5.   The mention of Plutarch—one of the early great historians—allows her a "silent" transition into an affirmation of the historical biographer's fundamental desires: "to express his own vision and to communicate it to the . . . consumer."

6.   A neat transition: "communicate" (here repeated) acts as a bridge between paragraphs 2 and 3.

7.   Extending through "exploding" the purpose of communication, she sees three elements: to please, to interest, and perhaps to edify (i.e., to improve, to raise to a higher level of moral awareness, to render more fully human). She then has a neat little debate with herself about the claims of edification (an idea *very* popular among nineteenth-century historians but regarded by many sophisticated twentieth-century historians as "old hat"). Again, as in paragraph 1, she takes on a possible role for her audience—"if you were to pin me down" —and responds to that challenge. She is thereby involving her audience more proximately in her argument and also presenting herself as open to challenge (a sign of her mature confidence).

4.   As a prism of history, biography attracts and holds the reader's interest in the larger subject.[8] People are interested in other people, in the fortunes of the individual. If I seem to stress the reader's interest rather more than the pure urge of the writer, it is because, for me, the reader is the essential other half of the writer.[9] Between them is an indissoluble connection. If it takes two to make love or war or tennis, it likewise takes two to complete the function of the written word. I never feel my writing is born or has an independent existence until it is read. It is like a cake whose only raison d'être is to be eaten. Ergo, first catch your reader.

5.   Secondly, biography is useful because it encompasses the universal in the particular.[10] It is a focus that allows both the writer to narrow his field to manageable dimensions and the reader to more easily comprehend the subject.[11] Given too wide a scope, the central theme wanders, becomes diffuse, and loses shape. The artist, as Robert Frost once said, needs only a sample. One does not try for the whole but for what is truthfully *representative*.[12]

6.   Coucy, as I began to take notice of him in my early research on the fourteenth century, offered more and more facets of the needed prism.[13]

---

8.   How does this first sentence of paragraph 4 work as a transition? What does it look back to, and echo? Note: **prism**: a piece of cut glass that reveals the presence of many colors in one (white light)—a neat metaphor:

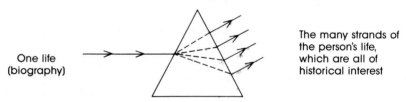

One life
(biography)

The many strands of
the person's life,
which are all of
historical interest

9.   A very clear and generous recognition of *the writer's need for readers*: no text is "complete" until it has been read by another person.

10.   Paragraph 5 takes up the theme of the general and the particular. Here Tuchman pushes it further by using the term "universal," claiming that other lives—however removed in time and place—have meanings that all others can recognize.

11.   The paragraph moves through a recognition of the danger of sweeping generalizations—diffuse and shapeless—to

12.   A recognition of the usefulness of truthfully *representative* samples (cf. examples). Tuchman looks at an age, an era, an epoch, by focusing on the particularities of the life of one *participant*—Coucy. By looking closely at particular episodes, events, actions, she brings us (spectators) very close to the participants. Tuchman herself remains a spectator and does not try to "become" Coucy, as Yourcenar does when she steps into the shoes of the emperor Hadrian (p. 93).

13.   (Enguerrand VII de) Coucy—the subject, or focus, of *A Distant Mirror*. This initiates an extraordinary paragraph, which runs on for more than a whole printed page—one of the most ambitious (extravagant?) paragraphs we have ever met. It offers an extraordinary number of specific details to support the generalizations that are placed at the beginning and the end of the paragraph.

From the time his mother died in the Black Death to his own marvelously appropriate death in the culminating fiasco of knighthood that closed the century, his life was as if designed for the historian. He suppressed the peasant revolt called the Jacquerie; he married the king of England's eldest daughter, acquiring a double allegiance of great historical interest; he freed his serfs in return for due payment (in a charter that survives); he campaigned three times in Italy, conveniently at Milan, Florence, and Genoa; he commanded an army of brigand mercenaries, the worst scourge of the age, in an effort to lose them in Switzerland, his only failure; he picked the right year to revisit England, 1376, the year of John Wycliffe's trial, the Good Parliament, and the deathbed of the Black Prince at which he was present; he was escort for the emperor at all the stage plays, pageantry, and festivities during the imperial visit to Paris; he was chosen for his eloquence and tact to negotiate with the urban rebels of Paris in 1382, and at a truce parley with the English at which a member of the opposite team just happened to be Geoffrey Chaucer; he was agent or envoy to the pope, the duke of Brittany, and other difficult characters in delicate situations; he was a patron and friend of Froissart and owned the oldest surviving copy of the *Chronicle*; his castle was celebrated in a poem by Deschamps; he assisted at the literary competition for the *Cent Ballades* of which his cousin, the Bastard of Coucy, was one of the authors; on the death of his father-in-law, King Edward, he returned his wife *and* the Order of the Garter to England; his daughter was "divorced at Rome by means of false witnesses" by her dissolute husband; he commanded an overseas expedition to Tunisia; he founded a monastery at Soissons; he testified at the canonization process of Pierre de Luxemburg; at age fifty he was challenged to a joust (in a letter that survives), by the earl of Nottingham, Earl Marshal of England, twenty-three years old, as the person most fitting to confer "honor, valor, chivalry and great renown" on a young knight (though from what I can gather Coucy was too busy to bother with him); he was of course in the king's company at the sensational mad scene when Charles VI went out of his mind, and at the macabre "dance of the savages" afterwards; it was his physician who attended the king and who later ordered his own tomb effigy as a skeleton, the first of its kind in the cult of death; finally, as "the most experienced and skillful of all the knights of France," he was a leader of the last Crusade, and on the way to death met the only medieval experience so far missing from his record—an attested miracle.[14] In short, he supplies leads to every subject—marriage and divorce, religion, insurrection, literature, Italy, England, war, politics, and a wonderful range of the most interesting people of his time, from pope to peasant. Among them, I may have rather reached for Catherine of Siena, but

---

14.   Only at this point does Tuchman draw together all the preceding particularities.

almost everyone else in the book actually at some point crossed paths with Coucy.[15]

7.   Once having decided upon him, the more I found out while pursuing his traces through the chronicles and genealogies, the more he offered.[16] The study of his tempestuous dynasty dating back to the tenth century, with the adventures in law, war, and love of his ungovernable, not to say ferocious forebears, made in itself a perfect prism of the earlier Middle Ages, which I needed for background. When I came upon the strange and marvelous ceremony of the *Rissoles*[17] performed each year in the courtyard of Coucy-le-chateau, with its strands reaching back into a tangle of pagan, barbarian, feudal, and Christian sources, I knew that there in front of me was medieval society in microcosm and, as I wrote in the book, the many-layered elements of Western man. . . .

(Here we omit eight pages in which Barbara Tuchman discusses her choices of subjects for her various books.)

8.   Whether in biography or straight history, my form is narrative because that is what comes naturally to me. I think of history as a story and myself as a storyteller, and the reader as a listener whose attention must be held if he is not to wander away.[18] Scheherazade only survived because she managed to keep the sultan absorbed in her tales and wondering what would happen next. While I am not under quite such exigent pressure, I nevertheless want the reader to turn the page and keep on turning to the end. Narrative, if the action is kept moving through every paragraph, has the power to accomplish this. It also has inherent validity: it is the spine of history and the key to causation. Events do not happen in categories—economic, intellectual, military—they happen in sequence. When they are arranged in sequence as strictly as possible down to month, week, and even day, cause and effect that may have been previously obscure, will often become clear, like secret ink.[19]

---

15.   Again, a sign of Tuchman's confidence: she can admit that by including Catherine of Siena, she was perhaps "stretching" Coucy's connections a bit far.

16.   How does this transition look both backwards and forwards?

17.   "The ceremony of the *Rissoles*": here Tuchman assumes, probably with good cause, that her audience would already have read her book. (The reference is to a complicated ritual in which the monks of the local abbey came to pay tribute to Coucy—a ceremony that was partly Christian and partly pre-Christian. For details, see *A Distant Mirror*, pp. 22–23.)

18.   "Whose attention must be held if he is not to wander away"—again Tuchman reveals her awareness of her reader's needs. It is this awareness that forms part of her great gift as a writer. Her book on Coucy is almost 700 pages long, and many readers agree that there's never a dull moment.

19.   Something of her excitement, the thrill of discovery, is revealed in this metaphor of "secret ink"—the revealing of mysterious secrets, long hidden.

9.   Sometimes, as in the Middle Ages, the necessary information to establish sequence is missing, whereas in recent history the problem is more likely to be too much information.[20] If the narrative is to be kept moving, this requires condensing, which is the hardest work I know, and selection, which is the most delicate.[21] Selection is the task of distinguishing the significant from the insignificant; it is the test of the writer as historian and as artist. The governing principle of selection is that it must honestly illustrate and never distort. By the very fact of inclusion or omission the writer has tremendous power to leave an impression that may not in fact be justified.[22] He must, therefore, resist the temptation to use an isolated incident, however colorful, to support a thesis, or by judicious omission to shade the evidence. Whether the historian is a Marxist or moralist, a psychologist or revisionist, is irrelevant. What matters is that he have a conscience and keep it on guard.[23]

10.   Unhappily, biography has lately been overtaken by a school that has abandoned the selective in favor of the all-inclusive. I think this development is part of the anti-excellence spirit of our time that insists on the equality of everything and is thus reduced to the theory that all facts are of equal value and that the biographer or historian should not presume to exercise judgment. To that I can only say, if he cannot exercise judgment, he should not be in the business. A portraitist does not achieve a likeness by giving sleeve buttons and shoelaces equal value to mouth and eyes.

11.   Today in biography we are presented with the subject's life reconstructed day by day from birth to death, including every new dress or pair of pants, every juvenile poem, every journey, every letter, every loan, every accepted or rejected invitation, every telephone message, every drink at every bar.[24] The result is one of those thousand-page heavies in which all the hard work has been left to the reader who can hardly be blamed if he finds the task unrewarding.

12.   Lytton Strachey, the father of modern biography at its most readable, if not most reliable, and an artist to the last pen stroke, would have been horrified to find himself today the subject of one of these laundry-list biographies in two very large volumes. His own motto was "The exclusion of everything that is redundant and nothing that is significant." If that advice is now ignored, Strachey's influence on psychological interpretation, on the other hand, has been followed to excess. In pre-Strachey biographies the inner life, like the two-thirds

---

20.   What of this transition? How does it work?

21.   Here she touches on two of any writer's most difficult tasks, condensation and selection. It's encouraging to know that even Barbara Tuchman finds them difficult. Again, her confidence (which she has earned) allows her to acknowledge her difficulties.

22.   Compare Grice, page 354.

23.   How does she build up, through paragraph 9, to this conclusion?

24.   What is the relationship between paragraphs 10 and 11?

of an iceberg that is under water, went largely unseen and uninvestigated. Since Strachey, and of course since Freud, the hidden secrets, especially if they are shady, are the biographer's goal and the reader's delight. It is argued—though I am not sure on what ground—that the public has a right to know the underside, and the biographer busies himself in penetrating private crannies and uncovering the failures and delinquencies his subject strove to conceal. Where once biography was devoted to setting up marble statues, it is now devoted, in Andre Maurois' words, to "pulling dead lions by the beard."

13.   A whole book is written to show that Martin Luther was constipated.[25] This may be fascinating to some, but is it, in fact, historically significant? Anyone who has studied John Wycliffe and the Lollard movement of the fourteenth century, and Jan Hus and the Hussite movement of the fifteenth century, knows that by the time Luther came along in the sixteenth, the Protestant breach with Rome was inevitable. If Luther had not pinned up his theses on the church door at Worms, someone else would have done so in Prague or Cologne or London. Luther's anal difficulties may offer the psychologist an interesting field of investigation, but they did not create the Protestant Reformation, and if they did not, then why should they concern us?

14.   Having a strong instinctive sense of privacy myself, I feel no great obligation to pry into a subject's private life, and reveal—unless it is clearly relevant—what he would have wanted to keep private.[26] "What business has the public to know of Byron's wildnesses?" asked Tennyson. "He has given them fine work and they ought to be satisfied." Tennyson had a point.[27] Do we really have to know of some famous person that he wet his pants at age six and practiced oral sex at sixty?[28] I suppose it is quite possible that Shakespeare might have indulged in one or both of these habits. If evidence to that effect were suddenly to be found today, what then would be the truth of Shakespeare—the new finding or *King Lear?* Would the plays interest us more because we had knowledge of the author's excretory or amatory digressions?

---

25.   What is the relationship between paragraphs 12 and 13?

26.   She establishes beyond doubt that when she is in role as a historian, her own *personal* values continue to operate. Her strong personal sense of moral decency, of decorum, continues to influence her in her public role as a historian. In this way, she demonstrates very clearly that taking on a role does not involve the abandonment of one's own principles.

27.   Byron, the Romantic English poet, was as celebrated for his wild living as for his writings. Many people were drawn to read his poetry by their curiosity about his bizarre exploits.

28.   Paragraph 14 finds Tuchman at her most assertive and passionate. Do you find her tone distasteful, indelicate, in a lecture given by a scholar with a great intellectual reputation in a highly prestigious national institution? Or do you find her frankness impressive?

15.   No doubt many would unhesitatingly answer "yes" to that question.[29] It seems to me, however, that insofar as biography is used to illumine history, voyeurism has no place. Happily, in the case of the greatest English writer, we know and are likely to know close to nothing about his private life. I like this vacuum, this miracle, this great floating monument of work that has no explanation at all.[30]

SIMON FRITH

Simon Frith, a former Berkeley graduate student, is a young English sociologist. He was trained as a historian, but his interest in rock music led him through social history—"How did this all start?"—to sociology—"What is happening here/now? What does it mean? What kind of sense can we make of it?" His articles on rock and punk have appeared in *Rolling Stone*, and he regularly visits the United States to take part in conferences on popular culture.

His chosen field, contemporary mores (**mores**: habits, ways of life, enthusiasms, trends), is especially tricky because what he is studying is ever changing, even as he observes it. In part, he uses historical perspectives to clarify current trends, as in his references to Shorty Snowden and Billie Holiday.

The following passage is from his book *Sound Effects* and comes from the chapter entitled "Rock and Sexuality."

We need to point out that Simon Frith's major overall interest in punk and other rock music is as *a set of signs* (like clothes, cosmetics, language, jokes, dancing, uses of money, etc.) through which a spectator can try to make sense of a subculture—in this case, the dominant urban countercultures of young people in the late 1970s and early 1980s.

Punk Sex and Disco Pleasure

1.   Punk was the first form of youth music not to rest on love songs (romance remained the staple of rock lyrics throughout the countercultural 1960s), and one consequence of this was that new female voices were heard on record, stage, and radio—shrill, assertive, impure, individual voices, singer as subject not object. Punk's female musicians had a strident insistence that was far removed from the appeal of most postwar glamour girls (the only sexual surprise of a

---

29.   She acknowledges that there are other points of view. Does she give those other points of view a fair hearing?

30.   Is her conclusion surprising? Why so? Is it effectively surprising? ("Effective surprise" occurs when one is not merely surprised, as such, but also provoked by the experience of surprise into thinking more.)

self-conscious siren like Debbie Harry, for example, was that she became a teeny-bop idol for a generation of young girls).

2.   Punk interrupted the long-standing rock equation of sex and pleasure, though the implications of this interruption still remain unclear.[1] British punk subculture itself hardly differed, in sexual terms, from any other working-class street movement—the boys led, the girls (fewer of them) hung on; and in the end it was probably punk's sexual effect on performers rather than on audiences that mattered—women were brought into a musical community from which they'd previously been excluded, and they brought with them new questions about sound and convention and image, about the sexuality of performance and the performance of sexuality. Whether these questions get answered we have yet to see, but at least punks opened the possibility that rock could be *against* sexism.

3.   Disco, which between 1974 and 1978 became the dominant sound of mass music across the world, had different origins and different effects.[2] The success of *Saturday Night Fever* simply confirmed the resonance of a genre that was already an $8-billion-per-year industry in the USA, already accounted for half the albums and singles in *Billboard*'s hot hundreds. Disco had changed the sound of radio, the organization of record companies, the status of club deejays, the meaning of a good night out, and all this has to be understood in the context of the 1970s' sexual mores.[3] Disco was not a response (like punk) to rock itself, but challenged it indirectly, by the questions it asked about music and *dance*.

4.   The dance floor is the most public setting for music as sexual expression and has been an important arena for youth culture since the dance crazes of the beginning of the century when Afro-American rhythms began to structure white middle-class leisure, to set new norms for physical display, contact, and movement. Dance has been, ever since, central to the meaning of popular music. Girls, in particular, have always flocked to dance halls, concerned not just about finding a husband, but also about pursuing their own pleasure. They may be attracting the lurking boys through their clothes, make-up, and appearance, but on the dance floor their energy and agility is their own affair. The most dedicated dancers in Britain, for example, the Northern soul fans, are completely self-absorbed, and even in *Saturday Night Fever* (in which dancing power was diluted by pop interests) John Travolta transcended Hollywood's clumsy choreography with the sheer quality of his commitment—from the opening shots of his strut through the streets, his gaze on himself never falters; the

---

1.   Frith willingly admits that some questions cannot yet be answered. As with Tuchman, Frith's admissions are a token both of confidence and of honesty.

2.   What type of transition is Simon Frith using here?

3.   Some years ago, the word "mores" would have been italicized to show that it was a foreign word. Since then, what must have happened that allows it *not* to be italicized?

essence of dance floor sex is physical control, and, whatever happens, John Travolta is never going to let himself go.

5.   Dancing as a way of life, an obsession, has a long American history. Shorty Snowden, the John Travolta of the Savoy Ballroom in the 1920s, suffered from "Sunday Night Fever":

> We started getting ready for Sunday on Saturday. The ideal was to get our one sharp suit to the tailor to be pressed on Saturday afternoon. Then we'd meet at the poolroom and brag about what we were going to do on the dance floor the next night. . . .

6.   The 1920s dance cult spread quickly to "hep" white teenagers who tried to dress, dance, move like these sharp black "dudes," and the Depression stimulated dancing among the non-hep too. Thousands of small, cheap bars with dance floors used pianos, record players, radios, and jukeboxes to fill the weekends with noise. Such working-class dance halls were crucial to the culture of courtship, but dancing meant something else even more important: it was an escape, a suspension of real time, a way in which even the unemployed could enjoy their bodies, their physical skills, the sense of human power their lives otherwise denied.[4] Such power does not need to be rooted in sexual competition (though it often enough is); parties, Friday and Saturday night bursts of physical pleasure, sex or no sex, have always been the most intense setting for working-class musics, from ragtime to punk.

7.   A party matters most, of course, to those people who most need to party, and, whatever else happened to mass music in the 1950s and 1960s, there were many people (black working-class Americans, British working-class teenagers, using much the same music) who never stopped dancing—1970s disco itself emerged musically from black clubs, depended commercially on its continuing white youth appeal. But, sexually, disco was most important as a gay aesthetic, and what was surprising, socially, was the appropriation of this aesthetic by the mass middle class.[5]

8.   Disco is dance music in the abstract, its content determined by its form. Middle-class dance music in the past, even in the 1930s, was a form determined by its content—there were still influential dance hall instructors, sheet music salesmen, and band leaders who laid down rules of partnership, decorum, uplift, and grace. There are no such rules in disco, but, on the other hand, individual expression means nothing when there is nothing individual to express. Disco is not, despite its critics, anything like Muzak. Muzak's effect is subliminal; its purpose is to encourage its hearers to do anything but listen to it. Disco's effect is material; its purpose is to encourage its hearers to do nothing but listen to it.

---

4.   Paragraph 6 relates the sense of power that dancers could enjoy to the sense of powerlessness that must have characterized their lives outside the dance hall. Is that the theme of the whole paragraph?

5.   Why "surprising"? (**appropriation**: adoption, takeover; **aesthetic**: the notion of what is beautiful)

9.   What do they hear? An erotic appeal, most obviously—what Richard Dyer calls "whole body eroticism."[6] All dancing means a commitment to physical sensation, but disco expanded the possibilities of sensation. Disco pleasure is not closed off, bound by the song structures, musical beginnings and ends, but is expressed, rather, through an open-ended series of repetitions, a shifting *intensity* of involvement. And disco, as Dyer suggests, shares rock's rhythmic pulse, while avoiding rock's phallo-centrism: disco is committed to the 4:4 beat in all its implications. Disco dancing is sinuous, it avoids the jerk and grind and thrust of rock; disco dancers hustle and slide, they use all their bodies' erotic possibilities.

10.   Dancing has always been a physical pleasure sufficiently intense to block out, for the moment, all other concerns, but disco pushed such enjoyment to new extremes:[7] the disco experience is an overwhelming experience of *now-ness*, an experience intensified still further by drugs like amyl nitrite, an experience in which the dancer is, simultaneously, completely self-centered and quite selfless, completely sexualized and, in gender terms, quite sexless. On the disco floor there is no overt competition for partners, no isolation; and disco (unlike bohemia) signifies nothing, makes no expressive claims—if bohemia suggests a different way of life, disco simply offers a different experience of it.[8]

11.   The disco version of eroticism and ecstasy is not, in itself, homosexual, but the aesthetic uses of these experiences did reflect gay consciousness. They were imbued, for example, with gay romanticism: disco sensations were associated with the fleeting emotional contacts, the passing relationships of a culture in which everything in a love affair can happen in a night. Disco eroticism became, too, the sign of a sexuality that was always being constructed. It was the process of construction, the very artificiality of the disco experience, that made it erotic. Disco was a version of camp: the best disco records were those made with a sense of irony, an aggressive self-consciousness, a concern for appearances.[9] There was an obvious link between the vocal styles of disco and 1930s torch songs: Billie Holiday and Donna Summer alike stylized feelings, distanced pain, opened up the texts of

---

6.   Note how deftly Frith borrows a useful phrase from Richard Dyer and acknowledges the loan.

7.   How does Frith get from paragraph 9 to paragraph 10? Is paragraph 10 an extension of paragraph 9, or a shift of emphasis or topic?

8.   Is this distinction clear? Significant? (Traditionally, many affluent young people, bored with hometown life, headed for a bohemian city [e.g., Paris] where the different life seemed so much more exciting, unpredictable, exotic, and satisfying.)

9.   Paragraphs 11, 12, and 13: Observe closely Frith's use of the semicolon (;) and the colon (:) and *from his uses*, try to frame guidelines for their use by writers unfamiliar with them. In two places, in paragraphs 11 and 13, he also uses parentheses. For what particular purpose does he seem to use them?

sexuality (and for this reason, disco, despised by punk-rockers on principle, had an immense appeal to the post-punk avant-garde).

12.   Mainstream disco, the Saturday night fever of the teenage working class, continued to operate according to the traditional street party line; teenagers danced in different ways, to different sounds than gays. But it was the gay disco aesthetic that middle-class dancers began to appropriate from 1974 on. If 1960s "permissive" sexual ideology had reflected new leisure and sexual opportunities, then 1970s disco culture reflected their emotional consequences. Disco was music for singles bars, sexual mobility, heterosexual cruising, weekend flings, and transitory fantasies. Gay culture reflected, in its own way, the problems and possibilities of sex without domesticity, love without the conventional distinctions of male and female. These problems and possibilities had become important now for heterosexuals too.

13.   Disco was about eroticism and ecstasy as material goods, produced not by spiritual or emotional work, God or love, but by technology, chemistry, wealth. The disco experience (the music and the mood, the poppers and the lights) revealed the artificiality and transience of sexual feelings—they were produced to be consumed; and disco pleasure, as it moved into the commercial mainstream, became the pleasure of consumption itself. This was obvious enough in the chic appeal of Studio 54, but was just as important for the strut of the factory girls, equally chic, up the steps of Tiffany's° in provincial Britain. Disco made no claims to folk status; there was no creative disco community. The music was, rather, the new international symbol of American consumer society. Chic discos sprang up around the world, each offering the secret of eternal American youth; the pleasures of consumption and the pleasures of sex became, in such settings, the same thing.

°**Tiffany's**: the name of a chain of commercial dance halls

14.   The problem with escapism is not the escape itself, but what's still there when it's over—the rain still falls when Monday morning dawns. Once something's been consumed it's gone; new goods are necessary, new experiences, new highs, new sex. As many observers commented, by the end of the 1970s, disco had become a drug, but it was leisure itself that had a new desperation.[10]

JEROME BRUNER

Jerome Bruner is probably the most distinguished and influential American psychologist of our time. Although his major interest is in how human beings learn, his work has ranged widely over many related fields. Much

---

10.   Is paragraph 14 upbeat or downbeat? How does Frith avoid representing its conclusion as merely his personal opinion?

Taking the text as a whole, how many of Frith's definitions were new to you? Did you find Frith's account of dance halls interesting? Has it effectively invited you to think about such matters in new ways? Do you find him fair, reasonable, cool? Or is he, for you, judgmental and disenchanting?

of his work is very specialized and appears in the psychology journals; but in 1966, he published *Toward a Theory of Instruction,* a collection of essays for a general audience about learning and teaching, which are, he says, "the efforts of a student of the cognitive processes trying to come to grips with the problems of education." In his preface, he acknowledges that "As always, it has been my wife whose partnership in dialogue helped the ideas take shape." We note this because it may help to draw your attention to the fact that *talking* about your ideas with a peer and receiving feedback, while working on a text, offers one of the most effective and congenial ways of shaping a text effectively.

In this paper, Bruner explores many questions about how we can best learn, and be taught, to acquire a fuller, more resourceful use of our own language. It is, therefore, a most appropriate text with which to bring this book to an end, since that is precisely what we have hoped to help you achieve throughout the book.

Notes   Using the same kinds of comments and questions as we have provided for Tuchman's and Frith's texts, write (a) comments to show what you appreciate in Bruner's *organization of his text* and (b) questions (to be put to other members of your class) that will promote closer attention to features of the text that we have highlighted (attention to audience, confidence, transitions, etc.).

Teaching a Native Language

1.   I have often thought that I would do more for my students by teaching them to write and think in English than teaching them my own subject. It is not so much that I value discourse to others that is right and clear and graceful—be it spoken or written—as that practice in such discourse is the only way of assuring that one says things right and courteously and powerfully *to oneself.* For it is extraordinarily difficult to say foolishness clearly without exposing it for what it is—whether you recognize it yourself or have the favor done you. So let me explore, then, what is involved in the relation between language and thinking, or, better, between writing and thinking. Or perhaps it would be even better to speak of how the use of language affects the use of mind.

2.   Consider this. As between reading, listening, and speaking, one falls asleep most easily reading, next most easily listening, and only with the greatest difficulty while writing or speaking—although I have seen both the latter happen among those deprived of sleep for long periods. There is an important difference between deciphering (as in listening or reading), and enciphering (as in speaking or writing). In listening or reading our span of attention typically lags behind the furthermost point where our eye or ear has traveled. We hold words and phrases in mind until we can tie the utterance together. A colleague of mine has been studying the retrospective integrating mechanisms involved in listening, and he finds his subjects holding decisions in abeyance until they see what is coming, which then permits them to go back over

what has been said in order to give it a final syntactical rendering. Of course, we aid our auditors and readers by reducing the amount of memorial baggage they carry to the end of a sentence. And so we write:

> This is the dog that chased the cat that killed the rat,

and avoid:

> This is the rat that the cat that the dog chased killed.

3.   In speaking or writing, the pattern is quite different: the arrow points forward. The speaker or writer rides ahead of rather than behind the edge of his utterance. He is organizing ahead, marshaling thoughts and words and transforming them into utterances, anticipating what requires saying. If the listener is trafficking back and forth between the present and the immediate past, the speaker is principally shuttling between the present and the future. The plight of the listener is to "fall behind"; of the speaker, to "get ahead of himself." Falling behind is a state in which the listener has insufficient processing time for decoding; getting ahead of oneself is a failure to anticipate properly. Pressed for time, the listener falls further and further behind, the speaker gets further and further ahead of himself. It is not surprising, then, that listening is soporific in the sense of blurring the present with the past. The tonic effect of speaking is that one thrusts the edge of the present toward the future. In one case anticipation is forced into abeyance. In the other, it dominates the activity.

4.   You will quite properly have guessed that I am about to urge that reading be rescued from its passivity and turned into a more active enterprise. Indeed, I do believe just that. But it is not a new theme. We have all discovered it (with delight) on our own. As a student, I took a course with I. A. Richards, a beautiful man and a great necromancer. It began with that extraordinary teacher turning his back to the class and writing on the blackboard in his sharply angular hand the lines:

> Gray is all theory;
> Green grows the golden tree of life.

For three weeks we stayed with the lines, with the imagery of the classic and romantic views, with the critics who had sought to explore the two ways of life; we became involved in reading a related but bad play of Goethe's, *Torquato Tasso,* always in a state of dialogue though Richards alone spoke. The reading time for eleven words was three weeks. It was the antithesis of just reading, and the reward in the end was that I owned outright, free and clear, eleven words. A good bargain. Never before had I read with such a lively sense of conjecture, like a speaker and not a listener, or like a writer and not a reader.

5.   I need not argue the virtues of reading oneself awake. Rather, I mean to pose a somewhat different problem, though a closely related one. Let me begin by stating rather baldly—though there is indeed ample evidence to support my point—that language is a major instrument of thought. When we are thinking at the far reach of our capacities, we are

engaged with words, even led forward by them. Take the first appearance of syntax in the life of the child. During his second year, he develops that curious but powerful construction, the one-word utterance or holophrase: *mummy, sticky, allgone, no, daddah.* If you study the course of growth, you will discover that on a certain day, and it should be celebrated with an anniversary party each year, the child mysteriously constructs a syntactical utterance. Mother washes jam from his hands. He says, *Allgone sticky.* If you keep observing you will discover further that during the next weeks he drives the new construction to its limit: a syntactic structure composed of a closed pivot class, *allgone,* and an open class that contains practically every other word in his vocabulary. *Allgone* what have you. Soon new pivot words emerge, always in this same kind of privileged position with regard to the other words in his vocabulary. In the first month after their appearance, there will be a few dozen utterances containing a pivot construction. A few months later they will number well over a thousand.

6.   What has this to do with our subject? It has precisely this to do with it: the child has acquired not only a way of saying something but a powerful instrument for combining experiences, an instrument that can now be used as a tool for organizing thoughts about things. It has been remarked that words are invitations to form concepts. It can equally be said that the combinatorial or productive property of language is an invitation to take experience apart and put it together again in new ways. Consider the new-found power and grace of the child we considered a moment ago. He returns from a trip in his stroller: *allgone byebye.* I am urging, in effect, that in some unknown but considerable measure, the power of words is the power of thought. There has been the teaching of English, as it has come to be called in the past half century. But it may well be teaching the calculus of thought as well. Indeed, I should like to urge that the closest kin to the teacher of English composition is the teacher of mathematics. The latter is teaching a somewhat artificialized calculus of thought that applies principally to what are called well-formed problems. The ill-formed problems for which the calculus of grammar is most useful are incalculably more interesting and strenuous. That is what the teacher of composition has in his charge.

7.   How conceive of language as a calculus of thought for ill-formed problems—problems, that is, without unique solutions? I should prefer to look at it from the point of view of the functions that language serves the speaker outwardly, and then to consider which of these functions also serve internally to help us organize our thoughts about things. My distinguished colleague and friend Roman Jakobson has some penetrating comments to make on this subject. He suggests that there are six discernible functions of language: emotive, conative, referential, metalingual, poetic, and phatic. It is a formidable list. He derives it from the nature of discourse, and if we assume that much of thought is internalized discourse or dialogue, it seems reasonable to suppose, does it not, that these functions should be represented in thinking. Discourse consists, in its essentials, of an *addresser,* an *addressee,* a *contact* that joins them, a *message* passing between them, a *context* to which the message refers and a

linguistic *code* that governs the way in which messages are put together and things referred to. The referential function of language has to do with the manner in which things are pointed to by utterances. "That is a man." "What happened to the team spirit?" The emotive function expresses the internal feelings of the addresser through words or intonation. "How nice to be here" is a banal example. "Damn" is better. The conative function seeks to produce behavior in the addressee. "Get thee to a nunnery," or "Please hold my hat." The phatic function has as its aim the maintenance of contact, and is best illustrated by the "uh-huh" uttered over the telephone when we wish to make it clear to the other that we are still there. Opening sentences between old friends long separated and newly met provide a treasury of phatic utterances. The poetic function has to do solely with the message for its own sake. "A girl used to talk about 'the horrible Harry.' 'Why horrible?' 'Because I hate him.' 'But why not *dreadful, terrible, frightful, disgusting?*' 'I don't know why, but *horrible* fits him better.' " Jakobson proclaims triumphantly, and quite correctly, "Without realizing it, she clung to the poetic device of paramasia." In the jargon of linguistics, the poetic function shifts the emphasis from rules of word selection to rules of word combination, the pure concern with the structure of the message, the delight of all who care about words. And finally the metalingual. It is jurisprudence applied to language: does this or that utterance fit the code—is or is not "mare" the feminine of "horse," and what is its contrast class? Or simply, "Do you know what I mean?"

8.   I hope I have not bored you with the technicalities of making a single point. The point is, simply, that language serves many functions, pursues many aims, employs many voices. What is most extraordinary of all is that it commands as it refers, describes as it makes poetry, adjudicates as it expresses, creates beauty as it gets things clear, serves all other needs as it maintains contact. It does all these things at once, and does them with a due regard to rules and canons such that a native speaker very early in life is usually able to tell whether they were well done or botched. I would like to suggest that a man of intellectual discipline is one who is master of the various functions of speech, one who has a sense of how to vary them, how to say what he wishes to say—to himself and to others. Too much contact maintenance and too little reference is a bore. Too much expression and too little anything else is a muddle. What is true of external discourse may also be true of internal discourse with oneself. But consider now the relation of external and internal language. Can one be clear to oneself and turbid in saying it?

9.   The shape or style of a mind is, in some measure, the outcome of internalizing the functions inherent in the language we use. Let me illustrate what is meant by internalization by citing two experiments, both by Russian psycholinguists. Each experimenter set a task that was straightforward enough. When one kind of display appeared, the young subjects were to press a bulb in their right hand; when the other appeared, the left-handed bulb was to be pressed. In the first experiment, conducted by Martsinovskaya, children between the ages of three and eight were the subjects. Their first task was to press one bulb when a red circle appeared, the other when a green appeared. The circles were presented on either

gray or yellow backgrounds. It is an easy task responding to a figure on a ground, and three-year-olds do it as well as the older children. Now, when the task was mastered, the children were told to ignore the red and green figures and respond instead to the backgrounds, one bulb for yellow and the other for gray, regardless of what color figure appeared on them. Under these circumstances, the younger children had great difficulty. They seemed unable to inhibit reactions to the figures, were somehow unable to instruct themselves properly. The older children took it in stride. And now the second experiment, this one carried out by Abramyan, again with children of the same age range. He argued that the difficulty experienced by the younger children in Martsinovskaya's experiment was that they were unable to encode the instructions in internal language in a fashion that would permit them to regulate their own behavior. Their internalized language went no further than concrete declaration. If the instructions could be converted into such a declarative form, then they would succeed. So he repeated the earlier experiment with only one variation: he substituted airplane silhouettes for the circles in the original experiment. Now when the child had to shift from figure to ground they were able to say, "Airplanes can fly on sunny days—yellow background; but they cannot fly on cloudy days—gray background. Press with one hand when the airplanes can fly, with the other when they cannot." With this small change, the three-year-olds could perform quite as well as the eights. Language, in short, provides an internal technique for programming our discriminations, our behavior, our forms of awareness. If there is suitable internal language, the task can be done.

10.   This is a very simple, perhaps too simple, experiment. It does, however, raise a deep question about the relation between being able to do or think something on the one hand and being able to say it to oneself on the other. That there is some intimate relationship is quite plain, though it is equally plain that we are only beginning to understand the nature of that relationship. The Chinese proverb can sometimes be reversed, and there are instances in which a single word is worth a thousand pictures— the word "implosion" was classified top secret by the Manhattan Project during the war. But words have limits. When we follow Mr. MacLeish in admitting that a poem is mute, what we are saying, I suspect, is that words do not fully exhaust the knowledge and sensibility contained in our acts and our images.

11.   I am not urging that the word is the summit of all intellectual discipline and cultivation. Rather, I would suggest that the way of language in knowing is the most powerful means we have for performing transformations on the world, for transmuting its shape by recombination in the interest of possibility. I commented earlier that there should be a special birthday to celebrate the entrance of the child into the human race, dated from the moment when he first uses combinatorial grammar. Each of the functions of language has its combinatorial necromancy, its enormous productiveness. It is with the cultivation of these combinatorial powers that I am concerned.

12.   Now let me return to instruction in one's native language and the degree to which it may also be instruction in the use of the implements

of thought. Let me exaggerate. If there is not a developed awareness of the different functions that language serves, the resulting affliction will be not only lopsided speaking and writing, but a lopsided mind. Like the children in the two experiments, the afflicted person will be restricted in his coping to events for which his stunted language provides suitable equipment. And one day he may be forced to fight a forest fire with a water pistol.

13.   But how does one achieve awareness, mastery, and finesse in the various functions to which language is devoted? How indeed does one become masterfully adept at the rules for forming functionally appropriate utterances for the consumption of others or for one's own consumption, *save by exercise*? Many of us have delighted over the years in the weekend competitions of the *New Statesman*. "Write the Declaration of Independence in the style of the Old Testament." Or, "Do a prose rendering of the 'Charge of the Light Brigade' in the style of Henry James." There is a comparable delight in Max Beerbohm's *Christmas Garland* or Raymond Queneau's *Exercises in Style*. To write in different styles and in different voices—a beseeching account of evolution, an expressive account of Newton's Law of Moments, whatever—surely this is one right path.

14.   I confess to having achieved one minor success in the teaching of English. The pupil was one of my own children. Several years ago she was applying for entry to a college that requires applicants to write an autobiographical sketch. She wrote one and brought the piece to me for comment. It was very much her—full of her warm enthusiasm—and yet the written document was almost a caricature of a warm-hearted girl. It is difficult to be graceful in one's comments about another's writing, and the more so when there is a close bond between critic and his charge. You cannot say to a seventeen-year-old girl, however gay your tone of voice, "My dear, this is gushy." The diagnosis of gushiness carries no remedial prescription with it. I stumbled on the happy formula. Could she rewrite the piece without a single adjective, not a one? Two hours later she returned with the news that her first draft had been disgustingly effusive, that I should have told her so, and that in spite of my failure in candor the sketch was being rescued from its original state. I suspect something more happened than just a change in writing.

15.   It is the case that the skills of speaking and listening precede those of reading and writing. Why does writing come so hard to the schoolchild? There is often a lag of from six to eight years between his "linguistic age" in writing and in speaking. Written speech is obviously a quite different enterprise from oral speech. The brilliant Russian psychologist Vygotsky suggested that writing and reading are second-order abstractions. In spoken speech there is more likely to be not only a referent present, but a great amount of steering provided by the social demands of the dialogue. Written speech may bear the same relation to spoken speech that algebra bears to arithmetic. A written word stands for a spoken word used in any context whatever. A spoken word "stands for" a thing or state or thought—not another word in a different medium. In written language, moreover, no interlocutor is presupposed and none is there. Spoken utterances are normally determined in large part by the demands of a dialogue,

with the interlocutor helping frame our decisions about what requires saying. Whoever uses written speech must detach himself from immediate social interaction altogether and conjure up in his own mind a situation appropriate to the written words with which he is dealing.

16. Let me suggest, then, that by virtue of its very separation from immediate dialogue, the act of writing creates a new awareness about the nature and powers of language. But if this is so, why is it that a man through his entire life as *Homo scribens* will continue to write with no improvement in his sense of craft and little improvement in his use of mind? It may well be that to become aware of what one has written requires that one hear it, listen to it, compare the spoken with the written version. Perhaps the paraphernalia of the "language laboratory" should be used, if only to have students read their compositions to a tape and then suffer the tape to read back aloud what they have written. There should be a tutor nearby, doubtless, to correct and encourage. But I am hard put to know what he would say to his charge. I would rather have the tutor play another role—not at the student's elbow but speaking from the tape. Let him take the student's composition and rewrite it in various styles, each capitalizing on different functions of language and on different techniques of saying or organizing what the student said. Then let the student write some more and listen, listen, listen.

17. It was Dante, I believe, who commented that the poor workman hated his tools. It is more than a little troubling to me that so many of our students dislike two of the major tools of thought—mathematics and the conscious deployment of their native language in its written form, both of them devices for ordering thoughts about things and thoughts about thoughts. I should hope that in the new era that lies ahead we will give a proper consideration to making these tools more lovable. Perhaps the best way to make them so is to make them more powerful in the hands of their users.

Answers to Questions

p. 8   Iris Origo's list of instructions to herself on how to behave as a mother-in-law.

p. 60   He/she corrected Michael Smith's spelling: Margret to Margaret, and awfull to awful.

p. 135   The next sentence in Rushdie's text is "The fever broke today."

p. 269   <u>Riddles</u>
1. Fire
2. River
3. Flea
4. Candle
5. Cow
6. Bottle of ale
7. Blacksmith

p. 270   a. Teeth
          b. Coal
          c. Bed
          d. Squirrel

           "By Morning": snow

p. 273   A kitten's view of a back yard and children.

p. 274   These aliens have landed in my kitchen. The linoleum has a symmetric floral pattern. There are cupboards (hinged structures) lining one wall. The stove is the prominent object standing alone against one wall. A small clock sits on the back of the stove, with a cord running down to a plug. The circular platforms are coils on the stove. On one coil is a metal pan full of boiling macaroni.

p. 275   An old dandelion top after the yellow has turned white and blown away.

p. 276   From sideburn to ear top.

p. 277   A member of a primitive culture with no written language, who has absolutely no concept of writing, observes a composition classroom. These were his thoughts.

p. 277   An alien from another galaxy, whose means of acquiring knowledge are extremely advanced but do not include reading books, finds himself observing earthlings at Utah State University. In Radio Report #2 he observes them in the library. In Radio Report #3 he observes a few sunbathers on the lawns around the dorms.

Photo Credits

Pages 16–19: From *The Hokusai Sketch-Books* by James Michener, Charles E. Tuttle Company, Inc., Rutland, Vermont, 1979.

Page 37: Above, The Bettmann Archive; *below,* Schlesinger Library/Radcliffe College.

Pages 38–40: From *20 Hrs., 40 Min.,* by Amelia Earhart, G. P. Putnam's Sons, New York, 1928.

Pages 55–56: Thomas Eakins, illustrated letter from Eakins to his mother, Paris, November 8 and 9, 1866. Hirshhorn Museum and Sculpture Garden, Smithsonian Institution.

Page 60: From *Words 3* by Geoffrey Summerfield and Richard Andrews, Cassell Ltd, London, England, 1973.

Page 94: Left, Photo by Christian Taillandier, courtesy of Farrar, Straus & Giroux; *right,* Art Resource.

Page 116: From *Devil Birds* by Derek Bromhall, Hutchinson & Co. Ltd., London, England, 1980.

Page 117: Photo by Clive Bromhall from *Devil Birds* by Derek Bromhall. Hutchinson & Co. Ltd., London, England, 1980.

Page 119: From the film *Devil Birds,* courtesy of The Marconi Co. Ltd., reproduced from *Devil Birds* by Derek Bromhall, Hutchinson & Co. Ltd., London, England, 1980.

Page 147: Christa Armstrong/Photo Researchers.

Page 148: Above, Joel Gordon; *below,* Timothy Egan/Woodfin Camp & Associates.

Page 149: Joel Gordon.

Page 169: The Museum of Modern Art-Film Stills Archive.

Page 176: Above, U.N. Photo; *below,* NASA.

Page 177: Above, AP/Wide World Photos; *below,* Library of Congress.

Page 181: N. R. Farbman/Life Magazine © 1946 Time, Inc.

Page 184: © 1966 by C. F. Peters Corporation. Used by Permission. Graphics by Roberto Zamarin.

Page 185: N. E. A.

Page 230: Above, Don Ploke/Las Vegas Sun; *below,* AP/Wide World Photos.

Page 231: Above, Ray Gora/Chicago Tribune; *below,* AP/Wide World Photos.

Page 248: William M. Harnett, *Mr. Hulings' Rack Picture,* 1888, courtesy of The Regis Collection.

Page 280: NASA.

Page 299: From *A Postillion Struck by Lightning* by Dirk Bogarde, Holt, Rinehart and Winston, New York, 1977.

About the Authors

JUDITH SUMMERFIELD (formerly Fishman) has taught composition and literature since 1963. At Queens College since 1972, she has served as director of the Writing Skills Workshop, co-director of the Queens English Project, a federally funded articulation project, and associate director of the composition program. A former member of the CCC Executive Committee, she has conducted workshops for teachers throughout the country. Coauthor, with Sandra Schor, of the *Random House Guide to Writing* and editor of *Responding to Prose: A Reader for Writers* (Macmillan), she is now at work on an interdisciplinary study of narrative as it informs autobiography, fiction, and non-fiction prose. Recent articles appear in *WPA, Linguistics and Stylistics, The Journal Book,* ed. Toby Fulwiler, and proceedings from the 1984 New Hampshire Conference on Reading and Writing, where she delivered a keynote address, "Framing Narratives."

GEOFFREY SUMMERFIELD is best known in his native England as coeditor of the poems and prose of John Clare (Oxford University Press), for his poetry anthologies, *Voices* and *Worlds* (Penguin), and for his work on Matthew Arnold (Cambridge University Press) and on composition (Batsford). In the United States, he was a member of the Dartmouth Seminar (1966) and has taught at the University of California, Berkeley, Northwestern University, New York University, and the University of Nebraska. He is currently an adjunct professor, teaching composition, at Queens College, New York. His most recent publications are *Welcome* (Deutsch/Dutton), poems for young readers, and *Fantasy and Reason,* a "prelude" to Wordsworth's *Prelude* (Methuen/University of Georgia Press). In 1980, he lectured in Australia and New Zealand; and in 1982, he settled in the States, marrying Judith Fishman.